THE EVOLUTION OF
WESTERN PRIVATE LAW

THE EVOLUTION
OF WESTERN PRIVATE LAW

EXPANDED EDITION

❧

Alan Watson

THE JOHNS HOPKINS UNIVERSITY PRESS

Baltimore and London

© 1985, 2001 The Johns Hopkins University Press
All rights reserved. Published 2001
An expanded edition of *The Evolution of Law*, published 1985
Printed in the United States of America on acid-free paper
9 8 7 6 5 4 3 2 1

The Johns Hopkins University Press
2715 North Charles Street
Baltimore, Maryland 21218-4363
www.press.jhu.edu

Library of Congress Cataloging-in-Publication Data will be found at the end of
this book.
A catalog record for this book is available from the British Library.

ISBN 0-8018-6484-4

For Olivia Robinson

Contents

Preface

An author who calls his book *The Evolution of Law,* or even *The Evolution of Western Private Law,* has taken a stance. He indicates a belief that law does not arise solely from the conditions of the society in which it operates, but that there is a pattern or patterns of development that transcend state or national boundaries. That there is such a pattern or patterns can, I believe, be demonstrated at a basic level even in a preface. Thus, most modern Western systems of law are traditionally and, I believe, properly divided into civil-law and common-law systems, from which it follows that any civil-law system has more in common with any other civil-law system than with any common-law system. The division, I must emphasize, relates to the system of private law, not to constitutional law or to police regulation. This division of legal systems, however, is not paralleled by social, economic, or political conditions in the countries in which the legal systems operate. Civil-law and common-law countries alike may have experienced similar economic and social circumstances, such as the Industrial Revolution, that have bypassed other civil-law and other common-law countries. And the nature of government, whether democratic or tyrannous, does not affect the classification of the legal system. Among civil-law systems are, for instance, those in France, Haiti, Argentina, the Netherlands, and, I believe, the nations that formerly were part of the Soviet Union. Common-law countries include England, Ghana, the United States, and Nigeria. Some other systems, such as Scotland and South Africa, are termed "mixed systems," partaking of elements of both common-law and civil-law systems. These last two countries are vastly different in racial mix, geography, and climate.

These basic differences between civil-law and common-law systems can therefore be explained only in terms of the legal traditions themselves: the differences result from legal history rather than from social, economic, or political history. But then we can be more precise. As it happens, the legal elements that have historically gone into modern Western systems are everywhere the same: Roman law, Germanic customs, canon law, and feudal law. Not only that, but how can it be that I can list among Western legal systems, for instance, Ghana, Haiti, and Nigeria—not usually regarded as Western countries—and more particularly place Haiti and Armenia among civil-law systems, Ghana and Nigeria among common-law systems? What puts them into one camp or the other? It must be some particular feature of the Western legal tradition: an emphasis on one strand of the tradition in one set of systems but not in the other. My answer is that a civil-law system is one in which parts or the whole of Justinian's Corpus Juris Civilis—to be discussed in Chapter 1—have been in the past or are at present treated as the law of the land or, at the very least, are of direct and highly persuasive force; or else it derives from any such system.[1] Common-law systems are those that have a dependency on English law.

In this book I seek to present a general and coherent view of the nature of legal change in the Western world that is largely independent of a particular time and place. I wish to explain why and how law changes in mature systems, in underdeveloped systems, and also in legal systems, even those possessing different levels of sophistication and derived from different societal roots, that come into powerful contact with each other. I hope and intend that the information I give, my arguments, and my conclusions will be useful tools for everyone interested in law and society, whether as legal historians (of any country or period), sociologists of law, anthropologists, or law reformers. I am well aware that in most chapters my conclusions are radical and will appear so especially to scholars who adopt conventional approaches to law in society. Yet this originality must be made explicit because, almost paradoxically, the conclusions seem to follow so simply from the evidence that they may appear all too obvious and even banal to the uninitiated in legal theory. As will appear, I believe passionately that any general theory of legal development must be grounded in actual historical data, observed as dispassionately as possible and considered comparatively. Hence come the individual, disparate themes of each chapter. For my goals to be satisfied, specialists in the field covered by each chapter must be convinced that my scholarship is sound and my particular conclusions plausible; and nonspecialists must be able to follow my arguments and believe that my conclusions can be generalized. The message of each chapter is wider than might at first appear.

The forces that determine the main outline of a legal system can be easily set down: the available sources of law; the nature of the legal process adopted;[2] the borrowing of law from elsewhere; and the combination of these factors. In the middle of the nineteenth century Thomas R. R. Cobb wrote in the context of American slave law that "philosophy is the handmaid, and frequently the most successful expounder of the law. History is the groundwork and only sure basis of philosophy. To understand aright, therefore, the Law of Slavery, we must not be ignorant of its history."[3] My subject is not slave law but law in general. Yet I believe Cobb was correct in claiming that one cannot understand law in society without philosophy and that only upon history can a philosophy of law be securely grounded. Cobb relied much on comparative legal history. Alas, the comparative history of law is still in its infancy.

The Evolution of Western Private Law was originally intended as a second edition of *The Evolution of Law* (Baltimore: Johns Hopkins University Press, 1985), but it varies greatly, especially in three respects. First, the arrangement is much altered, for ease of understanding. Second, although virtually all of the substance of *Evolution* is repeated with few changes, I have more than doubled its length with the development of themes. For this I have ruthlessly cannibalized other works of mine.[4] Third, realizing more clearly my limitations, I have retitled the book *The Evolution of Western Private Law,* from which my examples are drawn. I repeat my conviction that to understand the development of law one must proceed from history.

Part of my original aim for this edition was to make the book more reader-friendly, by increasing the examples. Yet, although I increased the examples, with reluctance I came to the conclusion that one cannot make a technical subject more appropriate by oversimplification. Still, I hope I have achieved some of my aim.

In this book I seek to show the evolution of Western law as a process, in which individual instances can be, and are, adduced as examples. This approach is most explicit in Chapter 5, on French tort law, and in Chapter 6, on water rights, but is to be found throughout; in Chapter 2, for instance, for lawyers' thinking impacting on legal development, and in Chapter 3, for the culture of judges. Still, I am very conscious of the force of particular events. That is the main reason I have altered the scope of this edition to the evolution of *Western* private law. Two events in that stand out. First, the Roman Twelve Tables of around 451 B.C., which established for the future the distinction between private and public law, gave the former predominance in juristic thought and established the main parameters of express legal reasoning. Second, Justinian's Corpus Juris Civilis, already mentioned, of the sixth century, which provided both a storehouse of legal institutions and rules that could be borrowed, divorced from specific Roman circumstances, and also, in the *Institutes,* a systematic structure for private law.

It is my hope that this volume will not be regarded as replacing *The Evolution of Law.* My aim in each book is different. In *The Evolution of Law* I wanted to indicate general *universal* traits in the development of law: that prominent lawyers, as distinct from the populace at large or the ruling elite, have great input on legal rules and institutions; that customary law often does not derive from what the people do; that borrowing of law from elsewhere is, in general, the most fruitful way in which law develops; and that a political revolution does not greatly alter the impact of some legal tradition but either modifies the existing tradition or substitutes a different tradition. I still believe my conclusions are correct but that I should have given more examples (which is what I set out to do for a second edition). When I came to give these additional examples, I found I was tying my argument rather specifically to Western private law. I decided to keep that emphasis.

Acknowledgments

From the beginning of my studies in law, a prime interest has been legal change: at first in Roman law, then more widely; at first on the fact of change, then on the factors of change. This book brings together my conclusions.

I have incurred too many debts to individuals and to institutions to list them all here, but they have my profound gratitude. Still, I must express my thanks for unfailing, warm, and friendly support to the University of Georgia Law Library staff and to other academic libraries that have generously sent me materials otherwise unavailable. It is more than a pleasure to thank Gracie Waldrup for her cheerfulness in typing many drafts.

I dedicate this book to Olivia Robinson for more than a quarter century of collegiality, friendship, love, and fierce criticism.

Abbreviations

BGB	Bürgerliches Gesetzbuch
C.	*Codex Justiniani* (*Code* of Justinian)
D.	*Digesta Justiniani* (*Digest* of Justinian)
G.	*Gai Institutiones* (*Institutes* of Gaius)
h.t.	The same title of *Code* or *Digest* as in the preceding text.
J.	*Institutiones Justiniani* (*Institutes* of Justinian)
TKM	Türk Kanunu Medenîsi
ZGB	Schweizerisches Gesetzbuch

THE EVOLUTION OF
WESTERN PRIVATE LAW

CHAPTER I

LEGISLATION

One cannot understand legal development in general without a new look at the history of individual legal changes. A new approach to legal development in general can, in turn, lead to a more just appreciation of individual legal changes. In this book my technique is to analyze particular legal events and facts, show that they have a significance beyond their immediate context, and generalize from them in order to construct a picture of how law evolves.

I emphasize the role in legal development of the formal *sources of law*, an ambiguous term, which I use here to indicate a formulation of law that is treated by courts as resting on a basis that the courts habitually regard as determinative for their decisions. Such bases, sources of law, differ from place to place and from time to time but in Western society they have been four in number: juristic opinion, legislation, custom, and preceding judicial decision. Although they each have their own particular impact on the development of the law, I do not treat them in the order of any supposed historical origin—in any event incapable of proof—but in the arrangement that makes them most easily accessible to the reader. Of course, they interact with one another.

As I insisted in the Preface, a concept of legal evolution in the Western world cannot be built up on a basis of abstract theory but on history; and general history cannot be discussed except as a result of examples. Because any author chooses the examples he considers most important, he may be biased by his prejudices. My starting point, based I believe on experience but perhaps on prejudice, is that for the development of law and for its relationship to society attention must first be given to the individual sources of law, their availability in a given society, and their interaction.

Of these sources I begin with legislation because, as an emanation of government, it should carry more weight than others. In a developed society, legislation has authority over all other sources of law, being constrained only by political reality.

But first we must consider the pivotal fact in the evolution of Western law, Justinian's Corpus Juris Civilis. It marks the end of the great Roman law tradition and the starting point for the subsequent Reception of Roman law. As we shall see later in the chapter, the compilation itself corresponds to one of the standard patterns of legislation.

CORPUS JURIS CIVILIS

Justinian became coemperor of the Byzantine Empire with his uncle Justin in 527. Later that year, when his uncle died, he became sole emperor. Probably even while Justin had been sole ruler, Justinian was contemplating a legal codification of some kind. He issued a constitution dated 13 February 528, establishing a commission to prepare a new collection, a *Codex,* of imperial constitutions. The word *constitution* here is a general term to include all kinds of imperial legal rulings. The compilers were given extensive powers to collect the constitutions, to omit any, in whole or in part, that were obsolete or unnecessary, and to remove contradictions and repetitions. They were not given power to make alterations in substance. The constitutions were then to be arranged by subject matter in titles, or named chapters, and within each title the constitutions were to be given in chronological order. The *Code,* which was published on 7 April 529, has not survived, but it was replaced by a second revised *Code,* which came into effect on 29 December 534. The revised *Code,* which has survived and is one of the four constituent elements of what came to be called the Corpus Juris Civilis, is divided into twelve books, subdivided into titles in which the constitutions appear chronologically. The constitutions range in date from Hadrian in the early second century to Justinian himself. A considerable proportion of the texts—2,019 as against 2,664—come from the time after the empire became Christian; in fact, the bulk of the Christian rescripts is much greater.

On 15 December 530, Justinian ordered the compilation of a collection of juristic texts, the *Digest,* and the work came into force on 30 December 533. This massive work, twice the size of the *Code,* is in fifty books, virtually all of which are subdivided into titles. Each title consists of fragments from the writings of jurists who lived between the first century B.C. and the third century A.D. About one-third of the whole work is taken from the jurist and civil servant Ulpian, who was murdered before the middle of 224; a further one-sixth comes from his contemporary Paul. In the opinion of some modern scholars, one jurist, Hermogenianus, was active in the fourth century, but otherwise no *Digest* text is attributable to any jurist who lived after the third century except for the rather obscure Arcadius Charisius.[1] The texts of the jurists include statements of principles, discussions of rules, commentary on the scope or interpretation of edicts and statutes, qualification of other juristic opinion, and the treatment of problem cases, real or hypothetical.

The compilers were instructed to cut out all that was superfluous or imperfect, all contradictions and repetitions, anything that was obsolete, and anything that was already in the *Code*.[2] Contrary, though, to a frequently expressed view, the compilers of the *Digest* were not given power to alter the substance of the law or to bring it up to date.[3] Indeed, any such alteration as occurred would have been contrary to the spirit of the instructions. There was very little juristic writing after, say, 235, and there are very few texts after that period in the *Digest*. Changes in the law after that date were almost entirely the result of imperial constitutions. But these constitutions were collected in the *Code*, and the *Digest* commissioners were expressly instructed not to repeat in the *Digest* what was contained in the *Code*. Significantly, the commissioners were to exclude from the *Digest* what was obsolete, meaning in large measure the rules that had been replaced by imperial constitutions, which were now collected in the *Code*.

This exclusion is one of the major differences of the *Digest* from the *Code*. The difference is not just that the *Digest* is a patchwork made out of juristic commentary and the *Code* a patchwork from imperial laws, or that the *Digest* is composed wholly of pagan originals and, unlike the *Code*, can be regarded as a Christian work only in a very limited sense. Even more, the two works stand at different points of legal and social evolution. The *Digest* presents a picture of law and of relevant social conditions as they were in Rome at the height of the empire; insofar as the picture of law at that time is inexact, this is because of excisions, not of later superimpositions, though some few of the alterations of the *Digest* texts do result in the presentation of postclassical law. The *Code,* on the contrary, mainly presents the postclassical world, where Rome was no longer the heart of the empire, and early Byzantium. Because of this difference between the two works, in subsequent history the *Code* was at times more emphasized, at other times the *Digest*. The Corpus Juris could speak with more than one voice.

The third part of the compilation is the *Institutes,* an elementary text-book for first-year students, which was planned from 530 and was published on 21 November 533. It is structured on the *Institutes* of Gaius, a work written about A.D. 160, and appears in four books, though, unlike Gaius's *Institutes,* the books are further subdivided into titles. The arrangements of topics—sources of law, persons, property, succession, obligations, law of actions—for which the credit should probably be given to Gaius, was the result of planning, and it differs markedly from the arrangement found in the *Digest,* which seems haphazard and is largely the unplanned result of the gradual growth of topics as they were rather unsystematically set out annually by the praetor in the later Roman Republic and early Roman Empire. The absence of a satisfactory arrangement in the *Digest* has long been a matter for unfavorable comment. Like the other parts of the Corpus Juris, the *Institutes* is statute law.

With the second *Code,* Justinian's work of codifying Roman law was complete. But he continued to legislate, and this subsequent legislation is now known as the *Novels.* No official collection of these constitutions was made, but there is considerable knowledge of three unofficial collections. Most of the constitutions were in Greek, some in both Greek and Latin, but translations of most of them into Latin also appeared. The bulk of the *Novels* relate to public or ecclesiastical affairs, although private law is by no means absent. Thus, *Novels* 118 and 127 reform the whole law of intestate succession, and *Novel* 22 sets out the Christian marriage law.

In the main part of this chapter I wish to establish, through examples, two propositions. Both are at first sight startling, but both are, I believe, firmly based in history. First, at most times, in most states, governments have been little interested in legislating on national law, especially private law but also much of criminal law; and, second, great lawmakers have had little interest in promoting a detailed political, social, or economic message.

PAUCITY OF LEGISLATION

Law is power. Law is politics. Law is politics in the sense that persons who have political power determine which persons or bodies create law, how the validity of law is to be assessed, and how the legal order is to operate. But one cannot simply deduce from that, as is frequently assumed, that the holders of political power determine what the rules are and what the sources of law are to be. The lesson of history, in fact, is that over most of the field of law, and especially of private law, in most political and economic circumstances, political rulers need have no interest in determining what the rules of law are or should be—provided always, of course, that revenues roll in and that the public peace is kept. Rulers and their immediate underlings can be, and often have been and are, indifferent to the nature of the legal rules in operation. This simple fact is not only overlooked; it is habitually denied. But failure to accept it is the greatest cause of misunderstanding the nature of law, the relationship of law and society, and the course of legal development.[4]

Yet, for Europe, the general accuracy of the proposition that the government is usually unconcerned with the precise nature of most of the legal rules in operation is easily demonstrated by facts that, I think, no serious legal scholar would consider denying, but which are not usually considered together.[5] I offer some examples.

First, ancient Rome's system of private law is regarded as the most innovative (and influential) that the world has ever known. But during its most formative time—the last two centuries of the republic and the first two and a half centuries of the empire—it was mainly the work of the jurists, private individuals who, in that capacity, had no ties to government.[6]

The last two centuries of the Roman Republic, until Octavius (later to be Augustus) was given tribunician power *in perpetuum* in 36 B.C., seem to have produced the greatest advances in private law that the world has known. But what role did statute law play in this?[7] If we begin earlier and rather arbitrarily at 300 B.C., we can take account of the *lex Aquilia,* whose final formulation is traditionally dated around 287 B.C.[8] This, the most important of all Roman statutes on private law, with the exception of the early codification, the Twelve Tables, is in three chapters. Chapter 1 deals with the killing of slaves and four-footed herd animals, chapter 2 with a small technical point of contract law, and chapter 3 (at least eventually—its original scope is disputed) with the wounding of slaves and four-footed herd animals, the killing or wounding of other animate property, and damage to all kinds of inanimate property.

There were various statutes covering personal guarantors, which should be taken together. By the *lex Furia,* of perhaps around 200 B.C., which applied only to Italy, the *sponsor* and *fidepromissor* (two kinds of guarantors) were relieved of liability after two years, and each was liable only for an aliquot share. The earlier *lex Appuleia* introduced a kind of partnership between *sponsores* and *fidepromissores,* and anyone who paid more than his share could recover from the others. The *lex Cicereia,* whose date cannot be established, declared that anyone about to take *sponsores* or *fidepromissores* had to give prior notice and declare both the matter and the number of guarantors. The *lex Cornelia,* of around 81 B.C., forbade the same person to be guarantor for the same debtor in the same year for more than 20,000 sesterces of loaned money.[9]

The *lex Cincia* of 204 B.C. forbade gifts in return for defense in court and gifts in general above a certain (unknown) amount to anyone outside of a specified relationship. Very shortly thereafter came the *lex Plaetoria* (or *Laetoria*), which gave an action against one who defrauded a minor and a defense to the minor if he were sued on the transaction.[10] The *lex Atilia* of uncertain date, but 210 is usually thought likeliest, allowed at Rome the praetor and a majority of the tribunes of the plebs to appoint a *tutor* to a person who had none.[11] The *lex Titia* of around 99 B.C. extended similar powers to magistrates in provinces.

There were four statutes concerning testate succession. The *lex Furia testamentaria* of somewhere between 204 and 169 B.C. enacted that no one, apart from certain classes of persons, could take more than 1,000 *asses* by way of legacy. The *lex Voconia* of 169 B.C. declared that a person in the first class of citizens according to the latest census could not appoint a woman as heir, and that no one could take, by legacy or *mortis causa* gift, more than the heirs took. The *lex Falcidia* of 40 B.C. enacted that a testator could not leave more than three-quarters of his estate in legacies.[12] The *lex Cornelia,* probably of 81 B.C., confirmed the validity of testaments made by those who, captured by the enemy, died in captivity.

The *lex Atinia* of the first half of the last century B.C. prohibited prescription of stolen property until it had first been returned to its owner. The *lex Minicia* of before 90 B.C. declared that children born of parents who did not have the right of civil-law marriage took the lower status. The *lex Scribonia* of around 50 B.C. prevented the prescription of servitudes.

These constitute all the statutes on private law at the time when Roman law was most inventive. Other governmental devices by the officials in charge of the courts introduced contracts such as sale, hire, mandate, and the modern form of partnership; good faith came to play an important role in legal thought; and a very great deal of the law of succession was made afresh by the Edict of the praetor. The higher Roman elected public officials had the right to issue edicts on how they saw their tasks. Those magistrates in charge of the courts, notably the praetors and curule aediles, issued edicts setting out the circumstances in which they would grant an action. Thus, though they did not technically have law-making powers, they had an enormous impact on legal change. But the innovations in the Edict were really the creation of the jurists.[13] The only statute of outstanding importance from the period, even for the Romans, was the *lex Aquilia;* some of the others, as we have seen, appear in groups, on guarantors or on testate succession.[14] Yet legislation on public law or on political matters was abundant. There are 16 known statutes on private law, at least 502 on political, criminal, or procedural matters.[15] The great majority of the latter are concerned with transient, particular issues; these cannot wait, but the broad eternal issues of private law can. The disproportion between private law and other legislation for this period can stand as an example—not extreme—of the typical interests of legislatures.

Second, from the eleventh century until the modern era of codification, the main feature of legal development in continental Europe was the Reception of Roman law. This could only occur, as it did, in the absence of legislation introducing much new law. It resulted above all from the work, the interpretation, of professors who again, as such, had no (necessary) ties to government. The Reception was seldom imposed by rulers; when it was, it was usually a recognition of the status quo. Moreover, what was imposed was the Corpus Juris Civilis as a whole or as glossed, not merely the rules favorable to princes.[16] But in general the Reception occurred at a lower level because the courts accepted Roman rules. The major part of Chapters 2 and 7 indicates both something of the scope of the Reception and the role of jurists in it.

Third, there was, as I just implied, a paucity of legislation on private law during the same period. This cannot be, as some will have it, because of lack of power or authority to legislate, because the same times and places saw much legislation on other matters.

Fourth, feudalism as a social and military system was coming to an end in the twelfth century or not much later, but it was only then that the feudal law (as set out in the *Libri Feudorum*), which was to be so influential, was coming into being.[17] Yet, despite a great degree of decentralization, feudalism, of all social systems, should be the one that most reaches from the highest level of authority downward because of the intense personal fealty it involves. The *Libri Feudorum*, which forms the basis of developed feudal law, was a private compilation, though it contains some statute law.

Fifth, European rulers have often been indifferent to communicating clearly the substance of law, even of criminal law, to their subjects, which explains the common scarcity of legislation and the consequent difficulty of finding or deducing the law from a mass of precedents or juristic writings. This indifference is incomprehensible if the rulers had much interest in the actual substance of the law.[18]

Sixth, even when great codifiers of private law emerge, they often are, like Justinian and Frederick the Great, much more motivated by a desire to make law more accessible than to make it conform to a particular political or social ideal. In their turn, with the civil codes prepared for their countries, Napoleon most wanted one law for all of France, and Atatürk in the 1920s wanted to modernize Turkey. The precise content of the law was generally of less concern to them.[19]

Last (for the moment), in England from the origins of the common law until the second half of the nineteenth century, law was left to be developed mainly by judicial precedent.[20] This made legal growth haphazard, slow, unresponsive to social and political conditions, incomprehensible to nonlawyers, and unsystematic.

GREAT LEGISLATORS

Even great lawmakers, famous for their legislation, have not been particularly interested in setting forth a detailed political, social, or economic message. Although legal historians, looking at an individual civil code, claim to find in it very specific relations with the political and economic order, the claims often lack substance. Examples of legislators' disinterest in giving a particular message can be chosen from Justinian, through Frederick the Great of Prussia and Napoleon, even to Atatürk. I am not, of course, claiming that these figures of history did not have precise political and other aims, but rather only that one cannot, at least in many contexts, uncover in their private law legislation a dominant concern to find the substantive law most suited for the conditions of their time. Massive legislation is itself a highly political act, but the legislators' main aim may be to clarify existing law and make it more readily available, to unify the legal rules within the state, or to modernize the law in order to help modernize the state. Such aims may fall far short of seeking the rules "most suitable" for the society.

For Justinian and his advisers one can discount, almost a priori, the notion that the substantive rules in the *Code, Digest,* and *Institutes* were in general geared to a precise societal ordering. If such had been his intention, then he would not have chosen to construct the *Code* and *Digest* on the basis of quotations of earlier law from emperors and jurists. No doubt the quotations are selective and reflect to some extent the concerns of the age, but to select statements from the past to give effect to conditions of the present is scarcely the way to set about providing legal rules precisely adapted to the contemporary world. Moreover, the *Digest* and, to a lesser extent, the *Code* reflect the pagan world of Rome, one of diverse economic conditions, not the Christian world of Constantinople. Indeed, the *Digest* and the *Code* to a considerable extent represent different worlds. Virtually no *Digest* text can be ascribed to the period after the death of the emperor Alexander Severus in A.D. 235, but by far the greater part of the *Code* belongs to the time after that date. Therefore, the former, unlike the latter, cannot reflect the economic collapse of the half century before Diocletian, the autocracy of that and subsequent rulers, the move to Constantinople, the rise of Christianity, and the absence of independent creative jurists.

These differences between the *Digest* and the *Code* become even more significant in the present context when we recall that the two works were prepared independently of each other. The surviving evidence indicates that when Justinian ordered the preparation of the first *Code,* he did not yet have the intention of collecting, abridging, and promulgating as law the writings of the classical jurists. Only if the *Digest* represents a second stage of his thinking on replacing the prior law can one explain the promulgation of the *Fifty Decisions*—to settle old, yet still existing, juristic disputes—*after* the completion of the first *Code* of 529, and their subsequent incorporation into the second *Code* of 534. But two such different works as the *Code* and *Digest,* conceived independently under the auspices of the same emperor, belie the notion that either of them, or both together, offered substantive legal rules that as a whole contained a precise political, social, or economic message. In addition, Justinian's instructions to his compilers and the other prefaces for the first *Code,* the second *Code,* and the *Digest* contain nothing to warrant the conclusion that he wanted the excerpted texts to maintain or bring about any particular image of society. Yet we have extensive information regarding what he stated he wanted in two prefaces to the first *Code,* one setting up the commission, the other confirming the completed work—a preface confirming the second *Code;* and in two prefaces to the *Digest,* one setting up the commission for it and the other confirming it.

So little does the massive *Digest* reflect early Christian Byzantium that astonishingly in the body of the work there is not a single reference to

Jesus, the apostles, or saints, and no arguments are drawn from the fathers of the church. The same is true of the *Institutes*, which introduced students to the law. Indeed, in the body of the *Digest* the word *deus* (god) occurs only twelve times, and apart from our other knowledge of Byzantium we could not tell if they concern a pagan god or the Christian God.[21] The position is rather different in the *Code*, but students began to study the *Code* only in their fifth and final year when their attitudes to law would be fixed.

For Frederick the Great of Prussia it is enough to call attention to the firstfruits of his attempts to codify the law, *Das Project des Corpus juris Fredericiani, d.h. S.M. in der Vernunft und Landes verfassungen gegründetes Landrecht, worin das Römisches Recht in eine natürliche Ordnung und richtiges Systema nach denen dreyen Objectis juris gebracht,* which was published at Halle between 1749 and 1751. The very title is instructive: "The Project for the Corpus juris Fredericiani, that is, the Territorial Law of His Majesty, Founded in Reason and the Territorial Constitutions, in which Roman Law Is Brought into a Natural Order and Right System in Accordance with Its Three Objects of Law." That is to say, it gives the *ius commune,* and it is in fact arranged in the order of Justinian's *Institutes.* No attempt is made to compose afresh a law peculiarly suited to the Prussian territories. Indeed, some paragraphs of the preface, particularly 15, 22, 23, and 28, make it plain that for the drafters the impetus for the *Project* was not dissatisfaction with the substantive *ius commune* but with the difficulty of ascertaining the law because of the poor arrangement of Justinian's Corpus Juris Civilis (apart from the *Institutes*) and of the multitude of writings by subsequent jurists. In the second section of part 1, book 1, Frederick claims it is only to be regretted that the German emperors when they received Roman law did not always systematize it. Frederick's primary intentions—at least as they were perceived by his famous chancellor, Samuel Cocceji—ought best to be revealed by the main thrust of this first production. The fact that, because of the Seven Years' War, it never came into force (which is regarded, for instance, by Franz Wieacker as rather fortunate) is not of consequence here. For later attempts at codification, ultimately crowned with success, with rather different aims, Frederick was indebted to a new generation of lawyers and philosophers.[22]

Indeed, even before, in the late fifteenth and sixteenth centuries, many German cities, towns, and even villages received reformed statements of their law. As Gerald Strauss has pointed out: "If one is to believe their preambles, municipal and territorial 'reformations' were undertaken in Germany for one overriding reason: to end the uncertainty affecting all areas of law by replacing the old rules with a single code combining the virtues of clarity and uniformity."[23] The main intention was not to incorporate particular political and social messages in the law, but to render intelligible the substance of the law. The fact that many "reformations" were Romanizing is not in conflict with this.

Napoleon, as is continually stressed, took a strong personal interest in the preparation of the Code civil.[24] In Chapter 5 I examine the construction of the articles on delict, which betray a French response to the Roman rules and show no sign of any particular political, social, or economic message. The same is true in other fields. Here we should examine a branch of the law in which customary law predominated and in which we should expect to find the impact of new ideas. What effect, one might wonder, did revolutionary and Napoleonic fervor have on the law of matrimonial property? And what growth of awareness is shown by the legislative history?

Article 1387 of the Code civil declares that the law does not regulate the conjugal association with regard to property except in the absence of special agreements that spouses can make as they judge fit, provided they are not contrary to good morals. This freedom to contract on matrimonial property is not ancient. Until the sixteenth century, the choice of matrimonial regime was unknown. Only one regime operated in each region in France: in the *pays de droit coutumier* this was community of property, and the precise arrangements varied from place to place; in the *pays de droit écrit* and also in Normandy, this was a system of dowry.[25] Article 1390 of the Code civil forbade spouses to stipulate in a general manner that their association would be regulated by one of the customs or other law that previously governed the different parts of French soil and that were declared abolished by the Code civil. Article 1391 states that the parties could declare in a general manner that they were marrying under the regime of community of property or under the dotal regime. In the first alternative, the arrangement was said to be governed by articles 1399 to 1539 of the Code civil (though actually it was governed by articles 1399 to 1496, the first part of the second chapter), and in the second alternative by articles 1540 to 1581 of the Code civil. Article 1393 enacts that, in the absence of special arrangements for the property of the spouses, articles 1399 to 1496 formed the common law of France.

Thus by the Code civil of 1804, spouses could make their own arrangements governing their property, but if they failed to do so, the marriage was with community of property under the particular regime described and enacted in articles 1399 to 1496. That same regime also applied if the spouses declared in a general manner that they were married with community. In terms of their freedom to make their own arrangements, the spouses could also agree that the wife would bring the husband a dowry. If they declared in a general manner that the marriage would have a dotal regime, then the parties' rights were governed by articles 1540 to 1581.

What, therefore, is this one regime of community property that was declared to be the common law of France, and this one dotal regime that applied when a dotal regime was declared but not further specified? How did the Code civil drafters come up with these rules, and what are the origins of the rules?

Of the various community regimes—and there were approximately sixty—at the time of the French Revolution, that of the Coutume de Paris was by far the most widespread and could even be described as the common law of France. The provisions of this *coutume* in very large measure formed the basis of the provision of the *communauté légale*. There seems to have been little determined search for other, better, or newer rules. The discussions in the Conseil d'Etat in September and October 1803 are instructive.[26] Apart from the preliminary issue of whether there should be a common law, there was relatively little discussion or disagreement about the substance of the provisions. By far the most lively argument was provided by Maleville in his unsuccessful opposition to what became article 1401. His arguments and those of Berlier, who opposed him, are significant. Maleville objected that by that provision, successions and gifts of movables to one spouse would be shared with the other. He argued:

> This principle is so extraordinary that even in the *coutumes* that accept community, it is usual to stipulate that spouses will not be liable for each other's debts; that their movables will remain their own in whole or in part; that the same will apply to successions or gifts that may come to them; that, in out of one hundred contracts of marriage made even in Paris, there are not ten where one is held to the statutory community as it is presented here. And one would like to give it as a rule to those who have always rejected it![27]

And the beginning of Berlier's response was:

> In reducing the conjugal community of property to a simple partnership of acquisitions, M. Maleville proposes to derogate from the most general

practices of the *pays de droit coutumier:* for the *coutume* of Paris, whose *ressort* was immense, and the majority of the others, brought together into the community the respective movables of the spouses. And that consideration has already some weight, for one must not innovate without serious reasons.[28]

Thus, Maleville was opposed to one provision in the Code civil that followed the Coutume de Paris on the precise ground that even in Paris the rules in it were not wanted and that, of those who made marriage contracts, more than 90 percent adopted different rules. The opposing argument, which was successful, was precisely that the provision did give the rules of the Coutume de Paris and of the *coutumes* in general, and that one should not innovate without strong reason. Nothing is more powerful than these arguments for demonstrating the absence of revolutionary zeal in reforming the law of marital property.

The rules for the dotal regime in articles 1540 to 1581 are equally significant in the failure of the Code civil to give a particular new political, social, or economic message, because in general they simply give the rules of Roman law as they had come to be understood in the *pays de droit écrit.* Indeed, article 1559 introduced Roman law that had not previously been received, according to Duveyrier, when the project was communicated to the *tribunat,* because the reasons for the Roman rule were foreign under the ancien régime but not under the new political institutions.[29] And it can scarcely be emphasized too much that the proposed rules on dowry had given rise to little debate in the Conseil d'Etat.

But we must go slightly further back. The *projet* for a code that the commission presented on 24 thermidor, an VIII, dealt only with the rules of community property, statutory and by special agreement, and were silent on dowry.[30] This omission caused such a furor in the Midi that the later *projet* contained numerous provisions on dowry.[31] Thus was confirmed the prophecy of Estienne Pasquier (1529–1615): "Ask those who are subject to the *pays de droit écrit,* they will tell you that separation of property is, beyond compare, better than community, and those of the *pays de droit coutumier* will give their judgment in favor of community of property. So much tyranny has a long and ancient usage over us."[32]

In no sense, however, am I claiming that the French Revolution and subsequent events had no impact upon French private law. Of course they did, notably with regard to personal status and the abolition of feudal notions of property. Rather, I am insisting that in the many fields in which there was no obvious, immediate, revolutionary promulgation, the drafters of the code, despite all their debates, gave rules that were rooted in the past, in the purely legal tradition at that, and that cannot be explained on the basis of some particular, political, social, economic, or moral message. It can in no way surprise us that legal change, indeed even drastic change, can be promulgated by statute: the surprising thing, to my mind, is the extent to which change does not occur.

A further example is Atatürk, who wished to reform and modernize Turkish life in so many ways (and was very largely successful). He promulgated in 1926 the Turkish Civil Code, the Türk Kanunu Medenîsi (TKM), which contained virtually all of the two Swiss codes, the Schweizerisches Gesetzbuch (ZGB) and the Obligationenrecht. Turkey in the same year issued its commercial code, which was a compilation of at least a dozen foreign statutes, and issued in 1929 its code of the sea, which is a translation of book 4 of the German Commercial Code (Handelsgesetzbuch).

The Turkish minister of justice of the time, Mahmut Esad Bozkurt, on the occasion of the *Festschrift* of the Istanbul Law Faculty to mark the civil code's fifteenth birthday, explained the reasons for the codification. First, the Turkish legal system was backward and primitive. Three kinds of religious law were in force, Islamic, Christian, and Jewish, each with its appropriate court. Only a kind of law of obligations, the "Mecelle," and real property law was common to all. Second, such an odd system of justice, with three kinds of law applied through three kinds of courts, could not correspond to the modern understanding of the state and its unity. Third and most important, each time Turkey had demanded the removal of the capitulation terms of the First World War by the victorious Allies, the latter refused, pointing to the backward state of the Turkish legal system and its connection with religion. When as a result of the Lausanne Peace Treaty the capitulation terms were removed, the Turks took it upon themselves to form a completely new Turkish organization of justice with a new legal system, new laws, and new courts. Bozkurt said that in one word the system was to be "worldly." The duties undertaken by the Turks under the Lausanne treaty had to be accomplished as quickly as possible. During the First World War commissions were already set up in Istanbul to prepare laws and they had started work. The results were examined in 1924. After seven or eight years the Turks had completed only two hundred articles on a law of obligations; the sections on succession, guardianship, formation of marriage, and divorce of a civil code; and between seventy and eighty articles of a criminal code; and even the code of land transactions was only a torso.[33] Consequently, after various systems had been looked at, the two Swiss codes were adopted virtually in their entirety.

Although the motivation was different from most earlier receptions—drastic modernization of society rather than the filling of gaps in the law—the Turkish reception was otherwise similar. Because the creation of new autochthonous law is difficult, it is much easier to borrow from an already existing, more sophisticated system that can be used as a model—above all, where the donor system is accessible in writing. By this time, of course, various excellent codes could have provided a model; notably the French, German, and Swiss were all greatly admired. Why was Swiss law chosen? Various answers have been given, but three strike me as most important: the Swiss laws were the most modern;[34] Switzerland had been neutral during the war, whereas French law was that of a former enemy and German law was that of a defeated ally; and Bozkurt had studied law in Switzerland, so Swiss law was most familiar to him. Hirsch, a German scholar who was a professor of commercial law at Istanbul and Ankara between 1933 and 1952, emphasizes what was to him the overriding importance of the last factor.[35] In any event, there is no reason to think that somehow Swiss law was more adapted than was French or German law to the society that Turkey wanted to become.

Hirsch stresses the nature of such a reception. What is important, he insists, is neither foreign law nor foreign codes, but foreign cultural property, which, only after its linguistic and systematic transformation, finds the appropriate external form; and only in the act of legislation is it fixed as a binding legal rule that comes into force.[36] Even after such legislation a reception is not a once-and-for-all act but a social process extending over many years. The result will not be Swiss law in Turkey, but Turkish law that owes much to Swiss legal culture, concepts, and rules.

The Turks did not accept some Swiss rules at all and changed others. For instance, whereas the legal regime in Switzerland for spouses' property is community property (ZGB 178), in Turkey it is separate property (TKM 170); the surviving spouse's right to a usufruct is smaller in Turkey (TKM 444 §2) than in Switzerland (ZGB 462 §2); the judicial separation of spouses may in Switzerland be pronounced for an indefinite time (ZGB 147 §1) but not in Turkey (TKM 139 §1); desertion as a ground of divorce in Switzerland must have lasted at least two years (ZGB 140), but in Turkey at least three months (TKM 132); the minimum age for marriage in the former is for males twenty, for females eighteen (exceptionally eighteen and seventeen), in the latter for males eighteen, for females seventeen. Other rules would be accidentally mistranslated and the final result need not be that of the donor nation. Others were deliberately given a different value in the translation. Still others remain a dead letter because they have no counterpart in Turkish conditions. The Turkish courts in giving flesh to the rules through interpretation may, as they usually but not always have done, follow the interpretation of the Swiss courts. Again, many rules have a different societal value in the two countries, such as those on a minimum age for marriage or on the requirements for a divorce.[37] Finally, such a reception, as fast as Atatürk wanted it to be, will, like that of Roman law and of other systems, be a slow process, and the speed and the extent of its success—never complete—will vary with circumstances.

Any new law resulting from such a massive transplantation has to be learned by judges and lawyers as well as by the people before it becomes effective. In the case of Turkey, where the new legal system was so different from what had gone before but was so closely attached to European models, the solution was to import foreign professors from Germany and Switzerland, notably Andreas B. Schwartz and Ernest E. Hirsch, to teach the new law, and to send budding lawyers and law professors to study law in Europe.[38] Also, aspects of traditional social life, such as marriage, respond only slowly to the pressures of new law, especially in country districts. Significantly, essays in a collection published to mark the thirtieth anniversary of the Turkish codification stress the extent to which the reception had not "taken,"[39] whereas those in another collection to mark the fiftieth anniversary accept the reception but emphasize its continuing nature and the fact that it is not, nor will be, complete.[40] In 1956 Kurt Lipstein could describe the extent of acceptance of compulsory civil marriage as "disappointing, to say the least."[41] In 1978 June Starr reported that in a particular village that she had studied, she found little evidence "that villagers are lax in obtaining state marriage licenses."[42]

The success or partial, yet still growing, success of the transplanting of Swiss legal ideas into Turkey gives many insights into what happens when a less "modern" or less "developed" system comes into powerful contact with a sophisticated modern system. These insights become almost blinding when we notice that Eugen Huber, who virtually alone was responsible for the ZGB, said that "the law must be delivered in speech out of the thought of the people. The reasonable man who reads it, who has pondered the age and its needs, must have the perception that the law was delivered to him in speech from the heart" (Das Gesetz muss aus den Gedanken des Volkes heraus gesprochen sein. Der verständige Mann, der es liest, muss die Empfindung haben, das Gesetz sei ihm vom Herzen gesprochen).[43] And Virgile Rossel declared that "in particular if one could say of the Code Napoléon that it was 'written reason,' we intended to work according to the sense of the national spirit, raising the moral level of our law so far as possible, and we would be happy if it was said one day of the Swiss civil code that it is, to some extent, the written internal moral sentiment" (En particulier si l' on a pu dire du code Napoléon qu'il était la 'raison écrite' nous avons cru travailler dans le sens de l'esprit national en moralisant notre droit autant que faire se pouvait, et nous serions heureux si l'on disait un jour du code civil suisse qu'il est un peu la conscience écrite).[44] Yet the same Virgile Rossel, was well aware that the differences in the laws of the various Swiss cantons could not be explained on the basis of religion, economy, language, or "race."

Thus, the Swiss codification was intended by those who worked on it to be the written moral consciousness of the Swiss people. The arbitrary rules of cantonal law were to be remedied by federal law appropriate to the conditions of the Swiss. The "Swissness" of the codification is stressed. Yet the Swiss codification could be taken over, almost in its entirety, some years later by Turkey, a country with a vastly different history, legal tradition, religion, culture, economy, political setup, and geographical and climatic circumstances. Turkey under Atatürk is a prime example not only of legal transplant but of revolution in law.[45] Substantive alterations were few and minor. But what is striking is that the two Swiss codes were regarded by their creators as particularly Swiss and in accordance with the Swiss national spirit and moral consciousness. Yet, writing in the context of Turkish marriage law, N. Y. Gürpinar can claim that "in addition, after the revolution in Turkey it was urgently necessary to create a law corresponding to the principles of the young Turkish republic. This for civil law was the Turkish civil code taken over from Switzerland." And in a more general context, after explaining the need for a modern Turkish code, B. N. Esen writes:

> That was the situation of fact. Now, Switzerland always was and is the land of democracy par excellence. As a land with a long democratic past Switzerland was quite especially called to serve as a model for the civil code. Turkey

did not hesitate a single second. And in 1926 the Schweizerisches Gesetz-buch and the Swiss Obligationenrecht were taken over with minor alter-ations as the statute law of the state. If these codes of foreign origin have been used in Turkey for a quarter century without the slightest difficulty, then it is on this account, because they mirror exactly the spiritual incli-nation of the social milieu, that they reflect the idea of law and justice of the place in which they are interpreted and used.[46]

Thus, insofar as private and commercial law are concerned, a revolu-tionary leader seeking democracy in Turkey could find almost precisely what he needed in codes framed for very different conditions in Switzer-land. I do not entirely agree with Esen. The making of a civil code for Turkey was proving difficult. So a model was borrowed. Swiss law was not easily accepted in practice. I do not believe that the Swiss codes mir-rored exactly what was wanted or needed.

CHAPTER 2

JURISTS

Legislation is the supreme power in law making. But legislation is often lacking or insufficient. The making of law is then up to subordinate law-makers who are tolerated by the government, but are not authorized to make law. These subordinate law makers—jurists, law professors, judges—make law *faute de mieux.*

In this chapter I explore the impact of juristic thinking on two very different fronts. First, I want to explain (as well as describe) the reasoning of jurists in the Western world. Second, in the context of the Roman law of contracts I want to demonstrate the enormous impact of thinking by law specialists, in this case by jurists, on the evolution of the law. But before that, I want to return to Justinian's Corpus Juris Civilis, the largest body of statute law that the Western world has known. The two major parts of the codification of Roman law, the *Code* and the *Digest,* were conceived of separately; when the *Code* was planned, the *Digest* was not in contemplation. The *Digest* was not to repeat anything that was in the *Code.* The *Digest* is very much an abridgment of juristic writings and is largely confined to private law, the interest of the jurists. The *Code* contains the rulings of emperors. Yet the *Digest* is twice as big as the *Code.* Nothing could better illustrate the impact of jurists on legal development, even when that development ends in statute.

ROMAN REASONING: MEDIEVAL AND
LATER AUTHORITY

Roman law is central to the evolution of Western law. Its own development was the product of particular historical circumstances, and the form of this development was determined at an early date. These circumstances fixed the basic modes of Roman legal reasoning, which then determined much of Western legal reasoning up to the present day.[1] The Reception of Roman law is not to be seen only in the borrowing of rules and institutions.

Astonishingly, the abiding characteristics of Roman law were fashioned mainly by events that occurred in a few years beginning around 451 B.C., in this early point in Rome's history.[2] After the expulsion of the last king, Tarquin the Proud, in 510 B.C. and the establishment of the republic in 509, government was primarily in the hands of two magistrates, later called consuls, who were elected annually. From early in the republic serious tension existed between the small number of leading aristocratic families, the patricians, and the great majority of the population, the plebeians. Presumably we should see in this tension the ambition of leading plebeians who wished to break into the patrician monopoly of high public office.[3] For the mass of the plebeians it could make no practical difference whether political and religious power was restricted to patricians or was also open to the wealthiest and most ambitious plebeian families.

The patrician monopoly of power, established by law, was all embracing. Thus, in the religious sphere, the main state priests, including the members of the leading College of Pontiffs and the College of Augurs, had to be patrician. Only after the Ogulnian law (*lex Ogulnia*) passed in 300 B.C., despite patrician opposition, could plebeians be pontiffs or augurs.[4] Control of the state religion was a powerful political weapon. In the administrative sphere, only patricians could be consuls—and consuls were the normal heads of state—until the Licinian-Sextian laws (*leges Liciniae Sextiae*) of 367.[5] Thereafter one of them had to be a plebeian, but this provision seems not to have been regularly implemented until 320. From 444 three military tribunes might hold the chief magistracy (in place of the two consuls) and plebeians could hold that office, but according to Livy (4.7.2, 5.12.9) no plebeian was elected until 400. Dictators, who could be appointed in an emergency, had to be patrician. The only other regular magistrates in the early republic were the quaestors, who were chosen by the consuls; plebeians became legally eligible in 421.[6] The office of praetor was created in 367, specifically to deal with legal issues. This office controlled the major lawcourts and had a great impact on legal change. Livy (6.42.9ff., 8.15.9) relates that the first plebeian praetor was elected in 337.

Of course, opening various offices to the plebeians was not a big step toward democracy. The powerful plebeians who sought election had more in common with the patricians than with the great mass of plebeians. With time, rich plebeians had more wealth than many patricians, and Rome was a society as money-conscious as today's United States.

The main political legislative body was the *comitia centuriata,* which could meet only when summoned by the consuls and could discuss only the business they put before it. The *comitia* could vote down legislation but not amend it. The *comitia* in early Rome was divided into five military classes determined by wealth, and voting was by the centuries or electoral units into which each class was divided. Above the first, wealthiest, class were centuries of cavalry (*equites*), and the cavalry and first class together constituted a majority of centuries.[7] Voting was in descending order, the *equites* first, the first class next, and voting stopped as soon as there was a majority for the positive or negative. According to Livy (1.43.10ff.), voting seldom went as far as the second class and almost never to the lowest class.

In their early struggle with patricians, the plebeians' political demands came to center on the need for law reform.[8] In 462 B.C. a tribune of the plebs, C. Terentilius Harsa, attacked the arrogance of patricians toward the plebeians and, above all, the powers of the consuls. There were, he claimed, no restraints on the consuls, and he proposed that five men be appointed to write down the law on the powers of the consuls, which in the future they should not exceed. Terentilius made no progress that year but proffered the same proposal the following year with the support of all the tribunes. Their demands encountered unfavorable religious omens. The Sibylline books were examined by the relevant two patrician officials, who found in them warnings against the danger of external attack and against factious politics. The tribunes treated these warnings as fraudulent and continued to press for their law reforms. Their demands were considered to be against religion—not surprisingly, given the composition of the priesthood—as well as against political order.

Around 454 B.C. the consuls declared that the passage of a law by the people and the tribunes would never happen. The tribunes, who were by now discouraged, proposed a compromise: if the senate would not accept a law passed by the plebeians, the patricians and plebeians should appoint a team of lawmakers drawn from both sides to make laws beneficial to both and equalizing the liberty of both. The senators were not against the idea of law making but insisted that they and they alone could make the law. The dispirited plebs accepted this, and a team was sent to Athens, says Livy, to write down the famous laws of Solon and to record the laws and customs of other Greek states. (In actuality, any

Greek influence may have come from Magna Graecia, in southern Italy.) When the delegation returned, it was decided to appoint ten officials, *decemviri*, as the sole magistrates, to draft the laws. After controversy over whether plebeians could be appointed to the office, the plebeians conceded that only patricians would be *decemviri*. The sources stress that the plebeians wanted the powers of the consuls to be limited and set down, and that they sought equality before the law.

These *decemviri* produced a code of ten tables which, after amendment, were successfully presented to the *comitia centuriata*. The *decemviri* proved to be very popular and, when it was felt that the code was incomplete, a second group of *decemviri* was elected for the following year. They produced two supplementary tables, and the resulting Twelve Tables became the basis of Roman law. Members of the second set, especially Appius Claudius, showed themselves to be tyrannous, remained in office after their term expired, but were eventually deposed.

The plebeians had demanded equality before the law. The Twelve Tables is remarkably egalitarian, but only because the patrician *decemviri* restricted its contents to the law they were willing to share with plebeians. Hence, there is no public law, no treatment of state public or religious offices.[9] This check created the distinction between public and private law that is so much a feature of modern law, especially in civil-law systems.

Statute requires interpretation. According to the jurist Pomponius (*D*.1.2.5–6), writing in the second century A.D., the task of interpretation, specifically of the Twelve Tables, was allotted to the patrician College of Pontiffs, which each year selected one member for interpreting private law. Ever afterward the subsequent Roman jurists concentrated on private law.

Such were the historical events that, above all, in my view, determined the spirit of Roman law. The major characteristics that shaped Roman law forever flowed from these circumstances.

Just as none of us make our history just as we like but carry our past with us, so the interpreters of the Twelve Tables carried over from their pontifical roles their sacred-law approaches to legal reasoning. Accordingly, legal judgments could not be reached expressly on the basis of what was reasonable, economically advantageous, useful, or just. As we shall see, a very particular form of internal legal logic was employed in reaching an opinion, with few references to social reality, which also explains the at least apparent remoteness from legal discussion of particular political, social, or economic circumstances or events.

The original role of interpretation given to the pontiffs and the choice of one of their number to give authoritative rulings are the basis of two other characteristic features of the system at Rome: the importance subsequently attached by gentlemen (i.e., the jurists) to the giving of legal opinions, and the acceptance by the state of the individual's important role in law making. Because becoming one of the (originally) four pontiffs was an important step in a political career and because giving authoritative rulings in law was a significant pontifical function, it was valuable for a gentleman to have legal knowledge and to provide legal opinions. Because the pontiffs were patricians and were appointed only after they had a known political track record, the ruling elite could usually feel confident in allowing them to declare what the law was. When the College of Pontiffs lost its monopoly of interpretation, tradition ensured that men of the same class regarded the task as important. Until the early first century B.C., the senators dominated the ranks of the jurists; and up to 95 B.C. eighteen jurists had held the consulate.[10]

The same facts explain fundamental approaches to legal sources. The role of interpretation given to the pontiffs entailed, as we will see, little scope for custom and judicial precedent in law making. That role and the high social status of the pontiffs, and subsequently of the jurists, ensured that there would be close cooperation between jurist and praetor and meant that once praetors began to create law by setting out in edicts how they perceived their legal functions, much of the detail could be left unstated, to be filled in by the jurists.

On the same basis, too, is to be explained the absence of concern with the realities of court practice. The jurists as such were not directly involved with litigation. Their prestige (and wealth) did not depend on the outcome of a trial, and they were not concerned with strategies for winning. Thus arose the extreme separation of substantive law from the technicalities needed to support it. Formalities, for instance, were required to create the contract of *stipulatio,* but they were of such a nature that they provided no evidence for a court that a contract had actually been made.

One text from the great Julian of the second century is sufficient to show the general style of Roman juristic reasoning.

D.9.2.51. A slave who had been wounded so gravely that he was certain to die of the injury was appointed someone's heir and was subsequently killed by a further blow from another assailant. The question is whether an action under the *lex Aquilia* lies against both assailants for killing him. The answer was given as follows: A person is generally said to have killed if he furnished a cause of death in any way whatever, but so far as the *lex Aquilia* is concerned, there will be liability only if the death resulted from some application of force, done as it were by one's own hand, for the law depends on the interpretation of the words *caedere* and *caedes*. Furthermore, it is not only those who wound so as to deprive at once of life who will be liable for a killing in accordance with the *lex* but also those who inflict an injury that is certain to prove fatal. Accordingly, if someone wounds a slave mortally and then after a while someone else inflicts a further injury, as a result of which he dies sooner than would otherwise have been the case, it is clear that both assailants are liable for killing. 1. This rule has the authority of the ancient jurists, who decided that, if a slave were injured by several persons but it was not clear which blow actually killed him, they would all be liable under the *lex Aquilia*. 2. But in the case that we are considering, the dead slave will not be valued in the same way in assessing the penalty to be paid for each wound. The person who struck him first will have to pay the highest value of the slave in the preceding year, counting back three hundred and sixty-five days from the day of the wounding: but the second assailant will be liable to pay the highest price that the slave would have fetched had he been sold during the year before he departed this life, and, of course, in this figure the value of the inheritance will be included. Therefore, for the killing of this slave, one assailant will pay more and the other less, but this is not to be wondered at because each is deemed to have killed him in different circumstances and at a different time. But in case anyone might think that we have reached an absurd conclusion, let him ponder carefully how much more absurd it would be to hold that neither should be liable under the *lex Aquilia* or that one should be held to blame rather than the other. Misdeeds should not escape unpunished, and it is not easy to decide if one is more blameworthy than the other. Indeed, it can be proved by innumerable examples that the civil law has accepted things for the general good that do not accord with pure logic. Let us content ourselves for the time being with just one instance: When several people, with intent to steal, carry off a beam which no single one of them could have carried alone, they are all liable to an action for theft, although by subtle reasoning one could make the point that no single one of them could be liable because in literal truth he could not have moved it unaided.

The issue arose under the *lex Aquilia,* which dealt with damage to property. Under chapter 1, for the wrongful killing of a slave, damages were the highest value the slave had in the past year. Under chapter 3, for the wrongful wounding of a slave, damages were the amount of loss to the owner.[11] A slave was wrongfully wounded so severely that he was sure to die. Then another person died, who had appointed the slave his heir in his will. Then someone else wrongfully killed the slave. The basic issue in the text is whether the first injurer is liable under the first or under the third chapter. Julian first reasons from the meaning of the verb, *caedere*, "to strike," and the noun *caedes*, "killing." He says in general a person is held to have killed if he furnished a cause of death in any way, but for liability under the *lex Aquilia* there are restrictions: there had to be an application of force, and this force had to be by the body to the body. This he claims to be the result of interpretation.[12] There is something strange in this because, so far as we know, neither *caedere* nor *caedes* appeared in the statute: the verb *occidere*, "to kill," did. And this should have allowed the wider interpretation. Perhaps some part of the statute has been lost. In any event, this restriction had been accepted by Julian's time. It meant in practice that for "furnishing a cause of death," the wrongdoer would not be liable under chapter 1, but to an action on the facts for which the damages would only be the owner's loss.[13] Presumably this distinction was first drawn by jurists and then accepted to restrict the possibility of windfall profits to the slave's owner. If this view is accurate, then the jurists were motivated by social concerns. But then we have an insight into their reasoning. Societal concerns of such a kind are not voiced in the discussions of the statute. They would be an inappropriate argument. Instead, the argument is from strict verbal interpretation. Julian deals with the point, but it does not really matter to him. He decides that both killed: the first because the blow was mortal, the second because the slave died sooner.

In fragment 1 Julian produces a different argument for developing his thesis. He cites, as is typical of jurists, the authority of earlier jurists. Where several struck a slave who died, and it could not be established who struck the fatal blow, all would be liable for killing. That is, each would pay the slave's owner the highest value the slave had in the past year. The owner would receive considerable windfall profit. Neither Julian nor any other jurist discussed the justice of the result nor, so far as our evidence goes, did any suggest reforming the statute. Justice or fairness seldom appears as an argument to reach a decision;[14] and law reform was not high on the jurists' agenda.[15] Significantly, when the *lex Aquilia* was received later in western Europe, this measure of damages was not accepted.[16]

In fragment 2 Julian relates that the penalty will not be the same in each case. The first wounder, or killer, will pay the highest value the slave had in the year prior to the wounding, the second will pay the highest price he would have fetched in the year prior to his death. The second, that is, but not the first, will have to pay the enhancement of the slave's price because of the inheritance. Julian is clearly aware that his decision will not satisfy everyone so he uses a standard juristic argument, the *reductio ad absurdum:*[17] it would be much more absurd to hold that neither should be liable or one more liable. But, of course, in this case by deciding the date of death differently, he has made the second wrongdoer more liable than the first. He had two other options. He could have held that both were liable for killing at the moment of death. This ruling would have been more rational, but then the owner would have received the windfall profit of the double inheritance, and Julian apparently wants to avoid that. Alternatively, he could have held the first assailant liable only for wounding. But then Julian would have had another problem. The first assailant would get off almost scot-free. Not only would he not have to pay for the inheritance but, because he only had to pay for the owner's loss, he would not have to pay on the slave's value for what the owner recovered from the second assailant. And the second assailant's wounding might have been slighter.

Although jurists usually avoided expressing social arguments, we have an exception here: "Misdeeds should not escape unpunished." We should note the context. Actions on the *lex Aquilia* were actions of private law but what they concern here would be a serious crime at Rome and elsewhere.

Julian, having great difficulty with his argument, continued to try to justify it: innumerable examples prove that the civil law has accepted things for the common good (*pro utilitate communi recepta*) that do not accord with pure logic. He indirectly admits that his solution lacks logic. Very seldom do the Roman jurists use utility as a reason toward a decision. When *utilitas* appears as an argument, it is almost always as an argument, as here, to justify past decisions. And what is accepted on the ground of utility is almost always an exception.[18]

Finally, Julian gives us one of these examples. But it is a simpler case. The Roman delict of theft, *furtum*, was committed by a wrongful touching, and did not require asportation. But if someone wrongfully handles something that he is incapable of carrying off, there is no *furtum*. Yet if two or more carried off, each of them is a thief. The only troubling issue is that the *actio furti* lay against a thief for a multiple of the value of the thing, not for the owner's loss. The text is instructive not only for what it says but for what it does not say: no direct allusion to societal issues. Julian's decision is illogical (and has often been held interpolated), and the correct solution had been given by Celsus, as reported by Ulpian:

> D.9.2.11.3. Celsus writes that if one man gave a slave a mortal wound, and another afterward deprives him of life, the former is not liable as if he had killed but as if he had wounded because he perished from another wound: the latter is liable because he killed. This is also the view of Marcellus, and it is the better view.

Julian's difficulty is made even clearer by another text of Ulpian.

> D.9.2.15.1. If a slave who has been mortally wounded has his death accelerated subsequently by the collapse of a house or by shipwreck or by some other sort of blow, no action can be brought for killing, but only as if he were wounded; but if he dies from a wound after he has been freed or alienated, Julian says an action can be brought for killing. These situations are so different for this reason: because the truth is that in the latter case he was killed by you when you were wounding him, which only became apparent later by his death; but in the former case the collapse of the house did not allow it to emerge whether or not he was killed.

The distinction drawn by Ulpian may be dubious. But what interests us in the present context is precisely that no social or economic argument is adduced. That was not the way of the jurists.

The compilation of Justinian described in Chapter 1, with the apparent exception of the *Institutes*, was lost to view in the West from shortly after Justinian's time to about the eleventh century. Thereafter, the study of it, and its Reception, are among the glories of the Middle Ages. Legislation, as often, was scarce, and governments left law to be made by subordinate lawmakers, again jurists but now mainly university professors, who were not appointed to make law and were not given power to do so. But make it they did by forms of reasoning approved of by their fellows and not objected to by governments.

Law created this way needs to be based on legal authority, and the professors found it in the great respect they attributed to Roman law and canon law. In many instances Roman legal rules or institutions could be taken over more or less without alteration, with the professors citing the Corpus Juris texts as authority. But even if law was needed for new social situations, Roman law could still be used. The professor might argue that a branch of Roman law, by analogy, supplied the law for the new situation. A striking example of this approach is a book that was published under a variety of titles, such as *Loci argumentorum legales* and *Topicorum seu de locis legalibus liber,* and first appeared at Louvain in 1516. It was the work of Nicholas Everardi (Everts), who was born in Zeeland in 1462 and died in 1532. He studied at Louvain University, graduating as doctor of civil law and canon law in 1493. He became professor of law there and later, in 1504, *rector magnificus.* In 1498 he was appointed "official," or ecclesiastical judge, representing the bishop of Cambrai, at Brussels, and from 1509 to 1527 he was president of the Court of Holland. In the latter year he became president of the Supreme Court of Holland, Zeeland, and Friesland at Mechelen. A professional of this type, a combination of professor and judge, of public servant and ecclesiastical officer, is not unusual for the period.

The *Loci argumentorum legales* is an innovation in legal literature in that, although interest in legal argument was not new, the author for the first time sets out fully and systematically the various kinds of argument that can be used in legal matters.[19] Of concern here are not the general *loci* (points for discussion) on drawing arguments from etymology, from the genus to the species, and from the whole to the part, but quite a number of *loci,* all based on argument by analogy and all dealing with individual legal subjects, whose arguments are drawn from Roman law to non-Roman law: thus, from slave to monk (*locus* 24); from freedman to vassal (*locus* 25); from *miles armatae militiae* (soldier of armed warfare) to *miles caelestis militiae* (soldier of heavenly warfare)—that is, from the rights and duties of a Roman soldier to those of a Christian cleric, priest, or bishop (*locus* 56); from soldier to church or *pia causa* (*locus* 57); from liberty (basically, presumption or interpretation in favor of liberty) to *pia causa* (*locus* 58); from fisc to church or *pia causa* (*locus* 61); and from minors to church or *pia causa* (*locus* 74). *Locus* 29, though entitled "from feu to emphyteusis" (Roman long lease of imperial land or of private land for a rent in kind), also deals with arguments from either one to the other.

In all of these the non-Roman element is in effect being delineated in terms of the Roman law. Roman law is regarded as providing a good analogy, and because it is fuller and more developed, gaps or presumed gaps in the other law can be filled. In the process, the non-Roman area of law receives rules of Roman law, and to some extent, the non-Roman element is seen in Roman law terms. More significantly, the system of Roman law is being extended to incorporate the later non-Roman elements. Roman law is being treated as living and developing law. It is appropriate that Everardi continually points out that the analogy is not complete—that, for instance, not on all points is the legal position of a monk identical with that of a slave. Everardi is by no means the initiator of the process, and among the many jurists he cites, the most frequent references are to the *gloss,* Baldus, and Bartolus.[20] Everardi's main role is that of systematizer.

Above all, the detail of the analogy is striking. For example, the *locus* from slave to monk reports that just as there can be no successor on death to a slave, so there can be none to a monk; a monk can hold property, as if it is his own, with the consent of his superior; there can be no valid transaction between monk and superior, though this claim is slightly qualified; as a slave acquires for his owner, so the monk acquires for the monastery; an action, when a monk has control of something, should be brought not against him but against the abbot or prelate; the monk cannot be a party to an action; monks cannot be witnesses to a will; and the superior must not cruelly punish the monk.

A more typical, and more important, approach was for the professor to act as if he was not innovating but merely explaining what was already there in the Roman texts. Here the texts are wrenched from their original context and given a new meaning in a different setting. Other professors were, of course, aware of what was going on, but they would not object because the goal was worthy—law was needed—and they were all doing the same thing. They might resist the particular result, but not the methodology. A prime example may be taken from conflict of laws, a subject that scarcely surfaces in Roman law, at least in a modern sense.[21] "Conflict of laws" is that branch of a state's law that comes into operation when a problem involves the possible relevance of the law of another state. For instance, a couple living in state A marry there where the marriage is legal, but subsequently move to state B where such a marriage if contracted there would be void. Is the marriage void in B? Is it still valid in A? If the husband dies with a will leaving his property in both A and B to his wife, will the wife receive it if an action is raised in A? Or if it is raised in B? Does it make a difference if the property is land or movables?

An early superb instance of this form of reasoning as if the law existed at Rome is the great Bartolus (1314–57).[22] One example may suffice. Section 7 of his gloss begins:

Eighth, about punitive statutes. This issue is to be investigated along many lines of question. First, whether they may extend their force expressly outside the territory? To which I say, that sometimes either the delinquent or he against whom the crime is committed outside the territory is a foreigner; then the rule is that the statute, though it expressly forbids the act, does not extend to those persons who are outside the territory, etc. [*D.*2.1.20; 1.1.9], because the statutes are the peculiar law of the city.

The proposition he is expounding would be widely accepted, and to this point he has based himself on two *Digest* texts. The first, *D.*2.1.20, runs:

One who administers justice beyond the limits of his territory may be disobeyed with impunity. The same applies where he purports to administer justice in a case exceeding the amount established for his jurisdiction.

The text is sensibly used by Bartolus, but it had no connection with conflict of laws. Its point is that an appointed magistrate has no jurisdiction to decide cases outside of his jurisdiction or for an amount higher than the financial limit set on his jurisdiction. It certainly did not mean that if a state enacted a statute that some act was criminal, then it could not hear a case within the state for the act committed outside of the state where either the wrongdoer or the victim was a foreigner. The other, *D.*1.1.9, is even less to the point:

All peoples who are governed under laws and customs observe in part their own special law and in part a law common to all men. Now that law which each nation has set up as a law unto itself is special to that particular civil society [*civitas*] and is called *jus civile,* civil law, as being that which is proper to the particular *civitas.* By contrast, that law which natural reason has established among all human beings is among all observed in equal measure and is called *jus gentium,* as being the law which all nations observe.

The jurist, Gaius, was making the point that in any state part of its law will be peculiar to that state, part of it will be found everywhere. He was considering these characteristics of law within one state and was not pronouncing on the impact of a state's legislation—in fact, legislation is not his specific concern—on behavior elsewhere. Again, the original text had no connection with conflicts of law.

In no sense am I criticizing Bartolus. He was not attempting to explain Roman law. Rather, he was dealing with the very practical problem that in fourteenth-century Italy there were many city-states with legal rules that often did not correspond. When a dispute arose between inhabitants of different states the issue of which law applied was of major importance.[23]

In the absence of legislation the approach was both useful and fruitful. Still, its artificiality did not escape the notice of learned nonjurists.
François Rabelais (c. 1483–1553) uses it to great comic effect. In chapter
39 of *Le Tiers Livre* Judge Bridoie defends his behavior in deciding lawsuits on the basis of his age and poor sight. He cast dice on the outcome
but he admits it could have been the case that he mistook a five for a
four or a three for a two. He insists that by the provision of the law im-
perfection of nature must not be imputed as a crime as appears from:
"ff. de re milit. l. qui cum uno, ff. de reg. jur. l. fere ff. de edil. ed. per
totum, ff. de term. mo. l. Divus Adrianus resolu. per Lud. Ro. in l. si
vero, ff. solu. marti." Very learned it seems, but not very funny until
we check his authorities. The first two are enough. The modern citation
of the first is *D.49.16.4.pr.*: "A man born with one testicle or who lost
one, may lawfully serve as a soldier according to the rescript of the de-
fied Trajan: for even the generals Sulla and Cotta are regarded as having been in that condition by nature." The other text is *D.50.16.108*: "In
almost all penal cases, relief is given for age and ignorance." Neither of
these texts would have availed Bridoie much in a real lawsuit. But Rabelais's fun consists in using Roman legal texts in precisely the way later
jurists did to argue cases or make new law. The humanist jurists, like
Cuiacius, who wished to reconstruct Roman law approached the texts
in a very different way. They expressed their contempt for this older
method—but still used—of the glossators and commentators. So did
Rabelais himself.[24]

Still, despite the contempt of the humanists, the main way jurists
could develop the law was precisely that of those who deliberately mis-
represented the sense of the Roman texts. This was true not only for Italy
and France but also for continental western Europe right up to codification. Let us return to conflict of laws. Many scholars proposed theories but none is so interesting for Britons and Americans than those of
the Dutchman, Ulrich Huber (1634–69), whose theory on the subject
was accepted in Scotland, England, and the United States alike. His
simple scheme was founded on three axioms.[25] *Axiom* is a mathemati-
cal term for a self-evident proposition, which accordingly needs no
proof. Axiom 1: "The laws of each sovereign authority have force within
the boundaries of the state, and bind all subject to it, but not beyond."
For authority he cites *D.2.1.20*, which I have already discussed. Axiom
2: "Those people are held to be subject to a sovereign authority who
are found within its boundaries, whether they are there permanently
or temporarily." The authority he gives is *D.48.22.7.10*, which by only

a little stretching is justifiable. Axiom 3: "The rulers of states so act from comity that the rights of each people exercised within its own boundaries should retain their force everywhere, insofar as they do not prejudice the power or rights of another state, or its citizens." For this he cites no textual authority; nor could he. The axiom is his own invention. But Huber is being wonderfully clever. First, by declaring axiom 3 to be an axiom he required no proof: the accuracy of an axiom is self-evident. Still, as support for his theory, the axiom ought to be part of Roman law. And so it was, he claimed, but as part of the *ius gentium,* not the *ius civile. Ius gentium* was that part of Roman law that was found everywhere, whereas the *ius civile* was restricted to Rome. Because it formed part of the *ius gentium,* Roman law found everywhere, absence of evidence for it at Rome itself could be discounted.

We should also look briefly at the German notion of *Pandektenrecht* (pandect law), so prominent in the nineteenth century. *Pandects* is another name (from the Greek) for Justinian's *Digest.* German universities had chairs for the teaching of the *Institutes* of Justinian, of the *Code,* and of the standard divisions of the *Digest.* They also had chairs of pandect law. The task of the professor of pandect law was not the same as that of professors of the various parts of the *Digest.* His job was primarily to teach modern German law on the basis of Roman legal texts. For instance, the most celebrated pandectist is Bernhard Windscheid, and his section on "Der Auftrag" (Commission) has in the title an asterisk pointing to a footnote that lists the sources, "*J.*3.26; *D.*17.1; *C.*4.35," which are the titles of the Corpus Juris that deal with the Roman contract of *mandatum.* The other sources listed are all secondary.[26] *Mandatum* arose when one person undertook to do something gratuitously for another. The actor could receive no reward, or the arrangement was not mandate. In fact, exceptions arose. Again, mandate was wider than our agency, because the undertaking did not have to involve making a contract for the principal. In the section Windscheid's treatment proceeds on the basis of the Roman texts and secondary material. The treatment of "Auftrag" is typical.

I would like to inject an autobiographical note. In 1957 I began to write my doctoral thesis on mandate in Roman law.[27] Then, as now, my focus was on primary sources, not the secondary literature. But, of course, I had to study the latter too, and found most guidance in Vincenzo Arangio-Ruiz, *Il mandato in diritto romano* (Naples, 1949). I also studied Windscheid's massive book but got nothing to my purpose. Indeed, I was rather slow to realize that he was not writing about Roman law and that his investigations were not geared to elucidating the meaning of the texts in their original context.

Windscheid begins the preface to the first edition (1862) by stating that the first impetus to the making of his textbook was the needs of his lectures. He subsequently states that he endeavored to speak German as much as possible, in expression as well as in matter—an interesting observation. He makes the problem patent. In the preface to the fourth edition (1874) he wrote "Whoever sets his strength on a textbook must assign himself to work for today." And in awareness of the preparation of the German civil code, the Bürgerliches Gesetzbuch, he stated that with its completion his work "would fall into the lap of the past, and the fruit of long and difficult work would be given over to oblivion." These words are quoted by the editor of the eighth edition, Theodor Kipp, in his preface.[28] That edition appeared in 1900, the year of promulgation of the BGB. Kipp left Windscheid's text, but appended at the end of each section a discussion of the law as it now was, with no apparatus to the supposed Roman law basis. Kipp expresses his belief that deeper knowledge of the modern law will for all time rely on the older foundations of German common law. But, significantly, the edition of 1900 was the last edition of Windscheid.

THE ROMAN SYSTEM OF CONTRACTS

I have three aims in this part of the chapter. First, I wish to add to our knowledge of the history of Roman law by producing a radically different view of the development of contracts, one that is, I believe, both consistent with the surviving textual data and plausible with regard to human behavior. Second, I wish to contribute to our general understanding of how and why law develops when it does develop, and explain the evolution of some very familiar legal institutions. I cannot accomplish the second aim without accomplishing the first. Little need be said about the importance of the subject. Third, and most important for present purposes, I wish to indicate the importance of juristic tradition on legal change.

Roman law has been the most innovative and most copied system in the West: the law of contract was the most original part of that system and the most admired. Private agreements and the relevant law occupy a central role in mercantile countries—indeed, in the Western world in general—and one would expect on a priori grounds that a particularly vivid light would be cast by this branch of law on the whole sub-

ject of legal development, and of law in society. This expectation should
be even greater because a contract is a private agreement, almost a private law, operating, say, between two individuals, but it requires state
recognition. The state may be slow or quick to give such recognition:
slow, as in England, where, by the late twelfth century, the king's court
exercised much jurisdiction over property law and criminal law but little
over contract;[29] quick, as at Rome, where, before 451 B.C., *stipulatio*
could be used to make a legally enforceable agreement. The state may
also have reservations about recognizing private agreements. It may restrict its recognition to agreements involving a specified minimum value,
only those being considered to have sufficient social or economic consequences to interest the state. Or it may restrict its recognition to agreements concluded with specified formalities, the implication being that
formalities could constitute evidence for others or bring home to the
parties the significance of what they were doing, and that only parties
sufficiently serious to make use of the formalities deserve to have recognition of their agreement by the state. Or it may restrict its recognition
to agreements on a particular subject matter—for instance, as at Rome,
an agreement to exchange goods for money but not an agreement to exchange goods for services. Or the state recognition may involve various
combinations of these restrictions: for instance, the French Code civil,
article 1341, provides that (apart from specific exceptions) any agreement
above a very tiny sum, although it is valid as a contract, is not susceptible of proof in court unless there is a written document either accepted
by a notary or signed by the parties; and the German Bürgerliches
Gesetzbuch, section 518, requires for recognition of a gift agreement that
it be recorded judicially or notarially.

The immediate thrust of this part of the present chapter is to account
for the recognition by the Roman state of the individual types of contract, such as deposit and sale; to show why they arose individually in
the chronological order that they did; to indicate why the dividing lines
between one contract and another are as they are; and to explain why
other contracts, such as a general contract in writing, did not arise or, as
in the case of barter, arose only late and with unsatisfactory rules. It will
become apparent that, although economic or social reasons demanded
the introduction of each type, it was the legal tradition that determined
the nature, structure, and chronology of every contract. The basic structure of Roman contract law then remained, long after there was any societal justification for the divisions.

This inquiry begins with the era shortly before the enactment of the Twelve Tables, the earliest Roman codification, which is traditionally and, I think, accurately attributed to around 451–450 B.C.[30] For present purposes I tentatively define *contract* as an agreement between two or more persons whose main legal consequence is an obligation with an effect personal rather than real. In any investigation of a legal system from a very different time and place there is, of course, always an initial difficulty of categorization. Specifically, here the question is whether the Romans of that time conceived the notion of contract as we do. The answer is probably no, that in fact the Romans had then no abstract concept of contract. The tentative definition includes, of the institutions existing in the early fifth century B.C., the contract of *stipulatio,* but it excludes conveyances like *mancipatio* and *in iure cessio* and security transactions like *nexum,* even though these include elements of obligation based on agreement.[31] This separation may seem unfortunate. But there are three grounds for accepting the tentative definition. First, our knowledge of the structure of the Twelve Tables is limited, and we have no evidence that the early Romans would have classified *stipulatio* with *mancipatio* and the others. Second, the tentative definition allows us to include all the obligations that the later Romans regarded as contractual, and to exclude all the obligations that the later Romans did not regard as contracts. Third, the modern perspective that is enshrined in the definition is a continuation of the ideas that the Romans came to develop.

It is often said that the Romans never developed a system of contract but only individual contracts,[32] and the attempt is sometimes made to explain in economic terms why each contract arose when it did. Such attempts are doomed to failure. No investigation into contracts one by one and separately can make sense in economic terms of the order of their appearance. For instance, deposit appears in the fifth century B.C., loan for consumption in the third century B.C. at the latest, but barter, insofar as it ever was a contract at all, had to wait at least another few hundred years; and all this while there was no contract of sale until about 200 B.C. Again, there was no specific contract for reward for looking after a thing, reward in return for another's use of one's thing, or reward for one's services until, after the advent of coined money, the introduction of the contract of hire sometime close to 200 B.C. In these circumstances, the early dating, before 123 B.C.,[33] of the invention of a contract of mandate according to which someone agreed to act gratuitously for another—and the essence of the contract was specifically that the performance was to be gratuitous—seems unlikely if the need for the contract is to be explained on economic grounds.

The truth is more complicated, but if one is prepared to grant legal tradition an important role in legal development, then the unfolding of the growth of Roman contracts is rational and simple to explain. The starting point is that from very early times the Romans did have a method—the *stipulatio,* in fact—by which parties could agree to create any obligation that was not positively unlawful. If one dares to speak probably anachronistically, one can say that in very early times the Romans did have a general theory of contract, not a law of individual contracts. The question to be resolved then is how this general approach to contract came to be lost. The clue to the development lies in a very strange fact that needs an explanation: apart from the very special and complex case of partnership, all Roman contracts either have a money prestation or no prestation. In this latter category are two kinds of contract: they may either be gratuitous of necessity or they are unilateral (in which case they may be matched with another contract). What does not exist, apart from that late and uncertain instance of barter, is a Roman contract according to which goods or services are proffered in return for goods or services. What is striking, moreover, is that in deciding which contract is involved, the touchstone is whether performance is necessarily (so far as the contract goes) for nothing or whether the performance is for money. For instance, the three distinct contracts of *depositum, commodatum* (loan for use), and *mandatum* all become contracts of hire (*locatio conductio*) if payment is promised. What is so significant about a prestation in coined money that a Roman contractual type must either contain it or be gratuitous? The solution to the problem of development, I submit, is that in most cases an individual type of Roman contract arose subsequently to *stipulatio* when, for whatever reason, a *stipulatio* was inappropriate or inefficient for that type of situation and when there was a societal need. Thus, almost every subsequent contractual type is a derogation from *stipulatio.* It should be noted that a legal remedy on an agreement is needed, not in accordance with the frequency of important transactions, but in accordance with the frequency of their going wrong.

The origins of the *stipulatio* (also known as the *sponsio*) are obscure and may have involved a libation or an oath, but they need not concern us now, nor should further conclusions be drawn from any hypothesis as to origins.[34] What matters is that it was well developed before the time of the Twelve Tables, under which the contract was actionable by the form of process known as *legis actio per iudicis postulationem* (*G*.4.17a). It was a formal, unilateral contract in which the promisee asked, "Do you promise [whatever it might be]?" necessarily using the verb *spondere*, and the promisor immediately replied "Spondeo" (I promise), using the same verb. Later other verbs could be used, but *spondere* could only be used by Roman citizens. The content of the promise was judged only by the words used, and the contract would remain valid and effective even if the promise was induced by fraud, was extorted by fear, or proceeded on an error. *Stipulatio* could be used for any lawful purpose: to promise a dowry, to make a sale (when mutual *stipulationes* would be needed), to engage one's services, and so on.[35] But when an agreement was not cast in the form of a stipulation, then, no matter how serious the intentions of the parties, no matter how important the subject matter of the transaction, there was no contractual obligation and no right to any disappointed party to bring a contractual action.

Stipulatio, by skillful modernization, could have become the root of a flexible, unitary contractual system. Writing, perhaps incorporated into two documents, could have been adopted as an alternative to the oral question and answer, or agreement (however it was proved) could have become the basis of a contract; remedies for fraud, intimidation, or error could have been made inherent in the contract; and implied terms could have been developed for specific types of factual situation. Instead, a number of other individual contracts arose, each defined in terms of its function. This definition by function and not by form separates them sharply from stipulation. They might even appear to be lesser breeds, particular rather than general. Each of the contractual arrangements, however, whether loan for consumption or sale, could be cast in the form of one or more *stipulationes* and then would be that type of contract.

One early contract was *mutuum,* loan for consumption. *Mutuum* was provided with the rather strange action known as the *condictio,* which lay when the plaintiff claimed that the defendant owned a thing that he was legally bound to deliver to the plaintiff. Many scholars believe *mutuum* to be very old, with a prehistory before it came to be provided with the *condictio*—and if so, the general argument of this chapter is strengthened—but much that is peculiar about the *condictio* is explicable, as we shall see, if we link the introduction of that action with the creation of *mutuum* as a legal institution. The form of action, the *legis actio per condictionem,* was introduced by the *lex Silia* when what was claimed was a determinate sum of money, by the *lex Calpurnia* when what was claimed was a definite thing (*G.4.19*). It is usually held that the *lex Silia* was earlier, on the basis that otherwise there would be no need for a law specifically covering money.[36] David Daube, as we shall see, adds a new dimension. In any event, whatever the priority of these two statutes may have been, the remedy of the *condictio* is old. As early as the composition of the *Rudens* by Plautus, who died in 184 B.C., the classical procedure by *formula* as well as the archaic procedure by *legis actio* could be used for the *condictio*.[37] And there would be little point in setting up fresh *legis actiones* once *formulae* were in being.

The peculiarities of the *condictio* are that it is abstract in the sense that the plaintiff does not set out in the pleadings the grounds of his case; that it is general in that it can be brought any time a nonowner believes that the owner of money or of a certain thing is under a legal obligation to give it him;[38] and that, apart from exceptional cases, there had to be a preceding delivery of the thing to the defendant by the plaintiff. Thus, the *condictio* could be brought both where there was and where there was not a contract.[39] The generality coupled with the abstraction requires explanation, and the simplest explanation is that the *condictio* was originally envisaged for one concrete situation so obvious that it did not have to be expressly set out—and then was found to be extendable to others. The most obvious concrete situation is *mutuum,* which, in fact, has always been treated as the primary use of the *condictio.* Loan for consumption would need to be given legal effectiveness when there was a breakdown in neighborly relations, when one friend failed to repay a loan: in an early agricultural community a loan of seed corn to be repaid after the harvest would be a common case. No stipulation would have been taken precisely because it is morally inappropriate for one friend, performing an amicable service, to demand a formal contract from another.[40] Where the loan was commercial, a stipulation would have been taken, to cover interest as well, and there would be no need for a specific contract of *mutuum.* We now see also why the action on *mutuum* was for the principal only and did not extend to interest: friends do not demand interest from friends.[41] The breakdown in neighborly relations might be related to an increase in Rome's size.

But the earliest action for a *mutuum* was apparently for money, not for seed corn. This is explained by David Daube in a wide framework. He stresses that "some transactions, originally belonging to the gift area of fellowship, 'Gemeinschaft,' tend to assume the more rigid, legalistic characteristics of partnership, 'Gesellschaft,' when money enters."

Specifically with regard to *mutuum,* the giving of an action—at first re-stricted to a money loan—marks for him a breakdown in the gift trade.[42] Earlier, a gift of seed corn or money to a friend in need was ex-pected to be returned by a converse gift at an opportune time. I would prefer to think that even before the *lex Silia,* the idea in *mutuum* was that of a loan to be returned in due course, but that is a minor matter. What is significant is that Daube offers a plausible explanation for the *condictio's* being originally restricted to a claim for money.

Another early specific type of contract, I believe, was deposit. The ju-rist Paul in the third century tells us that "on account of deposit an ac-tion is given by the Twelve Tables for double, by the praetor's edict for single."[43] It has long been held—by me as well as by others—that the action for double under the Twelve Tables, being penal, was not neces-sarily based on any concept of contract and was closer to delict,[44] and the further suggestion is then sometimes made that the delict is akin to theft.[45] But what must be stressed at this point is the very restricted scope of the action. It lies, if we believe Paul, where a thing that was deposited is not returned: according to Paul's words, it does not lie, nor does any similar ancient action we know of, where a thing that was hired out or was lent for use is not returned, nor even, deposit being neces-sarily gratuitous, where a fee was to be paid for looking after the prop-erty. Moreover, apart from questions of contract, there seems little need for the action. The owner would have the normal action (of the time) claiming ownership, the *legis actio sacramento in rem,* and he would have the action for theft—at least if the depositee moved the thing (and it would be of little use to him if he did not). There seems little reason to single out this particular situation for a specific action based on the no-tion of delict.

What then would impel the desire for a specific action? Deposit dif-fers from hire of a thing and loan for use, first, in that the object de-posited is being taken out of circulation—no one can use it, and cer-tainly not the depositee, because the contract is definitely not for the benefit of the depositee—and, second, in that it is precisely the recipi-ent who is bestowing the favor. It follows that the depositor is in no po-sition to demand that the recipient formally promise by contract to re-store the thing: the depositor cannot reward the depositee for his good deed by showing doubts about his honesty. Again, the reason the de-positor is willing to have his property out of circulation for a time is often that he finds himself in an emergency and cannot look after the property himself, and here too, he is in no position to demand the formality of a stipulation from his helper. But the depositor is particularly vulnerable to fraud, and it is reasonable to give him a forceful remedy with penal damages. In the late republic, the praetor issued a complicated edict on deposit whose main clauses gave an action for double damages against a depositee who failed to return property entrusted to him in what has come to be called *depositum miserabile*—deposit made as a result of earthquake, fire, collapse of a building, or shipwreck—and an action for simple damages in other cases.[46] Arguments have been produced both for the proposition that the provision in the Twelve Tables applied only to *depositum miserabile*[47] and also for the proposition that it applied to deposits of all kinds. The arguments seem inconclusive, though I tend to favor the second and more usual view, but in either eventuality the argument given here for an early specific action in fraud would fit. The strength of feeling that the depositor should have an action in the event of fraud would be intensified if, as seems likely, deposits were frequently made in temples or with priests (cf., e.g., Plautus, *Bacchides*, 306).

One of the great Roman inventions—it is now widely accepted that there were no foreign models[48]—is the consensual contract, a contract that is legally binding simply because of the parties' agreement and which requires no formalities for its formation. There were four of these, and it is generally presumed that the contract of sale, *emptio venditio,* was the earliest. It seems to me to have been fully actionable by around 200 B.C.[49] Numerous theories explain the origins of consensual sale.[50] Some, such as the hypothesis that at one time the agreement became binding only if the buyer had given the seller an earnest of his payment of the price, or only if the seller had delivered to the buyer, are now seen to lack support from the sources. Others, such as that of Theodor Mommsen, that state contracts (e.g., the public sale of booty) provided the example or model,[51] are concerned with the issue of what gave the Romans the idea that agreements without formality might be actionable, but provide no other insight into the transformation of private bargains into contracts of sale that, though made by private individuals, were enforced by the courts.

There may be more than one root in the development of the consensual contract. But whatever economic or social pressures one wants to postulate, whether one says consensual sale was wanted because (as some think) of an expansion of foreign trade and the need for contracts that could be made at a distance, or because (as others hold) of a need for a formless contract to accommodate foreign merchants unfamiliar

with Roman law formalities, or because (as still others argue) of a growing awareness of the worth of good faith in contract law for dealings
with both Romans and foreigners,[52] the same conclusion holds: consensual sale as a separate contract arose in part because of the inadequacy
of the *stipulatio* for the task. Of one thing there should be no doubt. Before the introduction of the consensual contract, parties to a sale-type
transaction who wanted legal enforcement of their agreement would
make their arrangements in the form of stipulations.[53] And further development would not have occurred if this way of making arrangement
had been satisfactory.

My own version of the origins of consensual sale and the connection
with *stipulatio* derives from the observation of two defects in the contract of sale, which were there initially and continued to exist for centuries[54]—namely, that the contract did not contain any inherent warranty of title or against eviction or any inherent warranty against latent
defects. Yet buyers did want the protection of warranties, as hundreds
of texts on the actual taking of warranties by *stipulatio* show. And the
notion of inherent warranties was not foreign to Roman lawyers because
they had already existed for centuries in the *mancipatio,* the formal
method of transferring certain types of important property. The absence
of inherent warranties would make the consensual contract far less valuable commercially. Whenever merchants wanted warranties—and the
evidence shows that they often did—the parties had to be face-to-face
to take a stipulation: hence, the contract could not be made by letter
or by messenger. Certainly, one could send a dependent member of one's
family to take or give the stipulation but that in itself would often be inconvenient and expensive.[55] The absence of inherent warranties for centuries, the strong Roman desire for warranties, and the knowledge that
warranties could be implied demand an explanation, which I believe can
be found only if we postulate an origin for the contract where the defi-
ciencies were not so obvious.[56]

If we go back beyond the origin of sale, the parties to a salelike
arrangement who wished a legally binding agreement would, as I have
said, conclude their business by stipulations. They had no alternative.
All terms, given the nature of *stipulatio,* would have to be spelled out.
The buyer would promise payment on a fixed date, with interest if he
delayed. The seller would promise that he would deliver the thing on a
fixed day, that he would pay a penalty if he delayed, that the buyer
would not be evicted from the thing, and that the thing was free from
hidden defects. Each *stipulatio* was unilateral, but the parties would want

their rights and duties to be reciprocal: hence the obligation to fulfill each *stipulatio* would have to be made conditional upon the fulfillment, or the readiness to fulfill, of the other. To make the problem still more difficult, this conditional reciprocity would have to be framed so as to take account of a partial but not complete failure to perform. For instance, if a sold slave was found to be suffering from some relatively unimportant defect, the buyer might still want to have the slave but pay only a reduced price. The drafting and taking of the stipulations would be extremely cumbrous and complex, and often it would happen that the parties' intentions would be frustrated.

So far we are on sure ground. What follows is a conjectural, but I think plausible, account of how the praetor, the magistrate in charge of the lawcourts, dealt with the problem. At some point a praetor accepted that he ought to grant an action in accordance with good faith to cover accidental interstices in stipulations concerned with a sale.[57] Above all he would seek to make the obligations reciprocal. In accordance with the Roman tendency to see law in terms of blocks,[58] the strict law *stipulatio* and the new action based on good faith would be kept separate. But the position would be reached that, provided there was a sale-type situation and at least one *stipulatio,* there would be an action to give the buyer or the seller an action against the other for an amount equal to what ought to be given or done in accordance with good faith. The separate contract of sale was in the process of being born. But what would be the content of the only necessary stipulation? In the simplest possible sale-type transaction there would be, immediately upon agreement, a handing over of the money and a handing over of the thing. The stipulation wanted would cover only continuing obligations, and they would be only of the seller and would consist only of a warranty against eviction and against latent defects. We know from the republican writer Varro (*De re rustica* 2.2.4; 2.3.4; 2.4.5) that these warranties were contained in a single stipulation. Eventually, an action on *emptio venditio* would be given even when no stipulation was taken, but because of the way the contract emerged, it long provided no remedy if the buyer suffered eviction or the object contained hidden defects, so long as the seller was in good faith. Heavy stress is placed on good faith in *emptio venditio* whether as a result of the way the contract emerged or, as many think, as part of the pressure for recognizing the contract. This suggested development has one further feature that renders it plausible. It avoids any sudden leap forward in legal thinking, and it is bedded firmly on how parties to a sale-type transaction would conduct their business and the gradual response of those in charge of law making to the problems that arose.[59]

A second consensual contract, hire (*locatio conductio*), has more obscure origins, but the usual assumption is that its beginnings are closely connected with those of sale and that sale was the more important case: either the example of sale was followed for hire, which is thus a later contract, or the impetus for recognizing a contract of sale impelled also, and simultaneously, the recognition of the less significant *locatio conductio*. The need to attach legal importance to good faith in contracts would, for instance, be one joint impelling factor.[60] If one grants priority to sale, whether in time or in legal importance, then one fact emerges unequivocally for hire, though strangely it appears never to have been noticed either by Romans or by later scholars. *Locatio conductio* is a residual category for all types of bilateral agreement that are not sale and where the prestation of one of the parties has to be in money. This fact and this alone can account for the peculiarity that at least three very different contractual situations are included within it: the use of a thing for a time in return for money; providing one's labor for a time in return for money; and the assignment of a specific task to be performed in return for money. In each of these situations the obligations of the party who is acting in return for money are very different. Any doubts that *locatio conductio* is a residual category must disappear when one notices that in the corresponding situations where no money is to change hands, this one contract is replaced by three: mandate, deposit, and loan for use.[61] It is in the highest degree illuminating for the force of legal tradition in legal development that such a figure as *locatio conductio* came into being, remained unchanged in its scope throughout the Roman period, and still flourishes in some countries, such as France, Chile, and Argentina, as one contract today.

As a further indication that one need not, even within the Western tradition, draw the line between one type of contract and another exactly as it usually is drawn, it is worth observing that in the second century B.C. at Rome an agreement to allow another to pasture his flock on one's land for the winter in return for a money payment was regarded as sale of the fodder (Cato, *De agri cultura* 149). Classical Roman and modern law would treat the agreement as hire. The republican position was perfectly sensible and would have remained so in classical law, given the fact that sale did not involve a requirement to transfer ownership but only to give quiet possession—in this case for the duration of the agreement. The standard warranties in sale against eviction and hidden defects would have been perfectly appropriate.

A third consensual contract, mandate (*mandatum*), was in existence by 123 B.C. and is different in its raison d'être from the two just examined.[62] Mandate is the agreement to perform gratuitously a service for another. It is thus not a commercial contract but an agreement among friends. It is thus again precisely the type of situation where a stipulation could not be demanded—either from the friend who was asked to perform the service or by the friend for repayment of his expenses. That the contract came into existence at all is a tribute to the great weight that the Romans placed upon friendship: friends were expected to do a great deal for one another. It may seem surprising that such a distinction is made between agreeing to act gratuitously for another and acting for reward, but the Roman attitude that found labor degrading is probably a sufficient explanation. That attitude, at least, led to the view that performance of *artes liberales* could not be the subject of *locatio conductio*.[63]

A similar explanation can account for the emergence of *commodatum*, a gratuitous loan for use, as a separate contract, probably around the beginning of the first century B.C.:[64] one friend who lends gratuitously to a friend cannot demand a formal promise for return. The same holds for the remodeled obligation of deposit, probably around the same date.

The origins of *pignus*, "pledge," as an individual contract are not so easily uncovered. As a real security transaction giving the creditor the right to a specific action pursuing the thing pledged wherever it might be, *pignus* appears to be relatively old, but this does not imply that *pignus* also gave rise to a contractual action. No evidence suggests the existence of a contractual action at Roman civil law,[65] but the praetor certainly gave one by his Edict no later than the first century B.C.[66] At the very least, the praetorian action is much more prominent than any presumed civil-law action, and its wording is revealing: "If it appears that Aulus Agerius [the plaintiff] delivered to Numerius Negidius [the defendant] the thing which is the object of this action, as a pledge because of money that was owing; and that money has been paid, or satisfaction made on that account, or it was due to Numerius Negidius that payment was not made, and that thing has not been returned to Aulus Agerius, whatever the matter in issue will come to . . . ," and so on. The so-called *iudicium contrarium* was also available to the creditor (*D*.13.7.9.pr.; 13.6.16.1), but there is no doubt that the primary, and perhaps at one stage the sole, contractual action lay to the debtor against the creditor. The main thrust of introducing the contract was thus the protection of the debtor. The real security of *pignus* could be made without delivery, but as the wording of the action indicates, there was a contract only if the pledge had been delivered to the creditor, and the contract gave rise to an action only when the debtor had repaid the loan or made satisfaction. Thus, in at least the great majority of cases, there could have been no physical obstacle to a stipulation. Even if delivery was not by the debtor personally, but by someone in the power of the debtor such as a son or slave, to the creditor, or delivery was made to someone in the creditor's power, a legally binding stipulation could have been taken. The *actio quod iussu,* which would (for our purposes) make a head of household liable for a *stipulatio* made on account of his transaction by one of his dependents, is unlikely to be much later than contractual *pignus.*[67] And because the transaction is commercial, moral obstacles to taking a stipulation of the kind already mentioned would not here have existed.

Tentatively, I would suggest a possible reason for the introduction of *pignus* within the tradition of Roman contract law. It rests on the premise that in the normal case, from the inside point of view, however unscrupulous or disreputable a lender might be, it is he who is doing the borrower a favor. The emphasis is on the fact that the borrower needs the cash, and the lender has it and is willing to lend. The borrower will not always be able to insist easily on taking a stipulation from the lender for the return of the thing after payment. The very request for a formal promise to do one's obvious moral duty implies distrust. Although it might be objected that an honest lender would have no qualms about giving a stipulation, the legal action is not needed for transactions that go well but for those that go wrong, and it is obviously aimed primarily at the dishonest creditor.[68]

But suppose one did not find an approach of this kind to be plausible, insisting instead that an explanation had to be sought in economic or social needs for the emergence of the contract of *pignus*? That explanation would not be found. It is difficult to envisage much economic or social pressure for the new contractual action even when no stipulation was taken. Thus, when the repaid creditor failed or refused to return the thing pledged, the former debtor would have the ordinary action available to an owner claiming his property, which by this date would be the *vindicatio.* Where the creditor's behavior was theftuous, the debtor would have in addition the action on theft, the *actio furti,* for a penalty. Even if one assumes that from the beginning, as certainly later, the *formula* was also intended to give the action where the creditor returned the pledge in a damaged condition—and given the wording the assumption seems implausible—then the debtor already had a right of action under the *lex Aquilia*, where it was the creditor or someone in his power who did the damage, negligently or maliciously. The one situation previously unprovided for but now covered by the contractual action (and within straightforward interpretation of the wording) is where the creditor failed to return the pledge because it had been stolen from him in circumstances in which he had been negligent. For much the same reasons, there can have been little economic need for the contract of *commodatum* or, as we have seen, of *depositum*.

It would not be surprising—though there is no positive evidence—if the praetorian actions on deposit, loan for use, and pledge are historically linked. The action of the Twelve Tables on deposit was the result of moral outrage, and, much later, the Edict moderated the damages in most cases to simple restitution. Loan for use was seen not to be dissimilar; hence, likewise, a contractual action was given where property in the hands of one person as a result of agreement was not duly returned to the owner; and *pignus* (which may or may not be older than *commodatum*) was seen as another example.

We have no indications of how or when or to what end the literal contract arose, and hence no argument can be drawn from it for or against any theory of the growth of Roman contract law. It was in existence by around the beginning of the first century B.C. (Cicero, *De officiis* 3.58) but may well be much older. In classical law it arose when a Roman head of family marked in his account books that a debt had been paid when it had not, then made an entry to the effect that a loan had been made when it had not.[69] It was thus not an originating contract but a method of transforming one kind of obligation into another. Whether that was also the case when the literal contract first came into being, and whether in the beginning the writing had to be in the formal account books are not clear.[70] The action was the *actio certae pecuniae* and therefore had to be for a fixed amount of money. The literal contract was flourishing in A.D. 79 when Pompeii was destroyed by the eruption of Vesuvius, but it had apparently disappeared from use by the end of the classical period.

Only one standard Roman contract, *societas* (partnership), remains to be dealt with, and its origins and growth are unique. The oldest Roman partnership, *ercto non cito*, is very old and came into being when a head of family died and his estate went to his *sui heredes* (G.3.154a)—that is, persons who were subject to his paternal power and on his death came to be free of any power. They were immediately partners in the inheritance and remained so until the inheritance was divided. Because in early Rome persons in the power of another owned no property, the *sui heredes* had nothing until the inheritance came their way: hence, *ercto non cito* is a partnership of all the property of the partners. This is not a contractual partnership, but, later, persons who wished to set up such a partnership were allowed to do so by means of a *legis actio,* the archaic form of process, before the praetor (*G.*3.154b). Eventually the praetor gave an action on a consensual contract of partnership, perhaps around the time he created the consensual contracts of sale and hire. But this consensual contract of partnership was modeled on the old *ercto non cito:* significantly, the praetor set out in his Edict only one *formula,* a model form of action, and that was for a partnership of all of the assets of the partners. Hence, the primary type of consensual partnership was not a commercial arrangement between merchants—they would want a much more restricted partnership—but between close relatives and friends, probably wishing to engage in a communal agricultural enterprise.[71] Rome had long been commercially active, a business partnership would clearly have been economically useful, but because of legal history and legal tradition the primary instance of consensual partnership was not mercantile. Whether from the outset, as certainly later, there could also be partnerships of a restricted kind cannot be determined.

This origin of partnership in succession and not in business accounts for a significant peculiarity in consensual partnership. An heir was liable for the debts of the deceased, even if they exceeded the assets. Coheirs would be liable for debts in the same proportion as they inherited. Hence, the jurist Quintus Mucius Scaevola (killed in 82 B.C.) claimed that it was contrary to the nature of partnership that it be so set up that one partner was to take a greater share of any eventual profit than he would take of any eventual loss (*G.*3.149). Mucius's view is expressly based on the nature of partnership as he sees it, not on fairness. Although Servius Sulpicius broke away from this approach and successfully argued that such a partnership—even one in which one partner was entitled to share in the profit but not in any loss—was valid because that could be a fair arrangement if his services were valuable, Sabinus and Ulpian held that such an arrangement was valid only if it was fair.[72] This is the sole instance in classical Roman law where a voluntary contractual arrangement entered into without error, coercion, or fraud was valid only if there was an equivalence of contribution and reward.[73] It owes its existence entirely to the internal logic of the legal tradition and not at all to economic, social, or political pressures. This same legal logic and the piecemeal development of Roman contracts, and not societal forces, prevented the necessity for equivalence from spreading to the other bilateral contracts or from being extinguished for partnership.

The force of this internal legal logic is apparent in another failure to develop. The contracts of deposit, loan for use, and mandate grew up one by one, but once they were all in existence, there was no reason for not subsuming deposit and loan for use under mandate, except that they were in fact thought of as separate institutions. That deposit and *commodatum* required delivery of the thing for the creation of the contract is no obstacle. The practical effect of the law would be unchanged if these contracts were incorporated into mandate: so long as nothing had been done on a mandate, either party was free to revoke or renounce unilaterally.[74] There might even be doubt at times, as Pomponius discovered, whether a particular arrangement was mandate or deposit (*D.*16.3.12–14).

But the force on legal development of the lawyers' ways of looking at problems is even clearer when we look at contracts that did not develop or developed only partially or late. To begin with, it is prima facie astonishing that the Romans never developed a written contract that would take its place by the side of *stipulatio* as a second contract defined by form, not by function. Such a contract would obviously have been very useful, above all for situations where the *stipulatio* would have been the obvious contract, except that the parties could not easily be present together: these situations would include sales where warranties against eviction or latent defects were wanted. Again, a contract whose validity depended on the existence of writing would usually be easy to prove. In fact, other contracts, including *stipulatio,* were often reduced to writing partly in order to provide proof,[75] partly to ensure that the terms were not forgotten. Nor can the Romans have been unaware of the possibility or the usefulness of written contracts: they had been standard even in classical Athens.[76] And the jurist Gaius in the second century A.D. was well aware of the existence of Greek written contracts and of the contrast between them and the Roman literal contract (*G.*3.134). The absence of such a contract demands an explanation, and that cannot be either economic or social. The most plausible explanation, I suggest, is that originally stipulation was the only contract, at a time when writing was not widespread. The habit of looking at *stipulatio* as *the* contract was so ingrained that other contracts arose as exceptions to or derogations from it only when *stipulatio* was obviously inappropriate. The idea of creating a new type of contract defined by form that could be used in all situations where *stipulatio* could be used and in other situations where it could not just did not occur to the Roman lawyers.

Likewise, it is equally astonishing that no contract of barter developed until the empire at the earliest. Until the introduction of coined money around 275 B.C.,[77] a barter-type situation must have been the most common type of commercial transaction. Even afterward, barter would be a frequent transaction. Yet barter, *permutatio,* as a legal institution is centuries later than the contract of sale, and it was never fully accepted into the Roman system of contracts.[78] As a contract it was very unsatisfactory: barter required for its formation delivery by one party, and an action for nonperformance lay only for the value of the delivered goods. Contrast this with the contract of sale, which required only the agreement of the parties, and where the action lay for a sum of money equal to what the defendant ought to give or do in accordance with good faith. Nor can one say that the all-purpose *stipulatio* made a contract of barter unnecessary, because the *stipulatio* required an oral question and answer, and hence required the contracting parties to be face-to-face. The only way two merchants in different places could make an agreement for a barter situation was for one of them to send to the other, often at considerable expense and inconvenience, a dependent member of his family, such as a son or a slave, to take delivery or engage in mutual *stipulationes.* To say that Roman merchants did not engage much in barter is to forget that the introduction of coined money into Rome is relatively late, and to say that the Roman merchants would not find the law relating to barter inconvenient is to render inexplicable the introduction of such a splendid contract as sale. But the individual Roman contracts emerged—certainly because of societal needs—at a pace and with characteristics dictated by legal reasoning.

Nothing illustrates this more clearly than a dispute between the Sabinian and the Proculian schools of jurists as to whether the price in a contract of sale could consist of a thing other than coined money (*G.*3.141; *J.*3.23.1; *D.*19.4.1.pr.). The Sabinians, who claimed that it could, relied on a text of Homer for the proposition that barter is the oldest form of sale:[79] the Proculians, who prevailed, claimed that the Sabinians had mistranslated and also argued that on that basis one could not determine what was the thing sold and what was the thing bought. At the root of the dispute is the serious business of extending satisfactory legal rules to barter. But the Sabinians, who were conscious of the economic realities, were bound by the rules of the legal game and could not come out and argue for more desirable rules for barter: the most they could do was argue that barter was included within the concept of sale. At no point, moreover, could they argue for legal change on social or economic grounds. The Proculians, who may or may not have been blind to the economic realities, also produced arguments of a purely legal nature for their successful position.[80] Law is being treated as if it were an end in itself, which indicates the existence of legal blindness. Apart from instances where it was morally impossible to demand a stipulation, the only derogations from *stipulatio* that were allowed to create a contract were those that involved an obligation to pay money: sale and the residual category of hire. It took even sale a very long time to break loose from the shackles of *stipulatio*.

Daube, as in the case of *mutuum*, feels that an explanation is needed for the failure to recognize a consensual contract of barter as early as sale, and even much later. And he finds that this "phenomenon is the result of the essentially intimate nature of moneyless barter as opposed to the distant aura in money-geared sale. Even at present, as a rule, an arrangement to swap records, cameras, houses (or partners) is more private and less law-oriented than one to transfer any of these possessions for money." And he offers a similar explanation for the failure to develop a contract akin to hire except in that neither of the prestations was in money.[81] Now there is, I believe, undoubtedly much truth in the argument, but the problem of the nonappearance of these contracts is perhaps greater than Daube suggests. First, intimate contracts not involving money prestations, such as deposit and loan for use, were recognized, provided always that they were gratuitous. Second, barter between merchants would be much less intimate than the modern examples Daube suggests, especially in the days before coined money. For the absence of these transactions from the list of contracts one must add to the fact of no prestation in money the legal tradition that recognized only the *stipulatio* as a contract except when sufficient pressure arose in a very specific type of situation for the acceptance of a derogation from the *stipulatio*. Except when money was involved, that pressure was greater where the obligation was seen to be obviously friendly, involving trust, hence gratuitous.

Perhaps as early as the first century A.D., the Roman jurists began to devise remedies to plug gaps in the contractual system (*D*.19.5); the remedy for barter seems to have been one of them. The jurist Paul in the second or third century A.D. eventually stated that an action would be given on any agreement of the following types provided the plaintiff had performed his side of the bargain: "I give to you in order that you give, I give in order that you do, I do in order that you give, I do in order that you do" (*D*.19.5.5.pr.). Thereafter, any agreement containing bilateral obligations that was followed by performance by one party gave rise to an action. It is sometimes said that this is a step toward a general theory of contract, but this claim seems incorrect. Each individual type of contract remained, each with its own major quirks. There was still no general contract law.

Finally, we should return to the oldest contract, *stipulatio*, which despite its long history never developed to its proper extent for reasons to be associated with the legal tradition. It is only to be expected that a very early contract is rigid, that the promisor is bound by what he says, and that the reason for his promise, even error, fraud, or intimidation, is irrelevant. But once it came to be accepted, especially for the consensual contracts, that the obligations could be based on good faith, then only lawyerly conservatism and tradition would keep *stipulatio* a contract of strict law. There are societal advantages for the law taking good faith into account for contracts, and there is no social class of cheats. But no remedy was provided with regard to *stipulatio* for extortion or fraud until the first century B.C. Remedies for extortion were introduced by a praetor Octavius around 80 B.C. and for fraud by Aquillius Gallus apparently in 66 B.C.[82] What concerns us are the special defenses, *exceptiones*, of extortion or fraud, which could be raised when an action was brought on a *stipulatio*. The point of an *exceptio* is precisely that the defendant is not denying the validity of the plaintiff's case. He is merely claiming that there is another fact that ought to be taken into account. In other words, extortion or fraud did not invalidate a *stipulatio*. It remained valid but its effects could be negatived by the use of the defense. *Stipulatio* always remained at this primitive level. Nor should it be thought that the distinction between invalidity and blocking by an *exceptio* is insignificant: if the defendant failed to plead the *exceptio* expressly at the appropriate time, he could not plead it later and would lose his case. No explanation for retaining a stipulation as valid but rendering it ineffective is satisfactory other than that of lawyers' ideas of what is appropriate in law.

The main thrust of this section of the chapter has been that it was Roman legal thinking, based on a tradition rooted in *stipulatio* as the original contract, that above all dictated the origins and nature of

Roman contracts. Although *societas* does not develop as a derogation from *stipulatio*, the mature contract, in its origins and nature, and also in a unique and important rule, equally demonstrates the enormous role of the legal tradition in legal evolution. None of this, of course, excludes an input by economic forces or by the politics of power. But this input of forces outside the legal tradition did not have a commensurate outcome. Nothing illustrates this more clearly than the relatively early actionability of contracts of *depositum, commodatum,* and *pignus,* on the one hand, and the late appearance and continuing unsatisfactory state of *permutatio,* on the other. It is not just that the first three, individually and collectively, are of much lesser commercial importance than barter; it is also that they were scarcely needed in view of existing actions in property and delict, whereas attempts to engage with legal protection in barter at a distance were fraught with inconvenience and expense. And it is surely hard to believe that the Roman merchants and others who engaged in barter had less political clout than the persons who deposited their property or lent it or used it as security for a loan.

The questions must be put whether one can generalize the enormous impact of the legal tradition on the evolution of the Roman law of contract and whether one should regard it as an exception in legal development. The second question can be dismissed out of hand, for two very obvious reasons. First, the development we have been looking at extended over more than a millennium, even though I concentrated only on the first five hundred years. Exceptional circumstances producing exceptional results are quite unlikely to last so long. Second, this is no unimportant, tiny branch of the law in a barren system, but the whole of contract law in the most imaginative secular legal system, a system that still has an impact almost fifteen hundred years after its demise with Justinian. All this is without taking into account the fact that similar patterns of development are to be found in many other circumstances.

But how far can one generalize? At this stage we should note three important reservations. First, we have been concerned with a mature legal system. How law develops in a system of customary law is the subject of Chapter 4. Second, we have been looking at one system, remarkable for its self-reliance. Borrowing from other legal systems, even a careful appraisal of other peoples' legal rules, is remarkably limited at Rome. Scholars do disagree on the impact of foreign law, especially Greek and Semitic law, in Rome,[83] but no one doubts that the input of the Romans themselves was exceptionally great. Hence it might be suggested that the Roman experience is unique, and that elsewhere the impact of the legal tradition is less pronounced. On the contrary, purely on a priori grounds—but the notion must be tested—one would expect that the more home-grown the product, the less would be the impact of the legal tradition of the legal elite. The reason is obvious. Speaking generally, only the legal elite of a society know anything about foreign law and can be in a position to organize a borrowing. Third, the Romans did not make much use of statute law, though it was available to them. Statute law is now the main vehicle of fundamental legal change. Perhaps it may be suggested that what happened at Rome has few lessons for the analysis of modern legal change. And I would be the first to concede that the sources of law, available and made use of, have an enormous impact on legal change. After all, that is the main argument of this book.[84]

It will have been noticed that, although this chapter is on development by jurists, many of the contracts appear as the result of statute, such as *depositum* and *mutuum,* or of the Edict, such as sale or mandate. There is no paradox. First, as will more fully emerge in subsequent chapters, the sources of law are often intertwined. In particular, juristic opinion can only become law when it is enshrined in statute, edict, or judicial precedent. Second, the praetor in developing law through his edict worked hand in glove with jurists.[85] Third, the pattern of development, very much piecemeal, betrays juristic input.

CHAPTER 3

JUDGES

Judges may make law in four vital ways. First, their decisions may become binding or authoritative as precedent. Second, judges interpret legislation. In practice, the meaning of a statute is that which they give to it. Third, juristic opinion, no matter how skillful and how authoritative it looks, has no practical significance unless it is accepted by judges. Fourth, as we shall see in Chapter 4, what counts as custom in law is primarily what judges say it is.

In the second part of Chapter 2 I showed that it is, above all, lawyers' thinking about law, not societal conditions, that determines the shape of legal change in developed legal systems. The thought pattern of the Roman jurists, rather than conditions in the society at large, determined the origins and nature of the individual Roman contracts, and the jurists were largely unaffected by society's realities. Of course, social, economic, political, and religious factors did have an impact, but to an extent that was very much less than their general importance in society. What was true for one main—perhaps the most original and the most important—branch of law, developed over centuries by jurists in one of the world's most innovative systems, is also true, I will now argue, for law in general developed over centuries by judges, in another of the world's innovative secular systems, the English medieval common law. After discussing the general impact of English judges, and the court system, on legal evolution, I then examine specific examples of judicial approaches in various Western systems.

ENGLISH COMMON LAW

In contrast to my handling of the Roman law of contract I do not want to produce a radically new theory of the development of the common law. Rather I want to demonstrate that my general thesis is implicit in standard accounts of the growth of the common law, especially as exemplified by the best-known modern account, S. F. C. Milsom, *Historical Foundations of the Common Law.* I would not want to accuse Milsom of sharing my viewpoint on legal evolution but, on very many pages on individual points and in the picture contained overall in his book, his argument strikingly confirms my thesis—if we assume, of course, he is correct in what he tells us of the history of English law.

Thus, in discussing feudal tenures—and feudal law was long at the heart of the English legal system—he can say: "The military tenures, of uncertain value as a provision for warfare, brought with them a logic which was to generate anachronisms throughout our history."[1] After the Norman Conquest, almost all those who held land directly from the king held it by knight service, which entailed the obligation of providing a fixed number of fully armed horsemen for forty days per year. The cavalry was so recruited for almost a century—though the military disadvantages of such a system are obvious—but eventually money payments called scutage were substituted. Although knight service was abolished in 1660, many of the incidents of the tenure resulting from its military origins remained until this century.[2] Again, at the low legal level of manor courts and manor law Milsom writes: "Some of this law was to perish, some to live to a sad old age as what came to be called copyhold."[3] Of the defects of copyhold many have written,[4] but much of the land of England was held by copyhold until 1925. "Although copyhold now [in the early seventeenth century] had equal protection, it retained its separate identity for three useless centuries, providing a measure of economic obstruction, traps for conveyancers, and puzzles for the courts. These puzzles concerned such matters as the entailing of copyhold, and they were of absorbing legal interest. Today their only value is as an object lesson in the great intellectual difficulty a legal system can encounter when it seeks to rejoin matters which became separated for reasons which are extinct."[5] On the evolution of land ownership he remarks: "It is hard to say which story is the more extraordinary: the evolution of the fee simple as ownership, with only its name and its necessary words of limitation to remind us of its tenurial beginnings; or the series of seeming accidents which produced the fee tail. But this juridical monster, beyond the desires of donors seven hundred years ago, beyond the intention of the legislator and far beyond reason, is with us yet" (p. 177). "The settlement, by which an owner of property can divide the ownership in time between beneficiaries who will take one after another, is the most distinctive creation of the common law, and perhaps the most unfortunate. . . . For the historian the special interest of the development is its repeated demonstration of the strength of purely legal phenomena. Results were reached which, although absorbed and exploited, cannot have been desired" (p. 106).

Examples can also be taken from the law of torts. Milsom points out that in the fourteenth century a suit in the royal courts against a blacksmith for negligence in shoeing a horse had to allege breach of the king's peace, and that this situation was remedied around 1370 when writs were issued which did not allege such a breach (pp. 290–91). But the *vi et armis* writ for cattle trespass "had been extended to the case of straying animals when wrongs still could not come into royal courts unless *contra pacem* was alleged; and in this case the writ was never modified as was the smith's to make an honest action on the case. Nor was this a curiosity without consequence: in the twentieth century the defendant owner would still be liable without the affirmative showing of fault which became necessary in an action on the case" (p. 291). And again writing of the period before 1370: "Or consider the sale of a diseased horse deceitfully warranted sound. As early as 1307 a buyer had sued in the king's court, but again only because he was on the king's service. The ordinary plaintiff could hardly represent the wrong as *contra pacem:* but it might seem capricious that he could not get to the king's court when the smith's ill-used customer could" (pp. 292–93). Slightly further on:

> Trespass, then, lost its original sense by being identified with trespass *vi et armis* and distinguished from case. It was from that distinction that the modern sense of trespass grew; and to hindsight the process seems perverse. When *contra pacem* lost its jurisdictional importance about 1370, its importance in the matter of process unhappily survived; and a chance of reuniting the law of wrongs was missed. A second chance came in 1504, when the same process was extended to all trespass actions. *Contra pacem* was thereafter without consequences in the real world except for a nominal fine to the king. But it was too late. The two categories existed in lawyers' heads, as the statute itself shows. It was certain there was a distinction even if nobody knew what it was; and a distinction is never without consequence in a law court. (pp. 308–9)

Discussing the system of civil judicature as it was around 1300 Milsom writes: "The system was to make some sense until the sixteenth century, to last until the nineteenth, and to leave its imprint in every common law jurisdiction today" (p. 33). Significantly for us, as we shall see, he adds: "But it was not devised as a national system of civil judicature. It was an accumulation of expedients as more and more kinds of disputes were drawn first to a jurisdictional and then also to a geographical centre. One result was to invest the machinery which controlled jurisdiction with an importance that was to outlive and to overshadow its reason." And on the fact that, in general, courts could not act without special authority, namely a writ from chancery in each case, he says:

> This jurisdictional accident was to be of growing consequence. In the middle ages it hampered the expansion of the common law by restricting the kinds of claim that could be brought before the court. If ordinary private disputes had continued to come before a jurisdiction like that of the eyre, to which plaintiffs had direct access, the common law could have reacted directly to changing needs; and in particular it could have continued to admit kinds of claims familiar in local courts but at first regarded as inappropriate for royal judges. But plaintiffs could not get to the court without a chancery writ, and the formulae of the writs, most of which were highly practical responses to the needs of thirteenth-century litigants, became an authoritative canon which could not easily be altered or added to. Important areas, some new but many older than the king's courts themselves, were in this way cut off from legal regulation, and they could later be reached only by devious ingenuity in the common law courts, or by resorting to the chancellor's equitable jurisdiction, to which once more the litigant could directly complain. . . . All this was no more than the constriction of red tape. But so complete did it become that in the eighteenth century it engendered a purely formalistic view of the law and of its development which has lasted until our own day. (pp. 36)

Speaking specifically of "trespass," but his meaning can be generalized, Milsom wrote that "the law itself was seen as based, not upon elementary ideas, but upon the common law writs, as consisting in a range of remedies which had as it were come down from the skies. If a case fell within the scope of one writ, then in general no other writ could be proper" (p. 309).

Many other passages could be cited to the same effect. Whether an action was available depended on a system (of writs) that had lost its meaning centuries before; whole parts of the law remained in effect though the societal structure at their base had disappeared centuries before; the scope of a remedy—whether for instance fault was an essential of a particular tort—depended and may still depend on devices and dodges invented centuries ago to meet difficulties dead centuries ago. Of one distinction, as we have seen, Milsom remarks that it "seems capricious." So it does, and so does the legal result in the other instances quoted; but only if we look at the law from society's point of view, from a consideration of the economic and social realities. It is not capricious if we look at law from the point of view of the legal elite, in this instance the judges who make the law. "But practitioners and judges do not normally give a pin for legal development. Their duty is to these clients and the proper disposition of this case" (p. 77). Precisely. Judges cannot dispose of a case just as they wish. They are boxed in, especially in a system based on precedent, by former decisions whether relating to jurisdiction or to points of substantive law. Writing specifically of land settlements Milsom declares: "The rules under which so much of the wealth of England was held for so much of its history were made and unmade by these processes, so extraordinary when looked at as a whole and backwards, so reasonable step by forward step" (p. 199).

In the attempt to give a decent remedy in a particular situation the judges may make matters worse both by complicating the law and by directing its course for the future. In judge-made law, the input of society at large—both in terms of the views of the inhabitants and of economic interests—is different from what it is in jurist-made law. At the very least the case comes before the judge only because there is a problem, and the issues are put vehemently—as vehemently at least as the system allows—by the interested party. But society's input is not matched by the outcome. That is determined by the judges' view of the law. It cannot surprise that there are rules of judging, that judges are blinkered by law that they see as existing in its own right, even if they can at times twist it to a rather different shape. If there is any cause for surprise, it is, as with the Roman law of contract, the acquiescence in this type of legal evolution by the ruling elite and society at large. But, then, if there was not this acquiescence most of the time, law would not evolve as largely autonomous, involved with its own culture, in the way that I claim.

The nature of legal evolution in England by judicial precedent leads to a fundamental question (which will not be answered here). Because of its emphasis on development by precedent and in ignoring Roman law, English law came eventually to be unique in western Europe, with different legal rules, divisions of law, legal structures, systematization, and hierarchies of lawmakers. What does this tell one about society in general and the ruling elite? Was England really different in social structure and values from the rest of Europe? And if it was, what were the significant social differences? Saxony, for example, taking the other route of building upon the Corpus Juris Civilis, was by the middle of the nineteenth century the possessor of a much more sophisticated, systematic, analytical system of law than England then had. I doubt that it tells one anything beyond the law—that is, until someone documents the differences in the societies that account for the difference in legal approach. What is one to make of the fact that for a long time, from 1714 until the death of King William IV in 1837, the king of England was the king of Hanover in Germany, where a very different legal system prevailed? Even then Ernest Augustus, duke of Cumberland, became king of Hanover and reigned until 1851. And was England, by avoiding the Reception of Roman law, more innovative in law than were the other western European states? If it was, what meaning does this have?

Law has, as Martin Kreigier emphasizes, a "pervasive traditionality," that to a considerable extent the legal past is a normatively and authoritatively significant part of the legal present. As he puts it, "In every complex tradition, such as law, what is present at any particular time is the currently authoritative or persuasive residue of deposits made over generations, recording and transmitting inconsistent and often competing values, beliefs, and views of the world. Current law is full of elements caught in and transmitted by legal tradition over generations. Dig into this diachronic quarry at any particular time, and the present will be a revealing mixture of fossils, innovations of the long gone, and recent deposits."[6] This incoherence is very obvious, as we have seen, in a system such as that of England built up by judicial precedent.

The incoherence also appears with astonishing clarity in a federal country where neighboring provinces or states, having much in common, build up over centuries very different legal rules on matters of fundamental concern. The law of the Swiss cantons at the time of the preparation of the Swiss Civil Code, Schweizerisches Gesetzbuch (ZGB), is a good example. Virgil Rossel (who prepared the French translation) was one of the two rapporteurs for the French language at the debate of the Conseil National in 1905 on the draft code of Eugen Huber, and he emphasized that the differences existing between the cantonal laws then in force had, almost always, origins that could not be explained by religion, language, or even by race. Then he continued:

> What is, for example, the matrimonial regime that is the nearest to that of the canton of Neuchâtel? Do not search too close by: go, on the contrary, to the extreme eastern frontier of Switzerland, in the canton of the

Grisons! Perhaps you think that the matrimonial regime of the canton of Thurgau and even the whole economy of its civil legislations is strongly attached to the neighboring canton of Zurich? The analogies are much more striking between the code of Thurgau and the *code Napoléon* than between the same code of Thurgau and that which Bluntschli drew up. Gentlemen, I borrow some other perceptions, no less characteristic, from the message of the federal council of 24 November 1896:

"The cantonal law gives the advantage to the sons to the detriment of daughters in the cantons of Lucerne, Fribourg, Zug and Thurgau. Schaffhausen and Neuchâtel give to ascendants and collaterals the right of property return according to the origin of the goods. Appenzell, Aargau, Basel, Fribourg and Solothurn make no distinction between the paternal and the maternal lines. Geneva, Thurgau, the Bernese Jura, Sankt Gallen, Vaud, Fribourg, Ticino and Solothurn make of ascendants a special class of heirs. Fideicommissary substitutions are forbidden in Geneva, the Bernese Jura, Lucerne, Glaris, in the Grisons and in Zug. Geneva, the Bernese Jura, Neuchâtel, Appenzell, Aargau, Valais, Bern, Vaud, Glaris and Fribourg give the illegitimate child a share in the inheritance to his father. Zurich, Geneva, Thurgau, Soleure, Ticino, Neuchâtel, Sankt Gallen and the Bernese Jura have permitted adoption. Bern, Thurgau, Aargau, Geneva, Soleure, Neuchâtel, Fribourg and Ticino give the mother, on the father's death, the paternal power and the guardianship of the children. Geneva and Nidwalden have instituted the family council whose task is to look after the tutor's administration. In the realm of the law of property, we find a land registry in Basel-city, Soleure, in the canton of Vaud, in Schwytz and Nidwalden . . ." I cut short my quotation. But is that not the best demonstration of what is artificial and fortuitous in our Swiss law? This mosaic, which seems the result of fantasy and chance at least as much as of ethical or moral influences, ought not to fill us with such veneration that we do not dare to lay hands on it.[7]

Here we are concerned with the fact of the incoherence of legal rules in neighboring cantons or states in a federal nation, not with explaining the causes of the differences. But investigation would show that many of the differences had their origins in particular events that were not deeply rooted in local consciousness. An individual dispute might require court resolution. And the court's decision might be followed in subsequent cases as being the best evidence of local custom, whether or not any local custom existed. A similar neighboring state might reach a contrary decision, possibly for reasons inhering in the particular case, and that decision in time might be treated as the basis of local custom. Or at the time of the codification of cantonal law a new rule might be adopted without much thought from an outside code, whether of a different canton or of a foreign state like France, which at the time had general prestige. And, once accepted for whatever reason, a rule lives on.

As the example of England also makes abundantly plain, legal development is greatly affected by the sources of law that are available. In this chapter on judges, I want to return to jurists, pointing out one aspect of development by juristic opinion that has been understressed, namely, the ability and power of jurists to react against the existing tradition and in part create a new one. They are, of course, still bound by what they know, but jurists can attempt to reject much of what has gone before. Much more freely than judges, they can decide whom they wish to regard as authoritative and whom they will despise. They do not have to give a ruling that will be acceptable in a particular case and, to be effective, they need not cause a change in accepted dogma or methodology at once. They can have long-term aims. The prime example of jurists adopting a new influential approach must be that of the great humanists of the Renaissance, such as Cuiacius and Donellus, with the rejection of the methodology of the glossators, postglossators, and, above all, the Bartolists. To assess the extent of their impact would require volumes but that need not detain us here.[8] What needs to be emphasized is only that jurists can powerfully affect the tradition. In this regard, naturally, the humanists do not stand alone.

One other example of the power of jurists is significant. It comes from the Kingdom of the Two Sicilies, and more particularly from Naples, from the late seventeenth well into the eighteenth century.[9] There was a change in attitude among the law professors, away from the traditional authorities to other international figures. Their works contain references to philosophers such as Bacon, Hobbes, Locke, Montesquieu, and Descartes, as well as to jurists such as Cuiacius, Donellus, Hotman, Brissonius, Bynkershoek, Pufendorf, Stryk, and Grotius.[10] The *Praelectiones ad Institutiones Justiniani* (1779) of M. Guarani may serve as one particular instance. The book contains, among legal citations, references to local case law and statute. Of references to foreign authors I make the following count: Noodt, 30; Bynkershoek, 22; Grotius, 20; Stryk, 19; J. Gothofredus, 17; Vinnius, 16; Cuiacius and Donellus, 15 each; Heineccius, 14; U. Huber, 11; Pufendorf, 10; and fewer than 10 to many others. To Italian writers I find: *Doctores*, 12, and *Glossa*, 3; Baldus, 5; Bartolus, 4; Irnerius, Accursius, and Julius Clarus, 1 each. Astonishingly, given the Spanish connection, I find only two references to Spanish jurists, one to Gomes, and one to Covarruvias; and more surprisingly still, none at all to the famous Neapolitan De Lucca. This rate of citation seems very lopsided. This new approach was slow to have an impact but was eventually powerfully felt as can be seen from the writings from the most important writer on the practice of the time, the advocate Giuseppe Sorge.[11]

This Neapolitan phenomenon is quite typical of what happens when jurists wish to change the existing tradition. To begin with, works that previously were treated as authoritative are either not cited or are cited only to be summarily dismissed; in either eventuality, the opinions contained in them are not properly considered. Then some other jurists are continually cited, to an extent that to an outsider seems extreme; it still seems astonishing that the Neapolitan Guarani cites the Dutchman Gerhardt Noodt more often than anyone else (apart from himself), and that he cites ten "foreigners" each more often than ten times and no Italian (other than reporters of cases) more often than five times. Finally, it should be noted that it takes time for their approach to have a practical impact. An example closer to home, and equally typical of development by juristic interpretation, is provided by the group in the recent United States known as Critical Legal Studies scholars. They, too, attempt to reject much of what has gone before, though they are bound by what they know. A glance at the footnotes in their writings will quickly reveal whom they wish to regard as authoritative—references to Roberto Unger and Duncan Kennedy are de rigueur—and whom they will despise. Indeed, some writings of the masters are always, in all contexts, treated as of the greatest relevance. A true believer reveals his faith by referring to these writings favorably in the opening pages of his own piece.[12]

From this and subsequent chapters it will be apparent that in uncovering the parameters of judges' reasoning and judicial decision making, one must take into account the legal tradition within which the judges work. Often, too, this also will involve taking a long, hard look at even remote legal history and at the law in our countries.

One factor makes this search particularly intriguing: judges are unable to give society what it expects from them. The populace expects from judges the correct legal decision as a result of their applying the law to the facts. How do good judges arrive at their decisions? It is easier to say what makes bad judges: their reasoning is lacking in logic, or they fail to know or to understand relevant law. But one cannot say that good judges, at least in most types of appellate civil cases, are those who arrive at the correct decision through the use of logic and the application of the legal rules to established facts.[13] Provided that the attorneys for the parties have done their work adequately and prepared their case, there is no answer that is necessarily correct. The case can go either way. The answer that is correct is the one the judges come to, but it is correct only after, and only because, they come to it. As Justice Robert H. Jackson put it: "There is no doubt that if there were a super-Supreme Court, a substantial proportion of our reversals of state courts would also be reversed. We are not final because we are infallible, but we are infallible only because we are final."[14] So, possibly, all judges who are not obviously bad judges ought to be counted as good judges? Yet insiders all believe that there are, in addition to bad judges, mediocre and good judges, and that among good judges some are better than others. What are the criteria for insiders? The answer I suggest is that for insiders a good judge is one who reaches the law to be applied to the facts by a mental process that is thought to be the most appropriate by his fellow judges and by well-placed attorneys and legal scholars. What the appropriate mental process is will be determined by the legal culture, and, like other aspects of culture, will scarcely be questioned by those participating in it. The outsider sees things differently. He may be impressed by the "foreign" culture, but some aspects strike him as incongruous.

JUDICIAL REASONING

To investigate the concept of judicial reasoning, I look at four approaches to deciding a case in different societies—contemporary England; uncodified civil-law or "mixed" systems (with an example from seventeenth-century Scotland and another from early-twentieth-century South Africa); nineteenth-century France after codification; and fifteenth-century Germany, with a glance at thirteenth- and fourteenth-century Spain—where the attempt is made each time to reach the correct decision by applying the mental process thought most appropriate. None of the approaches examined here is result-oriented, and to outsiders, especially to lawyers brought up in a different legal culture, the mental process seems artificial, even absurd, but not to those involved in the game. The approach in each case is not atypical for the particular legal culture, but I have tried to find striking examples.

Contemporary England

Anyone interested in the vagaries of legal evolution, whether as legal historian or law reformer, must be fascinated by the English doctrine of precedent, especially since the Practice Statement of the House of Lords issued in 1966.[15] From 1898 (according to the usual calculation but actually earlier)[16] the Law Lords regarded themselves as bound by their own previous decisions, but in the just-mentioned practice statement they announced that, while treating their previous decisions as normally binding, they would depart from a previous decision when it appeared right to do so.[17]

One recent House of Lords case, *President of India v. La Pintada Compañía Navigación S.A.* [1984] 3 W.L.R. 10, is instructive for its approach. The legal issue involved was whether, when no interest for delay in performance was specified in a contract, and payment was delayed but made before proceedings were begun, the other contracting party could claim interest for nonpayment among his damages. This issue is the "case 1" referred to by the judges.

Lord Fraser of Tullybelton, who delivered his opinion first, was brief: "I have had the advantage of reading in draft the speech of my noble and learned friend, Lord Brandon of Oakbrook. His reasoning seems to me irresistible and I feel myself driven, though with reluctance, to agree that this appeal must be allowed, with the consequences that the arbitrator's alternative award will be upheld."[18] Now, as I have said, in most types of civil cases at the appellate level, if counsel on both sides have done their work, it should not happen that one decision on the law is forced upon the judges.[19] Otherwise the case would not have got so far. All the more is this true where, as with the House of Lords, the court is not bound by its own or any other precedent. If the decision is not inevitable, then reasoning to it cannot be irresistible. Lord Fraser can only mean that by the type of logic or arguments that judges find persuasive, whatever these may be, Lord Brandon's reasoning to the conclusion is convincing. Nonetheless, Lord Fraser expresses regret at the decision he comes to. He accepts, that is to say, that there are principles that determine what is the law even when injustice is the result. Although he does not say so expressly, he accepts that "lawness" is to be fixed by these principles even when he is technically free to decide that the law is different. In other words, higher than the notion that judges decide what the law is, when they are free to do so, stands the idea that this decision has to be reached by the application of some conception of lawness—of what constitutes law—even when injustice results. That is, even those who can make law accept the standards of law as being different from their notions of justice. Lord Scarman's opinion reads:

> My Lords, I agree with the speech to be delivered by my noble and learned friend, Lord Brandon of Oakbrook, a draft of which I have had the opportunity of studying. But I wish to associate myself with the comments made by my noble and learned friend, Lord Roskill. I also reach with regret and reluctance the conclusion that the appeal must be allowed. The sooner there is legislation along the lines proposed by the Law Commission (or some other solution achieving the same end) the better.[20]

This takes us further than Lord Fraser. Again, Lord Scarman gives the unjust decision, although by exercising his judicial right of making law he need not have done so. Yet he expresses the desire that the law be changed, but by legislation. There is a hierarchy of lawmakers, and the legislature has greater powers of law making than have judges. Where the law ought to be changed, judges may feel that it is appropriate for the legislature to make the change, and not themselves, even when they can do so. This remains their position (or at least that of Lord Scarman in this case) even when, first, there is no certainty of legislative intervention and, second, when legislation, if any, will not rectify the present injustice. In furtherance of some notion of appropriateness in law making, judges are prepared to commit an injustice: not an injustice by some theoretical notion of justice but by the judges' own personal ideas of justice and injustice. Lord Roskill also finds Lord Brandon's reasoning compelling. Then he continues:

> But I freely confess that I have arrived at this conclusion though without doubt nevertheless with both regret and reluctance. It has long been recognised that *London, Chatham and Dover Railway Co. v. The South Eastern Railway Co.* [1893] A.C. 429 left creditors with a legitimate sense of grievance and an obvious injustice without remedy. I think the House in 1893 recognised those consequences of the decision, but then felt compelled for historical reasons to leave that injustice uncorrected. Since 1893 Parliament has intervened twice, first to remedy what my noble and learned friend has called case 3 and secondly to remedy case 2. On the latter occasion Parliament, with the Law Commission's report before it, had the opportunity also to remedy the injustice to creditors to which case 1 (a debt paid late but before proceedings for its recovery have been begun) can so often give rise. But Parliament neither accepted the Law Commission's proffered solution to case 1 nor provided any substitute solution of its own. It must, I

think, therefore be accepted that this inaction was deliberate. If so it cannot be right for this House in its judicial capacity by departing from the
London, Chatham and Dover Railway case to proffer a remedy which if applicable at all must apply to all three cases and not only to case 1 with the
consequence that as regards cases 2 and 3 there would be concurrent and
inconsistent remedies, one statutory and discretionary, the other at common law and as of right since once a breach of contract and damage caused
by that breach are proved a court has no discretion but must award the
damages claimed in full.[21]

The main authority set out for the decision is the case of 1893, ninety-
one years before, and Lord Roskill felt—rightly, as we shall see—that
the House of Lords at that time also thought its decision unjust.

Lord Roskill gives more argument for his decision. He accepts Lord
Brandon's view that the *London, Chatham and Dover* decision covered
three separate cases. Case 3 was remedied first by Parliament. Then, with
a Law Commission report in front of them that covered cases 1 and 2,
they remedied case 2 but did nothing about case 1. They neither accepted the Law Commission's recommendations nor proffered their own
solution. From this Lord Roskill draws the conclusion that Parliament's
inactivity was deliberate (and hence presumably that the House of Lords
would be acting against the will of Parliament if they changed the law).[22]

This type of reasoning, which is akin to an argument from silence, is
always dangerous. It becomes much more fragile when we take into account that British parliamentary drafting is notoriously bad,[23] that the
British House of Commons is famous for its lack of interest in legislating on matters with no party political impact,[24] and that many are the
factors extraneous to the deliberate intention of the House of Commons
that prevent the passing of legislation or the passing of complete and
well-rounded legislation.[25] Moreover, Lord Roskill's words "Parliament,
with the Law Commission's report before it" sound a trifle exaggerated.
Rather, the Law Commission had submitted a report to Parliament. But
that is not to say that members of Parliament were conscious of it, had
read it and understood it, or had it in contemplation. The reasoning—
from a failure to act, mind you—becomes downright absurd when we
consider that British courts at that time refused to consider legislative
history. There is arguably a case for seeking for the (fictitious) intention of the legislature only in the wording of a statute,[26] but there can
be none for interpreting a statute by seeking the intention of the legislature through the absence of clauses on a rather different issue.

Lord Roskill's argument at the end of that paragraph derives from that of Lord Brandon and is fundamental, and it is appropriate now to quote from Lord Brandon:

> There are three cases in which the absence of any common law remedy for damage or loss caused by the late payment of a debt may arise, cases which I shall in what follows describe for convenience as case 1, case 2 and case 3. Case 1 is where a debt is paid late, before any proceedings for its recovery have been begun. Case 2 is where a debt is paid late, after proceedings for its recovery have been begun, but before they have been concluded. Case 3 is where a debt remains unpaid until, as a result of proceedings for its recovery being brought and prosecuted to a conclusion, a money judgment is given in which the original debt becomes merged.[27]

It seems to me that Lord Roskill is correct. A remedy given in case 1 ought also to be given in cases 2 and 3. It would be wrong for there to be a greater right to interest in case 1 where no action was brought before payment, than in cases 2 and 3, where the debtor was being or had been sued. But is there really an argument for saying that the creditor's claim should be greater in cases 2 and 3 than in case 1? Is there any justification for holding that a creditor who has started an action is entitled to interest on the debt, but one who has not is not so entitled? Common sense and justice—which may have little to do with law—would suggest not.

But much may depend on the nature of this legal right in cases 2 and 3. The Law Reform (Miscellaneous Provisions) Act of 1934, section 3(1) covers case 3 and provides: "In any proceedings tried in any court of record for the recovery of any debt or damages, the court may, if it thinks fit, order that there shall be included in the sum for which judgment is given interest at such rate as it thinks fit on the whole or any part of the debt or damages." The court may, "if it think fit," give interest on the debt where there is a judgment. Schedule 1 of the Administration of Justice Act of 1982 covers case 2: "Subject to rules of court, in proceedings (wherever instituted) before the High Court for the recovery of a debt or damages there may be included in any sum for which judgment is given simple interest, at such rate as the court thinks fit or as rules of court may provide, on all or any part of the debt or damages in respect of which judgment is given or payment is made before judgment." The court "may" award interest. Thus, in cases 2 and 3 the court has discretion to award interest.

But what is the nature of this discretion? It is surely not to be exercised arbitrarily but—like the right of the House of Lords not to follow its own decision—to be exercised according to sound standards of judging.[28] What are the appropriate principles to be applied? I think we can state that interest is not to be awarded as a penalty: first, because one would expect that if an award could include a penalty, that would be expressly stated in the legislation; second, because an appropriate penalty would not always correspond to an interest sum; third, because the primary purpose of interest is compensation or recompense; and fourth (and above all), because both statutes expressly declare that their provisions do not apply if interest had been fixed by agreement between the parties or otherwise, a rule that is inappropriate if the judges were in fact being given power to award a penalty.

If interest may be awarded, but neither arbitrarily nor as penalty, the award must be to take account of loss suffered by the plaintiff: the interest is to be awarded as damages. It is relevant that under both statutes the discretion of the court, "if it thinks fit," extends not only to the award of interest but also to the rate of interest and the period of time for which it runs.

Let us now return to the question whether there is an argument for saying that the creditor's claim should be greater in cases 2 and 3 than in case 1. If the foregoing analysis is correct, and courts should award interest in cases 2 and 3, where part of the plaintiff's loss is precisely loss of interest that he would have obtained if he had received payment of the debt, then they ought also to award interest in case 1. And, on principle, apart even from cases 2 and 3, interest ought to be awarded in case 1. As we have seen Lord Roskill arguing, at common law, "once a breach of contract and damage caused by that breach are proved a court has no discretion but must award the damages claimed in full." On that sound principle, no one would now doubt—whatever may have been the situation in 1893 and earlier—that in the usual situation a creditor on receipt of payment will invest it, at least in a bank. Where he was likely not to have done so, and hence not to have sustained further loss, the court should not grant interest as damages.

Thus, on general principle, in the absence of the 1893 decision—which could have been set aside—and apart from cases 2 and 3, the court could and should award interest as damages in case 1. But Lord Roskill sees a problem: all three cases would be covered by the common law and would give a remedy as of right, but cases 2 and 3 are also covered by statute that gives only a discretionary remedy. The inconsistency is more technical and aesthetic than substantive. By common law, interest would be given as of right, but only where loss is presumed to have followed from nonpayment or late payment of the debt; by statute, the court, if it thinks fit—and the discretion must not be taken from the judges—is to include interest in the award, but it must not act arbitrarily or make the award as a penalty, but only on account of loss, actual or presumed. The remedies have different bases but they ought not to lead to inconsistent results. Lord Roskill concludes:

> My Lords, it would be idle to affect ignorance of the fact that the present state of the law in relation to case 1 places the small creditor at grave disadvantage vis-à-vis his substantial and influential debtor. The former may fear to offend the latter by instituting legal proceedings either swiftly or indeed at all and it is notorious that some substantial and influential debtors are not slow to take advantage of this tactical strength, especially in times of financial stringency. It has taken two pieces of legislation, one some 50 years after 1893 and the other almost another half-century later, to remedy the injustice in cases 2 and 3. I venture to hope that whatever solution be ultimately adopted in case 1, whether the Law Commission's somewhat complicated solution or something simpler, that solution will be found promptly and the remaining injustice in this branch of the law finally removed.[29]

The first part of that paragraph shows clearly the need to give the creditor in case 1 as much protection as creditors in cases 2 and 3. The unlikelihood of legislative activity to remedy case 1 is brought out by the length of time it took to remedy cases 2 and 3. Neither Lord Roskill nor any of his brother judges are likely to live to see legislative reform of case 1, a reform they themselves refused to make.

Lord Brandon of Overbrook gives three main reasons for his decision:

> My first main reason is that the greater part of the injustice to creditors which resulted from the *London, Chatham and Dover Railway* case has now been removed, to a large extent by legislative intervention, and to a lesser extent by judicial qualification of the scope of the decision itself. My second main reason is that, when Parliament has given effect by legislation to some recommendations of the Law Commission in a particular field, but has taken what appears to be a policy decision not to give effect to a further such recommendation, any decision of your Lordships' House which would have the result of giving effect, by another route, to the very recommendation which Parliament appears to have taken that policy decision to reject, could well be regarded as an unjustifiable usurpation by your Lordships' House of the functions which belong properly to Parliament, rather than as a judicial exercise in departing from an earlier decision on

the ground that it has become obsolete and could still, in a limited class of cases, continue to cause some degree of injustice. . . .

My third reason is this. Suppose that your Lordships were to depart from the *London, Chatham and Dover Railway* case [1893] A.C. 429 in such a way as to give all creditors, whose debts either remained unpaid or were paid late, whether before or after action brought, a cause of action for interest by way of general damages for breach of contract, what would be the result? The result, as it seems to me, would be that such cause of action would be available to a creditor not only in case 1, in respect of which he still has no remedy except where he can prove special damages, but also in cases 2 and 3, in respect of both of which, since the coming into force of the Act of 1982, he already has a statutory remedy. What is more, the new cause of action so applicable to cases 2 and 3 would constitute a remedy as of right for a creditor, whereas the statutory remedy would remain discretionary only. There would, accordingly exist, in relation to cases 2 and 3, two parallel remedies, one as of right and the other discretionary; and the likelihood would be that creditors would, because of this difference, come to rely mainly on the former, rather than the latter, right. It is, in my view, plainly to be inferred, from the form of the relevant provisions in the Acts of 1934 and 1982, that Parliament has consistently regarded the award of interest on debts as a remedy to which creditors should not be entitled as of right, but only as a matter of discretion. That being the manifest policy of the legislature, I do not consider that your Lordships should create, in relation to cases 2 and 3, a rival system of remedies which, because they would be remedies as of right, would be inconsistent with that manifest policy.[30]

The first main reason is quite unconvincing and has no force. If a legal rule works unjustly in three situations and is corrected in two, that is scarcely an argument for leaving it uncorrected in the remaining situation. For those who find themselves in that unfortunate situation, it is scarcely consolation that in related situations, but not in theirs, injustice will not be done.

The third reason we have already seen, and it also weighed with Lord Bridge of Harwich. Even as set out so expertly by Lord Brandon, it seems a trifle forced. The common-law rule need not be that, in all actions on breach of contract for nonpayment of the debt, interest on the debt would necessarily be included in the award of damages, but that, where part of the plaintiff's loss was interest on the unpaid debt, the award of damages would include an amount by way of interest.

To estimate the value of the second main reason we have to consider the 1982 act. The beginning of the act sets out its contents.

An Act to make further provision with respect to the administration of justice and matters connected therewith; to amend the law relating to actions for damages for personal injuries, including injuries resulting in death, and to abolish certain actions for loss of services; to amend the law relating to wills; to make further provision with respect to funds in court, statutory deposits and schemes for the common investment of such funds and deposits and certain other funds; to amend the law relating to deductions by employers under attachment of earnings orders; to make further provision with regard to penalties that may be awarded by the Solicitors Act 1974; to make further provision for the appointment of justices of the peace in England and Wales and in relation to temporary vacancies in the membership of the Law Commission; to enable the title register kept by the Chief Land Registrar to be kept otherwise than in documentary form; and to authorise the payment of traveling, subsistence and financial loss allowances for justices of the peace in Northern Ireland. [28th October 1982]

No mention of our topic! That is slipped in as part 3 of the act after a part entitled "Damages for Personal Injuries, Etc.—Scotland" and before a part on "Wills." Part 3 reads:

15. (1) The section set out in Part 1 of Schedule 1 to this Act shall be inserted after section 35 of the Supreme Court Act 1981.
(2) The section set out in Part II of that Schedule shall be inserted after section 97 of the County Courts Acts 1959.
(3) The Crown Proceedings Act 1947 shall accordingly have effect subject to the amendment in Part III of that Schedule, being an amendment consequential on subsections (1) and (2) above.
(4) The provisions mentioned in subsection (5) below (which this section supersedes so far as they apply to the High Court and county courts) shall cease to have effect in relation to those courts.
(5) The provisions are—
   (a) section 3 of the Law Reform (Miscellaneous Provisions) Act 1934; and
   (b) in the Administration of Justice Act 1969—
      (i) section 22; and
      (ii) in section 34(3) the words from "and section 22" onwards.
(6) The section set out in Part IV of Schedule 1 to this Act shall be inserted after section 19 of the Arbitration Act 1950.
16. The following subsection shall be added after section 23(5) of the Matrimonial Causes Act 1973 (financial provision in orders in connection with divorce proceedings etc.)—
   (6) Where the court—
      (a) makes an order under this section for the payment of a lump sum;

and

(b) directs—

    (i) that payment of that sum or any part of it shall be deferred; or

    (ii) that the sum or any part of it shall be paid by installments. The court may order that the amount deferred or the installments shall carry interest at such rate as may be specified by the order from such date, not earlier than the date of the order, as may be so specified, until the date when payment of it is due.

The statute has much of the charm hinted at by many observers of United Kingdom legislation: several subjects are dealt with in one statute; the law on one subject is dealt with in several statutes; legislation is by reference to other legislation (thus increasing the obscurity); and there is flight from the body of the statute to schedules.[31] Above all, the statute does not indicate that Parliament had given full, rounded consideration to the issue of when interest should be awarded for the nonpayment of a contractual debt.

R. H. S. Crossman records that when he was minister of housing and local government he never bothered to read any of the bills he got through the House of Commons, that "he never bothered to understand the actual clauses, nor did many Members, not even the spokesman for the Opposition."[32] Lord Brandon's argument would have us believe that the members of Parliament not only bothered to read and understand section 15 of the Administration of Justice Act of 1982—and understanding the section involves reading and understanding the schedule and the six statutes referred to in the section—but understood what was not covered by the section and had made the deliberate decision not to have the injustice of case 1 corrected; and this deliberate decision involves them knowing the previous law, including case law. I, for one, remain skeptical and therefore find unpersuasive the second main reason for Lord Brandon's decision. Parliament's treatment of the Law Commission's 1978 Report on Interest (Cmnd. 7229) and section 15 of the 1982 Administration of Justice Act do not encourage me to expect speedy reform by legislation. Incidentally, there is something almost inconsistent in Lords Scarman and Roskill accepting Lord Brandon's reasoning as compelling (that Parliament did not want reform of case 1) and their expressed hope for legislative reform. It is worth recalling that if the lords had reformed case 1, they would not have been flouting the expressed wish of Parliament but altering the basis of a decision of their own of 1893.

A consideration of *President of India v. La Pintada Compañía Navigación S.A.* as an example of the judicial approach to law making would be excessively incomplete without a glance at *London, Chatham and Dover Railway Co. v. The South Eastern Railway,* the case of 1893 from which their Lordships decided not to depart. In that case Lord Herschell, L.C., said:

> I confess that I have considered this part of the case with every inclination to come to a conclusion in favour of the appellants, to the extent at all events, if it were possible, of giving them interest from the date of the action; . . . But I have come to the conclusion, upon a consideration of the authorities, agreeing with the Court below, that it is not possible to do so.

And Lord Watson:

> I regret that I am unable to differ from your Lordships.

And Lord Shand:

> I confess that I have looked with very great anxiety to the possibility under the law of England, as I have heard it argued, of giving interest in this case, for I cannot help thinking that a gross injustice is the result of witholding it. It appears to me that it is a defective state of the law.

Thus a judgment of 1893 that was regarded as unjust by the judges who issued it and was treated as settling the law leads judges who are not bound by it, ninety-one years later, to issue a judgment that they repeatedly expressly condemn as unjust, when there was no intervening legislation on the point in issue. The 1893 judges, of course, were particularly concerned with cases 2 and 3.

In discussing this case as a specimen of the House of Lords' approach to law making, I am not suggesting that the approach taken in the case is unique or even unusual—far from it. Nor is it relevant to inquire whether *sub specie aeternitatis* the decision ought to be regarded as unjust. Rather the aim is to indicate that law was treated as existing in its own right, that judgment was to be reached by a mental process appropriate to establishing lawness, not by the judges' own feelings of what was just or what the law ought to be. The decision was unjust in the judges' own express opinion. They could have reached what they believed was the just decision by reversing a decision of their own of almost a century earlier, and they had the power to do so. Instead, they felt bound to come to the unjust decision because of a particular process of legal reasoning. First, they held that the law was previously settled. Second, they accepted that there is a hierarchy of lawmakers: legislators rank above judges. From that they reasoned that if legislators had not made a change in the law when they had the chance, then the judges ought not to make the change, because that would be to usurp the role of the legislators. And they deduced from the simple failure of the legislators to act a deliberate intention not to act.

The argument is a legalistic one and will be acceptable to many within the tradition. But the artificiality—and the legalistic nature—of the reasoning is revealed both by the accepted refusal to inquire into the state of intention of the legislators and by the expressed hope that the legislators would change the law. (One cannot, I believe, escape from this conclusion by postulating that the judges were shedding crocodile tears, that in fact they had reached the conclusion most acceptable to them for social, economic, or political reasons. First, if they had so thought, they need not have stressed that their judgment was unjust or have expressed a hope for legislation, thus calling attention to the shortcomings of the decision. Second, it is difficult, and for me impossible, to understand what political, economic, or social bias would have motivated their decision. Third, one of them, Lord Scarman, had been chairman of the Law Commission, which recommended reform.)

It will usually be outsiders, and especially outsider lawyers, who see the absurdity of legal reasoning in this fashion, who will ask how people can be paid and highly regarded for reasoning in this way. To the insider the form of law making is hallowed by tradition; he cannot explain why it has come to be as it is, and he will be surprised if he is even asked to explain it.

Uncodified Civil Law Systems

But the approach of the English judges should not be singled out. They are not alone in seeking a route to an answer they can justify not by the quality or suitability of the result but by a notion of lawness; a route that is artificial and seems bizarre to outsiders, and one the judges need not take.

One striking case of this kind is the Haining's case, from seventeenth-century Scotland (described in Chapter 6). Striking though it is, it represents a common attitude of the times both in Scotland and in continental Europe. A landowner had caused the pollution of a tributary of the river Tweed, which resulted in the deaths of Tweed salmon, thus causing loss to the Tweed commercial fishers. The fishers brought an action. The main arguments on both sides of the case proceed on the restrictions on the use of rivers in Roman law, and especially on the issue of whether a riparian owner had the right to pollute flowing water. The societal economic factor at the heart of the case, where Scottish conditions were different from Italian—namely, the existence of large commercial river fishery—was never discussed in order to determine the relevance of Roman law as a guide. Yet Roman law was not part of Scots law and need not have been employed. But it had become common practice to look to Roman law where there was a gap in Scots law. The arguments proceeded on a view of lawness established by the legal tradition, an approach that owed much to prevailing fashion and was definitely not mandatory. We do not know the outcome of the case. Nor does it matter. What concerns us is that the attorneys on both sides thought the case ought properly to be adjudged on the basis of Roman rules and that the appropriateness of these rules for Scottish conditions was not brought into issue.

Even today in countries where the Corpus Juris Civilis and subsequent developments from it are still regarded as being in some sense part of the law of the land, or at least highly persuasive, the same problem of tradition may arise; judges may be so imbued with their legal culture that they approach their decision making through rules that were made to apply elsewhere and in very different circumstances, without always giving sufficient weight to the particulars of the case before them. The Republic of South Africa, now the predominant civil-law country (though with an admixture of common law) where the law is uncodified, presents, naturally enough, the most obvious examples. One, from before independence, will suffice. By way of background it is enough to note that on the orthodox view, Roman-Dutch law, and in particular the law of the Province of Holland in the seventeenth century, is authoritative in South Africa even without the impress of South African case law.[33] This Roman-Dutch law includes the Corpus Juris Civilis so far as received in the Netherlands (or perhaps so far as not abrogated by subsequent statute or a contrary custom), the writings of the Dutch jurists, and the decisions of the Dutch courts.

Mann v. Mann [1918] C.P.D. 89 was a case in which a woman living separate from her husband but without a judicial separation, and where there was no community of property, brought an action against him for assault both on the grounds of loss and of pain and suffering. As part of his judgment Searle, J., said:

With regard to the Roman-Dutch Law on the subject, the absence of any known civil action ever having been brought in this Court on such grounds as these by a wife against her husband goes far to show that it has been tacitly recognised as not allowed by our law, but of course this is not conclusive. Under Roman-Dutch Law, marriages ordinarily take place in community of property, all the property of husband and wife is joint, though each may be regarded as entitled to half; the husband has the administration of the whole. Consequently, I do not see how there can be civil actions between them involving the payment of money by the one spouse to the other. If the wife sues the husband, the latter is entitled to have the amount of the judgment paid over to him, as long as the marriage subsists and there is no legal "separation"; it would be of no advantage to the wife to get a judgment against her husband for he still would be entitled to the administration of the proceeds.[34]

The statement is clear and reasonable, but not very helpful for the present case, where, as I have mentioned, the issue was precisely an action for assault where the parties were not married in community. Searle then goes on:

There are not many Roman-Dutch authorities which I have been able to find on this point, other than those quoted by the Magistrate. *Voet* (bk. 47, tit. 10, para.2) says, as translated in Mr. Melius De Villiers' Book on *Injuries:* "It is indisputable, moreover, that a husband has marital power over his wife, but if he abuses that power by inflicting upon her any 'real' injury of a more serious kind, there is nothing to prevent her according to a decision reported by *Sande* suing him on account of the injury, provided that the action, for the sake of the respect due to the estate of matrimony, be couched in moderate and temperate language." *Voet* explains in paragraph 7 that by "real injury" he means a serious injury, and undoubtedly the assault here charged, if it be proved to have taken place, would be sufficiently serious to be styled "real." The learned author of this Book on Injuries in commenting on the above passage says at p. 42: "It is very questionable, however, whether a wife can sue a husband in a civil action for an injury done to her by him," and he refers to Brouwer *de Jure Connubiorum* (On the Law of Marriage) (2, 29, 12). This author says: "The Jurisconsults deny the *actio iniuriarum,* which is '*famosa,*' to a wife who has been severely and excessively beaten, without reason, but they allow the *actio in factum,* to the effect that the husband pay compensation for the injuries he has brought upon her. The former is correct, but the latter is not, for the law has provided a fixed penalty for this delict, and we ought to be content with the punishments contained in the laws." He then refers to a penalty prescribed in such case by Justinian, namely that the husband should give out of his own goods to the wife the third part of the goods settled by antenuptial contract; and points out that nowadays wife-beaters are handed over into custody for correction and emendation by the authorities, and that Justinian's penalty has never been adopted in practice, i.e. the practice of the Courts of Holland.

The discussion by the Dutch authorities largely concerns points of Roman pleading affected by substantive Roman law. Under Roman law a spouse could not bring an action against the other that would cause the unsuccessful defendant to be *infamis,* to suffer a kind of technical legal disgrace.[35] Such an action was the *actio iniuriarum,* the private action appropriate to assault. To avoid *infamia,* and to give the injured spouse an action for redress, the Romans granted an action on the facts, an *actio in factum:* an action for damages for assault would be allowed, but the unsuccessful defendant would not become *infamis.* The Dutch had not received the notion of *infamia,* nor the technical aspects of Roman pleadings. The Romans, it is worth noting, had no system of matrimonial property regimes.

On the face of it, therefore, there should have been no obstacle in Holland to an injured wife, married without community, suing her estranged husband for assault. The opinion of à Sande and Johannes Voet would therefore seem to be vindicated. Hendryk Brouwer, whose opinion is cited without analysis, seems a trifle confused. If Justinian's penalty had not been accepted (in Holland) as he says, then the Roman jurists could not be inaccurate (for Holland) in allowing the *actio in factum* because that action could not have been displaced (in Holland) by the action with penalty.

Searle continues with further Roman-Dutch authority:

The decision in *Sande* to which *Voet* refers is to be found in *Dec. Fris.* (bk. 5, tit. 8, def. 9). After referring to an action against the wife as to which there was some difference of opinion among legal experts, he says: "And therefore Castellianus Catta lays down that a wife cruelly beaten by her husband ought not to proceed by the *actio injuriarum* but only by the *actio in factum,* in order that the '*fama*' of the husband may still remain." One difference between the *actio injuriarum* in Roman law and the *actio in factum* ("on the case") consisted in the circumstance that the consequence of a defendant being condemned in the former action was that he suffered "*infama*" [sic], involving the loss of certain important civil rights (see *Hunter's* Roman Law, p. 546) whereas the *actio in factum* did not entail these consequences.

Ulrich Huber in *Heedensdaegse Rechts Geleertheyt* in pt. 2, bk. 3, ch. 10, para. 21, says that the *actio injuriarum* does not obtain between spouses, because he who is condemned in such an action loses reputation, or at all events has reputation lessened, and such a result ought not to obtain as between spouses. As is pointed out by Mr. De Villiers the authorities thus do not seem to agree. *Voet* seems to think that the *actio injuriarum* lies, but quotes *Sande,* who says that it does not, but that an *actio in factum* does. *Huber* simply says that the *actio injuriarum* does not lie, and *Brouwer* says that neither action lies, because a specific punishment has been provided. *Sande* and *Huber* are Frisian authorities, and the Frisian law seems to have followed the Roman law more closely than the law of Holland, of which *Voet* and *Brouwer* are exponents.

Grotius in his *Introduction* (bk. 1, ch. 5, para. 20) says: "A husband may not beat his wife or otherwise illtreat her; and whichever of the spouses forgets himself or herself as against the other, is liable to such fine as is prescribed at each place for such offence, and is occasionally even more severely punished. In case of protracted quarrels, a separation from cohabitation may be granted by the Court.

Perezius on the *Code* (bk. 9, tit. 15, para. 4), after laying down that it is conceded according to prevailing custom that a husband may give moderate correction to his wife, says that if the husband vents his rage against his wife he may be restrained according to the discretion of the judge; and that it is always open to the wife on account of the intolerable cruelty of her husband to leave him and to live apart; and that in like manner a son who is badly treated by his father, may compel the father to grant him emancipation.

Groenewegen, *De Leg. Abrog.*, commenting upon *Novel* 117, para. 14, says that if any one vents his rage against his wife without cause, by our customs he does not fall into this legal penalty (referring to divorce, and Justinian's rule as to the third part of the property, above cited) but he is wont to be fined according to the Judge's discretion; and that the husband may be made liable to pay alimony to a wife suing for it, away from her home; but he adds that it is lawful for a husband to chastise an erring or delinquent wife, and quotes a considerable number of authorities to that effect.

The argument of Ulrich Huber would seem to have little relevance because *infamia* did not exist in Holland. That the possibility or otherwise of a private action between spouses for damages for assault is not mentioned by some Roman-Dutch authorities is not surprising, no more than is the absence in South Africa in 1918 of a precedent, because in seventeenth-century Holland, too, marriage usually entailed full community of property. Thus Hugo Grotius, *Inleidinge tot de Hollandsche Rechtsgeleerdheid*, 2.11:

8. Marriage contracted in Holland or West Friesland produces community of goods between the spouses at common law, except in so far as community is found to be excluded or restricted by ante-nuptial contract; except when a young man beneath the age of five and twenty, or a girl beneath the age of twenty, marries without consent of parents, friends, or of the magistrate, as has been said above in treating of marriage; since in the case of such marriages, though the marriage proceed, there is no community of goods.

Upon dissolution of the marriage the joint estate is divided equally between the spouses or their heirs: and if there are children who during the marriage have received anything from their parents to advance their marriage or trade and commerce, they must bring this advance into the common estate before any division: and this bringing-in (*collatio bonorum*) enures for the benefit not only of the other children (we shall speak of this below) but of the surviving spouse as well.[36]

Searle himself immediately continues:

It certainly would seem to be an intolerable state of things that if a husband grievously assaulted his wife who was earning her own living apart from him in such manner that she was no longer able to earn it—as for instance if he broke her arm—she should only be able to prosecute him or bind him over to keep the peace, but should have no remedy of compensation for the loss she had sustained. For it would surely not be sufficient answer that the husband was bound to maintain his wife; he might be in a very poor position whilst she might be able to earn a large income. But probably the most reasonable view to arrive at is that suggested by Mr. Melius De Villiers in his work quoted above. He says (p. 42), "Where husband and wife have been divorced or judicially separated there can be no reason why an action should not lie on account of injuries committed subsequent to the claim for divorce or separation being granted." It is true that the text writers do not appear to lay down this rule. Of course it goes without saying that when the parties are divorced and the marriage dissolved a civil action of damages for assault would lie; and although after a judicial separation the parties are still husband and wife, and the order is granted in hope of reconciliation I can see no reason why, as long as the order is in force, the relations between them should not be treated as so distinct that an action of compensation for an assault committed after the date of the order should lie.

It is precisely here that Searle shows himself to be unnecessarily influenced—overinfluenced, in fact—by the cultural tradition of referring to Roman-Dutch law, which in this case was primarily concerned with

a different factual situation. Certainly, as he says, "the law cannot provide for every individual case." But it can provide for marked categories,
such as where the couple were married without community. The opening sentences of the paragraph just quoted, where Searle voices his opinion on a husband assaulting a wife living apart, apply equally well where
the spouses are married with community or without, and logically in
the latter case whether the separation is judicial or not. Searle, however,
expressly adopts the opinion of Melius De Villiers, with its restrictions:
"Where husband and wife have been divorced or judicially separated
there can be no reason why an action should not lie on account of injuries committed subsequent to the claim for divorce or separation." But
he need not have done so, as he immediately goes on to show: "It is true
that the text writers do not appear to lay down this rule." In the absence
of a rule established by precedent or jurists he could have stated that
an action for damages also lies against a spouse where the couple have
separated and were not married in community of property. Further
along in his opinion Searle says:

> Upon the whole, therefore, and not without some hesitation and some re-
> gret I come to the conclusion that there is no sufficient authority to show
> that this action is allowed by Roman-Dutch Law or that in the Courts of
> Holland it has been recognised; that it does not appear to have been recog-
> nised by our practice in the Supreme Court; that the bringing of such an
> action is hedged about with such great difficulties that we must hold that
> the remedy by way of civil compensation for assault should only be allowed
> to a wife living apart from her husband under an order of Court for judi-
> cial separation.[37]

He is not entirely happy with the outcome of his judgment. But his decision is primarily culture determined and not result oriented. His decision, which was not forced on him by the state of the law, is geared
to show that he is a good judge concerned to come to the result by the
mental process appropriate to establishing "lawness" (although, writing in 1918, Searle may have been less sensitive to wife abuse than would
often be the case today).

But his approach is artificial in the extreme and takes little account
of changed conditions in the law or social behavior. The starting point
is the refusal of the Romans to grant an *actio iniuriarum* between
spouses. But the reason for this refusal—that the action was infaming—
was long gone before seventeenth-century Holland, not to mention
early-twentieth-century South Africa. With the reason for the restric-

tion gone, the restriction should also have gone. More could also have been made of the Roman ad hoc remedy of the facts. The absence—by no means total—of evidence for the action in Roman-Dutch law, in the courts of Holland, and in South Africa is explicable on the basis that the standard marriage was with community of property, whereas the Manns' marriage was without community. The changed factual situation makes the absence of authority of little relevance. The difficulties that hedge about an action between husband and wife in South African law are largely, as the first quotation from Searle shows, the result of community of property: any award to one against the other involves a withdrawal from joint property coupled with the addition of the same sum to the joint property, with no alteration in the allocation of resources.

Before we leave the case we must backtrack a little and return to a paragraph of Searle's slightly before that last quoted:

> Voet, in his book on the Lex Aquilia, the action allowed under the Roman-Dutch Law to recover compensation in damages for wrongs done (9, 2, 12), says: "These direct and equitable actions lie against those who have occasioned the damage, even against a wife or husband if the action does not bring about *infamia.*" This, as has been stated, would be the consequence if the *actio injuriarum* succeeds. He quotes in support of this the *Digest* (9, 2, 56) which lays down that a wife may be sued if she damages her husband's property. But *Voet* points out (in 47, 10, 13) that cases of assault to the person all fall under the class of *injuriae* proper; so that the fact that an action under Lex Aquilia can be brought between husband and wife does not take this matter much further.[38]

Mrs. Mann's case, though based on assault, was actually for medical expenses and for pain and suffering. Grotius, in the *Inleidinge* (3.34.1, 2), says:

> Wrongs against the body are acts whereby someone loses a limb; is maimed, wounded or otherwise hurt. From this arises obligations to compensate for the surgeon's fee, for damage sustained and profit lost during the recovery, and also afterwards if the injury is lasting. Pain and disfigurement of the body, though properly incapable of compensation, are assessed in money, if such is demanded.

And the appropriate action for pain and suffering as well as for medical expenses was accepted by the Roman-Dutch authorities as being provided by the *lex Aquilia,* though the remedy is a post-Roman development.[39] And the *actio legis Aquiliae* did lie between husband and wife because it was not infaming. Mrs. Mann should have succeeded. *Mann v. Mann* was effectively overruled by *Rohloff v. Ocean Accident & Guarantee Corp., Ltd.* 1960 (2) S.A. 291 (A.D.), and it seems now to be accepted that an action based on the *lex Aquilia* will lie.[40]

The outsider from another legal tradition may find it bizarre to see judges struggling to interpret law put forth by authorities hundreds of years ago;[41] even more when the appropriate action is hard to discover; still more when the old law, when discovered, is not binding. But when judges in such a position fail to take much account of changes in the reason for the law or in societal conditions, then their approach is incomprehensible except in terms of the enormous impact of legal culture.

France after Codification

A third type of approach is occasioned by one effect of the dominating event in most civil-law countries, the promulgation of a civil code. In almost all cases the promulgation of a code involves a break with the past. The civil code is now the law, and gaps ought not to be filled with references to the preceding law.[42] The reason is clear: what is wanted is a new beginning, and one of the main reasons for codification has often been a desire for simplicity in the law, and especially in the sources of law.[43] Reference to the old law obstructs the fulfillment of this desire.[44] Thus, sooner or later, even for the interpretation of the code, judges and jurists will put a distance between the code and the older rules, even when the latter formed the basis of the code provisions.

Yet sometimes there ought to be reference to the old law—for instance, when a contract was made before the codification. Then there might be an obvious conflict, to be resolved only in terms of legal culture, between the need to recognize that the old law is deeply relevant and the overwhelming desire to restrict its impact. The issue arises in a particularly striking form when, for example, at the heart of a dispute is a continuing contract, such as a lease, made many years before the code but entailing obligations even into the future.

Such a case is that of the French Cour de Cassation, Chambre Civil, 6 March 1876,[45] *De Galliffet v. Commune de Pélissane.* Insofar as it concerns us here, the Civil Court of Aix found on 18 March 1841 that by a contract of 22 June 1567 Adam de Craponne agreed to construct and maintain an irrigation canal and to irrigate the lands of the commune of Pélissane. In addition, it was agreed that for the irrigation of each carteirade, three sols would be paid to Adam de Craponne or his heirs, and the commune was not to levy taxes on the revenues from the canal. Adam de Craponne agreed to maintain the canal and bridges over it in perpetuity. The court further found, in addition to the terms of the contract, that the costs of irrigation and of maintenance of the canal had risen to such an extent that the cost of irrigation was out of all proportion to the payment and that the enterprise would have to be given up unless the payment for irrigation of each carteirade was raised. The court ordered the cost to be raised to sixty centimes (i.e., about fourfold), and justified this on the ground that when a contract involves successive performances over a long period the court may on equitable principles revise the contract in the light of changed circumstances that make the contract unjust.

After some related actions the Court of Appeal of Aix on 31 December 1873 affirmed the decision of the civil court, declaring: "It is recognized in law that contracts resting on periodic performances may be modified by the court when a balance no longer exists between the performance of the one party and the obligation of the other." The commune of Pélissane then raised a *pourvoi* before the Cour de Cassation. The ground that concerns us is based on article 1134 of the Code civil, which states:

> Legally formed agreements take the place of law for those who made them.
>   They can be revoked only by their mutual agreement or for reasons that the law authorizes.
>   They must be executed in good faith.

The relevant part of the opinion of the Cour de Cassation reads:

> But, on the first ground of the *pourvoi:*—article 1134 of the Code civil duly considered. Whereas the provision of that article is only the reproduction of ancient principles followed in the matter of obligations by agreement, the fact that the contracts giving rise to the lawsuit are anterior to the promulgation of the civil code cannot be, in the instant case an obstacle to the application of the said article;—Whereas the rule that it promulgates is general, absolute, and governs the contracts whose performance extends to successive ages just as it does those of a quite different nature; that in no case is it the function of tribunals, no matter how equitable their decisions may appear to them, to take into account time and circumstances to modify the agreements of the parties and substitute new clauses for those freely accepted by the contracting parties; that in deciding to the contrary and in raising the irrigation charge to 30 centimes from 1834 to 1874, then to 60 centimes from 1874, fixed at 3 sols by the agreements of 1560 and 1567

under the pretext that the sum payable was no longer in relationship with the costs of maintenance of the canal by Craponne, the judgment under attack formally violated article 1134 above considered.

And the court went on to quash the decision of the court of appeal. The court's response should perhaps be amplified for a non-French audience. Inherent in the argumentation, though not made express as self-explanatory, is a principle of French interpretation that "one must not draw a distinction where the law draws none."[46] Hence, since article 1134 draws no distinction between contracts executed by one single performance and continuing contracts, the court must draw none.

The Cour de Cassation seemed to agree that the decision of the lower court could appear equitable but quashed it nonetheless on the ground that it is not for the court to set aside the agreement of the parties. But the decision was not forced on the court, which might have fixed its gaze on the good faith of the parties under article 1134 rather than on the equitable approach of the courts. It could possibly have held that when changed circumstances rendered the balance between one party's performance and the other's obligation to pay so disproportionate that performance would be impossible for any standard commercial enterprise, then it was contrary to good faith for the second party to insist on the continued performance of the contract; or that changed circumstances external to the parties rendered its performance impossible by a *force majeure* that could not be imputed to the successors of Adam de Craponne.

But our interest lies in a different matter. Obviously for the decision, the law as it was in Pélissane in 1567, when the last contract was made, cannot be irrelevant; and the court says of article 1134: "Whereas the provision of this article only reproduces ancient principles continually followed in the law of obligations . . ." It evinces no desire to show any authority for these ancient principles—how widely held they were, what exceptions there were to them, and, above all, whether they applied to contracts made in Pélissane in 1567. All the judges want to do is to make article 1134 the main governing law for the contract. They have to make a bow in the direction of the older law, but in reality they are, again for cultural reasons, taking the Code civil as the starting point of the law. They might get an apparently fairer answer by looking at the older law, but, though they need not do so, they adopt an approach to discovering the law that excludes the possibility.

In fact, there were no ancient principles in Pélissane in 1567 corresponding to article 1134. Pélissane lies in the *pays de droit écrit,* and in the absence of a local rule of customary law (which probably could not have been discovered by the court in 1876), recourse would be had to the Corpus Juris Civilis and its common interpretation. Roman law knows no such ancient principle as that indicated by the court. On the contrary, although there is no text exactly on the point of a contract extending over centuries, there is ample evidence for the contract of hire (*locatio conductio*)—admittedly texts relating to hire of a thing—to show that changed circumstances could change the contractual obligations. Thus, if in the lease of land, exceptional climatic conditions such as drought or a force external to the land that could not be avoided such as a plague of starlings ruined the crop, then the tenant was excused from paying the rent for that year (*D.*19.2.15.1, 3). Again, if the windows of a leased building were subsequently obscured by a neighbor, the tenant could avoid the lease (*D.*19.2.25.2). Subsequently instances such as these came to be categorized; for instance, for Robert Pothier (1699–1772) the lessor implicitly guarantees that windows will not be obstructed by a neighbor, if the light is needed by the tenant.[47]

What Roman law did have, however, which is the historical ultimate source of article 1134, is the rule that parties to a contract might by agreement impose standards different from those settled in law. Thus, in the *Digest,* 16.3.1.6: "If it is agreed in a deposit that there will be liability even for negligence, the agreement is ratified: for the contract becomes law by the agreement."[48] Normally there was liability in deposit only for fraud. The immediate source of article 1134 is in Jean Domat (1625–96), *Les Loix civiles dans leur ordre naturel,* 1.1.2.7: "When the agreements are completed, whatever has been agreed on stands in place of law to those who made them; and they cannot be revoked except by the mutual consent of the parties, or by the other ways to be explained in the sixth section." Domat refers to the *Digest* text just quoted and to others that are, at the most, to the same effect (*D.*50.17.23; 2.14.1; 50.17.34). There is no indication that Domat was going beyond the Roman law to reach the proposition that judges have no right (as they had in Roman law) equitably to alter the terms of contract when conditions have drastically altered. Indeed, Domat accepts at 1.4.2.18 that if, as result of *force majeure,* the lessee is unable to enjoy the object of the lease, he is excused paying rent. French law before the Code civil did not know these "ancient principles" spoken of by the Cour de Cassation.

The wording of article 1134 follows that of Domat closely, and from that alone one would probably be justified in thinking that the draftsmen of the Code civil also were not going beyond Domat and the Roman rules. But we have the *travaux préparatoires,* which also contain no indication that the draftsmen considered themselves to be departing from Domat.[49] The Cour de Cassation either misunderstood or deliberately (and without express recognition) extended the scope of article 1134. The decision was a consequence of the legal culture, which put a distance between the Code civil and earlier French law. Not surprisingly, the decision, which might appear inequitable, was applauded by the French jurists of the time on account of the judges' mode of reasoning.[50]

Fifteenth-Century Germany

Examples even more remote from us in the legal tradition bring home in a particularly clear manner the absurdity of judges unnecessarily adopting a mental process to establish that their decisions are governed by principles of lawness. Thus, it was common in medieval Germany for a town to adopt a "mother" town to which it looked for legal opinion, even though it was in no way politically dependent on the mother. The mother might have been chosen for the "daughter" town by the founder when the town was established, or it might have been voluntarily selected. Especially in the latter case another mother town could be subsequently chosen, and mother towns in their turn often selected a mother town for themselves. Magdeburg in Saxony is the prime example of a mother city, and its law prevailed in most of the towns of Ostfalen, Mark Brandenburg, Mark Meissen, Lausitz, Silesia, Lithuania, the Prussian territories of the Teutonic Order, and the kingdom of Poland, in Stettin, and, for some time, in Stargard in Pomerania and in some towns in Moravia. In general, moreover, it was the main influence on the law in Bohemia and Moravia. Many of the towns, though, had a very different law of family property, and hence of succession. Magdeburg had the old Saxon arrangement of the administration and use of the wife's property by the husband with direct descent and widow's portion in the event of death, whereas many towns of Thuringia had the Frankish system of common property in all acquisitions or of general community of property.[51] This difference in law did not stop judges of daughter towns from presenting problems on such matters to the *Schöffen*—the title given to the nonprofessional judges—of Magdeburg. The following case gives a fifteenth-century opinion rendered by the *Schöffen* of Magdeburg to the court of Schleiz in Thuringia:[52]

The honorable *Schöffen* of Magdeburg: A legal reply made for the court at Schleiz relating to succession.

Because you sent us writings of two parties, namely the charge and accusation of Hans Krebis and the counterplea and reply of Hans Helwig as guardian of his wife, and requested us to state the law, etc., and as each of the two parties in their writings allege some privilege [i.e., a particular right of a legal community, and especially of a town] and town custom, which appears to state, express, and be to the effect that "If a man die without heirs of the body, if the same man graces his wife with all his goods, to enjoy them personally after his death until the end of her life"—of such custom it does not please us to take notice in law. But we, the *Schöffen* of Magdeburg, give our reply on the matter in accordance with law on the complaint and answer.

If Hans Helwig, defender of this matter as guardian of his wife, demonstrates with the testimony of the court and completely, insofar as is correct, that Hans Krebis in sound body and good mind gave by way of inheritance, delivered and properly left to his wife before the court, in fear of his death, a meadow situated in Ollssenicz [Olsnitz(?) in Saxony, 60 kilometers south of Leipzig], a barn, a garden, and in addition all his movable goods, that she might do with them as she pleases; if he proves that completely, if the same woman [Frau Helwig] has held the gift and possession for a year and a day and longer without the legal objection of anyone, then the same gift must in law remain in effect; and the widow of Hans Krebis, now the wife of Hans Helwig, has a closer title and better right to such aforementioned goods, namely the meadow, barn, garden and all movables, than that Hans Krebis, the nephew of her deceased husband can prevent her and claim from her on account of succession.

The judges of Schleiz did not need to take the case to the *Schöffen* of Magdeburg, but they did. They also did not need to follow the opinion of the *Schöffen*. The pleadings sent by the Schleiz court made it plain that the law at Schleiz on that issue was not the same as the law in Magdeburg. The *Schöffen* of Magdeburg made it equally plain that they were giving their opinion based only on the Saxon law. Nor were the Magdeburg *Schöffen* here following a course unusual for them: they did not usually decide according to the law of the petitioners.[53] The judges of Schleiz were unlikely to have been unaware of the Magdeburg practice. We do not know if the judges of Schleiz eventually decided according to the ruling from Magdeburg or not. If they did, then they were overturning the established and usually followed local custom when they did not need to do so and for reasons not inevitably connected with the welfare of the populace or the expectations of the parties to the lawsuit. If they did not, then an outsider might wonder at the odd, superfluous behavior of the Schleiz judges in approaching the *Schöffen* of Magdeburg. Whether they did or did not follow the opinion of the Magdeburg *Schöffen*, the judges of Schleiz were, for the insider, establishing that they were following the proper principles for lawness. It was appropriate but not necessary in a difficult case to have the opinion of the Magdeburg *Schöffen*, and it was appropriate, though not necessary, to accept that opinion. The Schleiz judges were adopting the appropriate course even when the laws of Schleiz and Magdeburg differed and when the Magdeburg *Schöffen* would base their opinion solely on the law of Magdeburg.

A system similar to that in Germany of applying to the *Schöffen* of a mother town also existed elsewhere, in Belgium, for instance, from the twelfth century[54] and in parts of Spain between the twelfth and fourteenth centuries. In Spain, the *fuero* (i.e., the town charter or town privileges) of one town might be granted to others by the king or some other lord, or the redactors of a *fuero* might take another as a model. A town whose *fuero* was highly regarded by others, whether it had been granted, borrowed, imitated, or simply admired, would be visited by notables from the other towns. For instance, Alfonso II of Aragón said in 1187 that people continually came from Castile, Navarre, and other lands to Jaca to learn the good customs and *fueros* and take them home.[55] In fact, such was the reputation of the extensive *fuero* of Jaca (of 1063) and of its lawyers that towns inhabited by *francos*—a term indicating foreigners on whom had been bestowed particular privileges—such as Estella (whose *fuero* of 1164 received part of the law of Jaca elaborated until that date), San Sebastián (in Viscaya, whose *fuero* authorized by King Sancho el Sabio of Navarre [1150–94] derived from that of Estella), Fuenterrabía (in Castile), and Pamplona (which was granted the *fuero* of Jaca by Alfonso I in 1129), not only consulted Jaca on the interpretation of certain rules but in the case of litigation actually sent appeals to the authorities of Jaca as the true interpreters of the law, although the law in their towns was by no means identical with that of Jaca. King Sancho el Fuerte of Navarre (d. 1234) forbade appeals to Jaca. But later the *jurados y hombres buenos* of Pamplona wrote to the judges and notables of the city of Jaca that they had many books of *fueros*, supposedly of Jaca, that, however, did not always give the same law, and they asked that their *fueros* be corrected by the master *fuero* held by the judges of Jaca. The reply of 27 August 1342 refused the request, pointing out that the habit of appealing to Jaca was observed also by cities ruled by the king of Navarre and referring to the ancient bond of love between Jaca and Pamplona.[56] Presumably, the judges of Jaca refused because if the jurists of Pamplona had the correct text, they would not need to send appeals to Jaca.[57]

No doubt the judges of Jaca, like the *Schöffen* of Magdeburg, deserved their high regard, but it would be stretching human credulity to believe that at times the appeal to them was not also inappropriate.[58] The approach to Jaca seems unnecessary, but again, it was intended to show that the judges of the other towns had a proper attitude to judging.[59]

Summary

Thus, contemporary House of Lords judges in England have such regard for the will of the legislature that they interpret absence of legislation as indicating a deliberate intention not to act and therefore follow, when they need not, their own ancient precedent to a judgment that they declare unjust; in uncodified civil-law or "mixed" systems, courts in seventeenth-century Scotland and twentieth-century South Africa rely on Roman or Roman-Dutch law, which is not binding on them, even when circumstances are very different and the reliance is inappropriate; judges in France a half century and more after the promulgation of the Code civil so wish to keep themselves removed from the law earlier than the code that they do not look for it when it is relevant and hence come to misinterpret the basis of provisions of the code; judges in fifteenth-century Germany have such regard for the *Schöffen* of a mother town that they consult them, though they have no obligation to do so, even in a case where they know their law is different and can expect an answer based on the mother's law; in thirteenth- and fourteenth-century Spain judges even sent their appeals to the town whose *fuero* was at the root of their own.

The cases discussed in this part of the chapter have been put together not for the purpose of comparing or contrasting the approaches but to bring out a common theme within the Western legal tradition. Judges set out to establish themselves as good judges, to show that they are correctly analyzing the legal implications of the case before them by a particular mental process—which may differ from system to system. This process shows a high regard for "lawness," for the establishment of the decision on a foundation other than that of the judges' authority or of their right or power to make law. The process has a legitimating function: the judges have the right and power to choose their decision, but they must not exercise their choice arbitrarily. The process involves going beyond the boundaries of the existing law, and it is culturally determined. The mental process, of course, belongs to the culture of the judges and those who practice before them, not specifically to the culture of the population at large or the ruling elite. The influence of the legal culture is so powerful that the mental process is used even when it leads to results that are inappropriate, either because the decision—which is not inevitable—is unjust in the eyes of the judges themselves, or societal conditions have altered in a significant regard, or the legal basis for the approach has gone. Of course, it is precisely when the results are inappropriate that the impact of culture on the judges' attitudes is most apparent, but the cases are not otherwise atypical.

One subsidiary, but rather uncomfortable, conclusion follows. It is not possible to read any judgment so as to understand fully a judge's approach without considerable understanding of the legal culture in which he or she operates, which means in effect that a great deal of knowledge of legal history is needed—legal history, in fact, that in many instances involves the history of other legal systems.

CHAPTER 4

CUSTOM

A proper understanding of the nature of customary law—a source of law that has not yet been much discussed in this book—is important for Western legal historians. From post-Roman times to the beginning of the modern legal age in the eighteenth century, the two main elements in European law were Roman law and legal custom, the learned law and the other. In large measure, the main task of lawyers of that long stretch of time was the unification or harmonization of the two strands of Roman law and custom. Naturally, customary law was important even before—in Rome before the Twelve Tables no doubt, and among the Germanic tribes before the codes beginning in the fifth century. But evidence for these days is slight, so the stress in this chapter is on explaining the nature of customary law as it appears from, say, the eleventh century onward.[1] Customary law is not all of one piece. It operates, for example, among wandering small groups, temporarily settled tribes, rather small permanent communities, and so on right into economically developed modern Western societies where there is also much statute law.

CUSTOMARY LAW IN EUROPE

Customary law, of course, most flourishes in circumstances where law is likely to be least theoretical. Yet there must be theoretical underpinnings for the nature of any source of law, even if these underpinnings are implicit and never expressed. For custom to be regarded as law in Western private law, more must be and is required than simple usage, even if the usage is general and has long been frequent. The issue, of course, is that one cannot simply equate an *ought* and an *is*. The fact that people so behave does not indicate that they should so behave, and be subject to some sanction if they do not. What is it, above mere behavior, that makes the behavior normative? The main problem for any theory or understanding of customary law seems to be the determination of this additional factor. The Roman sources clearly imply that some additional factor is needed, even if the nature of this factor is not apparent. Thus, *Epitome Ulpiani*, 4: "Custom is the tacit consent of the people, deeply rooted through long usage." Here the additional factor is expressed by the otherwise tautological "tacit consent" or "tacit agreement" (*tacitus consensus*). But to what has tacit consent been given? Certainly it is not to the long usage itself: the tacit consent is rooted in the long usage. And *J*.1.1.9: "Unwritten law is that which usage has approved. For long-practiced customs, endorsed by the consent of the users, take on the appearance of statute." This time the additional factor is expressed by "endorsed by the consent of the users" (*consensu utentium comprobati*). The vagueness of Ulpian has not been dissipated.

> *D*.1.3.32.1 (Julian Digest 84). Deeply rooted custom is observed as a statute, not undeservedly; and this is what is called law established by usage. For because statutes themselves bind us for no other reason than because they have been accepted by the judgment of the people, then deservedly those things which the people have approved without writing will bind all. For what does it matter that the people declare its wish by vote or by positive acts and conduct? Therefore, it is very rightly accepted that laws are abrogated not only by the vote of him who purposes law, but also through desuetude, by the tacit consent of all.

We need not discuss here the accuracy of Julian's account of the people's role in statute making, or of custom bringing about the desuetude of statute. This time the nature of the additional factor seems to be clearer: for Julian it appears to be that the custom is law because the people accept it as law.[2]

For a long time after Justinian there seems to have been little advance in coming to grips with the issue,[3] but the idea of *opinio necessitatis,* which may by implication have its roots in the text of Julian, did eventually appear[4] and, despite some opposition, still appears to be dominant. The idea of *opinio necessitatis* is precisely that the persons involved purposely follow a certain rule because they believe that it is a rule of law. The idea has been explained by modern theorists like K. Larenz:

> One can say the practice must be the expression of an "intention of legal validity" of the community or of a "general conviction of law," provided only that one is clear that this "intention of legal validity" or the "general conviction of law" is not solely a *"psychological fact,"* but the *"sense of ful-*

filling a norm" (of a legally commanded behavior) developing or dwelling in the individual acts of conduct according to the judgment of those sharing the same law.[5]

On this view then, custom becomes law when it is known to be law, is accepted as law and practiced as law by the persons who share the same law. But suppose that, once the custom is known to be law and is accepted as law, the practice changes. Does the old law cease to be law, and the new practice come to be law? If this does happen, at what moment does it happen? And what is the machinery for change?

There are two different problem situations. First, the past custom is remembered. Second, the past custom is forgotten.

In the first situation, which is the one that is really important both in theory and in real life, it must be the case that the law cannot be changed by a contrary practice. So long as the past custom is remembered as being law, there can be no point on the continuum at which the new practice is used in consciousness that it is law. The outmoded practice must cease to be law before a different law can begin to emerge from customary usage; and within the theory there is no mechanism for deleting law that no longer commands approval.

One might try to get around this difficulty by postulating a doctrine of desuetude inherent in customary law: when a practice that has become blessed as law ceases to be followed or to be regarded as law, then, it may be claimed, it ceases to be law. At that stage, but not before, the road becomes clear, it might be suggested, for the creation of new customary law. The performance of the new custom before the old customary legal rule became obsolete is a factor in making the old legal rule obsolete, but not (always following the doctrine of *opinio necessitatis*) in creating a new legal rule because the new practice was not followed in "the general conviction of law." So at the moment of desuetude, there is no law on the point at all. But against this arises here in a particularly sharp form the objection raised by Friedrich von Savigny against *opinio necessitatis* within the framework usually attributed to custom.[6] Custom should not rest on error, a point expressly made in the Roman sources.[7] But then, he says, there is a contradiction without solution. For the rule of law should arise first through the custom, but at the time of the first behavior the law was, of course, not in existence. But the first relevant behavior should be accompanied by the *opinio necessitatis*. Consequently the first behavior rested on an error and should not be counted for the creation of the customary law. But this also applies to the second act of behavior, which now becomes the first, and so on through all subsequent acts.

On this basis, under the received doctrine of *opinio necessitatis* and custom, it is logically impossible for customary behavior to create law. A fortiori, when the new customary behavior was being adopted when there already existed a different rule of customary law, any belief that the new behavior was to conform to law was clearly grounded on error. If custom cannot create a legal rule, even less can it both create and substitute a new legal rule for an established rule that it abolishes.

In fact, if *opinio necessitatis* is at the root of customary law, it is very difficult to admit the possibility of desuetude of a customary legal rule, provided always that the legal rule is remembered. Customary law is, we are told, a "general conviction of law"; hence it corresponds to what people generally do, and they do it because it is the law. To act contrary to this would be a deviant act, unacceptable and contrary to law.[8] The point, it should be remembered, is not that customary behavior does not change but that, under the doctrine of *opinio necessitatis*, where a rule of customary law exists and is remembered, it cannot become obsolete by desuetude: contrary acting that is known to be contrary to the rule cannot affect it.

There is a further and more important logical difficulty in admitting the possibility of desuetude of customary law under a theory of *opinio necessitatis*. A legal rule can fall into desuetude only if it has been replaced by another legal rule, even if this later rule is only to the effect that the first rule no longer applies. But by the theory of *opinio necessitatis*, the new rule can come into existence only after it is established that the old known rule is extinct, since otherwise there could be no general conviction that the new behavior corresponds to the law. There is thus no scope for desuetude.

In the second situation also, where the past custom is forgotten, the law is not being changed by a contrary practice. If customary law is completely forgotten, then for all intents and purposes it does not exist and has not existed. There is not even any need to bring in here a theory of obsolescence. What would be involved is the creation of law where none existed before. Also the total forgetting of the customary law can happen only in particular circumstances.[9] Either the past behavior occurred very seldom in practice, in which case one must doubt whether it had ever become law as a result of common consciousness that it was law. Or the people had in this regard adopted a very different life-style—perhaps as a result of migration—in which case it should be argued that the new practice is law not because new law has replaced old law but because law has been created for circumstances where no law existed before. In any event, where a rule or supposed rule of customary law has been completely forgotten, one cannot admit that a subsequent contrary practice has, as law, replaced previously existing customary law.

Thus, the doctrine of *opinio necessitatis* excludes the possibility of changing customary law by subsequent practice, especially in the situation where the customary law is remembered. If one wishes to hold, as I believe theorists would wish to hold, that customary law should be in correspondence with what people do, then one would want any theory to countenance the possibility of changing the law by contrary practice. *Opinio necessitatis* must then on this basis be dismissed.

Savigny, despite his powerful argument against *opinio necessitatis* within the framework usually attributed to customary law, retains the notion. His solution rests on his general view of law as the "spirit of the people." Law does not arise from individual acts of behavior but from common consciousness. Thus, individual acts of behavior are not the cause of creation of customary law, but are the appearances or indications of a preexisting common conviction of law.[10] Hence, the *opinio necessitatis* exists before the first relevant act of behavior, which therefore does not rest on an error of law.[11] *Opinio necessitatis* is thus saved but only for a very different doctrine of the nature of customary law. The validity of Savigny's view of custom and *opinio necessitatis* depends on the plausibility of his general theory of law, which is today universally rejected, I think, by legal philosophers.[12] Hence it will not be further discussed here.

Thus, if we wish to retain as an element in customary law the power to change when practices change—and even perhaps if we wish a power in customary behavior to create law—we must abandon *opinio necessitatis*. A further conclusive objection against the theory will emerge implicitly from the following pages, namely that *opinio necessitatis* just cannot explain what actually happens in practice. A different theory, which may prove to be more acceptable, is suggested to me by the work of John Austin. According to him, customary laws considered as rules of positive morality arise from the consent of the governed; but considered as moral rules turned into positive laws, customary laws are established by the state, either directly by statute, or circuitously when the customs are adopted by its tribunals.[13] Thus, customary behavior does not make law; law is made by legislation or by judicial decision. Custom becomes law only when it is the subject of statute or judicial decision.

Before we consider the value of this, we should first recognize that the proposition is not necessarily or obviously correct except to someone who, like Austin, holds that law is the command of a sovereign. Statute is law even before it is enforced by a decision of a court.[14] Hence, if other sources of law, such as custom, exist in possibility, then that law, too, may in possibility exist without benefit of a court decision. It may well be argued that "it is precisely the binding force of custom which challenges [Austin's] initial assumption itself," and that "he failed to explain satisfactorily why the body of rules which he classifies as 'positive morality' . . . lacked the true character of law."[15]

A second point that may be made is that societies that do not regard judicial decisions, even a consistent line of them, as binding precedents—that is, as law—may nonetheless treat decisions establishing a custom as binding. On this basis one might claim that judicial precedent is not law; custom is law. When a court finds that a custom exists, the decision in itself is not binding, but the preexisting custom that already is law has as a matter of fact been established; hence the decision (which is not law) expressed the law.

These two points have, or may have, great weight against Austin, but there are other factors that seem to lend support to his position.

In the first place, customary law very often does not grow from a "general conviction of law." In this case, legal decisions play a fundamental role in determining what is the rule of customary law. Thus, it is a standard complaint of those living under customary law who wish to reduce it to writing that the law is difficult to find, or know, or remember. Thus, to give a few examples, the famous Philippe de Beaumanois (d. 1296) gives among the reasons for his *Coutumes de Beauvaisis*: "It is my opinion and of others also that all customs that are now used be written down and recorded so that they be maintained without change from now on, because through memories that are liable to fade and human life that is short what is not written is soon forgotten" (Prologue, sec. 71). In his *Conseil* (c. 1260), which concerns the customs of Vermondais, Pierre de Fontaines claims that the old customs are much destroyed and almost all are defective, partly because of judges who prefer their own wishes to using the customs, partly because of those who are more attached to their own opinions than to the acts of earlier generations, and almost entirely because the rich despoiled the poor and now the poor despoil the rich. The country, he says, is almost without custom (chap. 1, sec. 3).

At the beginning of this century J. A. Brutails, in his celebrated work on the custom of Andorra, also brought out the difficulty of knowing customary law. He stresses that in a small place the number of lawsuits is limited, and in the absence of any methodical collection of decisions, the law in the cases fluctuates. He points out that even on contemporary and important matters there is at times a disconcerting incertitude. For instance, he asked prominent people, magistrates, former magistrates, and judges what were the rights of the widow over the property of her husband; and he received five different answers.[16] Indeed, he claimed often to have heard that Andorra had no custom, but Andorra seemed to him no different from other customary systems. Despite the numerous and significant gaps in the law, it was not certain whether they were to be filled first by looking at Roman, canon, or Catalan law. The common view was the first, but he sought to demonstrate that in fact it was Catalan law that had usually prevailed.[17] It seems to me that Andorran legal sentiment now favors Roman law, though in practice Catalan law may prevail.

King Charles VII of France's Ordonnance de Montil-les-Tours, dated April 1453, records that "it often happens that in one single region, the parties rely on contrary customs, and sometimes the customs are silent and vary at will, from which great hardships and loss affect our subjects" (art. 125).

In such situations, in the absence of official redactions of the customs, which then hold sway as statute, court decisions embody the rules. As Philippe de Beaumanoir says for his unofficial redaction, "We intend to confirm a great part of this book by the judgments that have been made in our time in the said county of Clermont" (prologue, sec. 6). Well worth quoting are the words of the Maître Echevin in the preface to the official redaction of the customs of Metz in 1613, after the work had supposedly been under active preparation since 1569:

> At last, gentle people, here is the methodical disposition, so passionately wanted, so impatiently awaited, the hard-won redaction of the customs according to which our ancestors so happily administered public business. The customs here, of course, cost much time to lift from the dust; if so many thorns (that you know about) had not been met with, you would be right to be less pleased with your official, because, truth to tell, one is not at all indebted for what one has dragged out rather than received. But apart from the incredible work employed simply to set out various opinions so that they agree on the same matter, there was need of several Hercules to overcome the difficulties, common and frequent, as much in seeking out the articles in each chapter, as in verifying them. This was not done by giv-

ing way to the opinions of individuals, but by a precise and painful reading through of the judgments, memorials, and instructions which mossy
antiquity left in the strongboxes of the town. Despite all this, the customs
are dear to us for the utility the public will receive from them.

The Maître Echevin's words make clear both the great difficulty of finding the customary law and the belief that it is embedded in judicial decisions. There is also the belief that customary law is useful.

Brutails claimed, and he has been followed by Ourliac, that the idea
of legality is very obscure in Andorran brains.[18] Now if this means, as I
think it does, that these scholars believe that there is often great doubt
in Andorra as to what legal rules are appropriate to a given situation,
and that ascertaining the precise legal rule does not rank as a high priority in general Andorran thinking, then their position should be generalized. For obvious reasons, it is often the case in customary systems
that the legal rules are uncertain and that this is not treated as a matter
of great concern. Customary law most flourishes in small communities
with a high degree of kinship, and the law is not an academic learned
law. Hence, to begin with, there will be a relatively small number of disputes, and, in a customary system, disputes delimit the scope of legal
rules. Again, in the necessary absence of a strong academic tradition,
there will be a reluctance to generalize from the cases and extract principles that can be used in other, rather different, situations. Moreover,
what few important decisions there are may not be adequately recorded
or be easily accessible. To give one example from a living customary system: the first published Andorran decisions appeared in a journal, *Re-
vista juridica de Cataluña,* only in 1963,[19] and there are still only two collections in book form. That of Carles Obiols i Taberner covers the years
1945 to 1966 and contains only ninety-six appellate decisions.[20] That of
Ourliac, already mentioned, also contains his commentary and covers
decisions on appeal to Perpignan for the years 1947 through 1970. Significantly, both sets of reports occupy each only one fairly slim volume.
Above all, there is relatively little demand for a precise knowledge of the
legal rules in a customary system because so many disputes in the small
community are among relatives, friends, or neighbors who have to live
with one another afterward and who therefore often have recourse to a
less formal means of dispute solving. Respected friends or relatives may
be invited to adjudicate, or there may arise in a village a recognized approach to adjudication. In any case, those appointed to judge will often
decide by their opinion of what is fair and reasonable rather than search

for a definite legal rule. Formal legal rules do not necessarily give the most accepted solution. But if a problem situation occurs often enough, and if the same solution is usually reached (which need not be the case), a custom may emerge.

In the second place, often the customary law does not come from what the people do but is borrowed from elsewhere. The standard practice, particularly common in medieval France, of one jurisdiction accepting the law of another system as its residual custom is striking testimony to this, whether the outside system is the Coutume de Paris or of a neighboring custom, as in the *pays de droit coutumier*, or of Roman law, as in the *pays de droit écrit*. This wholesale reception, though it is residual, is particularly revealing, both because it cuts down the discretionary choice in the individual situation and because the outside system may have originated for a very different society (in economic and political terms), such as ancient Rome, or for a much larger, more commercial, and more anonymous center, such as Paris. The same phenomenon occurs even when a local patriot prepares an unofficial collection of the customs. For instance, modern scholars agree that by far the greatest part of the *Conseil* of Pierre de Fontaines comes from Justinian's *Digest* and *Code*,[21] even though it was meant to be a practical work for training a friend's son in the local customs (*Conseil*, chap. 1, par. 2). The same can be said for the contemporary *Livre de Jostice et de Plet*, a product of the Orleans area, where the Roman and canon-law origins of the rules are hidden and ascribed falsely to French notables.[22] Of course, when these works were unofficial they would not themselves create the customary law, but they could be, and were, frequently treated by the courts as evidence of the custom. Here, too, court decisions have particular relevance: by adopting the rules in the books, whatever the origin of those rules, they declare the rules as custom. Again, in perplexing cases the courts themselves frequently based their decision on customs from elsewhere. Thus, Philippe de Beaumanoir also wished to confirm part of his book "for doubtful cases in the said county, by judgments of neighboring lordship." Here not only was a "foreign" source of law borrowed, to be treated as the custom of the borrower,[23] but the borrowed foreign rule was actually that embedded in the foreign judgment. Again, the borrowed rule would have (at least in authority) the force of law only when it was incorporated in a judgment or judgments of the borrower.

Thus, it often happens that the acceptance of rules as local customary law comes from local judgments and not from preceding local behavior.[24] When this happens, the basis of the law is treated as custom, not judicial precedent. What then is the role of judgments in creating customary law? The nature of the question becomes clear, and so perhaps does the answer, if we set out a series of propositions, beginning with those already established.

1. To be law custom needs more than behavior.
2. *Opinio necessitatis* fails to provide the extra factor.
3. Court decisions declare customary law even when (a) custom is uncertain (and there is no *opinio necessitatis*) and even when (b) there is no custom.
4. Proposition 3 is accurate even when (as in many systems) court decisions themselves do not make law; hence, we cannot simply say the court decision is the basis of customary law.
5. Custom officially written down as law is law as statute, though that is not proof that the custom was not law before.

Propositions 1 to 4 have been established. Proposition 5 is self-evident. But we can now go on:

6. If court decisions are not law and therefore are not the basis of custom becoming law, but decisions declare custom as law even when there was no preceding practice (i.e., taking propositions 3 and 4 together), then it is the official declaration of a rule as customary law that makes it law (whether the behavior was customary or not).

Therefore, it is official recognition that particular normative behavior is customary that makes it law. But official recognition also entails official acceptance. Hence, the validity of this custom as law depends on its official recognition and acceptance. The custom was not law before.

The objection may be made that though official recognition makes law as custom what was not the practice before, nonetheless habitual normative behavior may be law as custom even before official recognition, especially if the practice is universally regarded as the custom. The objection, though prima facie plausible, is ultimately untenable. Suppose a case involving the practice comes before the court and the court rejects the behavior as incorporating customary law; then one must hold that the custom cannot be changing the law; hence, the normative behavior was not customary law before the decision. It still remains that it is the official recognition of normative behavior as customary law that makes it law.

7. It follows that, in societies where customary behavior can be treated as law, there is an attribution to the people of the power to make law by their tacit behavior, but this law is created only when it is officially recognized or accepted.

8. Just as the opinion of a sovereign is not law until it is institutionalized—as statute, for example—so behavior of the people is not law until it is institutionalized by being recognized and accepted by an official court decision.

"The will of the emperor has the force of statute" in Justinian's *Institutes* 1.2.6 means, as the text goes on to explain, that his will comes to have that effect when it is couched in the proper institutionalized form. "Deeply rooted custom is observed as a statute" (*D*.1.3.32.1) similarly means, as we have seen, that custom comes to have that effect when it is expressed in the proper institutionalized form, namely in judicial decision.

If the will of the emperor is mistakenly set out in the statute, it is the meaning that is accepted as being in the statute that prevails; likewise, if there was no custom, it is the meaning that is accepted as being in the judicial decision that prevails.

On this understanding of the nature of customary law there is no difficulty either for its creation or alteration. Normative customary behavior becomes customary law when it is recognized by the courts as such. There is no need for a belief among the actors that they were already acting in accordance with an existing rule of law. So long as the courts treat the custom as law, it is the customary law, but should the courts hold that the custom has changed, then the new ruling becomes the customary law.

This leads on to the question—which, for our purposes, actually need not be asked—whether these findings might be used to support the theory of John Austin that law is the command of a sovereign that is backed by a sanction, when a sovereign is defined as someone whose commands are habitually obeyed and who is not in the habit of obedience to anyone else. At a first stage we should not be concerned with the validity of that theory as a whole, and we should for the sake of argument accept Austin's proposition that when judges make a legal rule, that rule is established by the sovereign legislature.[25] Our concern at this point is thus only with the question whether, if there can be no customary law without a court decision, that means that customary law is at least as much a command of the sovereign as binding precedent is.

Only three factual situations need be considered. First, it is argued by some writers, notably Vinnius (d. 1647),[26] that there can be no customary law under an emperor. Where there is an empire and this doctrine is accepted, there is no problem for Austin with regard to custom.[27] Second, where customary law is accepted and judicial precedent is binding, there is also no problem for Austin. One can say custom forms a rule of law because it is incorporated in a binding precedent. Third, where customary law is accepted and judicial precedent is not otherwise binding, the people as a whole is not the sovereign in Austin's sense. The people's behavior makes law, but only at the moment when it is recognized and accepted by the court. That acceptance is necessary. Hence, insofar as Austin's argument is correct that court decisions accepted by the sovereign as creating law are commands of the sovereign, custom regarded as law when it is accepted as such by decision of the court is equally a command of the sovereign. The point is significant because, as we have seen, it is frequently urged that one of the major weaknesses in Austin's theory is precisely the difficulty of fitting customary law within it.[28]

But when one proceeds to a second stage, there remains a difficulty for accepting Austin's theory as a whole. Binding judicial precedent and customary law are on a level as forms of law making in the sense that both require the consent, the acceptance, and the tolerance of the sovereign to be law. That consent, acceptance, and tolerance might be withheld. Nonetheless, it seems farfetched to equate consent, acceptance, and tolerance with a command.

It seems to me that Austin is saying in effect that all law is legislation and that judges, insofar as they are lawmakers, are legislators. My position is different. I would accept that binding judicial precedent amounts to law making in its own right—it is a source of law distinct from legislation—but it has the requirement that it be accepted by the sovereign as an appropriate method of creating law. Likewise, custom is a separate source of law distinct from both legislation and judicial precedent. But like judicial precedent, custom in order to make law has the requirement that it be accepted by the sovereign. As is the case both with legislation and with binding precedent, custom to become law has to be clothed with the requisite form (which marks its official acceptance by the sovereign). For custom this form is indeed that it is incorporated in a judicial decision. But that custom as a means of making law is not simply subsumed into binding precedent is shown by the fact that a society might accept custom as law (when set out in a judicial decision) but deny law making effect to precedent.

The conclusion—that to a great extent customary law does not derive from what the people of a locality habitually do and that official judicial decisions declare the law—may illumine other aspects of the issue.

To begin with, we can now understand the situation described by F. Pollok and F. W. Maitland (one that has long puzzled me), that in the Middle Ages neighboring villages might be inhabited by persons of the same race, religion, and language, subject for centuries to the same economic conditions, yet have very different rules for the central institution of matrimonial property.[29] In fact, the villages may well have shared a number of ways of arranging family property holding, but in each village one way will have become fixed as law following upon a judicial decision. The final result in any one place will contain some element of the arbitrary.

Second, the common German medieval practice of one independent town that was governed by customary law selecting another as its "mother" town for settling disputed legal issues and submitting issues to the "mother's" *Schöffen* (nonprofessional judge-jurists) takes on a different aspect.[30] However the question to the *Schöffen* might be framed, the "daughter" town was not really seeking to know its own customary practice. Rather, the daughter town had no custom or the custom was unsettled or unknown, yet the town wanted a ruling because of this dispute and preferred it to be given by the mother town, whether because the latter's *Schöffen* had high prestige or because the local judges preferred to distance themselves from local disputes. The practice, in fact, is one particular example of the more general phenomenon that often there is a lack of interest in establishing the local custom. The frequency of borrowing another's custom (already adverted to) is itself an example of this lack of interest. The popularity of the *Sachsenspiegel* is a further illustration. This unofficial statement of practice in the bishoprics of Magdeburg and Halberstadt in the early thirteenth century was widely used in northern Germany, Poland, the Low Countries, and elsewhere. Of its two parts, one survives in over 200 manuscripts, the other in almost 150, and it was translated numerous times.[31]

Yet another example is the enormous length of time that occurred before French local customs were reduced to writing even after the royal command. The Ordinance of Montil-les-Tours of Charles VII of 1453 required the redaction of the customs in each district, but a century was required before most of the work was done.[32] The delay is to be explained not just by the magnitude and difficulty of the task, but by a frequent lack of interest in establishing the custom.

All this alerts us to a possible danger of interpretation. It is well known that there are "families" of customary law. We should not therefore deduce that the members of one family group are closer in economic, social, and political structure to the other members than they are to members of other legal families.

Finally, in this context, a further explanation is required for the fact that, in many territories in the Middle Ages, there was no or little legislation on private law. The explanation so often given is that there were lacking great foci of centralized power and that kings and other magnates were weak.[33] For some places and times this explanation may be complete, but often it clearly cannot be. To begin with, there are very many instances of magnates' granting charters to towns and of their issuing statutes on matters relating to public law. Clearly magnates often had the power to legislate. And we cannot say the magnates' power to legislate on private law was bitterly resented by the people, who were fiercely attached to their customs. As we have seen, frequently there was no great attachment to the customs.[34] The simplest explanation is that magnates were often not concerned to legislate private law for their subjects. Magnates frequently have more interesting, more exciting, and perhaps more important things to occupy their time.

Of course, to show that customary law often does not derive from preceding local behavior is not to claim that it never, or only infrequently, does. To a great extent, even if not to a commonly measurable extent, it must do so. But when we turn to the most notable attempts in the Middle Ages to treat customary attitudes as determining customary law, namely the *Weistümer* in Germany and the *enquête par tourbes* in France, we find striking confirmation of the main claims of this chapter.

A *Weistümer* involved the fixing of the local law through persons sharing the same law and was performed by the posing of formal questions in the law and giving of formal answers. Which persons were summoned varied from place to place. Often, some questions were left unanswered (some to be filled at a later date or by an *Oberhof*),[35] but the result was rather like a restatement or code. *Weistümer* collections are extant from the eleventh century. In the course of time the *Weistümer* had to be in writing, executed by a notary. *Weistümer* were prepared only at the smallest local level, that of the village.[36]

In medieval France, when a judge was unaware of an alleged custom, he had to inquire into its existence by an *enquête par tourbes*. This involved a number of persons of good repute—ten was established as the minimum within the *ressort* of the Parlement de Paris—who had the legal question put to them, deliberated, and then (as an ordinance of 1270 puts it) "they will say between whom they observed that custom, in what case, in what place, if there was a court decision and in what circumstances." Their reply, which was to be in writing and sealed, was given as one voice.[37]

The very attempt to try to find out by *Weistümer* or *enquête par tourbes* what the custom was amply shows that particular behavior was not known to be law and accepted and practiced as law by the persons sharing the same law. Hence, here too we cannot regard *opinio necessitatis* as providing the factor needed to turn behavior into law. They both show that it was often difficult to know what the law was. As the *Weistümer* system indicates, in cases where answers were not given, there were gaps in the law even with regard to basic matters. The reduction of *Weistümer* to writing indicates an awareness that the law should be (at least relatively) fixed for the future and is another indication of the awareness that knowledge of law could easily be lost. Of course, under both systems, it would still be the case that if courts refused to recognize a custom as law and would not enforce it, then it would not be customary law.

The importance of courts in the development or recognition or statement of customary law ensures a significant role for the legal tradition, especially that of the judges, in shaping the law.

Fueros, the name given in Spain to collections of local municipal law, often containing particular privileges, are usually classed as short (*breves*) or extended (*extensos*). The majority of the former date from the eleventh and twelfth centuries, the majority of the latter a little later. It is a peculiarity of the *fueros* that the most successful were, totally or partially, granted to or borrowed by other municipalities. The main outlines of the transfer of *fueros* from town to town are well known; in fact Ana Maria Barrero Garciá in her *Fuero de Teruel* publishes a map with arrows showing the direction, and dates indicating the time, of the movement of *fueros* from municipality to municipality.[38] So long as *fueros* are regarded as containing customary law, it is hard to see how their movement can be regarded as consistent with the traditional notion that customary law emerges from norms people obey in the belief that they are law. Yet F. Tomás y Valiente, the most highly regarded of the younger generation of Spanish legal historians, writes: "Because they contain the customary law, alive in that place; because they are in part the fruit of the municipal autonomy and at the same time its guarantee, given that they contain the privileges on which this autonomy is based and the rules for the choice by the locals of judges and town officials; and because of the complete and self-sufficient nature of the order contained in them, the municipal *fueros* were considered by the town and cities as their own property and very important, and accordingly were defended against other types of law (that of the king and that of the learned jurists because, as we shall see, both began to develop in the thirteenth century)."[39] With no apparent awareness that he is contradicting his first clause, his next sentences run: "Just as happened with short *fueros,* the extended *fuero* of one town was often enough granted directly to another. At times the redactors of the *fuero* of one city utilized as a model the already written text of the law of another." The rest of his first passage just quoted is more convincing for the importance attributed to *fueros.* Inhabitants defended their *fuero* because it granted them privileges, not because it contained the good old norms derived from their habitual behavior.

Nor was this movement of municipal customary law from town to town confined to Spain. It occurred frequently elsewhere—in Normandy, for example. Thus, Eau borrowed the privileges of Saint Quentin; at Les Andelys the rules were copied from those of Mantes. And in general the rules of Norman towns derived from those of Rouen.[40]

There is another problem with the traditional view: the spatial limits of customary law coincide with the political frontiers. Robert Besnier, writing of the Coutume of Normandy, puts it this way:

> The political framework becomes fixed at the moment when the necessity of a *coutume* imposes itself upon the Normans. Hence comes the parallelism between the creation of the institutions and the elaboration of the law. The limits of the dukedom and the jurisdiction of the custom coincide: the latter is essentially fixed by the repetition of identical acts in similar situations, it develops everywhere, simultaneously, as well in the courts of justice as in daily relations or in the presence of officers charged with administrative, military or financial matters. At a time when functions are not yet clearly specialized there are no organisms which do not play their role in this slow elaboration.[41]

This spatial coincidence is more easily explained, as I argued on other grounds, if one says that, where customary law is recognized, it is created only when it is officially recognized or accepted, and this recognition is signaled by court decisions. Court jurisdictions and political boundaries then necessarily coincide.

I also argued that a difficulty for believing that customary law rested on a general conviction that it was law was that often the custom was difficult to find even when it could be said that there was something that could be designated as the custom. A striking instance of the difficulty of knowing the custom even when there was one is given by the Coutume de Toulouse. This was written down in the *livre blanc* which was kept in the town hall, but it was written in Latin. Cazaveteri published an edition in 1545 with short notes but still in Latin. François-François in 1615 published selected titles with commentary, this time in French, but the work contained less than half of the Coutume de Toulouse. In the eighteenth century very few copies of these (long out-of-print) books were to be found in lawyers' offices or at booksellers. Only at the very end of the eighteenth century was the whole work translated into French and published by Soulatges with the express intention of making it accessible to lawyers and others.[42]

Toulouse was by no means the only place whose custom was written in Latin; the same occurred elsewhere, for instance in Spain. Thus, the Costumbres de Lérida which were the first redaction of local laws in Catalonia, were written in Latin in 1228 by Guillermo Botet. Subsequently they were turned into Catalan, but significantly that version has not survived though there are five manuscripts of the Latin.[43] And if one accepts, as I think one should, that *fueros* ought to be regarded in part as containing customary law, then one should include as customs written in Latin those of, for instance in Extremadura, Calatayud (1131), Daroca (1142), Teruel (1177), and Cuenca (1188 or slightly thereafter).

Of course, often in a customary system law is needed where there is no law or, if there is, it cannot be found. The law has to be created. To give one further example: King Liutprand of the Lombards in several years of his reign issued a number of laws. In some of the preambles he expressly states that the laws that follow are enacted precisely because the custom is not known or, if it is, is not wanted by persons other than him. Thus, for his thirteenth year (A.D. 725): "Because I remembered that subjects of ours coming into our presence brought causes in controversy among themselves which we were not certain how to bring to an end according to custom nor were provided for in the body of the edict."[44] The Lombards were fortunate that theirs was a society with statutory law as well as custom; otherwise a custom would just have been imagined to exist.

Also, as I maintained, the whole notion of customary law being what people do is undermined by the usual approach in medieval and later France of accepting the law of somewhere else, usually of Rome as the law was set out in the Corpus Juris Civilis or of Paris as the law was to be found in the Coutume de Paris, as subsidiary law when the local coutume failed to give the answer. Whichever was chosen, conditions in early Byzantium or the capital of France were very different from those, say, in parts of Brittany or the Auvergne. And there is no doubt that gaps often had to be filled in the local coutume. But what is the standard doctrine of customary law to make of the fact that just before the French Revolution (which was to put an end to local custom) it could still be questioned in general whether recourse was to be had to the Corpus Juris Civilis or the Coutume de Paris?[45] In circumstances such as these one cannot even say that, in the absence of a custom, it was the custom to look at the custom or other law of some other particular place.

Apart from any other considerations, one reason makes it very difficult for my thesis on the nature of customary law to become acceptable. The reason is very practical. No society that accepts a system of customary law can operate it on the open basis that I postulate because the law would lack authority. Such societies operate in law by a myth. In general they have no legislation, do not accept judicial decisions as binding precedent, either have no law books, or do not see them as authoritative. How then do they resolve disputes? The legitimate answer for those living under such systems can only be that they look for the norms of practical behavior that are generally regarded by the populace as binding. There cannot be open recognition that there may not be a custom, that a rule may be accepted as law simply because it exists elsewhere, or that a judge is just making up a rule. But a myth to live by is to the outsider no less a myth.

To illustrate the preceding paragraph we can turn again to the Costumbres de Lérida. Botet lists at the beginning of the work the sources of law in Lérida and he includes *mores,* customary behavior. But he says he was urged by his fellow consuls and other citizens to write down the custom, and he explains in the opening paragraph why he did so: "I Guillermo Botet have put in some little effort in order to collect in one place and set out in writing the various and different customs of our city in order to take away the opportunity of evil doing from some people who declare, when a custom is in their favor, that it is the custom. If it is alleged against them in a similar case, they insist that it is not the custom. Hence, proof of customs delays the progress of lawsuits and thus litigants incur severe costs."[46] If the difficulty of finding and knowing the custom can plausibly be given by Botet as his reason for writing down the customs, then in fact he incidentally gives the lie to the notion that customary law arises from normative behavior which occurs because people believe it is the law. Yet, as we have seen, Botet himself says that in this connection it is the *mores* that are law. He also tells us in paragraphs 168 and 169 that among the sources of law ranking after customs are inter alia Visigothic law, then Roman law. Visigothic law is seldom followed, he says, but Roman law often is, especially in matters that do not arise every day. In effect he is saying that in the absence of custom, custom assumes that Roman law will be assumed to be the custom. There is no other basis for accepting that Roman law is authoritative.

Equally significantly, the *fuero* of Cuenca—as do many other collections of customs—gives as the justification for their redaction into writing: "because therefore human memory is transient." Again, if customs cannot be remembered, they cannot be obeyed because of a consciousness that they are law.[47] Even if the transience of memory is not a reason for the redaction of custom, it is significant that it is given.

CUSTOMARY LAW OUTSIDE EUROPE

We have been looking only at European law, and Western law is the subject of this book, but I believe that at least the following propositions have general application.

1. The extent of a customary rule is frequently very unclear.
2. Cases often arise for which the preceding custom, or even whether there was a preceding custom, is quite uncertain, but judgments have to be given as if according to custom. In the absence of writing, customary rules have a relatively limited survival rate, because knowledge of them is uncertain.
3. The unofficial writing down of customary law will be treated as giving evidence—often of great weight—of the law.
4. Decisions of a tribunal, though not binding precedent, come to carry great weight as a statement of, or the best evidence for, a legal custom.
5. Customary behavior that will not be given support by a tribunal will not come to be accepted as having the normative status of customary law.

6. The combined effect of propositions 1 through 5 is that it is the official recognition of normative behavior as customary (whether it was or not) that makes it customary law. This is so even though official recognition of custom be not accepted in any jurisdiction as the basis of customary law's being law.

7. Borrowing from other legal systems is frequent.

Because I believe my view on the nature of customary law is largely original, I would not expect to find it set out thus in any treatise on, say, modern African customary law, or to appear to be acceptable to any author of a treatise. Yet much that is inherent in the principles does seem to be contained, implicitly perhaps, in statements about African law. I should like to quote from authorities whom I would not charge with agreeing with my principles. I begin with J. F. Holleman, in his *Shona Customary Law:*

By far the greater part of the information so collected consisted of case material, the facts of which could be checked and cross-checked when necessary. The majority of these cases were supplied by alternating teams of carefully selected informants, practically all of them people who were taking an active part in the tribal administration of justice as assessors to a chief's or headman's court, and who could therefore quote from personal experience. A great number of cases I witnessed myself by regularly attending the sessions of the local tribal courts.

These actual cases formed a realistic basis for a discussion and analysis of the legal principles involved. As one case report led to another, and the pile of factual data grew, the various aspects of Shona law emerged, not as a clear pattern of strictly defined rules, but as a collection of broad concepts and guiding principles, the practical application of which varied with virtually every case in which they were reflected. Only in exceptional circumstances, when no actual cases could be supplied to illustrate certain points of law, were hypothetical cases submitted to different teams of informants in order to ascertain their views.

It thus became possible, on the basis of a vast stock of case material, not only to conceive and formulate the general principles of an indigenous system of law, but to reveal its great flexibility as one of its essential characteristics. This explains the collection of case reports included in this volume. They have been selected, not because they are always correct interpretations of Shona law (many of them are not), or because they carry the weighty authority of a legal precedent such as is found in our legal system (they are never, in fact, interpreted like that), but because they are illustrations of an indigenous administration of justice in which a satisfactory solution of the conflict between the parties often matters more than a correct interpretation of the legal principles involved.[48]

Next, from L. Shapera, *Handbook of Tswana Law and Custom:*

The Tswana themselves speak of their laws as having always existed, from the time that man himself came into being;[49] or as having been instituted by God (*Modimo*) or by the ancestor spirits (*badimo*). This does not imply that no laws at all are held to have been made by man. But it does serve to direct attention to one important fact: the mechanism of the courts is used for the most part to enforce the observance of usages which have already established themselves in practice and become accepted through tradition. . . .

The existence of the courts has created another important source of law, in the form of judicial decisions. The courts in the first place must declare what the law is. A custom, until brought before them, operates as part of the general system of behavior incumbent upon members of the tribe. If brought before the courts, and held to be valid, it obtains recognition as good law, and henceforth is supported by the additional sanction of judicial enforcement. The courts do not create the custom: they merely recognize, and by so doing strengthen, the obligatory character of a rule already in existence. Sometimes, however, the courts will hold that a custom, even if generally observed, is incompatible with the existing conditions of tribal life, and will refuse to regard it as legally binding. Here the role of the courts in defining the law is even more apparent. Decisions of this nature have become fairly frequent as Western civilization has penetrated more deeply into Tswana life.[50]

F. A. Ajayi writes of Nigeria, that "in spite of both judicial and legislative attempts to ensure the development of customary law, there are still, as most people would agree a number of *lacunae* in the whole system."[51]

Hans Cory declares in his *Sukuma Law and Custom:*

These variations [in law] had developed within the tribe primarily because of its size. In times when communications between the populated areas were poor, when permanent inter-tribal warfare existed, when wild animals endangered the life of the traveler, and superstitious fear was dominant, exchanges of cultural achievements were not common. Therefore, partly owing to the influence of neighbors in the boundary chiefdoms and partly through the action of autocratic rulers, laws underwent local changes. Many recent examples can be found where a chief has decided upon a beneficial change of anachronistic laws for his own area; such changes have seldom been accepted by others, even if their advantages were clear, because jealousy has been greater than insight.[52]

These quotations show that the authors are aware of one or more of the following: that there are important gaps in customary law; that customary legal rules are not clear or precise; that customary law is not easily known; that case law, though not binding as precedent, declares what the customary law is; that customary law can be affected by the influence of neighbors; that a powerful magnate can change or deliberately fail to change law; that courts may not accept customary behavior as law and it is then not law. That they do not seem to question that customary law exists even before it is declared by the courts is only to be expected given the traditional view of the nature of customary law.

Instances of the impact of Western law, even when it is not imposed, are too numerous and well known to require exemplification.[53]

The very numerous restatements of tribal law, of which Cory's book is one,[54] have striking similarities to *Weistümer;* they betray the feeling that customary law requires to be (relatively) fixed for the future, and that it is easily lost. Restatements may be formed after inquiries similar to those used for *Weistümer,*[55] and then they bear similar implications.

CHAPTER 5

LEGISLATION AND JURISTS
French Délit

We have now seen something of the impact of the four sources of law on legal evolution: juristic opinion, legislation, custom, and preceding judicial decision. Of course, the sources interact: above all, judicial precedent has a fundamental role in the life of the other three. In fact, its impact plays out differently with each of the three. In this chapter I want to focus on one aspect of the impact of jurists on legislation. Although legislation can be autonomous with no input except from the legislators themselves, in practice it does not work like that. The input of jurists may be enormous. This is especially true of some of the most famous legislation.

While I again deal with particular examples, my intention is to raise issues of much wider implication. The focus here is on the impact of purely juristic thinking on the rules on delict and quasi-delict in the French Code civil of 1804, but the underlying issue is legal borrowing or legal transplants, an issue that concerns us throughout this book. *Transplants* is a dirty word for many scholars. If borrowing is standard practice then sociologists of law have a problem. How then can law reflect society?[1] Legal historians also have a problem; they have to understand the borrowed law, the language in which it was written, and why it was adopted.

During the eleventh to eighteenth centuries, the two primary intersecting strands in Western legal development were local customary law and Roman law (often in the form of the *ius commune*), with the latter, gradually or more swiftly, acting to fill gaps in, modify, render more sophisticated, or replace the former. The modern civil codes are largely the result of this intertwining. But the specific contribution of each strand is not easily determined. Thus, to estimate the force of the Roman law strand, one must find the answer to a question that I have never seen raised. What was the impact of Roman rules on the legal rules in modern civil codes when the Roman rules were inappropriate either because of changed societal conditions or attitudes or because for some reason the Roman rules themselves were underdeveloped? If the Roman rules were not accepted, must one simply deny any input and restrict the Reception of Roman law to instances of direct borrowing? Is nonacceptance rejection? This certainly seems to have been the attitude of some distinguished scholars who have, perhaps, not quite seen the issue. Thus, Jean Brissaud regards codification in France as a victory for customary law over Roman law.[2] For Paul Viollet, "Our codes, considered from the historical point of view, are the concentration and unification of the old French law, dispersed, and often divergent, in the royal *ordonnances* and the customs."[3] And Rudolf B. Schlesinger bluntly states:

> On one point, however, there can be no reasonable difference of opinion: The old adage, all-too-frequently repeated, that the civilian codes presently in force are merely a modernized version of Roman law, is simply nonsense. In many respects, the solutions adopted by the codifiers were not traditional; and of the traditional ones, many were not Roman. The late Professor Reginald Parker was probably right when he said: "I seriously believe it would not be difficult to establish, if such a thing could be statistically approached, that the majority of legal institutes, even within the confines of private law, of a given civil law country are not necessarily of Roman origin.[4]

The implication seems to be that if Roman solutions were not adopted, Roman law had no impact. A further implication seems to be that the impact of Roman law was not as great as has been supposed and hence, for an understanding of the modern law, may be safely ignored.

The matter, I believe, is not so simple. I intend no paradox, but this chapter will be devoted to an investigation of the Reception of Roman law when the Roman rules were not received. The issue is, What happens to the law upon codification when the Roman legal rules are obviously inappropriate and hence not accepted? Each situation of fact and law is different, and I do not intend to build up a general theory. By temperament and training, I can only proceed from detailed analysis and I wish here to concentrate on the articles that appear in the French Code civil of 1804 under the heading "Delicts and Quasi-Delicts":

> 1382. Every action of a human that causes injury to another binds the person through whose fault it occurred to make it good.

1383. Everyone is responsible for the injury he caused not only by his action, but also by his negligence or imprudence.

1384. One is responsible not only for the injury one causes by one's own action, but also for that which is caused by the action of persons for whom one is responsible, or of things one has under one's guard.

The father, and the mother after the death of the husband, are responsible for the injury caused by their minor children living with them;

Masters and employers for the injury caused by their servants and agents in the functions for which they employed them;

Teachers and craftsmen for the injury caused by their pupils and apprentices during the time that they were under their surveillance.

The above responsibility lies, unless the father and the mother, teachers and craftsmen prove that they could not have prevented the action that gives rise to the responsibility.

1385. The owner of an animal or the person who makes use of it, while it is subject to his use, is responsible for the injury which the animal has caused, whether the animal was under his guard, whether it had wandered off or escaped.

1386. The owner of a building is responsible for the injury caused by its fall when that occurred as a consequence of a defect in maintenance or by a fault in its construction.[5]

To begin with, we take these articles at face value on the subject of the basis of liability. The relationship among the five provisions is by no means clear. Articles 1382 and 1383, dealing with responsibility for one's own actions, make liability clearly dependent on fault, including negligence; and, though this is not expressly said, the normal burden of proving negligence lies with the plaintiff. But how can one understand the basis of liability in article 1384 for the behavior of persons for whom one is responsible or for things under one's guard? With one crucial exception, nothing is said about the basis of liability. The first issue to which no answer is given directly is whether the person for whom one is responsible must have been at fault for liability to accrue. One might at first say no, because minor children will often be under the age at which any fault could be attributed to them. Nothing is said to divide minor children into categories, and it is a principle of French law that one cannot make a distinction where the law makes none.[6] Nevertheless, in favor of a positive response is the fact that a master is liable for injuries caused by the action of a servant. Is a master liable for his own behavior only if he is at fault, but is to be automatically and strictly liable for the injury caused by a servant who was without fault? Common sense would suggest not. Thus, this article does not yield a clear answer, negative or positive. Nor is there any indication on the face of the article whether for liability to be caused by a thing, the thing must have been defective.

When we look elsewhere for the basis of liability in the behavior of the "superior," we are left in just as great a state of confusion. For injury caused by the behavior of servants and agents and things, there is no clear indication whether for liability the "superior" himself had to have been at fault. One might feel that the "superior" here was always absolutely liable, even if free from fault, because the sole exception to liability—applying expressly to parents, teachers, and craftsmen—is not stated so as to apply to the master of servants and agents or the guardians of things. But it might be rash to draw such a conclusion. And does article 1384 really equate the liability of the "superior" for the behavior of persons with his liability for the behavior of things? We should suppose so, because they are treated without distinction in the same article. But that conclusion seems unpalatable. The exception, too, causes problems. Parents, teachers, and craftsmen are excused from liability for injury caused by their children, pupils, and apprentices only if they can show that they could not have prevented the action. The basis of liability is not that for one's own actions in articles 1382 and 1383; at the very least, the burden of proof here has been shifted to the defendant.

More than that, it seems that the defendant is not free from liability if he proves he was not negligent; he must show that he could not have prevented the behavior. And we must remember that we cannot tell whether the behavior in question had to be negligent or worse on the part of the actual doer. Article 1385 in its turn does not on its face provide us with an answer to the two relevant questions: whether the animal had to be at "fault" for liability to be imposed on the master or operator, or whether for liability the master had to be at fault in allowing the animal to cause injury. Article 1386 is clearer in its meaning but leaves us no less confused. The owner of a building that collapses and causes injury is liable for the damage in either of two cases: where the collapse was the result of poor maintenance (fault on the part of the owner) and where the collapse was the result of a fault in the construction (a defect in the building). But this second case leaves us with several problems to which the articles, on their face, provide no solution.

First, why is the owner liable even when he is without fault—he may have had no part in the construction and may have been unable to check for defects in construction—when for his own behavior he is liable only when at fault? Second, why is a distinction made with regard to a building in article 1386 and things under one's guard in article 1384—and what is the nature of that distinction? Third, why does article 1386 speak expressly only of buildings and not of immovables in general? For example, a tree may fall if it has not been properly looked after or if it is defective. In enumerating the problems of the basis of liability under the five articles, we should finally note that the heading refers to both delicts and quasi-delicts, but neither term appears in the text of the articles.[7] The terminology is not further elucidated, nor is any difference in the basis of liability for one or the other.

We are still not yet concerned with the intention of the drafters of the code. But in light of what has just been said, it should be admitted with regard to the basis of liability both that the articles were poorly drafted and that the drafters either were hopelessly confused or had no consistent policy. What explanation can be found for these facts? It should be emphasized here that the issue is not just of theoretical significance. The basis of liability under these five articles is one of the most controversial issues in the interpretation of the Code civil as the merest glance at the battery of apparatus, from both "doctrine" and "jurisprudence," laid out in the *Petit Code Dalloz* edition, would show.

In response to the confusion, two answers must be given: the short and the long one. The short answer offers a basic explanation. The long answer then demonstrates the accuracy of the short answer and adds detail.

First, the short answer. The confusion occurs above all in situations in which Roman solutions, as set out in Justinian's Corpus Juris Civilis, were inappropriate and could not be expressly used because of changed social conditions and societal attitudes—but in which those solutions or texts had a hidden impact.

Thus, in articles 1382 and 1383, the basis of liability for one's own behavior—of which rather more must be said later—is obviously based on fault. This was the position in Roman law, especially under the *lex Aquilia* (e.g., *D.9.2*). But the first problem that concerns us arises only in article 1384, which covers liability for the actions of persons for whom one was responsible. Under Roman law, the dependent person for whom a superior was responsible would be a son in the power of his father (a *filiusfamilias*) or a slave. A slave had no legal standing in private law and could not be sued directly, and a *filiusfamilias* owned no property and was not worth suing. The head of the family, the *paterfamilias,* was logically the only person who could be sued, and liability vested in him—as did, for example, rights regarding the contracts of sons or slaves—because he was the head of the family. Roman law gave the victim an action against the owner or father as the *paterfamilias* for the wrongful behavior, whether malicious or negligent, of a slave or son, but the defendant could avoid condemnation in the money sum by handing over the slave or son to the victim in noxal surrender before judgment was pronounced (e.g., D.9.2.27.3; *h.t.* 32.*pr.*; *h.t.* 44.1; 9.4.2.*pr.*, 1; *h.t.* 4.2; *h.t.* 6). The notion was therefore a primitive form of limited liability. The wrongful behavior of a dependent could result in a loss of his or her "superior" but only up to the worth of the wrongdoer. Fault on the part of the "superior" was irrelevant—because liability was based solely on his position as head of the family—except that it might in some circumstances exclude his right to hand over the actual perpetrator in noxal surrender.[8] Fault on the part of the dependent was necessary, just as fault alone made a person of independent status (*sui juris*) liable for injury caused by his or her behavior. The absence in France of noxal surrender (and of anything equivalent to the Roman *patria potestas*) meant that this neat and satisfactory solution could not be adopted. This inability resulted (as will be shown in the long answer) in some confusion of thought both among the drafters of the Code civil and among the French legal scholars who preceded them—hence the failure in the Code civil to make liability depend clearly either on fault on the part of the dependent perpetrator or on fault on the part of his or her "superior."

Similarly, there was no obvious, appropriate solution to be found by the drafters of the Code civil in Roman law regarding liability for damage caused by things under one's guard. There was no general overriding principle in Roman law concerning liability for damage caused by an inanimate thing—nor was one much needed before the days of steam boilers, the internal combustion engine, and high explosives—but liability for movables occurred in two situations, both of which were classed by the Romans as quasi-delicts. In one, an action was given against a householder from whose dwelling something was thrown or poured onto a way that was commonly used, resulting in damage (D.9.3). The action lay against the householder—simply because he was the householder—whether he did or did not do the throwing, knew of it, or could have prevented it (see, especially, $D.9.3.1.4$). Ownership of the thing thrown or poured was irrelevant ($D.9.3.1.4$); the action was given in effect against the person who had the thing under his guard. And, of course, there can be no question regarding the injury resulting from a defect in the thing. The Roman approach is sensible, especially in view of the difficulty of proof and because the occupier on any approach would be liable not only for his own behavior but also for that of his sons or slaves; if the occupier had not thrown or poured out the thing, they might have done so.

In the other situation, an action was given against the occupier of a building from or on whose eave or projecting roof something was suspended or placed, above a way commonly used, and whose fall could cause damage ($D.9.3.5.6$ff.). The action did not lie specifically against the person who placed the thing in its dangerous position, and, since no injury had yet occurred, there could be no relevance in the condition of the thing.[9] The approach is reasonable as a preventive device. These are both special cases. If one generalized from them—which obviously one ought not to—then one would come up with the proposition that a person was liable for things under his guard whether or not his own behavior was wrongful, and irrespective of any defect in the thing. Article 1384 of the Code civil seems to have been framed in this way, but if this were the intention of the drafters, it would be highly inappropriate for the following reasons. It conflicts first with the basis of liability for one's own acts, under articles 1382 and 1383; second, probably with article 1384 regarding the acts of persons for whom one was responsible; and third, with article 1386 concerning the collapse of a building. But Roman law provided no general solution that could be borrowed regarding liability for damage caused by a thing. (As an aside, I wish to interject that it would be truly amazing, would it not, if the formulation here in the Code civil resulted from the Roman *actio de effusis vel deiectis* [action for pouring out or throwing down] and *actio de positis ac suspensis* [action for placing or suspending]? Yet that is what I want to show.)

Under Roman law, when an animal caused damage and could be said to be at "fault," a remedy under the *actio de pauperie* lay to the victim against the owner of the animal for the amount of harm done—but, again, the owner could escape further liability if he chose to surrender the animal ($D.9.1$). The device of an owner's limited liability was again used. Given that fact, and the fact that the victim had, indeed, suffered loss, it is perfectly understandable that for the *actio de pauperie* to be available the negligence or otherwise of the owner in keeping the animal from causing harm was not an issue. But noxal surrender did not exist in France, so the total acceptance of the solution of the *actio de pauperie* was not obviously appropriate. Yet article 1385 on its face says nothing about whether the owner or user of an animal is liable without fault for any damage it causes or whether, as in the case of the owner's or user's own behavior, he is liable only if he is at fault. Either interpretation is possible. (It should be remembered that at this stage we are concerned not with the intention of the drafters but rather with their formulation in the Code civil.) A pattern in the drafting seems to be emerging. The solution—noxal surrender—of the Roman *actio de pauperie*, in which the owner's negligence in preventing the animal from causing harm was irrelevant, was not acceptable in nineteenth-century France. But because the Romans did not discuss this issue of the owner's negligence regarding the *actio de pauperie*, then neither did article 1385 clearly set out the basis of the owner's or user's liability.

Two other remedies were available in Roman law for damage caused by animals, and both are relevant here. The *actio de pastu* gave an action when animals fed on the acorns on another's land. This action is not prominent in the Roman sources, the texts are relatively uninformative, and one of two views may be held. On one view (which I favor), the action was available only when a person actually sent his animals to feed on another's land (*D.*10.4.9.1; 19.5.14.3). On another view, which has textual support in the postclassical juristic *Pauli Sententiae*, the action allowed noxal surrender,[10] in which case fault on the part of the owner would be irrelevant. The second action was given under the edict of the curule aediles against someone who had kept a fierce animal (presumably often for gladiatorial games) in such a way that it caused damage where people commonly walked. The basis of liability was exposing people to damage, and no other fault was necessary. Hence the action was penal: a fixed sum was payable if a free human being was killed; the judge decided what was fair if a free human being was injured; and in other cases the penalty was double the loss inflicted (*D.*21.1.40; *h.t.* 41; *h.t.* 42). Thus, there were three Roman actions, though the action that was prominent in the Roman sources was the *actio de pauperie*.

The existence of a pattern is confirmed when we look at article 1386. The "setting in life" of the provision, as a glance at Jean Domat (1625–96) and the discussion of the draft code reveals[11]—and as we shall see in the "long answer"—is in the Roman remedies for *damnum infectum*, that is to say, loss that is threatened but has not yet occurred.

In general, as has been mentioned, Roman law gave no remedy for damage caused by a thing, even for the collapse of a building (e.g., *D.*39.2.7.1, 2). But if a neighbor felt threatened by defective elements on another's land, he might approach the praetor, who would command the latter to give security for restitution if the damage occurred—the so-called *cautio damni infecti.* The *cautio* was given on account of threatened injury, which means there must have been a defect in the thing. Hence, even if the injury for which the *cautio* was taken occurred but the defect was not the cause of the injury—for instance, when a storm was so strong that even a sound building might lose its tiles—the owner of the defective property was not liable under the *cautio* (e.g., *D.*39.2.24.4–11; *h.t.* 43.*pr.*). If the owner of the dangerous property failed to give the *cautio,* the praetor would grant the threatened neighbor *missio in possessionem,* or detention of the property.[12]

Because French law did not adopt either *cautio damni infecti* or *missio in possessionem,* there was no remedy for future, threatened damage. Nonetheless, the Roman treatment of *damnum infectum* was the focus for subsequent French discussion of damage by immovable property; there was no other possible part of Roman law to which discussion could be attached since, in the absence of the *cautio,* there was no general remedy for damage caused by an inanimate thing.[13] This setting enables us to provide answers to the three problems set out earlier in connection with article 1386. First, the owner in France might be liable without fault on his part, because liability in Roman law was based on a defect in the property (which might cause damage). For the Romans, of course, because the defect was observable and the injury foreseeable and made known to the owner, the owner would be at fault if he had failed to carry out the necessary repairs. Second, article 1386 deals only with immovables because threatened damage by immovable property alone was covered by the Roman remedies. The third problem—why article 1386 speaks expressly of buildings and not also of trees—requires greater elucidation.

The Roman *cautio de damno infecto* was available not only for damage threatened by defective buildings and other human works but also for threatened damage from defective trees (*D.*39.2.24.9). But whereas the praetor provided model *formulae* in his edict for threatened damage from human works, he appears not to have given one for damage resulting from trees. Likewise, the jurists did not discuss threatened damage by trees and other natural objects on land in their own right, but only in passing in connection with human works.[14] Most important perhaps, *missio in possessionem* was never discussed in connection with damage threatened from natural objects but only regarding human works, and especially buildings. Subsequent French discussion, therefore, came to speak only of damage by human works, above all by buildings. If the argument up to this point is correct—and detailed evidence will be provided in the long answer—then we have a particular twist in legal development in article 1386. The basis of liability in article 1386 was determined by Roman remedies that were not accepted in France, yet because of the emphasis in the Roman sources the French provision appeared to be restricted to damage caused by human immovable works and not also (as in Roman law) to damage from trees.[15]

At this stage, some preliminary conclusions may be drawn, if only to show where the argument is going. In the field of wrongful damage, although Roman law provided a coherent set of remedies, some of those remedies were inappropriate for the France of a later era, partly because of changed social conditions and partly because of the rejection of certain Roman legal notions, such as surrender of dependent persons and animals or the concept of threatened damage. Still, the discussion in France that formed the basis of the articles of the Code civil proceeded on the basis of Roman law, resulting in the appalling confusion apparent in the articles—whether the confusion was mainly in the drafting or also in the minds of the codifiers. Now the corollary to these conclusions is most important. When Roman law was inappropriate, and even when it was rejected, the drafters were not necessarily freed from its dominance. They did not always find solutions in local custom. They did not always proffer their own coherent solutions.

Now the long answer. To keep it brief, I will deal expressly and at length with only four issues: liability for a thing under one's guard under article 1384; liability regarding persons for whom one was responsible; liability for an animal under article 1385; and liability for the fall of a building under article 1386.

We may find a satisfactory starting point in Jean Domat's *Les Lois civiles dans leur ordre naturel* (which first appeared between 1689 and 1697). Domat's grand plan was to set out a scheme of Christian law for France in an easily comprehensible arrangement. Four kinds of law, he said, ruled in France.[16] First, the royal ordinances had universal authority over all of France. Second, customs had particular authority in the place where they were observed. Third, Roman law had two uses: first, as custom in some places in several matters and, second, over all of France and on all matters, "consisting in this that one observes everywhere these rules of justice and equity that are called 'written reason,' because they are written in Roman law. Thus, for this second use, Roman law has the same authority as have justice and equity on our reason." Fourth, canon law also contained many rules accepted in France, though some had been rejected. Domat went on to claim that he drew up the plan of the book and the choice of subject matter because the natural law of equity lay in the Roman law and because the study of Roman law was so difficult.[17] He introduced the discussion of wrongful damage in book 2, title 8:

> One can distinguish three sorts of wrongs from which some damage may arise: those wrongs which amount to a crime or an offense; those wrongs of persons who fail in their agreed on obligations such as a seller who does not deliver the thing sold, a tenant who does not make the repairs he is bound to do; and those wrongs which have no relation with agreements and which do not amount to a crime or an offense, as if light-mindedly one throws something out of a window which spoils a suit; if animals not properly guarded do some damage; if one carelessly causes a fire, if a building which threatens to collapse, not being repaired, falls on another and there causes damage.
>
> Of these three types of wrong, only those of the last category are the subject of this title; because crimes and offenses ought not to be mixed with civil matters, and everything that concerns agreements has been explained in the first book.[18]

The scene is set for the discussion of the topics that interest us, damage caused by things, animals, and buildings. The discussion under this one category seems very lopsided. The headings of the title are: (1) on what is thrown from a house, or can fall from one and cause loss; (2) of loss caused by animals; (3) of the loss which may result from the collapse of a building or some new work; and (4) of other kinds of damage caused by fault, without a crime or offense. Pothier, in his *Traité des obligations*, gives very short shrift to *délits* and *quasi-délits*, dismissing the subject in half a section.[19] This approach, which was not restricted to these two lawyers, indicates a disregard for the subject, which was to have enormous consequences and which must be explained. Domat was discussing other kinds of loss caused by fault, "sans crime ni délit." The translation of the word *délit* is by no means immediately obvious. It is not clear whether it is the Roman *delictum* or the *délit* of later French law. Whatever it is, like "crime" it should not, in the eyes of Domat, be mixed with civil matters. The basic idea can be discovered in a roundabout way by looking at what Domat in fact does not treat—because he is concerned with civil law—and examining how other writers, even at a later date, approached the issue.

Domat did not deal with the wrongs that the Romans, as in Justinian's *Institutes,* classed as *delicta,* presumably because, as other writers make plain, they partook of crime. Thus, to take a few examples from other jurisdictions, Sir George Mackenzie, in his *Institutions of the Law of Scotland* (first edition, 1684), did not deal with delicts, but in the final chapter of the book "Of Crimes" (4.4), he wrote: "*Private crimes,* called also *delicta,* in the *Civil Law,* oblige the Committers to repair the Dammage, and Interest of the private Party." But he says no more about private crimes. And Marino Guarano in his *Praelectiones ad Institutiones Justiniani in Usum Regni Neapolitani* (1779) claimed (4.1.3): "Vitiositas actus in veris delictis est dolus, in quasi delictis est culpa" (The wickedness of the act in true delicts is malice, in quasi-delicts it is negligence). (See also his 4.5.1.) Giambattista de Luca (1614–83), discussing delicts in *Instituta universale di Tutte le Leggi* (4.2, 3, 4, 5 §1), said, "oggi in pratica resta più comoda l'azione Criminale" (today in practice the criminal action is more helpful). He even claimed (at §7) that it was not worthwhile to spend time on the action of the *lex Aquilia,* which was rarely used.

The main Roman delicts were *furtum* (theft), *rapina* (robbery with violence), *damnum iniuria datum* (wrongful damage to property), and *iniuria* (which covered both defamation and physical assault). In later law (if not also in Roman law), all of these were covered above all by criminal law, because, with the sole exception of *damnum iniuria datum,* they all required deliberate malicious conduct on the part of the malefactor. For *damnum iniuria datum,* the wrongful action had to be either malicious or simply negligent. In western Europe in the later Middle Ages, specific difficulties hindered the Reception of the Roman law of delict. In France, there was no Reception of the Roman law on this subject.[20] The tragedy for France was that in excluding *delicta* from discussion as being above all crimes and as being law that was not received, the French writers also deprived themselves of a treatment of the *lex Aquilia,*[21] since that is the context in Roman law in which one finds the treatment par excellence of negligence in all its aspects and of negligent injury to things and human beings. (Injury to human beings comes under *damnum iniuria datum* because slaves were a prime kind of property, and to a great extent dependent children in law could be analogized to slaves.) Hence, subsequent treatment by the jurist who took this approach is weak regarding the basis of liability for tortious wrongdoing.

Domat discusses liability for things poured or thrown out of windows or dangerously suspended, but there is no other case of liability for injury proceeding from an inanimate movable thing or from a person's wrongful act except in the most general terms and without analysis— as in book 2, title 8, section 4. Robert Pothier (1699–1772) says not a word on the basis of liability for damage by a thing, and in the discussions before the Conseil d'Etat concerning the draft of the Code civil no time was spent on the meaning of "dommage . . . causé par le fait . . . des choses que l'on a sous sa garde." Significantly, the draft contained two other specific articles that would have appeared immediately after the existing article 1381:

> Article 16. If, from a house inhabited by several persons, water or something which causes damage is thrown onto a passerby, those who inhabit the apartment from which it was thrown are all liable in solidarity, unless he who did the throwing is known, in which case he alone has the obligation of restoring the loss.

> Article 17. Guests who only inhabit in passing the house from which the thing was thrown are not bound to repair the loss, unless it has been proved that it was they who threw; but he who lodges them is bound.[22]

These two draft articles have supreme significance for understanding the drafting of this part of the Code civil. They both relate only to the circumstances of the Roman *actio de effusis vel deiectis,* and they both concern particular situations: where there is more than one principal inhabitant and where the inhabitants are temporary guests. As particular cases, they illuminate the main notion and reveal the context of the discussion. Article 16 was at first accepted without discussion in the Conseil d'Etat, but in discussing article 17, Citizen Miot claimed that the enunciation of the principle sufficed and that examples should be cut back.[23] Not a word was said in the Conseil d'Etat regarding liability for damage by things under what is now article 1384. Likewise, when that part of the Code civil was presented before the Corps législatif on 19 February 1804, not a word on the subject was spoken by Treilhard in his presentation or by the tribun Tarrible in its discussion.[24]

Indeed until the importance of the rule showed up in practice, liability for damage caused by things attracted little scholarly attention. For instance, the long-winded commentator on the code, Toulier, who devoted twenty-one articles to a discussion of damage by animals, gave only one to damage caused by inanimate objects—and that, after a brief mention of article 1384, is devoted to article 1386.[25] Likewise, even as late as 1877, F. Mourlon in his published lectures on the Code civil dealt under article 1384 only with persons for whom one is responsible, and under the heading of things under one's guard only with articles 1385 and 1386.[26] Indeed, so little was made of liability concerning things under one's guard in the debates, so little attention was paid to it in practice before the Teffaine case of 1896,[27] and so obscure is the background to the clause, that it can be said to be the unanimous opinion in France that the drafters' intention was to establish liability only for animals and collapsing buildings, and that the relevant part of article 1384 simply announced the particular cases in articles 1385 and 1386.[28]

But we cannot leave article 1384 yet. We must still consider some aspects of liability for the acts of persons for whom one is responsible. Domat says in *Les Lois civiles* (1.2.8.7): "Schoolmasters, craftsmen and others who receive into their homes students, apprentices or other persons to train them in some art, manufacture or commerce are liable for the behavior of these people."[29] We have here an early statement regarding liability for other persons' behavior in French law. As it stands, removed from its context, it has no parallel in Roman law. In Roman law, one was responsible for the conduct of one's slaves and sons-in-power, not for pupils, apprentices, and others whom one was training. But the context is important for Domat. The text arises out of the discussion of things poured or thrown out of windows and probably should be restricted to that (for Domat), though no restriction is expressed. Then there would be absolute liability in Roman law, and Domat expresses the liability in absolute terms. Interestingly, Domat cites in support *D*.9.3.5.3, which in fact has a rather different effect. What is at issue there is who is to be regarded as a *habitator* (inhabitant), and the text indicates that an action on the facts will be given if one rents a building to have work done there or to teach pupils there (and one does not sleep there) and damage ensues.

The issue is taken up again by Pothier, who asserts that one is also liable for the acts of persons subject to one's power, as fathers, mothers, tutors, and teachers when the delict or quasi-delict is committed in one's presence, and generally when one could have prevented the injury but did not. But if one could not have prevented it, there is no liability. Pothier adds that one is liable for the wrongs caused by servants and employees even when one could not prevent the wrong, provided the wrong was committed in the exercise of the functions for which the servants or employees were employed.[30] This brings us closer to the rules set out in the Code civil. For Bertrand de Greuille, addressing the Tribunat on 6 February 1803, teachers and craftsmen were responsible for the acts of their pupils and apprentices, because they took the place of the parents—not at all the Roman position.[31]

The line of historical development from Domat is fairly plain. He stated absolutely the liability for pupils and such others (and this was proper in its context). Pothier generalized this approach, whether he had Domat or an equivalent statement in his mind. But in a general context the liability had to be restricted—to wrongs that the parent to teacher could not have prevented. And then Pothier added his treatment of liability for servants and employees. But, as was said before, the basis of one's liability for the acts of children, pupils, and apprentices had consequently become stricter in the Code civil than the basis of liability for one's own acts. The main reasons for this lie first in the removal from the French discussion of any treatment of the *lex Aquilia,* where the principle of no liability without fault is laid out, with the consequent blurring in French law of this all-important principle. The second reason lies in Domat's unqualified statement of absolute liability (but in the limited context of the *actio de effusis vel deiectis*), and Pothier's having had before him some discussion such as Domat's to which he added qualifications (untrammeled by too much consideration of the *lex Aquilia*). Third, Pothier's views were adopted by the code commission without too much evidence of independent thought.

For article 1385, the *travaux préparatoires* make the best starting point for the long answer, since the codifiers' intent there is readily apparent. Treilhard said nothing in the Conseil d'Etat, but Bertrand de Greuille was explicit:

> The draft then considers the cases where an animal, led by someone or escaped from his hands or having simply wandered off, has caused some wrong. In the first two hypotheses, the draft intends that the person who uses the animal, and in the third it orders the person who is its owner to be held liable for the reparation of the loss, because the loss must be imputed either to a lack of guard and vigilance on the part of the master, or to the rashness, clumsiness, or lack of attention of him who used the animal and because, in addition, within the general thesis, nothing belonging to someone can injure another with impunity.[32]

Thus for de Greuille, the liability of the owner or user of the animal was absolute, and he had two basic arguments. The first is one of imputed fault, and the second is that liability for animals falls within the general category of liability for things (under article 1384), and that liability is absolute. Tarrible's remarks are shorter but base liability on negligence that, however, may be very slight.[33] Thus, there seems to be some conflict regarding the interpretation of the article, even among the legislators. But Bertrand de Greuille is the more explicit, and his intention was to establish absolute liability for the acts of animals. This approach would correspond very accurately to the three remedies of Roman law if one assumed that the *actio de pastu* was not limited to the situation in which the owner sent his animals to feed on another's land and thus that the action would be noxal. Domat certainly takes this broad view of the *actio de pastu,* though he says nothing about noxal surrender. This view is in keeping with the approach that he says he is taking with regard to damage by animals; because customs varied so much, he set down only general rules that might be of common use, not what was particular to local customs or what was contained in Roman law but not in those customs (hence he does not deal with noxal surrender).[34] In fact, what he gives is Roman law, with omissions.[35] There is again in this context no recourse by the drafters to local customary law, though customary law was extensive, especially with regard to pasturage.[36] Here, too, the formulation of article 1385 can be said to be the result of Domat's treatment, which was based on Roman law. From this, however, was excised noxal surrender, which had given the Roman rules a different impact.[37]

To establish the connection here concerning liability under article 1386 for the collapse of a building and the very different remedies for *damnum infectum* in Roman law, we need do nothing more now than consider the remarks of Bertrand de Greuille in the Conseil d'Etat:[38]

> It is also as a consequence of that incontestable truth that the last article of the draft holds that the owner of a building is responsible for the loss that is caused by its collapse when that occurred through defective maintenance or by a flaw in its construction. This decision is much less rigorous and more equitable than the provision which is found in Roman law. That authorized the individual whose building could be damaged by the fall of another which was in danger of collapse, to put himself in possession of this neighboring heritage, if the proprietor did not give him guarantees for the loss one had reason to fear. Thus apprehension of the harm itself gave an opening for the action, and could bring the dispossession into play: the

draft to the contrary intends above all that the harm be present. It is thus the collapse alone that can legitimate the complaint and the demand of the injured party, and determine a condemnation for his benefit. It is after this collapse that he is allowed to examine the injury, to decide its importance; and it is then that the judge gives a decision on its reparation, if it is established that the negligence of the owner in maintaining his building or the ignorance of the workmen whom he employed in its construction were the cause of the collapse.

Thus, Bertrand de Greuille expressly links liability under article 1386 with the very different Roman remedies for *damnum infectum*. Whether the Roman remedies were or were not less equitable need not concern us. What does matter is a feature that was inappropriately carried over, to a different effect, and that made imbalanced the French liability for wrongful damage. The Roman remedy was given for threatened future damage. That means that the future collapse was apparent if nothing were done; for the owner then to do nothing to prevent the collapse would in fact be negligence, even if the defect arose from a fault in construction. But the French action was for past damage and was given even for a fault in the construction that was unknown to the owner. Thus, French liability came to differ from liability in Roman law. More than that, liability under article 1386 differs from liability under articles 1382 and 1383 in not requiring negligence and from article 1384 in requiring a defect in the thing (in the absence of negligence).

The obduracy of the inappropriate Roman *damnum infectum* clearly appears when we examine the 24 November 1803 discussion in the Conseil d'Etat and notice that Regnaud wanted to excise the offending "par une suite du défaut d'entretien ou par le vice de la construction" (in consequence of defective maintenance or by a flaw in the construction) and substitute "par sa faute" (through his fault). This attempt to make liability depend on fault was rejected.[39]

With these five articles on wrongful damage in the French Code civil, we are thus face-to-face with a very complex and peculiar phenomenon in legal development. They do not at all harmonize on the subject of the basis of legal liability. But this lack of harmony does not seem to be the result of careful thought on the different situations by the legislators, or simply the result of poor draftsmanship. Rather, it is the outcome of past legal history and above all the consequence of a reliance on a discussion of liability largely in the context of inappropriate Roman law, which had been rejected in large measure. There was no recourse to the rules of customary law. One can say that Roman law here was not received, but it nonetheless was the initial factor—and the dominant factor—in determining the shape of the French rules in the Code civil.

To avoid misunderstanding, one point ought to be made explicit. I am, of course, not claiming that there is no place for different standards of liability to operate in different situations for wrongful injury. Nor am I claiming that the French rules were necessarily grotesque for the French in 1804. But I am claiming that the various bases of liability in the French articles were adopted, without much thought or social purpose, from rejected Roman originals of which traces survived in old French books, and that the drafting, based as it was on preconceptions deriving from the old works, failed to achieve clarity. A glance at the corresponding articles in sections 823 to 853 of the German Bürgerliches Gesetzbuch (BGB)—themselves much influenced by Roman law—or, for the United States, at any edition of *Prosser on Torts,* shows that very different rules could just as easily have been accepted.

These rules of the Code civil illustrate a proposition that I regard as being of the highest importance and that is already inherent in past work of mine. The proposition is that in any country, approaches to law making (whether by legislators, judges, or jurists), the applicability of law to social institutions, the structure of the legal system, and the formulation and scope of legal rules are all in very large measure the result of history and overwhelmingly the result of legal history, and that the input of other, even contemporary societal forces is correspondingly slight. Thus, for instance, to understand why a piece of legislation or a judicial decision is as it is, we must know the legal tradition within which the lawmakers operate. And, given the prevalence and importance of legal borrowing and the ancient roots of much of law, to a very great extent, attitudes toward law making, the structure of legal systems, the parameters of legal rules, and the outlook of lawyers can be explained only if we examine the law in its historical relation to other law and over a period of centuries.

One final problem should be considered. Article 1382 reads: "Tout fait quelconque de l'homme, qui cause à autrui un dommage, oblige celui par la faute duquel il est arrivé, a le réparer." *Fait* may reasonably be translated as "action" and in itself does not seem to carry a connotation of blame or of wrongful action. The wrong that gives rise to an action is denoted by *faute,* or fault, a word that does not necessarily imply deliberate wrongdoing. But article 1383 reads: "Chacun est responsable du dommage qu'il a causé, non seulement par son fait, mais encore par sa négligence ou par son imprudence."

If we take "fait" in this article also to mean action and not to connote blameworthiness, then "par sa négligence ou par son imprudence," appearing in contrast to it, should mean that one is also liable for not acting and should denote a liability for nonfeasance even when there was no affirmative duty to act. "Négligence" is not contrasted with "dol." Article 1383 has "fait," not even "faute," which, in a pinch, to give a proper sense to "négligence" one might even want to translate as "deliberate wrong." Yet we know from the *travaux préparatoires*[40] that it was not the intention to give an action for nonfeasance, but rather to make clear that the action for wrongful loss existed both when there was malice and also when there was merely negligence. Thus, article 1383 was poorly drafted. But what, in any event, is the point of having these two articles? Why not simply have one reading: "Tout fait quelconque de l'homme, qui cause á autrui un dommage, oblige celui par le dol ou la négligence ou l'imprudence duquel il est arrivé, a le réparer." The answer lies in a previous French distortion of Roman law. As early as Pothier, a sharp distinction was made: a "délit" was a wrongful act done maliciously; a "quasi-délit" was a wrongful act done negligently.[41] The point—unexpressed—of article 1383 was to indicate that a negligent act that causes harm also creates liability.[42]

But there is an element of failure in the legal imagination. Whose imagination failed? Not obviously, I think, that of the Roman jurists. Certainly, that of Domat, in treating all *delicta* as crimes when he need not have done so. Even if he did not wish to discuss the *lex Aquilia,* he could have made use of the Roman discussion of negligence and liability. By failing to include the basic scenarios of damage caused by someone responsible for his or her own behavior, Domat lost the emphasis on the basic framework of liability only for fault including negligence; the exceptional cases were not fitted into the scheme of things with their rationales and boundaries explained. Subsequent French jurists, like Pothier, in following such a model also failed to set out an adequate treatment of private wrongs. A considerable failure of the imagination must be attributed to the drafters of the Code civil, who seem to have been blithely unaware of the inconsistencies in the articles and of the history of the rules they were perpetuating, especially since they stood at the point at which satisfactory law most easily might have been made. Failure of imagination is one of the themes of this book.

But failures of the legal imagination have consequences: they entail future failures. Law has practical effects, but, as I have argued elsewhere,[43] it has to a very considerable degree a life of its own. Law has functions related to the practical life, but it also operates at the level of culture, especially regarding the culture of the law-making elite, which has the power to make changes in the law. And a living culture is not examined by those who live it. Three typical features of law as culture are pertinent to the present failure of legal imagination, though none will be examined here in depth. First, codified legal rules are resistant to removal or replacement. Second, society and lawyers on a day-to-day basis can tolerate much inappropriate, even absurd, law. Third, legal rules, when available in an accessible form, can readily be borrowed often without an inquiry into their effectiveness.

With regard to the first feature, four of the five articles remain unchanged in the current French Code civil, though there has been subsequent relevant legislation. Article 1384 has undergone modification but mainly with regard to liability for persons for whom one is responsible, and for things under one's guard, though only in minor respects.

With regard to the second feature, we should perhaps talk less of a failure of the legal imagination than of an excess of the legal imagination. S. F. C. Milsom has well stated the issue for the history of English common law:

> The life of the common law has been in the abuse of its elementary ideas. If the rules of property give now what seems an unjust answer, try obligation; and equity has proved that from the materials of obligation you can counterfeit the phenomena of property. If the rules of contract give what now seems an unjust answer, try tort. Your counterfeit will look odd to one brought up on categories of Roman origin; but it will work. If the rules of one tort, say deceit, give what now seems an unjust answer, try another, try negligence. And so the legal world goes around.[44]

Much of Milsom's book, however, serves to demonstrate that though the counterfeits (as he calls them) work, they do not work well; and often indeed the counterfeits cannot be created at the right time. In France, articles 1382 and 1383 have always been interpreted as meaning that for one's own act, liability was based on fault that the victim-plaintiff had to prove. At first, liability for animals under article 1385 was based on fault that was presumed but, by the late nineteenth century, liability was strict and the owner or the person using the animal was liable unless he could show *force majeure*, the act of a third party or the fault of the victim. Interpretation of article 1386 has been reasonably stable: if a building collapsed,[45] the owner was not excused from liability just because he established that he was free from fault, for example, if he had charged a competent builder with the maintenance of the building or if it was humanly impossible to uncover the defect. The greatest variation in interpretation—desperate attempts to make some social sense of the provision—has occurred with regard to liability under article 1384 for things under one's guard. The range of interpretations has been enormous and will not be examined here, but it has swung from liability only if the keeper could be shown to be at fault, through liability if the thing was defective even if this was not known to the keeper, through strict liability that can be rebutted only if the keeper proves *cas fortuit, force majeure,* or a *cause étrangère* that cannot be imputed to him. It has even been held that when a thing in motion (such as an automobile) is under the control of the keeper, the keeper is liable under article 1384 for damage caused by the thing (even when it is not defective) unless he can show *cas fortuit, force majeure,* or *cause étrangère.* Under this interpretation, an automobile driver may be liable without fault under article 1384, ignoring articles 1382 and 1383.[46]

As to the third typical feature of law as culture—the easy transplanting of rules without an inquiry into their effectiveness—we can even make a random choice of examples. Thus, the Code civil for the lands of the king of Sardinia of 1837 gives the French provisions verbatim.[47] The Dominican Republic took over the Code civil in 1845 and translated it into Spanish only in 1884; the French provisions remain unaltered to the present day as articles 1382 to 1386 of the Codigo civil. The Italian Codice civile of 1865 simply translated the French articles as articles 1151 to 1155 but with the addition of article 1156 fixing liability *in solidum* if several persons were liable for the delict or quasi-delict.

I wish to clarify what I am claiming from the example of articles 1382 to 1386. I am not asserting that the French Code civil is nothing but a modernized version of Roman law—the articles themselves show that much was not received—nor am I claiming that the explanation of each article of the Code civil is to be found in Roman law. I am claiming that the articles of the Code civil (and I would extend this to all legislation, I think) can be fully understood with regard both to their form and their substance only if there is an inquiry into the cultural history behind them, and this inquiry must often span centuries and countries. I would also claim that the force of a reception, in this case of Roman law, is not to be judged simply by the acceptance of rules and structures, but by the extent of dependence on a foreign system.

Articles 1382 to 1386 do not stand alone in this regard. I should like to mention only a few other oddities in the French Code civil without, however, detailing their history. The first paragraph of article 1110 reads: "Error is not a cause of nullity of the agreement unless it falls upon the very substance of the thing that is its object." The meaning of "substance" is not further clarified and is the subject of much doubt. Scholars likewise dispute the obscure *error in substantia* in Roman law, its meaning, its acceptance by jurists, and its scope.[48] The model or models for the French drafters are not apparent nor is their intention. The article in the *projet,* article 8 of "Du Consentement," was accepted in the Conseil d'Etat without discussion on 11 Brumaire, an 12 (1803).[49] In explaining the reasons for the article in the Code civil before the Conseil d'Etat, Bigot-Préameneu, after mentioning "la substance même de la chose," said: "It is by following this rule that one must decide with Barbeyrac and Pothier that error in the motivation of the agreement is only a cause of nullity in the case where the accuracy of these motifs can be regarded as a condition on which it is clear that the parties intended their contract to depend."[50] And Mouricault said: "It is necessary that the error bore on the very substance of the thing or on the motive which determined the agreement," and he referred to Pothier twice in the immediately succeeding discussion.[51] Likewise, Favard, though he is less explicit regarding the meaning of "substance," cites Pothier in the connected context of the avoidance of contract because of fraud or force.[52] And subsequent commentators[53] and judges have considered Pothier's views to be very relevant in the interpretation of the article. But it must be doubtful if Pothier's formulation was immediately before the eyes of the *projet*'s drafters. Pothier wrote: "Error avoids the agreement, not only when it is as to the thing itself, but also when it is as to the quality of the thing that the parties had principally in mind, and which constitutes the substance of that thing."[54]

Pothier thus clarified the notion of substance, giving it a meaning it never had in Roman law. Although it can be assumed that the French codifiers intended to follow Pothier's view, the absence from article 1110 of anything resembling his formulation of the meaning of substance suggests that they had a simpler model before them, such as perhaps G. Argou, *Institution au droit françois:* "With respect to error, that only vitiates the contract of sale when it is met with in regard to the substance of the bought thing."[55] In the seventeenth and eighteenth centuries, throughout Europe there were many books like Argou's that one might term "Institutes of local law," and which in their arrangement and subject matter had their foundations in Justinian's *Institutes.* French books of the institutional type seem to have had a strong influence on the structure of the Code civil.[56] Thus, we have here another, but simpler, instance of a reception of Roman law in which the Roman rules were rejected. The compilers presumably followed the opinion of Pothier, which was not that of any Roman jurist. But Pothier retained the use of the Roman terminology, "substance," and some later writers, like those of the institutes, did not expound on the nature of error with regard to substance. Lack of clarity as to the meaning of the simple-sounding Code civil provision ensued. There were at least two failures of the legal imagination: of Pothier, in retaining the Roman terminology (at least when he was not much more explicit as to the extent that his theory diverged from the Roman), and of the codifiers, in failing to see the full ambiguity of the word *substance,* given its past history.

Another example could be the famous doctrine of "cause." Article 1131 reads "The obligation without cause, or on a false cause or on an illicit cause, can have no effect."

I do not need to say much here, since the story is well known. As is agreed, the modern idea does not appear in Roman law or in early French law.[57] *Causa* does, of course, make its appearance in the Roman legal sources, but its role in the field of obligations is ambiguous at best. *D.*2.14.7.4 tells us that when there is no *causa,* there is no obligation on account of agreement. And *D.*15.1.49.2 reads to the effect that whether a master is debtor to his slave or vice versa is to be computed *ex causa civili. Causa* appears more prominently as a basis for acquisition of ownership by delivery or prescription.[58]

In French law, the notion basically goes back to Domat (though there are canon-law forerunners),[59] who sets out a precise scheme, with contracts divided into types: bilateral, unilateral but for a consideration, and gifts.[60] Pothier was rather less explicit,[61] the discussions of the article in the Conseil d'Etat were not a little confused,[62] and article 1131 lacks all clarity on the meaning of *cause.* Not surprisingly, the early commentators called attention to the obscurity of article 1131.[63] More recent writers have concentrated their efforts not only on defining and refining the nature of cause but also on discovering its practical value and theoretical validity. Although it seems likely to retain some place in French law, cause, for many French legal writers and for more outsiders, is thought to have little practical value and to be theoretically incorrect and unnecessary.[64] At the very least, there would, I think, be general agreement that the practical importance of cause has often been grossly exaggerated and that theoretically its significance is difficult to explain. But, as the treatment in Domat and others shows, it obviously is another example in which Roman law rules were not accepted but formed the basis of discussion in French law until codification,[65] and to some extent influenced the later rules.

What I have been concerned with here is above all legal rules and their formation, not law in action, not how in lawsuits or administrative dealings the law can be manipulated for the benefit of particular individuals or groups. And it must be admitted by all, I think, that though law in action may differ from law in books, law in books has, at the very least, a very powerful effect on how law can be manipulated in practice.

It is extremely significant that both the legislators of Napoleonic France and powerful academic theorists of earlier ages were so little interested in the impact of the rules of delict on particular groups or in the social effect of the rules concerning the basis of liability. The rules were taken over, with no apparent interest in their effect, from ancient roots from which some parts have been chopped. Admittedly, the legislators at times used language such as "nothing belonging to someone else can injure another with impunity," but this seems intended to be a justification of a predetermined rule, not an argument toward a rule.

With liability for things under one's guard under article 1384, there is undoubtably social awareness among both professors and judges in their interpretations. But there is also a legal culture, as the cases indicate. An interpretation, whether of judges or professors, becomes established and may remain stable for years, despite a failure to achieve the social result sought by those who originally favored the interpretation.

There is thus an underlying theme in this chapter as in this book as a whole: the legal tradition, as an intellectual, cultural force, plays an extremely important but largely unrecognized role in law making—even in legislation and even at a time when a new beginning is stressed. Legal rules, even in legislation, have an intellectual, dogmatic history, not just a social, political, or economic history. Law is not an end in itself but can only be a means to an end. Yet often the end or ends to which the law is a means do not stand clearly before the eyes of the lawmakers.[66]

Moreover, as I argue more fully in Chapter 6, legal academics, too, are often so blinded by the tradition in which they work that they misconceive what they are doing. Thus, it is not particularly surprising to find modern French scholars claiming that certain applications of the *lex Aquilia* can be explained according to the modern theory of risk. Still it is off-putting to find the same scholars declaring that the Roman praetorian edict *de effusis vel deiectis* can only be explained by the theory of risk, by responsibility for the acts of things under one's guard (article 1384), while they show no awareness that liability for things under article 1384 derives from that edict.[67]

CHAPTER 6

JURISTS, JUDGES, CUSTOM, LEGISLATION

Water Rights

This chapter considers the interrelations of the four sources of law as they relate to one subject—water rights. I concentrate, in turn, on the impact of the legal tradition itself on the development of law, as well as the scarcity of legislation; juristic reasoning, especially in the absence of authority in the local system; fake authority; and the complex course of legal development, whose study often requires comparative legal history.

Aspects of water law are the subject matter, but the reader will understand that the subject is by way of example only. I concentrate on one aspect of law in various systems to show the richness of the material.

WATER AND NEIGHBORS' RIGHTS

The general issue for consideration is, To what extent, in what ways, and with what remedies, may an owner of land be restrained by his neighbor from using his land in a way that is otherwise lawful in order to avoid causing a financial loss or reducing a financial benefit to the neighbor? In this section, I look only at one issue concerned with water law: flow to a neighbor's land. The problem, of course, is that almost any agricultural, domestic, commercial, or industrial use of water by one landowner will have an impact on other landowners.

The starting point in the granting of legal remedies has a considerable impact on the unfolding of the law. Legislators, judges, and jurists alike are so blinkered by the legal tradition that it is hard for them to change the thrust of the law. In addition, in the absence of comprehensive, satisfactory legislation, subordinate lawmakers such as judges and jurists may well hold differing analyses of the law over a long period of time. It is not always true that one successful approach replaces another. The older approach may also continue. In reviewing the issue of water rights, I consider first Roman law, then French law.

Roman Law

The Roman approach to the water usage problem is, at first glance, deceptively simple. The Twelve Tables, the famous codification of Roman law around 451–450 B.C., gave a remedy *si aqua pluvia nocet* (if rainwater does damage; *Tab.* VII. 8a). Precision on the original scope of the remedy is not possible,[1] but this clause of the Twelve Tables set the scene for future development. By the first century B.C. at the latest, the praetor (the elected official in control of the courts) had issued a model *formula* for the action: "If it appear that the work was done on the estate at Capena, from which rainwater injures the estate of Aulus Agerius (plaintiff), on account of which Numerius Negidius (defendant)[2] ought to ward off that water from Aulus Agerius, if that matter is not restored at the discretion of the judge, etc."[3] This formulation of the issues remained the basis of the law even in the sixth-century reign of the emperor Justinian. The cause of action was available only when the injury was the result of "work done" (*opus factum*), it was restricted to injury in the country (*D.*39.3.1.17, 19–20; Ulpian, Edict 53), and the thrust of the action was for restitution of the status quo ante. Consistently with this, even in the republic of the first century B.C., jurists interpreted "if rainwater does damage" to mean "if it can cause damage" (*D.*40.7.21, Pomponius, Plautius 7; *D.*39.3.1, Ulpian, Edict 53). Pecuniary damages were awarded only for loss occurring after the beginning of the action.[4]

As was usual in Roman law, this brief formulation in the praetor's edict depended for its impact on interpretation by the jurists. Key elements of the remedy are not described. Still, the *formula* set the ground rules, and it must be emphasized at the outset that never again in the development of this area of the law did the Roman state intervene by legislation—though, as noted later, three interdicts of limited significance were issued by the praetor.

Only a few of the main elements of the water usage law need be considered here: the nature of the *opus factum,* which would give rise to the action; the impact of the formulation *si aqua pluvia nocet* (if rainwater does damage); and the harm that was treated as actionable.

The following discussion from Ulpian, a jurist active in the early third century A.D., is probably the most significant description of the requisite *opus factum:*

Quintus Mucius says this action is not available on account of that work which was done with a plow in order to cultivate a field. But Trebatius would make an exception not for work done with a plow to cultivate a field but only for plowing to secure a crop of grain. 4. But Mucius said that even ditches made to drain fields were made in order to cultivate a field, but they ought not to be made so as to cause the water to flow in one channel. Thus, one ought to make one's own field better in such a way that one does not make one's neighbor's worse. 5. But if he can plow and sow even without water channels, Mucius says he is liable for such, although he seems to have acted in order to cultivate the field: but if he could not sow unless he made the channels he is not liable. But Ofilius says it is lawful to make water channels for the purpose of cultivating a field if they are all made to run in the same direction. (*D.*39.3.1.3–5 ; Ulpian, Edict 43)

As in other areas of the law, the basic legal positions seem to have been fixed as early as the last century of the republic. Of the three jurists mentioned in the texts, Quintus Mucius was consul in 95 B.C., Trebatius was a protégé of Cicero, and Ofilius belonged to Julius Caesar's inner circle.[5] Even the differences of opinion between them expressed in the texts seem, surprisingly, never to have been resolved.

What is striking at first glance (and remains so even after reflection) is the extremely wide scope that the jurists gave to *opus factum*. Almost all works done by humans on land that would increase the flow of harmful water on another's land would give rise to an action. Although Quintus Mucius would allow an exception for plowing for agricultural purposes, Trebatius would restrict even this to the shallow plowing needed for grain crops, and apparently would not even make an exception for the rather deeper plowing needed for vines and olive trees (Columella, *De re rustica,* 2.2.24). Mucius would also allow an exception for making water channels only when they were needed for planting and sowing; but even then he would permit an action against a landowner who allowed the surplus water to run onto a neighbor's land in one channel. Ofilius, however, would seem to be rather more lenient toward a landowner's using water for irrigation, even though a neighbor suffered loss from the surplus.

Alfenus, another jurist of the first century B.C., is recorded as having expressed a clear view simply (*D.*39.3.24; Alfenus, Digest 4). A landowner could not be restrained from plowing as he wished, even if by placing his furrows in a different direction his neighbor would be uninjured. On the other hand, if he made water channels that did, or even might, injure a neighbor through the flow of water onto his land, he could be compelled to fill them in ($D.39.3.24.1-2$). Thus, plowing was unexceptional, but irrigation or drainage was not. Pupils of Servius, of whom Alfenus himself was one, are recorded as holding that the action to ward off rainwater could be brought when someone planted willows and as a result water overflowed and injured a neighbor's land ($D.39.3.1.6$; Ulpian, Edict 53). A slightly broader view of unexceptional activity may have been current in the first century A.D., when Labeo disallowed the action when the work was done for the gathering of fruit crops of any kind ($D.39.3.1.7$).

There is an element of ambiguity in the treatment of the subject by Ulpian, the jurist whose works were most used by the compilers of Justinian's *Digest.* At one point Ulpian writes that Sabinus and Cassius, both jurists of the first century A.D., held that man-made works all came within the scope of the action unless they were for the purpose of cultivating a field ($D.39.3.1.8$). Almost immediately afterward, however, Ulpian says that the same jurists wrote that the action would lie when man-made water channels caused injury by an increased or changed flow ($D.39.3.1.10$). Presumably these jurists, Labeo and Ulpian, intended that all nonagricultural work would give rise to the action where damage might result, and that some, but not all, agricultural work would be excluded from the scope of the action. Their view, then, would not represent a change from some views expressed in the preceding century.

As has been said, the action required *opus factum,* a man-made work that increased or changed the flow of water onto neighboring property in such a way that harm could result ($D.39.3.1.1$). Some jurists, however, were prepared to interpret this requirement in a manner giving a very wide scope to the action.

It is recorded in Namusa that if flowing water blocks its channel with dung and from its overflowing it damages a higher field, an action can be brought against the lower proprietor that he allow the channel to be cleared: because this action is available not only for constructions made by man, but in all circumstances which we do not want to occur. Labeo approves a view contrary to that of Namusa, for he declares that the very nature of the field may change of itself, and everyone ought to bear this with equanimity whether his position was made better or worse. Therefore, he says even if the condition of the ground is changed by an earthquake or great storm, no one can be compelled to allow the place to be restored to its former condition. But even in this case we admit the claim of fairness. ($D.39.3.2.6$; Paul, Edict 49)

Namusa would allow the action even when water flowing in a natural channel became blocked, but only to compel the proprietor to allow it to be cleared, not to force him to clear it. Labeo, however, would refuse the action to clear a natural channel, but, as we know from other texts (*D*.39.3.2.2, 5, 7), would grant the action to clear a man-made ditch or allow it to be cleared even when no record existed of when the ditch was made.[6] Alfenus took the rather more restrictive position that no action would lie when a man-made dam burst if no record existed of when it was constructed (*D*.39.3.2.5).

This discussion alerts us to a further point: the work in question need not have been done by the defendant proprietor. Thus, for example, Sabinus and Ulpian agree that if an owner is injured by a neighbor next-but-one, he can sue either the constructor or the intervening proprietor through whose land the water flowed (*D*.39.3.6; Ulpian, Edict 53).

One further comment on this *Digest* passage is appropriate. Immediately after citing Labeo for the proposition that the *actio aquae pluviae arcendae* would not lie if the condition of land changed without human intervention (for instance, if there were an earthquake or great storm), Paul says that even in this case he would admit the claim of fairness (*D*.39.3.2.6). What he means is not further explained, but by admitting the claim of fairness Paul hints that an action or an ad hoc remedy might be given sometimes even beyond the scope of the law.

As demonstrated by the texts so far examined on *opus factum,* the law remained remarkably static; the opinions expressed in the republic in the first century B.C. were valid in the classical law of the third-century Roman Empire as well as in sixth-century Byzantium when Justinian's *Digest* was published. Odder still, perhaps, is the inescapable conclusion that issues disputed in the first century B.C. were no nearer settlement in the sixth century A.D. But the most surprising fact of all is the wide interpretation given in this context of *opus factum.* Virtually any operation on land, except the most basic agricultural use, that increased the flow of rainwater onto a neighbor's land, or changed its course so that the water did damage, would give rise to the *actio aquae pluviae arcendae,* an action whose primary purpose was the restoration of the status quo ante. No encouragement whatever was given to the improving landlord. Alternatively, one might find the surprising fact to be the very opposite: some agricultural uses of land would not give rise to the action even if a neighbor suffered loss as a result. Certainly, if the law was that a neighbor had a right to an action for loss caused by water flowing onto his land because of *opus factum,* there was no logical reason for refusing the action where the work done was plowing for the cultivation of grain while granting it on account of other plowing, or for refusing the action where the work done was making channels for the purpose of planting while granting it where the channels were for irrigation.

Law frequently develops with a logic of its own that seems independent of social and economic needs, and so it was in regard to yet another aspect of the availability of this action. The Twelve Tables' wording provided legal redress "*si aqua pluvia nocet*" (if rainwater does damage), and all subsequent juristic attention for wrongful damage by water in the country focused on this provision. But water actually injured only when it increased or flowed in a different channel, not when it diminished or disappeared. Hence, the *actio aquae pluviae arcendae* did not apply when your neighbor cut off or reduced your water supply:

> *D.*39.3.1.11. The same jurists [Sabinus and Cassius] say that everyone has the right to retain rainwater on his own land or to channel surface water from his neighbor's onto his own, provided no work is done on another's land (for no one is prohibited from benefiting himself provided he does not injure another) and no one is liable on this account. 12. Then Marcellus writes that no action, not even the action for fraud, can be brought against one who, while digging on his own land, diverts the stream of his neighbor. And certainly the latter ought not to have an action[7] if he acted not with the intention of injuring his neighbor but to improve his land. . . .

> *D.*39.3.12.21. But just as work done in such a way that rainwater does one damage gives rise to this action, so likewise the opposite question arises whether one can bring the action for warding off rainwater if the neighbor does work that prevents water which otherwise, flowing onto my land, would be beneficial, from conferring this benefit. Ofilius and Labeo think the action cannot be brought even if it be in my interest that the water comes to me: for this action lies if rainwater damages, not if it fails to confer a benefit.

So, for reducing a neighbor's water supply the *actio aquae pluviae arcendae* did not lie, nor did any other action except perhaps the action for fraud (*actio de dolo*) when one acted deliberately to injure one's neighbor and not to benefit oneself. This law dated from the earliest times and remained the law in the age of Justinian. Just as the scope of the action for increasing the flow of water seems extraordinarily wide, that for diminishing the flow seems extraordinarily narrow. And not only is it obvious that a water supply is needed, but we know from numerous texts on the servitude of drawing water or of aqueduct that water from a neighbor's land was frequently wanted.[8] No satisfactory explanation for this phenomenon can be drawn from economic or social conditions. An explanation must be sought within the law itself.[9] The wording of the Twelve Tables and the name of the action were directed to warding off rainwater, and governments were so little interested in private law that the Roman state never again intervened to provide a further remedy (except for the interdicts still to be discussed).[10] And jurists were so blinkered by their legal culture that they never sought to interpret the Twelve Tables' clause to include damage caused by deprivation of water.

Similarly, only legal tradition can explain why the law did not change to allow the judge in some circumstances to award compensation to the injured neighbor, rather than to order the defendant to destroy or permit to be destroyed the offending works. Obviously, it would frequently happen that potential gain to the maker of the work would be greater than loss to the neighbor, yet the latter would not agree to any deal. In other contexts judges were given discretion in the way the decision was formulated.[11] In still others, they were able to issue a money judgment for a sum equal to what the defendant ought to give or do in accordance with good faith.[12]

One related area in which the law and legal terminology are not clear should be addressed. A number of texts use the terminology of servitudes. Thus, Paul states, "in short there are three ways by which lower land is under a servitude to higher: by an agreed regulation, by the nature of the place and by a long period of time" (D.39.3.2; Paul, Edict 49). But the classical Roman legal concept of servitude was properly applicable only to one of the three—namely, where the neighbors reach agreement that an increased flow from the dominant land will be accepted by the servient, and the servitude is then created in proper legal form. Thus, Paul's first manner of creating a servitude presents no problems for us. But under the classical scheme no legal servitude really existed by the "nature of the place," although the basic outline of Paul's thought is plain. By the very nature of things, without human intervention, some water flows from one person's land to another and it is reasonable that the owner of the land onto which the water flows is bound to accept it, and not bar its progress in such a way that the water injures the higher neighbor.[13] The classical Roman approach, though, seems to have had at least one legal consequence: if there was a man-made construction and it was removed, and the water consequently flowed in its natural channel more vigorously, then the owner receiving the water had no right to an action (*D*.39.3.1.22; Ulpian, Edict 53).

Moreover, in Roman law there was no legal servitude by the lapse of a long period of time after the *lex Scribonia* (of around 50 B.C.) abolished the usucapion of servitude.[14] It is precisely here, however, that difficulties arise, because the jurists in the later classical period did give some effect to the passage of time. Thus Ulpian wrote: "If no servitude is found to have been imposed, the person who made use of a 'servitude' for a long time, and did so not by force or by grant at will [*precarium*] nor stealthily, seems to have acquired a servitude by long custom just as if it had been lawfully imposed."[15]

The limits of Ulpian's notion are by no means clear. What is involved, however, is not really a servitude acquired by prescription. Acquisition by prescription in classical law was by *usucapio* and required physical control begun in good faith by someone holding with the intention of being owner. For the requirement of good faith (*bona fides*) Ulpian substituted "not by force or by grant at will or stealthily," a formulation found in various other contexts. Moreover, in classical law the period of *usucapio* was two years for land and one year for movables, and both Paul and Ulpian clearly have in mind a much longer, if not indefinite, period of time, which they express by the term *vetustas*. The development of the notion of *vetustas* here is unclear.[16] Yet indications are that in late classical law, as Ulpian's words suggest, very long use created a presumption of previous grant, provided the use was not by force, stealth, or *precarium*. By the time of Justinian, the acquisition of servitude was wholly under the regime of *longi temporis praescriptio:* the right was acquired by use in ten years if the owner of the servient land was present in the region, in twenty if he was not.

This question of a servitude right by *vetustas* might arise in various contexts. Perhaps the most important was that of the landowner who suffered the increased water flow for some long time without protest but then, wishing to use his land differently, required a reduced flow; because of *vetustas*, however, he might find that his right to have the flow reduced was blocked. For if a servitude was found, however it was created, the important opinion of Ofilius, approved by Paul, would apparently apply: when land was under such a servitude, its owner lost the right to the *actio aquae pluviae arcendae* "so long as the damage is not excessive" (*D*.39.3.2.10; Paul, Edict 49). Reasonableness seems to have been the test.

So far we have been concerned only with private law. The Roman jurists, in fact, drew a remarkably sharp distinction between private law and public law, and dealt almost exclusively with the former,[17] by which they meant the interaction between one individual and another. In this instance consideration of a public-law dimension turns out to be illuminating. The Romans treated some rivers as public, and the praetor issued an interdict concerning these: "Do not do anything in a public river or on its bank, do not put anything into a public river or onto its bank, by which its position or its course for shipping becomes worse" (D.43.12.1; Ulpian, Edict 68). What counted as a public river was not entirely settled, but for Cassius, Celsus, and Ulpian it was a river that flowed all year round (D.43.12.1.3). Because this edict dealt only with interference with navigation, its effects were restricted to navigable rivers (D.43.12.1.12) or, in the view of Labeo, to public rivers that visibly contributed to making navigable the river into which they flowed. For such public (or navigable) rivers, then, the right of landowners to use the water was restricted in the public interest. But this restriction would also benefit their neighbor. The landowner could not divert the public river or reduce its flow considerably. Thus, for such rivers the neighbor would in practice have equal right to a reasonable use.

Much more to our purpose would seem to be the second interdict. Ulpian gives its wording: "The praetor says: 'I forbid anything to be done in a public river or on its bank or anything to be put into the river whereby the water flows in a different manner than it flowed in the previous summer.'"[18]

This interdict applied to any public river, including those that were not navigable (D.43.13.1.2). Ulpian explains its purpose in a text in which the manuscript reading is insecure: "The praetor provided by this interdict that rivers do not dry up [exarescant] by channels that are not allowed or that a changed river bed does not cause some injury to neighbors" (D.43.13.1.1). *Exarescant* is the reading of the inferior manuscripts,[19] and it seems to be generally preferred. But the prime manuscript, the Florentine, actually reads the questionable word as *excrescent,* "that rivers do not increase in volume." If that were accepted as the proper reading, this part of the provision would be similar to the law for the *actio aquae pluviae arcendae.* In either case, however, the interdict seems to have been given a very limited scope, for Ulpian explains that it was not applicable where a neighbor changed the volume of the water's flow alone, but only where a neighbor changed the manner and direction of the current (D.43.13.1.3; Ulpian, Edict 68). Thus, provided the neighbor did not use up all of the water in the public river, he could use and diminish the supply, as long as he did not change the manner of the water's flow. There was no attempt to strike a balance in the amount of use of water by, or of injury to, neighboring proprietors.[20] This interdict contained only a prohibition, but it was closely associated with another interdict ordering restitution where something had already been done that changed the water's flow (*D*.43.13.1.12f.13; Ulpian, Edict 68).

These last two interdicts thus did have an impact on the water rights of neighboring proprietors. What seems surprising, however, is the lack of interest shown in them in Justinian's *Digest,* and hence apparently by the classical jurists. There is none of that detailed and subtle discussion that we find for the *actio aquae pluviae arcendae*. The relevant *Digest* title is very short and consists of only one text, by Ulpian in thirteen fragments, and he refers only once to another jurist, Labeo (*D*.43.13.1.13). The title on the *actio aquae pluviae arcendae* is much larger, with twenty-six texts. The thrust, then, was always on that action. The neglect of the interdicts is most easily explained on the basis of the sharpness of the distinction between public and private law and the jurists' emphasis on the latter.[21] At any rate, this juristic focus on the *actio aquae pluviae arcendae* had a great impact on subsequent discussion in French law.

French Law

Now I turn to the law as it was in France at the time of the promulgation of the Code civil in 1804. My aim will be to explain the law as it was then after centuries of development by local customs and the Reception of Roman law, to estimate the impact of the Justinianian formulations, and finally to relate the Code civil's provisions to preceding French law, to the draft codes of Cambacérès, and to the discussion of, and debates on, the draft codes.

The most striking thing about the relevant French law on the eve of codification must be how little it had developed since the time of Justinian. Our starting point for warding off rainwater should be Robert Pothier (1699–1772),[22] whose works have long been recognized as a source of inspiration for the draftsmen of the Code civil. In his *Traité du contrat de société,* Pothier claimed that the *actio aquae pluviae arcendae*—he kept the Latin name—lay to the proprietor or possessor of a lower-lying field against his neighbor in a higher field when the latter, as a result of some work done on his land, collected water that fell onto the lower field in greater quantity and with greater rapidity than it naturally would have fallen, and so caused the proprietor of the lower field some loss. But if the water descended naturally onto the lower land there was no action, for it was not the higher proprietor but the nature of the land that caused the fall. Nor could the lower landholder complain on account of furrows that the superior landholder made when the furrows were only the ordinary furrows necessary for the plowing of the field. The superior landholder could not make the furrows deeper or more on a slope than was necessary, however, even if by doing so he would improve his land; he could not improve his own land to the detriment of his neighbor. Pothier then quoted Quintus Mucius: "Thus, one ought to make one's own field better in such a way that one does not make one's neighbor's worse." In the following article, Pothier claimed that, vice versa, the holder of the higher ground had an action against the lower proprietor who, by building a dam, caused the water to flood the higher ground. The plaintiff brought the action, said Pothier, for the destruction of the work that caused his loss: the destruction was to be at the cost of the defendant if the work was done by his order or by that of someone from whom he inherited; otherwise the defendant only had to allow the destruction at the cost of the plaintiff.[23]

Thus, all the law Pothier gave was to be found in the *Digest* title on the *actio aquae pluviae arcendae* and, indeed, he gave references to no other sources. He made no mention, however, of the creation of a servitude right. Pothier also said nothing about the Roman rule that held that there was no remedy if a proprietor by work on his land caused an injurious reduction of water to his neighbor. Nor did he say anything akin to the content of the Roman interdicts.

The case of Jean Domat is different. As already noted, in *Les Loix civiles dans leur ordre naturel* he did not deal with the water rights of neighboring proprietors. But Domat was inclined to draw a sharp distinction between private law and public law,[24] and in his *Le Droit public,* which is a continuation of his work on civil law, the following passage occurs:

> The use of rivers being public, no one can make any change that is harmful to that use. Thus, one cannot make the current of the water slower or faster, if this change injures the public or individuals. Thus, one who has property divided by a watercourse or who possesses two distinct properties on the two banks cannot for his use make a bridge which joins his two properties. Likewise, although one can divert water from a stream or a river to water one's meadows or other land, or for mills or other uses, he must use that freedom in such a way that he does no harm either to the navigation in the river whose water he diverts, or in another that is made navi-

gable by the water of the first, or to some other public use, or to neighbors who have similar need and a like right. And if there is not enough water for all, or if the use that some make of it is injurious to others, all will be provided for, according to need, by the officers who have that responsibility.[25]

Thus, in general, Domat incorporated the law found in the Roman interdicts and, indeed, all his references were to the relevant *Digest* texts. Two innovations occurred at the end of the passage, however. As we have seen, a Roman remedy was not available against a proprietor who simply reduced the volume of water to a neighbor, thus causing him injury. The two Roman texts that Domat cited as authority for his whole sentence were not relevant for this point. Further, Domat cited no authority—such did exist, but not in Roman law—for the other important innovation: when there was not enough water for the use of all, officers would be charged with deciding the relative needs and uses.

The Roman failure to rationalize and reconcile the sources on water rights thus resulted in a split tradition in French juristic writing. The principal source of the innovation in French law was Colbert's Ordonnances des eaux et forets of April 1669, written for Louis XIV. Title 27, article 42 forbade any individual to erect a mill or other structure, or to throw anything that might cause loss in navigable rivers. The penalty was a fine.[26] Article 44 of that title forbade anyone to divert the water of navigable rivers, to lessen their flow, or to alter their course under penalty of having to restore matters to the way they were before. The law was thus not quite that set out by Domat, primarily in its restriction of application to navigable rivers rather than all those whose use was public. Domat's inclusion of all public rivers, of course, was influenced by the concepts of Roman law.

Domat's "river whose use is public" was, of course, a wider notion than "navigable river" and was, indeed, imprecise. Case law was to bring precision to the notion of "river whose use is public," producing a solution that still exists but can hardly be justified on social or economic terms. A person on whose land a spring arises could use it as he willed, even diverting it or using it up completely, according to cases from different parts of France, of 13 August 1644, of September 1698, and of 22 August 1766, set out by P. A. Merlin in his celebrated *Répertoire de jurisprudence*.[27] In the last case, the Parlement of Paris judged that the baron de Vitry had the right to change the course of springs that were on his land despite the immemorial possession of enjoyment that the curé of Chide had for watering a meadow of his cure. In the case of all other rivers that passed through or bordered a person's land, the rule was that the landowner could not divert them but could use them for irrigation.[28]

The law that was thus developing is well set out in the three draft codes that were prepared by Cambacérès for the French revolutionary assemblies but never accepted. It is enough for our purposes to quote the third, of 1796.

> 447. Lower-lying places are subject to the higher places, to receive the water that flows by itself from them; to suffer all the disadvantages that the position of the higher ground can cause them naturally and without the work of man.

> 448. The owner of the higher land cannot divert the course of water whose spring is not in his property.
>
> He is not free to increase the rapidity of flowing water, nor to hold it back in such a way that it can cause damage by its sudden release.
>
> He can use it as he judges appropriate, for the irrigation of his property, as it passes through.[29]

Before codification France was a land of very many different legal systems. The main legal divide in the nation was between the southerly *pays de droit écrit*, where by custom Roman law was subsidiary law, and very potent; and the northerly *pays de droit coutumier*, where Roman law was either not so directly law or not so influential, or both. On this point of water law, however, the difference between the regimes seems not to have been great.

The Conseil d'Etat's definitive redaction of the Code civil was presented on 5 January 1804:

> 633. Lower-lying lands are subjected to those which are higher to receive the water that flows naturally therefrom, to which the hand of man has not contributed.
>
> The lower owner cannot erect a dam that hinders this running off.
>
> The higher owner can do nothing that aggravates the servitude of the lower land.[30]

This article corresponded exactly to article 636 of the previous draft, which came before the Conseil d'Etat on 27 October 1803 and was accepted without discussion.[31] It had very much the thrust of the Roman *actio aquae pluviae arcendae*. The servient land was required to receive naturally flowing water from the dominant land, and the proprietor had a remedy only if the hand of man contributed to the flow. The stress in the article was on the burden on the lower-lying land, and the second sentence showed that the owner of the lower-lying land could not create an obstruction that caused flooding on the higher ground. The law was that of Rome, but its formulation corresponded to that of Pothier and Gabriel Argou. Even the specificity of *digue* (dam), for the obstruction on the lower land, was the wording of Pothier.[32]

The article, however, did not seem to free the superior owner from liability where the damage by water was caused to his neighbor as a result of plowing. This seems intentional and corresponds to subsequent interpretation. The substance of the article was, as noted already, adopted without discussion in the Conseil d'Etat on 27 October 1803, and none of the three *projets* of Cambacérès showed any sign of the Roman exception for plowing; nor did the work of Argou.[33] Earlier, as we have seen, Pothier had allowed the exception for plowing, but to a very limited extent: only when the furrows were ordinary furrows and were necessary for the plowing of the land; and the furrows could not be deeper or more sloping than was necessary, even when to make them so would have improved the superior land. Moreover, before the Code civil there was no reference to the exception in the case law which was cited by Merlin.[34]

The next five articles of the definitive redaction should be considered together.

> 634. He who has a spring in his lands can use it as he wishes, except for the right that the owner of lower-lying land might have acquired by grant or prescription.
>
> 635. Prescription in this case can be acquired only by uninterrupted enjoyment for a period of thirty years, counting from the moment when the owner of the lower land made and completed obvious works intended to facilitate the fall and course of the water on his property.
>
> 636. The owner of the spring cannot change its course when it furnishes to the inhabitants of a commune, village, or hamlet the water that is necessary to them: but if the inhabitants have not acquired or prescribed the use, the owner can claim an indemnity that is fixed by experts.
>
> 637. He whose property borders on running water, other than that which is declared a dependency of the public domain by article 538, . . . can use it as it passes for the irrigation of his properties.
> He who had property through which water passes may similarly use it during the time it passes through, but on the condition of restoring it, when it leaves his land, to its ordinary channel.

638. If a dispute arises between owners to whom this water could be useful, the courts, in declaring their judgment, must reconcile the interest of agriculture with the respect due to ownership; and, in every case, particular and local regulations on the channel and use of water must be observed.[35]

The superior landowner could use the water from a spring on his land at his pleasure, but he could not change its course when the owner of the lower land had acquired the right to use it by grant or by prescription. Prescription required uninterrupted use for thirty years from the time the lower proprietor had completed obvious (*apparents*) works that facilitated the coming of the water onto his property. The right of the lower proprietor to receive the flow of water was thus a real servitude, and the period of prescription ran not from the time he began to enjoy the improved flow but from the time he finished a construction intended to use the improvement in the flow.

This acquisition of a servitude by prescription seems to have been an innovation in French law. It was forbidden by the Coutume de Paris (article 186) and by the Coutume d'Orléans (article 225). It did not appear in Pothier, or in the projets of Cambacérès, or even in the draft laid before the Conseil d'Etat on 27 October 1803. Previous decisions in French courts had held that long use of water flowing from a spring on a neighbor's land did not hinder the neighbor from cutting off the flow.[36] Articles 637 to 639 of the draft (which correspond to articles 634 to 636 of the definitive redaction) read simply:

637. He who has a spring on his land can use it as he wishes.

638. He whose property borders running water, other than that which is declared a dependency of the public domain by article 531, can use it as it passes for the irrigation of his properties.
    He who has property through which water passes can similarly, during the time it passes through, use it as he wishes, but on the condition of restoring it when it leaves his property to its ordinary channel.

639. If a dispute arises between owners to whom this water could be useful, the courts, in declaring their judgments, must reconcile the interest of agriculture with the respect due to ownership; and, in every case, particular and local regulations on the channel and use of water must be observed.

Articles 637 to 639 of the draft gave rise to extensive debate. In front of the Conseil d'Etat, Berlier, accepting the principle in article 637 of the draft, suggested as an addition: "but without prejudice to the rights or the owner of the lower property when it has received the water from that spring for a period sufficient for the prescription of use." This gave rise to the expression of various opinions: that prescription of water use was a logical impossibility (Treilhard); that such a servitude existed in France in neither the *pays de droit écrit* nor the *pays de droit coutumier* (Tronchet); that taking away a habitual water supply from lower land could greatly diminish its value; and that villages depended at times for their water on a supply from land belonging to a single owner (Regnard). Maleville seemed to favor the wording of the article, but he took it to mean that time alone did not diminish the rights of an owner to a spring except where the lower proprietor had works made for the use of the water for thirty years. Case law, he said, had softened the rigor of this approach and this softening was, he said, now confirmed by article 639. He expressed strong approval of that article in a subject matter where, he argued, it was dangerous to lay down principles that were too abstract. He added that "equity, the public interest, and the very destination of the water required that lower lands not be arbitrarily deprived: Providence created for the use of all that element which is necessary to all." Tronchet was impressed by the argument from equity, but insisted that Maleville was departing from established legal principle and that neither in the *pays de droit coutumier* nor in the *pays de droit écrit* could one acquire by prescription a servitude to have water flowing on to one's land. He proposed in effect that prescription of servitude be based on the notion of a grant that had been lost and replaced by possession, and hence prescription would be hard to prove except where there were "ouvrages extérieurs." After much further discussion, a new draft resulted, which became articles 634 to 636 of the definitive redaction.[37]

The resulting articles contained at least three different bases for acquiring the right to have water flow onto land. First, an individual could acquire the right by positive prescription. Second, a community could acquire the right on the basis of public utility. Third, by article 638, when a dispute arose between owners to whom the water was useful, the tribunals had discretion—that is, they could look to the equity of the situation. This last was reminiscent of the opinion expressed by the Roman jurist, Paul (*D*.39.3.2.6), as well as that of the *ordonnances* of August 1669. Moreover, the words of Regnaud show that he was thinking of competing agricultural uses.[38] In addition, the only express usage granted to the proprietor was for irrigation, and the remainder of the water was to be returned to its original channel.

What was needed for the acquisition of the servitude right must be further explicated. The rule in article 635 of the definitive redaction did not correspond to the proposal of Berlier. Article 635 of the definitive redaction required positive prescription;[39] Berlier's proposal, merely negative prescription. For Berlier it was enough that the lower-lying land had received the water for the required period, but article 635 demanded that there be works on the lower land for the required period and that they be obvious, hence knowable, to the owner of the higher land. This distinction between negative and positive prescription could not exist in practice for the Roman *actio aquae pluviae arcendae*. But the distinction was basic in the general context of Roman servitude. Thus, in general an urban praedial servitude was extinguished only by positive prescription, whereas a rustic praedial servitude could be extinguished by negative prescription.[40]

On the subject of any servitude right, it should be reemphasized that what was under discussion was foreign to Roman law. The right under the French Code was the right to receive flowing water, whereas any Roman servitude right with regard to the *actio aquae pluviae arcendae* was the right to discharge flowing water in greater volume or in a more injurious way onto a neighbor's land.

Thus, the Roman perspective dominated French law on this part of the law of property until the making of the Code civil.[41] In some ways the Code civil marks a new beginning, but there may even be fresh reminiscences of Roman law in the resurgence of servitude rights. What cannot be overemphasized, though, for an understanding of the way law develops, is that the innovations on servitude came at the last possible moment for their appearance in the Code civil, as a result of the debate in the Conseil d'Etat on 27 October 1803. Moreover, when previous drafts of the Code civil were sent to the parlements and other bodies, there was virtually no comment on this part of property law.[42] In other words, the innovations almost did not occur in the Code civil. Indeed, given this history, we can be sure that, in the absence of comprehensive legislation on private law such as the Code civil was, there would have been no change in riparian rights for some time to come.

JURISTIC APPROACHES

The examples in Chapters 2 and 3 showed how jurists build up law by their reasoning on—so far as we know—theoretical issues. Now I want to consider an actual argument in court by a famous jurist who was also a skilled and successful practitioner. The example, from seventeenth-century Scotland, is not atypical. It is the pleading of Sir George Mackenzie (1636–91) before the Supreme Court of Scotland for the defender Haining, which also quotes the arguments for the pursuers, the fishers upon Tweed.[43] Advocates' speeches of the period are much fuller than are the reports of the judicial decisions. In Mackenzie's collected works this is the first pleading on Scots law.

Scots private law in the seventeenth century was custom or consuetude when there was not (as there often was not) a statute.[44] Judicial decision was also very pertinent. Stair, in the second edition of his *Institutions of the Law of Scotland* (1.1.16), seems in fact to regard a number of decisions as forming a custom.[45] Thus, Scots law of the time can properly be regarded as a mature system of law which was largely customary. For both Stair and Mackenzie, in the absence of local custom, canon law and especially civil law carried great weight because of their high quality.[46]

Mackenzie's pleading, "For Haining against the Fishers upon Tweed," runs as follows:

> How far a Man may use his own, tho' to the Prejudice of his Neighbours?
>
> Haining being prejudged by a Lake which overflow'd his Ground, and which by its Nearness to his House, did, as is ordinary for standing Waters, impair very much the Health of his Family: He did therefore open the said Lake, whose Waters being received by *Whittater,* did at last run with *Whittater* into *Tweed.* The Fishers upon that River, pretending that the Water which came from that Lake did kill their Salmond [*sic*], and occasion their leaving the River, do crave that *Haining* may be ordain'd to close up that Passage. This being the State of the Case, it was alleged for *Haining.*
>
> That since Men had receded from that first Community, which seem'd to be establish'd amongst them by Nature, the Law made it its great Task, to secure every Man in the free and absolute Exercise of his Property, and did allow him to use his own as he thought fit, and whatever did lessen this Power and Liberty, is by the common Law term'd a Servitude, or Slavery; nor can a Servitude be imposed upon a Man without his own Consent. And suitably to this Principle, every Man may raise his own House as high as he pleases, tho' he should thereby obscure the Lights of his Neighbour's House: Or if I should abstract from my Neighbour's Ponds, that Water which formerly run into them from my Lands, the Law doth not think him prejudged, nor me obliged to prefer his Conveniency to my own Inclinations, as is clear by *1.26.ff de damno infect.* For as that Law very well observes, he is not prejudged who loses a Benefit, which flow'd from him who was no Way ty'd to bestow it, *1.26.ff. de dam. infect.* Proculus *ait, Cum*

quis jure quid in suo faceret quamvis promisisset damni infecti vicino, non tamen eum teneri ea stipulatione: Veluti si juxta mea aedificia habeas aedificia eaque jure tuo altius tollas, aut si in vicino tuo agro cuniculo, vel fossa aquam meam avoces. Quamvis enim & hic aquam mihi abducas, & illic luminibus officias, tamen ex ea stipulatione actionem mihi non competere: scil. *quia non debeat videri is damnum facere, qui eo veluti lucro quo adhuc utebatur, prohibetur: Multumque interesse utrum damnum quis faciat, an lucro, quod adhuc faciebat, uti prohibeatur.* And if I dig a Well in my own House, which may cut off those Passages whereby Water was conveyed to my Neighbour's Well, one of the greatest Lawyers has upon this Case resolved, that my Neighbour will not prevail against me; *For,* saith he, *no Man can be said to be wrong'd by what I do upon my own Ground, for in this I use my own Right,* 1.24. §12. *ff eod. In domo mea puteum aperio quo aperto venae putei tui praecisae sunt, an tenear?* Ait Trebatius, *Me non teneri damni infecti, neque enim existimari operis mei vitio damnum tibi dari, in ea re, in qua jure meo usus sum:* Where the Gloss observes, that *in suo quod quisque fecerit, in damnum vicini id non animo nocendi facere presumitur.* And if by a Wall or Fence upon my Land, the Water was kept from overflowing my Neighbour's Land, I may throw down my own Fence, tho' my Neighbour's Land be thereby overflowed, *l. 21. ff. de aqua pluvia.* And therefore, seeing the Ground doth belong to *Haining,* and that the Fishers of *Tweed* have no Servitude upon him, he may use his own as he pleases, especially seeing he doth not immediately send his Water into *Tweed,* but into another Rivulet, which carries it very far before it doth disgorge there. So that if the Fishers upon *Tweed* did prevail against *Haining,* they might likewise prevail against all from whose Ground any Moss-water runs into *Tweed,* tho' at Fifty Miles Distance; and they may forbid all the Towns from which any Water runs into *Tweed,* to throw in any Excrements, or any Water employ'd in Dying, lest it prejudge their Salmon-fishing; whereas, *Alteri prodesse, ad liberalitatem, non ad justitiam pertinent* [sic].

It is (My Lords) referr'd to your Consideration, that public Rivers have been very wisely by Providence, spread up and down the World, to be easie, and natural Vehicles for conveying away to the Sea, (that great Receptacle of all Things that are unnecessary) Excrements, and other noxious Things, which would otherwise have very much prejudged Mankind; and that they may the better perform this Office, Providence has bestow'd upon Rivers a purifying and cleansing Quality, so that after a little Time, and a very short Course, all that is thrown in there, doth happily lose their noxious Nature, which is wash'd off by the Streams by which they are carried.

Rivers are Nature's High-ways by Water, and we may as well forbid to carry any Thing that smells ill, upon our High-ways by Land, as we may forbid to throw in stinking Waters into our Rivers. The proper Use of

Rivers is, that they should be portable, and fit for Navigation, or for trans-
porting Things from one Place into another, and Salmon-fishing is but an
accidental Casuality, and therefore the only Interdicts or Prohibitions pro-
pon'd by the Law, relating to public Rivers are, *Ne quid in flumine ripave
ejus fiat, quo pejus navigetur, tit. 12 lib. 53.*[47] and, *ut in flumine publico nav-
igare liceat, tit. 14. ff. eod. lib.* But in Rivers that are not navigable, the Law
has forbidden nothing, but that their Course and natural Current be not
alter'd, *Ne quid in flumine publico fiat, quo aliter fluat aqua, atque uti pri-
ore estate fluxit, tit. 13. ibidem.* So that since the Law doth not forbid the
throwing in any Thing into public Rivers, it doth allow it; for it is free for
every Man to do what the Law hath not prohibited: And if upon such
capricious Suggestions as these, Men were to be restrain'd from using their
own, no Man should ever adventure to drain his Land, to open Coal-sinks,
or Lead-mines, or to seek out any Minerals whatsoever, whose Waters are
of all other the most pestilentious, because after he had bestow'd a great
deal of Expence, he might be forc'd to desist, for satisfying the Jealousy,
or Imagination of melancholy or avaritious Neighbours. And if this Pursuit find a favourable Hearing, Malice and Envy will make use of it, as a
fair Occasion whereby to disturb all successful and thriving Undertakers.
But your Lordships may see, that the World, both learn'd and unlearn'd,
have hitherto believ'd, that such a Pursuit as this would not be sustain'd, in
that tho' Interest and Malice did prompt Men to such Pursuits, yet no one
such as this has ever been intended, for ought I could ever read, save once
at *Grenoble,* where an Advocate did pursue a Smith to transport his Forge
from the chief Street, because it did by its Noise disturb not only him, but
the People who frequented that Street; from which Pursuit the Smith was
absolved, as *Expilly* observes in his Pleading.

Yet, my Lords, the Fishers upon *Tweed* want not some apparent Reasons
which give Colour to the Pursuit; and it is urg'd for them, "That no Man
is so Master of his own, but that the Commonwealth has still an Interest
with him in it; and Law being invented to protect the Interest of Societies,
as well as to secure the Property of private Persons; Therefore tho' every
private Man inclines to satisfy his own Humour and Advantage, in the Use
of what is his own; yet it is the Interest of the Commonwealth, that he do
not abuse his own Property; and therefore it is, that the Law doth interdict
Prodigals; nor will the Law suffer that a Man use his own *in emulationem
alterius, 1.3. ff. de oper. pub.* and a Man is said to do any Thing *in emulationem alterius,* when others lose more by what is done, than the Proprietar can gain: As in this Case, tho' *quilibet potest facere in suo,* yet *non potest
immittere in alienum,* which is their Case; and all the Arguments brought
for *Haining* do not meet, seeing they only prove, that a Man may use what
is his own as he pleases, *ubi nihil immittit in alienum;* as is clear by the In-

stances given, of throwing down his own Wall, or the digging up a Well in his own Land, which differs very much from our Case, wherein *Haining* doth pour in his poysonous Water into the River of *Tweed*.

That Men are restrain'd for the Good of the Commonwealth in the Use of their own Property, is very clear from many Instances in our Law, as Men are discharg'd by Acts of Parliament to burn Moors, to kill Smolts; the Way and Manner of Fishing upon *Lochleven* is prescribed to the Heritors by Act of Parliament, and Men are forbidden to steep Lint by public Acts likewise. Likeas, the common Law will not suffer Men so to use Water running thro' their own Land, as that they may thereby prejudge Mills belonging to their Neighbours, which use to go by that Water: and whatever may be alleged in favour of any Innovation in running Waters; yet Lakes being appointed by Nature, seem to have from Nature a fix'd Being; nor should they be open'd to the Prejudice of others, contrary to their Nature.

These Objections may (my Lords) be thus satisfied. To the First, it is answered, That the only Two Restrictions put upon Men in the free Exercise of their own, are, *ne in alterius emulationem fiat, vel materiam seditionis praebeat,* as is clear by the foresaid *1.3. ff. de oper. pub.* neither of which can be subsumed in this Case. And when the Law considers what is done *in emulationem alterius,* it acknowledges, *illud non factum esse in emulationem alterius, quod factum est principaliter ut agenti profit, et non ut alteri noceat, 1. fluminum § fin. ff. de dam. infect.* and the Gloss formerly cited upon that Law determines, that *Animus nocendi* is not presum'd, if any other Cause can be assigned: And in this Case, *Haining* can ascribe his opening this Lake to the Prejudice it did to his Land, and to his Health; whereas it cannot be alleged, that he ever express'd any Malice against the Fishers upon *Tweed,* many of whom are his own Relations. As to the Instances given, wherein the Law doth restrict the free Use of Property, the Principle is not deny'd but it is misapply'd. For the Law only bounds the Proprietar's Power in some Cases, wherein his Loss may be otherwise supply'd; as in Moor-burn, and killing of Smolts at such a Season of the Year, and in steeping Lint in running Waters, which may be as commodiously done in standing Pools; but these Pursuers crave this Lake to be stopt at all Times. Nor is there an apparent Reason here as there, this Pursuit being founded only upon a conjectural Prejudice; and in these Cases, the Prohibition is made necessary by the Generality and Frequency of Occurrences, and yet tho' so circumstantiated, there is still a public Law necessary. And when a public Law discharges the free Exercise of Property, it ordains him in whose Favours the Prohibition is, to refound his Expenses who is prohibited. Nor is the Commonwealth here prejudg'd so much by this, as it would be by the contrary; for thereby all Coal-heughs, Lead-mines, and the winning of other Minerals would be discharg'd: Whereas it is uncertain if this Water chaseth away the Salmon, which are at best but a Casuality, and which will go but from *Tweed* to other Rivers in *Scotland;* for they cannot stay in the Sea. Salmon-fishing is but an Accident to Rivers, but these being the common Porters is their natural Use. Thus (my Lords) you see that we contend for what is natural to Rivers; they for what is but casual; we are founded upon the Nature and Privilege of Property, they upon mere Conjectures.

> The *Lords enclin'd to sustain Haining's*
> *Defence; but, before Answer, they granted*
> *Commission for examining upon the Place,*
> *what Prejudice was done.*

If we restrict our gaze only to the law and legal argument, the first thing to be noticed in the case is that on this relatively large issue—especially as expressed at the outset as the legal question to be answered—there is a complete gap in the law. No Scottish statute or legal decision is cited for the general issue of how far one may use one's own property although another is injured. The same holds true for another question: how far may one, for one's own benefit, cause deterioration in the quality of flowing water. As often in a customary system, there is no established law, and also there is no way—or at least no way is sought—to determine what practice is followed as a norm. So Mackenzie moves straight to the citation of Roman law. He offers no justification for this, even though Roman law was no binding authority. But it is, first of all, the admired system; second, it is an accessible system in writing, and much fuller in detail than Scots law; third, the tradition among advocates and judges has been to turn to this system; and fourth, Scots law has already filled gaps from Roman law, thus making further borrowing seem harmonious. We can appreciate how natural it becomes to develop law in this way.

But something that may appear vital is missing in this appeal to Roman law for the filling of gaps, namely societal concerns or the relationship of law to society. With respect specifically to the free use of public rivers. Mackenzie seeks of Roman law only knowledge of the remedies given for interference with their use. And he finds interdicts relating to hindering or preventing navigation and with regard to rivers that need not be navigable, only a legal prohibition against changing their course. But he does not ask whether the societal interests of the ancient Romans were the same as those of the contemporary Scots. Significantly, neither he nor his adversary apparently thought fit to include the question and an answer in their pleadings, despite the presence of important societal rights involving rivers in Scotland that had no counterpart in Italy, commercial salmon fishing, precisely the societal right adversely affected by Haining's behavior. And these societal rights were governed by law long before the time of Mackenzie.

Although legislation in general was relatively uncommon, legislation on salmon fishing was frequent, existing as early as the thirteenth century.[48] Salmon fishing was distinguished in law from the fishing for all other river fish.[49] It was indeed a royal right, though different from all other royal rights. The details need not detain us here, but Baron David Hume in his lectures (1786–1822) could say:

> But, as to all the higher and more profitable modes of fishing for salmon, with long net and coble—or with currachs,—or by cruives, and standing nets,—and in short the different whole-sale ways of taking them—the right is a Royal right—and which none of the lieges, heritor or not, can exercise on a proper public river—or any river, that is large enough to afford those profitable modes of fishing,—without a grant and title from the Crown.[50]

Such a grant from the crown was held by the fishers upon Tweed. The point I wish to make is that if, in the absence of pertinent Scots law, discussion of legal problems had centered on what legal rules would be best for Scottish societal conditions, and not—as was dictated by the legal tradition—on what were the Roman legal rules and the principles behind them, then the thrust of the debate, and possibly the result of the trial, would have been different.

We have not finished with Mackenzie's defense, but now we should consider the pursuers' case. A man, they say, cannot use his own property just as he likes: society also has an interest. Hence he cannot abuse his property, and it is for this reason that prodigals are interdicted. Scotland had long known the interdiction of prodigals,[51] a notion probably itself derived from Roman law. The argument is not a strong one and is not insisted on. The second point is expressed in Roman law terms—one must not deal with one's property *in emulationem alterius*—with a Roman law citation. But the law is wrongly stated, both for Rome and Scotland.[52] Neither country accepted the notion that one so acted when the loss to others was greater than the possible gain to oneself. In both, the decisive issue was the intention. The pursuers had no real argument here, which might explain why they cite no authority from Scots law. Mackenzie, be it noted, correctly rebuts the argument, and he likewise cites no Scots law.

The next argument is apparently in rebuttal of an argument for Hain-

ing: one may use one's own as one pleases only *ubi nihil immitit in
alienum* (when one does not send something onto another's property).
And Haining, the pursuers claim, poured his poisonous water into the
Tweed. Two separate legal points may be involved here, and Mackenzie
certainly refers to both of them. The first seems to turn on the issue of
a servitude, with the pursuers claiming they were not subject to one.
As Stair puts it, "What hath been said of stillicides, holdeth more apparently in sinks either for conveying water, filth, or any thing else, upon
or through the neighbour's tenements, which cannot be done, unless
there be a servitude thereupon either by consent or prescription."[53] But
the requirement of a servitude to send water through another's property
applied only to towns. In the country, one could let water drain onto or
through a neighbor's land with impunity.[54] Mackenzie turns the argument around: Haining can send his loch water into the rivers, because
he is not bound by any servitude to the fishers of Tweed. And, of course,
he could not be, since a servitude existed only over bounding property.

The second legal point is perhaps ignored by the pursuers: at least it
is not pressed with vigor. The Roman *actio aquae pluviae arcendae,* as we
saw in the first section of this chapter, gave a remedy where, as a result
of human activity, water resulting from rain would flow onto another's
land and cause loss. The Roman action was worked out in great detail:
not every human activity would give rise to the action, since certain
kinds of agricultural work were exempt from liability,[55] and what
counted as rainwater was much disputed. But for the present case, draining the loch would not be an exempt activity; loch water would be rainwater; and the action was available in the country (but not in towns).
The Roman action was intended primarily to have the defendant prevent future damage by the water,[56] and this is precisely what the fishers
of Tweed demanded. The point where difficulties might arise for the
pursuers is that the Roman texts are concerned with resulting injuries
on another's land, not in the water itself. But an extension might have
been argued for. From this distance one might think that the *actio aquae
pluviae arcendae* would have given the pursuers their best legal argument, but the fact is that neither the action nor an equivalent was
prominent in Scots law. It does not appear in Stair or Mackenzie.

Very instructive is the treatment a century and a half later by Baron
Hume in his lectures:

> With this rule coincides that precept of the *Roman* Law (and observed in
> ours), "*ne immittas in alienum,*" that one shall not send, throw or direct

any thing, such for instance as a stream of water, into the property of one's neighbour, to harm him. The operation, it is true, commences *in suo,* within the bounds of one's own tenement; but it has an instant, an intended, and a foreseen, a necessary continuation into the next one and is much the same in substance as the doing of something there. Take the case of one who has a lake, or loch in his grounds and who wishes to drain the loch. Now here, if there be no natural runner into which to conduct the water, he is not at liberty to open a vent for it through his march, leaving it to his neighbour to rid himself of the water as he best may. He must buy the necessary level or channel from his neighbour, who may refuse to deal with him if he please; and, when bought, it must be scoured and kept in condition for its uses, and at his own expense. I refer you on that head to the case of *Gray v. Maxwell,* 30 July 1762 (Kaimes).[57]

He begins as if discussing the servitude already mentioned, but then goes on as if he is treating of the *actio aquae pluviae arcendae.* He allows it, though the circumstances he relates are significantly different from Haining's case. And a few pages further on he seems to express a different view:

> Last of all, as to water collected in a Loch or Lake, which is a subject of a different condition from a stream. If a lake be encompassed by the lands of one heritor only, and there be no sort of stream or discharge from it, certainly he is owner of the lake, as much as of the lands, and may drain or dispose of it at his pleasure, if he have the means of carrying off the water through his own lands. This, I say, holds in his favor unless, by usage of watering, or otherwise, his neighbours have established a servitude of some sort, to restrain him.[58]

The obvious conclusion to be drawn is that even by this time the *actio aquae pluviae arcendae* had not become well established in Scotland. Even much later in the century it was still very questionable whether draining a lake so that the flow of water was hurtful to lower ground gave rise to an action.[59] The reason for this is obscure: the utility of the *actio aquae pluviae arcendae* had been known to the Romans as early as the fifth century B.C. Perhaps the difference in climatic conditions is relevant: the need for proper drainage of higher land would be more apparent in Scotland,[60] and because rain there falls less torrentially than in Italy, lower-lying proprietors would be affected less dramatically. But this explanation does not seem too persuasive. The Scots also failed to adopt to any extent the related Roman remedies for *damnum infectum,* future loss, which would have been as useful in one country as in the other. In any event, the interest of the matter for us is that a borrower need not take all its law from the prime outside authoritative source, and a failure to borrow may at times be as difficult to explain on societal terms as borrowing can be.

Mackenzie makes the point that if there were restraints on polluting rivers, the working of coal pits and lead mines would be inhibited, and that these are more valuable to the society than salmon fishing. Quite so, and the Romans were as aware as the Scots of the pestilential effluvia of lead and silver mines, and such workings were at least as economically valuable to the Romans. But the important societal difference between Scotland and Rome was precisely that the rights of salmon fishing in the former but not the latter were economically valuable and, in this regard, were left unprotected.[61] The growth of law in Scotland restraining the pollution of water was, in fact, slow. The earliest case in which an interdict was granted against polluting a stream was decided in 1791, and the owners of salmon fisheries were being protected by 1886.[62] Not until late in the nineteenth century was it well established that a stream was not to be polluted "so as to be made unfit for the use of man or beast."[63]

None of the legal arguments adduced on either side, apart perhaps from that of Mackenzie just discussed, rely on local societal conditions. Rather they show the importance of the legal tradition. One final argument of Mackenzie is rooted in the legal tradition and is independent of place but not of time. He contends, he says, for what is natural; the other side, for what is only casual. The reference to the Law of Nature of this type is to be expected only in the Age of Reason.[64]

Many thousands of cases, from all over western Europe from the twelfth century at the latest onward, could be chosen to illustrate the same points. But any choice of examples would of necessity be arbitrary; nothing is gained by offering a few more cases, and this one case may stand for all, exemplifying both success and failure of legal development and of legal borrowing.[65]

No case of Haining's type—and, I venture to believe, no case at all— can be fully understood as an instance of law in action unless one takes into account the thrust of the preceding chapters: that the legal tradition sets the parameters of the debate, that customary law may well not emerge from local normative practices, and that some "foreign" legal system may be so admired in general by the lawyers that they are dazzled and half blinded to local concerns. Not all cases are affected by such factors to the same extent. Some cases do not concern customary law; in some the impact of law from another time and place is much in the background (though scarcely ever entirely absent). But none is ever independent.

JUDICIAL APPROACHES

Borrowing is often creative. This creativity may be very open as, noted in Chapter 3, when Everardus writes a treatise on how to use textual arguments from Roman law to build up a different branch of law:[66] from a law for slaves to a law for monks for example. Or the creativity may be more hidden (but still not obscure or unacceptable to the hearers): as when Bartolus uses a Roman law text on *forum conveniens* to found jurisdiction in conflict of laws on the concept of domicile.[67] My favorite example is Ulricus Huber's own theory of conflict of laws, which he founds, as already noted, on three axioms all ostensibly based on Roman law. For the first two he relies on *Digest* texts, which said something very different in the original context. He has no Roman authority, no matter how fake, for the third axiom (which he says has never been doubted).[68] His argument is wonderful. The rule comes, he says from the *ius gentium;* in the sense common in his time of "law found everywhere," or "everywhere among civilized nations." Huber took the term *axiom* from mathematics, and used it to mean a proposition that is so self-evident that it need not be proved. Thus, his axiom 3 is from the *ius gentium,* hence found everywhere so the lack of relevant Roman texts is irrelevant; besides, as an axiom it is self-evident and needs no proof.[69]

But this very creativity presents us with an apparent paradox. If one is going to change the rules around, why bother to appear to borrow at all? The answer is that all law making, apart from legislating, desperately needs authority. That appears for scholars like Everardus, Bartolus and Huber, as in the instances just adduced. It is also true for judges, as the two modern cases that I discuss in this section, from Scotland and South Africa, demonstrate.

Roman law, as was mentioned in the first section of this chapter, drew distinctions between types of rivers. A river was to be distinguished from a stream by its size or by the opinion of those who lived round about (*D.*12.1.1.1). Some rivers were perennial, others were torrential. A perennial river was one that flowed all year round (even if it occasionally dried up); a torrent was one that flowed only in winter (*D.*43.12.1.2). Some rivers were public, others private. The jurist Cassius defined a public river as a perennial river: his opinion was followed by Celsus and found acceptable by Ulpian (*D*.43.12.1.3; cf. *D*.43.12.3.pr.). Some public rivers were navigable, others were obviously not (e.g., *D*.43.12.1.12).

As was standard in Roman law there was no legislation on the subject but, as already noticed, there were edictal clauses providing interdicts. One read: "Do not do anything in a public river or on its bank or put anything in a public river or on its bank by which the passage or landing of a boat is or shall be made worse."[70] Another had: "I forbid the use of force against such a one to prevent him from travelling in a boat or a raft in a public river or loading or unloading on its bank. I will also ensure by interdict that he be allowed to navigate a public lake, canal or pool" (*D*.43.14.1.pr.). The other interdicts are similar: they are concerned with navigation (*D*.43.13; 43.15), which comprised passage not only by boat but also by raft.

Still, a navigable river is nowhere defined, nor are its characteristics described. Likewise, we are nowhere told what are the public rights in a public—but nonnavigable—river, except that there is a right to fish (*J*.2.1.2). What can be logically deduced is only that there must have been some such rights, for otherwise there would scarcely be a distinction between a public and a private river; and that these took precedence over the rights of the riparian owners, for otherwise they would not be rights (yet we never find out what these rights are).

The Roman rules became the basis of the law of both Holland and Scotland.[71] The Roman-Dutch authorities, like the Roman jurists, concentrated on navigation rights, and both Johannes Voet and Huber repeat that anyone can fish in a public river.[72] Likewise the stress in the Scottish sources is on navigation.

The two cases that we look at here are instructive in a number of ways. First, they report that in both Scotland and Holland what had been *res publicae* had become part of the regalia under feudal law.[73] The ruler's "right in them," wrote Erskine for Scotland, "is truly no more than a trust for the behoof of his people."[74] This right was inalienable. Thus, what we are faced with is a common but curious phenomenon, the borrowing from two distinct and very different systems of law, Roman law and feudal law, for the same institution. Feudal law became the basis for landholding, but the quality of the attributes—the extent of these rights—was taken from Roman law.[75] Of course, the class of *regalia* was wider than that of Roman *res publicae*, and some *regalia* such as a salmon fishing were alienable. But we are concerned with the descendants of the Roman *res publicae*. Yet it is noteworthy that, in contrast to Scotland, fishing was public at Roman law in a public river.

Second, the cases show that, in systems that develop by scholarly opinion and judicial precedent, whole areas of law may remain unclear for centuries: from the second century right through to the twentieth. Presumably problems arose but did not interest the scholars or reach a court at a high enough level.

The Scottish case, *Wills' Trustees v. Cairngorm Canoeing and Sailing School Limited,*[76] involved riparian owners on the River Spey seeking a declarator that they had exclusive rights of navigation in the stretch that ran through their lands, and asking for an interdict to prevent the sailing school company from sailing its canoes on that stretch. For our purposes the House of Lords held that the Spey was a public navigable river, and that the crown could not have alienated the right of navigation that it held in trust for the public. Thus, the public right of the sailing school to navigate took precedence over the riparian owners' private right to salmon fishing.

Although there was much citation of old authority such as the *Regiam Majestatem,* Stair, Erskine, Bankton, and Baron Hume, that authority was extremely vague as to what made a river "navigable."[77] Part of the riparian owners' contention was that to be treated as "navigable," a river had to be navigable in both directions, and in the days when the Spey was used commercially for floating timber, it was navigable only toward the sea. Baron Hume had drawn this distinction between "proper navigable rivers" and rivers like the Spey; but his discussion does not show in what ways the public rights in them differed in substance.[78] Indeed, the whole implication of what he says is that there was no difference.

The relevant facts of the South African case, *Transvaal Canoe Union v. Butgeriet,*[79] were not dissimilar. The plaintiff claimed that it and its members were entitled to paddle their canoes on the Crocodile River. The defendant riparian owner argued that when they paddled over her property they were trespassing (and she had taken extreme practical steps to stop them). The plaintiff maintained that the river was perennial and a *res publica;* the defendant claimed the river was not *res publica.*[80] The court held that by the common law the river was public, and that Roman and Roman-Dutch writers stressed the importance of navigation on public rivers. The court also held that it did not matter that the river was not navigable in the sense understood by the Roman and Roman-Dutch jurists: navigability was a relative term, and the Crocodile River allowed the passage of canoes.

The judge, Eloff DJP, noted that it was not really disputed that the river was perennial. Hence, at Roman law the river was public. The only real issues were therefore (1) was the river navigable, and (2) if not, what rights would the plaintiffs have? Much Roman and Roman-Dutch law was cited, but in terms of the issues the great bulk of the citations is entirely irrelevant. This is true of *Digest* 39.3.19.2 (Ulpian); 43.12.2 (Pomponius); Johannes Voet, *Commentarius ad Pandectas* 43.12.title; 43.12.sole text; 43.14 title; 43.14.sole text; Grotius, *Inleidinge tot de hollandsche Regtsgeleertheyt* 2.1.25; Huber, *Heedensdaegsе Rechtsgeleertheyt* 2.1.16, 17; Simon van Leeuwen, *Het Roomsch Hollandsch Recht*, 2.1.12; Dionysius Godefridus van der Keessel, *Praelectiones juris hodierni ad Hugonis Grotii introductionem ad jurisprudentiam Hollandicam* 2.1.25. The only relevant citations were to the works already named of Voet, at 1.8.8, and of Huber, at 2.1.19, who stated that one can fish in public rivers, thus showing that navigation was not the only right in public rivers.

The real issue in the case was disposed of very shortly and with no citation of direct authority:

> It will, I think, be in keeping with this approach [i.e., of Innes CJ] to recognize the right of the public in South Africa to make use of the waters of our public rivers for such modest and limited forms of navigation as those rivers permit. Navigability is a relative concept, and it can be said of the Crocodile River that it allows the passage of small craft such as canoes. It should furthermore be borne in mind that the type of use of rivers which, e.g., *Huber* (supra) and *Voet* 1.8.8 refer to, indicate that even pleasurable activities may be indulged in by the public. In my judgment, members of the public, such as Dr. Monteith and the canoe clubs affiliated to the Canoe Union, have at common law the right to paddle on the Crocodile River.

The issue that previously had faced Innes CJ was very different, namely the ownership of the riverbed and of minerals contained in it.[81] Still, Eloff quoted Innes with approval:

> The elasticity of the civil and the Roman-Dutch systems has enabled South African Courts to develop our law of water rights along lines specially suited to the requirements of the country. Their result has been a body of judicial decisions, which though eminently favourable to our local circumstances, could hardly be reconciled in its entirety with the law either of Holland or Rome. To take a point bearing upon the present enquiry— the definition of a public stream has been extended far beyond its original limits. And the Legislature has set its seal upon the work of the Courts.

Every stream is now public, the water of which is capable of being applied to common riparian use, no matter how frequently it may run dry. The Union, therefore, though practically without navigable rivers, is covered with a network of public streams, the majority of quite small size.[82]

With this quotation we are back to the beginning of this part. Climatic conditions made rivers very different in character in Rome, Holland, South Africa, and Scotland. In Roman terms, some Roman rivers would be public, many private; almost no South African river would be public; very few Scottish rivers would be private. In South Africa the notion of public river was expanded. Still, what would surprise a non-lawyer—and perhaps should surprise a lawyer, too—is the enormous attention paid to Roman law in very changed circumstances, especially when that law itself was very unclear. Attention also focused in Scotland on old Scots authority although economic circumstances were different; and in South Africa on Roman-Dutch law although climatic conditions were different. The enormous need for legal authority for legal decisions and reasoning is again unveiled.[83] It is this need for legal authority that often lends strength to transplants (or apparent transplants).

I would not want to be misunderstood. In no sense am I arguing that Roman law is today a potent source for new law in Scotland. Too much law has been created since the time of Justinian, and that more recent law usually provides the authoritative source for further development. Roman law will be seldom referred to, and even less often will it be conclusive.[84] My point is different. Both Scotland and South Africa have a shared tradition of both Roman and English law. That tradition is there even when it is unremarked and unacknowledged. The truly remarkable thing is that in the absence of a local statute or judicial precedent, recourse is expressly made to *Roman* law, even in very different economic conditions, and when the Roman law cannot be really established.

A major theme of this book is the importance in two regards of tradition in legal evolution. First, the weight of authority of a foreign system has come to be the source that is to be turned to in time of need. Even if the law from there is unclear and inappropriate, even if the system is seldom expressly referred to, still it is there. Second, the impact of the past on present law is enormous. Even when past law is changed its influence continues. Change in law when society changes is to be expected and needs no explanation. What needs to be explained is the paucity of change.

For this second point I should like to refer to Rudi Schlesinger, whom

I greatly admire as a scholar and loved as a man. He was, as already emerged in Chapter 5, not enamored with the idea of the academic study of Roman law. The importance of the influence of Roman law, it would appear, was for him long gone.[85] He was the real instigator of the now fashionable notion of a "common core" of European private law.[86] Indeed, the highly organized program at the University of Trento searching for the "common core" with the ultimate goal of a general codification for the European Union is named in his honor. But what can be any "common core" of European private law? The only answer is those parts which most clearly give Roman law rules or derive from such Roman law rules. In the seventeenth and eighteenth centuries, in the Age of Reason, one basic approach to natural law was the claim that it was knowable to everyone by reason, but without much thinking, because it was the law found everywhere.[87] But what was this "law found everywhere?" Again the answer is that part of law borrowed from Roman law, or derived from it. A recent energetic exchange shows a modern scientific study of Roman law has a low priority for some scholars but not others. As a practical matter, the outcome of the debate is of limited significance. The influence of Roman private law continues through the DNA of its descendants.

WATER AND NEIGHBORS' RIGHTS: AGAIN

The preceding discussion of Roman and French law in the first section of this chapter may serve us in good stead when we look at the American law on the same subject. We have seen how difficult it may be to frame laws regulating neighboring landowners' rights to use up water, or to divert it onto or from another's land. It is hard to find one principle that gives satisfactory results in all situations; and several principles, operating at the same time, may underlie the operation of the law. We have seen also that the law may have its own momentum, and be—at least to some extent—separate from social and economic realities.

With these thoughts in mind, I now turn to water rights in American common law up to the middle of the nineteenth century. I discuss the main cases treated by Morton Horwitz in his distinguished chapter, "The Transformation of the Conception of Property,"[88] with his account of the law as a backdrop. This approach is selected not to criticize Horwitz, but to show that from a starting point in comparative legal history a very different understanding of the law is much more plausible.[89] Horwitz finds an almost linear development in the law from point *A* through point *B* to point *C.* But the law on this topic from ancient Rome and France may suggest that all three points could exist at the same time, or that one could appear, disappear, then reappear.

First it should be stated that Horwitz begins with a serious mischaracterization of the earlier law. He writes:

> The productive development of land and natural resources at the beginning of the nineteenth century drew into question many legal doctrines formulated in an agrarian economy. In the eighteenth century, the right to property had been the right to absolute dominion over land, and absolute dominion, it was assumed, conferred on an owner the power to prevent any use of his neighbor's land that conflicted with his own quiet enjoyment. Blackstone, in fact, asserted that even an otherwise lawful use of one's property could be enjoined if it caused injury to the land of another, "for it is incumbent on a neighboring owner to find some other place to do that act, where it will be less offensive." Not until the nineteenth century did it become clear that, because this conception of ownership necessarily circumscribed the rights of others to develop their land, it was in fact, incompatible with a commitment to absolute dominion. Logical difficulties had been easily concealed by experience, since the prevailing ideal of absolute property rights arose in a society in which a low level of economic activity made conflicts over land use extremely rare.[90]

In fact, no such idea that "the right to property had been the right to absolute dominion over land" existed. On the contrary, Horwitz relies for his statement on Blackstone's *Commentaries on the Laws of England* (1765–69).[91] But here Blackstone was trying to explicate how it had come about that, from a state of nature in which everything was held in common, private individuals had now come to have exclusive rights of dominion over external things. This was no idle issue. It was a common question how, by the law of nature, one could own anything because originally there was no such thing as private ownership.[92] Although eighteenth-century apparent rhetoric may mislead, Blackstone was giving an explanation of the social fact of ownership, not describing its legal extent. Indeed, no landowner in eighteenth-century England could imagine a right to absolute dominion over land when the paramount features of landholding were the feudal tenures and the doctrine of estates in the land.[93] Blackstone's treatment of such matters dominated his volume 2, *Of the Rights of Things.* Moreover, his chapter 3, "Of Incorporeal Hereditaments," was devoted to a discussion of other restrictions on exclusive or absolute ownership, of which he listed ten different sorts.

Nor was it the case, as Horwitz asserts, that this notion of absolute ownership gave an owner power to restrict, nor were there logical difficulties to be concealed. The notion of property in land just did not correspond to Horwitz's description of absolute dominion.

For the specific issue of water rights in America we should start with the English background in Blackstone:

> With regard to other corporeal hereditaments: it is a nu[i]sance to stop or divert water that uses to run to another's meadow or mill; to corrupt or poison a watercourse, by erecting a dye-house or a lime-pit for the use of trade, in the upper part of the stream; or in short to do any act therein, that in it's consequences must necessarily tend to the prejudice of one's neighbor. So closely does the law of England enforce that excellent rule of gospel-morality, of "doing to others, as we would they should do unto ourselves. . . ."[94]

> Thus too the benefit of the elements, the light, the air, and the water, can only be appropriated by occupancy. If I have an ancient window overlooking my neighbor's ground, he may not erect any blind to obstruct the light: but if I build my house close to his wall, which darkens it, I cannot compel him to demolish his wall; for there the first occupancy is rather in him, than in me. If my neighbor makes a tankard, so as to annoy and render less salubrious the air of my house or gardens, the law will furnish me with a remedy; but if he is first in possession of the air, and I fix my habitation near him, the nuisance is of my own seeking, and must continue. If a stream be unoccupied, I may erect a mill thereon, and detain the water; yet not so as to injure my neighbor's prior mill, or his meadow: for he hath by the first occupancy acquired a property in the current.[95]

Blackstone's stance was very different from that of Roman law. His starting point was not something akin to the *actio aquae pluviae arcendae* but the tort of nuisance. To do something on one's own property that was lawful gave the neighbor an action if the neighbor was caused loss in a way that was regarded as unlawful. On that basis, the action for nuisance was available regardless of whether more or less water was sent onto the neighbor's land. Indeed, the relevant example for us is precisely the harmful reduction of a flow of water, say, to a mill or meadow. Although we need not be too precise, the neighbor's right was a property right acquired, Blackstone said, by prior occupancy. Some such rights, such as ancient lights, were acquired only by prescription, "that is, [they] have subsisted there time out of mind."[96]

Because this part of the chapter is on the development of American law we should not go too far into English legal history. But it is pertinent to observe that Blackstone's own opinion on this aspect of water law (as involved with the trespass of nuisance) goes back at least as far as Bracton in the thirteenth century. In his *De Legibus et Consuetudinibus Angliae,* Bracton held that one could not be prevented from doing on one's land something that caused loss (*damnum*) to a neighbor but that was without wrongdoing (*iniuria*), such as building a mill that took away customers from a neighbor's mill, "provided he does not raise the level of one's pond in such a way that the neighbor's land is flooded. Likewise he cannot dig a ditch on his land by which he diverts the water of his neighbor so that it cannot return to its previous channel, in whole or in part."[97] In the same context, a littler further on, Bracton had a similar treatment under the specific heading "of wrongful nuisance, of servitude."[98] In addition, it should be observed that the context generally was his discussion of the Assise of Novel Disseisin;[99] and specifically when one was disseised of things that were among the appurtenances of a free tenement, such as rights.[100] His concern, therefore, was with property law.

Thus, English law in the time of Bracton and Blackstone and American law in the eighteenth century had reached a point never reached by Roman law and not fully even by the French Code civil with regard to a neighbor's right to continue to receive a supply of water necessary for the continued, similar use of his land. The obvious explanation is that both approaches were rooted in their starting point. The Roman (and French) law began from the *actio aquae pluviae arcendae,* which gave the neighbor only the right to ward off damaging water. English (and American) law began from the general concept of nuisance, which was actionable whether the flow of water was increased or diminished.[101]

There is, of course, a real problem for neighboring landowners, one that involves a conflict of rights and that probably can never be satisfactorily settled in practice by any one particular legal rule. In the remainder of this chapter I, like Horwitz, primarily consider one aspect of the problem: the circumstances in which the owner of a mill can prevent a neighbor from performing acts on his own land that will adversely affect the supply of water to the mill, thus causing the owner economic loss. In Bracton and Blackstone, as well as in eighteenth-century America, such rights to restrict a neighbor's activities existed, apparently based on priority of use.[102] When we look at the English and early American law from this perspective provided by comparative law, we see clearly how misdirected is Horwitz's statement that "[t]he premise underlying the law as stated was that land was not essentially an instrumental good or a productive asset but rather a private estate to be enjoyed for its own sake. The great English gentry, who had played a central role in shaping the common-law conception of land, regarded the right to quiet enjoyment as the basic attribute of dominion over property."[103] The great English gentry, it turns out, seem to have been less interested in this so-called quiet possession as the basic attribute of dominion over land—at least in this regard—than were, as we saw in the first section, the ancient Romans or the French before and during the Revolution.

A consideration of Bracton and Blackstone also shows that Horwitz's discussion of the general view of property rights in the nineteenth century is misdirected. He says:

> Two potentially contradictory theories of property rights underlay eighteenth century legal doctrines for resolving conflicts over uses of property. The first, an explicitly antidevelopmental theory, limited property owners to what courts regarded as the natural uses of their land, and often "natural" was equated with "agrarian." For example, in cases involving the conflicting claims of two riparian owners, courts usually gave precedence to appropriation of water not only for domestic purposes but often for agriculture and husbandry as well.
>
> Natural uses of land were probably favored also by strict liability in tort: any interference with the property of another gave rise to liability; only the lowest common denominator of noninjurious activity could avoid a suit for damages. The frequency with which eighteenth century courts solemnly invoked the maxim *sic utere tuo, ut alienum non laedas* is a significant measure of their willingness to impose liability for injury caused by any but the most traditional activities.
>
> The second theory of property rights on which courts drew in the eighteenth century, though it appeared in a variety of legal forms, amounted to a rule that priority of development conferred a right to arrest a future conflicting use. Sometimes this rule was simply stated by the long-standing maxim "first in time is the first in right." More refined formulations required that the first user be engaged in this activity for a period of time sufficient to ripen into a prescriptive property right against interfering activities.[104]

Horwitz's treatment is beside the point for several reasons. First, because Blackstone (like Bracton) treated the working of a mill (Horwitz's main concern) as an instance where priority of use gave a right, two potentially conflicting theories did not exist in the precise context considered; the theories would both give the same result. Second, the doctrine of strict liability—provid:ng that when dangerous substances were brought onto land (even for such natural uses as supplying water to a mill), their escape which caused damage to a neighbor would give rise to an action—had not yet developed. The great English case, *Rylands v. Fletcher*,[105] which established the strict liability doctrine in England and was of great importance also for the United States, dates only from 1865, much too late for Horwitz's analysis, and is thus hostile to Horwitz's thesis. Third, the doctrine of natural use itself seems to appear later. There was, for example, no mention of natural use in the early editions of J. K. Angell, *Treatise on the Law of Watercourses*,[106] nor in those of Chancellor Kent, *Commentaries on American Law*.[107]

Thus, there was no such thing as two theories. In fact the earliest explicit distinction between natural and artificial use occurred in the case of *Evans v. Merriweather* (which Horwitz does not discuss) before the Illinois Supreme Court in 1842.[108] Moreover, the distinction between natural and artificial use that flowed from that important case seems to be not quite as represented by Horwitz. Natural use there was not equated with agricultural use, nor were proprietors limited to natural uses of their land. This issue and this case were so important to the development of the rights of riparian owners that a substantial part of the *Evans* judgment is quoted later in this chapter. In addition, what Horwitz calls natural uses (using the term anachronistically), such as watering cattle and irrigating, *could* (and did) give rise to an action if the water was used wastefully or unreasonably, as in *Cook v. Hull*,[109] a case involving wasteful irrigation that unlawfully diminished the flow of water to a mill. Nowhere did the cases say that mills were more or less important than irrigation, or watering cattle. The concept discussed in the cases was natural *flow*, or natural *rights* connected with natural flow. Justice Williams put it this way in *Buddington v. Bradley*:[110]

> In this case, the plaintiffs have a right to have the water come to them in its natural and accustomed course, not by their artificial channel or into their artificial reservoir, but to flow within its banks, through their lands, as it was wont to flow. This right they claim, not as mill-owners, but as riparian proprietors. The defendant objects, that the plaintiffs have not used the water, in the same manner as they now use it. The answer to that is, that the plaintiff's right to the water does not depend upon their use of it, or their prior occupancy, but upon their *natural* right to have it flow as it has been accustomed to flow.[111]

The first American case to which Horwitz devotes space is *Merritt v. Parker*.[112] It is in this context that Horwitz wrote of the "great English gentry" in the passage quoted earlier. The defendant possessed a mill dam for several years before the plaintiff cut a trench to the dam, a trench that passed through the defendant's land, to convey water to his own land for the use of a mill. The defendant, to prevent the increased flow of water through his land—by means of the trench cut by the plaintiff—erected banks that caused a reflow of water onto the plaintiff's land. The principles adopted by Chief Justice Kinsey in *Merritt* were wholly in line with the law set out in Blackstone. A landowner had the right to have water that was flowing in its natural channel reach him without diversion, diminution, or increase because of activity on the part of his neighbor.[113] When a landowner had by prior activity acquired a flow of water, priority gave him the right to maintain the flow.[114] But the rather unusual facts gave the words of Kinsey in the *Merritt* decision an emphasis that was easily misunderstood.[115] It was, after all, the plaintiff in *Merritt* who dug a trench on his neighbor's land taking water from his neighbor's land, thus diverting water from his neighbor's mill, and increased the flow on another part of his neighbor's land. Then he brought the suit against the neighbor because the neighbor, to prevent the increased flow on his own land, built banks that caused a reflow of water onto the plaintiff's land. Kinsey wrote:

> In general it may be observed, when a man purchases a piece of land through which a natural water-course flows, he has a right to make use of it in its natural state, but not to stop or divert it to the prejudice of another. *Aqua currit, et debet currere* is the language of the law. The water flows in its natural channel, and ought always to be permitted to run there, so that all through whose land it pursues its natural course, may continue to enjoy the privilege of using it for their own purposes. It cannot legally be diverted from its course without the consent of all who have an interest in it. If it should be turned into another channel, or stopped, and this illegal step should be persisted in, I should think a jury right in giving almost any valuation which the party thus injured should think proper to affix to it. This principle lies at the bottom of all the cases which I have met with, and it is so perfectly reasonable in itself, and at the same time so firmly settled as a doctrine of the law, that it should never be abandoned or departed from.[116]

Here Kinsey set out the general principle found in Blackstone, which he regarded as settled. The action would lie, of course, only where the landowner suffered loss. The basis of the action would be the tort of nuisance.

> Upon the best consideration which it has been in our power to bestow upon the subject since the commencement of the trial, we are of opinion

that the plaintiff had no right to cut the trench or canal, and thus to draw out the water, which the defendant by the erection of the dam had appropriated to his own use, and had acquired a property in, some time before.

Should this however be doubtful, and admitting the plaintiff had a right to use the water, and to cut the trench in order to enable him to use it, still we think, that he could not exercise his right in such a manner as to cause the flow of an additional quantity of water over the defendant's land without his consent.

Further, we think, that if one man by any contrivance causes to flow over the land of another a greater quantity of water than it is naturally subjected to, against his will, or without his consent; such other has a legal right to resort to any device, or may erect any banks, dams &c. on his own land, to prevent this additional current of water; and if any consequences injurious to the first wrong-doer result from this course, he must submit to them, and cannot recover compensation in damages. In the present case it is impossible that Parker could discriminate between the water that was drawn from the creek, and that which belonged naturally to the rivulet; neither could he prevent the one from flowing in to his land without keeping out the other also.

It is unreasonable, and the doctrine cannot be countenanced, that when one has erected a dam, and at a considerable expense has appropriated water to his own use, another person by cutting a canal shall be permitted to diminish his supply, and avail himself of the labor and work of the original owner, without defraying any portion of the expense that had been incurred, or undertaking to assist in keeping these works in repair. It would be equally unreasonable that one man should have a right to turn more water over the land of his neighbor than would naturally go in that direction; and so far as regards the rights, it is altogether immaterial whether it may be productive of benefit or injury. No one has a right to compel another to have his property improved in a particular manner; it is illegal to force him to receive a benefit as to submit to an injury.[117]

The same general principle was again used. But with it appeared Blackstone's principle of priority of use. The defendant had previously appropriated the water to his use and thus had acquired property rights in it.

What gave the case the appearance of an exceptionally restrictive view of water use was Kinsey's insistence that a landowner had the right to refuse an increase or diminution of the water flow even when the increase or diminution was beneficial. He accepted that the defendant was legally justified in erecting the banks to ward off the water and, hence, in refusing the plaintiff's action. What Kinsey was not saying was that a landowner who was not injured would nonetheless have a right to an action.

It is worth noting Horwitz's statement that "the New Jersey court regarded the legitimate uses of water as those that served domestic purposes and husbandry, requiring insignificant appropriations of the water's flow."[118] Nothing in the case restricted the legitimate use of water to domestic purposes and husbandry, however, and priority could establish the right to considerable appropriations.[119] Although Kinsey was well aware that a principle that would safeguard everyone's rights would not be easy to find, his decision was in line with the writings of Blackstone.

That the law was not easily settled is shown by a glance at other cases.[120] Thus, slightly earlier in the Connecticut case of *Perkins v. Dow*,[121] a landowner was held entitled to the use of water running through his land "as to answer all necessary purposes to supply his kitchen and for watering his cattle, etc. also he had right to use it for beneficial purposes, such as watering and enriching his land." He was so entitled even if by his use a neighbor's mill, which was "anciently erected," could not properly be used; but he was not entitled to deprive the proprietor of any surplus. The extent to which the proprietor could make use of water for beneficial purposes was not further clarified.

Horwitz regards the 1805 New York case of *Palmer v. Mulligan* as the start of a new development. In estimating its importance we should notice that the court was not only divided as to the law (as Horwitz says), but was also divided as to the facts or as to the implication of the facts. The plaintiffs had mills on the Hudson; the defendants erected mills and constructed dams higher up the river, thereby diverting the water from its previous course. Sufficient water remained for the working of the plaintiffs' mills, but the working was rendered more expensive and the milldam had to be run out farther into the stream. The majority found for the defendants, and it was the majority opinion that was important for any new beginning. Judge Spencer wrote for the court that the defendants' activities were only "slightly injurious" to the plaintiffs, who were remediless. He continued:

> The erection of dams on all rivers are [*sic*] injurious in some degree to those who have mills on the same stream below, in withholding the water, and by a greater evaporation in consequence of an increased surface; yet such injuries, I believe, were never thought to afford a ground of action. In any and every view of the subject, the verdict was legal and just.[122]

If we take Judge Spencer at face value, then he believed his opinion was nothing new. The reasonable use of flowing water—and this would apply to irrigation as well as to mill building—diminished the quantity available to lower proprietors. But this was inevitable and not actionable if the loss to other proprietors was slight.[123] Seen in this way, Spencer's opinion was no different from the judgment in cases such as *Perkins v. Dow,* because even in the time of Bracton and Blackstone the use of water to run a mill was regarded as normal practice. The issue of priority, so important for Bracton and Blackstone, did not come up because Spencer regarded the loss to the plaintiffs as trivial. Judge Livingston took up the point of priority:

> But as the plaintiffs' mills were first erected, it is said, that if the defendants have any right of this kind, they must so use it as not to injure their neighbors. Without denying this position, which is indeed become a familiar maxim, its operation must be restrained within reasonable bounds so as not to deprive a man of the enjoyment of his property, merely because of some trifling inconvenience or damage to others—of this nature is the injury now complained of, so far at least as it is supported by proof. It is not pretended that the water is diverted, or that less business can be now done at the plaintiffs' mills than formerly, but they are obliged to bring their logs a very little farther round in the river, (in order to get them into the dam), which is the principal, if not only inconvenience they are exposed to by the defendants' conduct. Were the law to regard little inconveniences of this nature, he who could first build a dam or mill on any public or navigable river, would acquire an exclusive right, at least for some distance, whether he owned the contiguous banks or not; for it would not be easy to build a second dam or mound in the same river on the same side, unless at a considerable distance, without producing some mischief or detriment to the owner of the first. Were this not permitted for fear of some inconsiderable damage to other persons, the public, whose advantage is always to be regarded, would be deprived of the benefit which always attends competition and rivalry. As well, therefore, to secure to individuals the free and undisturbed enjoyment of their property, as to the public the benefits which must frequently redound to it from such use, the operation of the maxim *sic utere tuo ut alienum non laedas* should be limited to such cases only, where a manifest and serious damage is the result of such use or enjoyment, and where it is very clear indeed that the party had no right to use it in that way. Hence it becomes impossible, and, indeed, improper, to attempt to define every case which may occur of this kind. Each must depend on its own circumstances; and the fewer precedents of this kind which are set, the better.[124]

Judge Livingston, thus, did not dispute that priority of use confers rights, but stated that an action was available only when the damage was "manifest and serious." Again, it is difficult to believe there was anything new in this, even if the argument had never been so clearly put before. It is in the nature of things that neighboring proprietors will suffer loss from the use of water on other land, even when that loss is otherwise entirely lawful. The issue for the tort of nuisance in such circumstances—which would have been raised in countless instances before—was really how much damage must be caused before it was actionable.[125] For Livingston this could depend only on the circumstances; thus, he was averse to the existence of a fixed rule. The reasonableness doctrine in this position is akin to the formulation of article 645 of the French Code civil.

But was Livingston's consideration of the public good something new? In one sense the answer must be a resounding no. Bracton had already written:

> And note that there may be a wrongful nuisance because of the common and public welfare, which would not be such because of the private welfare, as where one having lands on both sides of a stream builds a fishery or pond, when his land is in every way free and under no obligation to neighboring land, below or above; by so doing, though he causes damage to his neighbours, he commits no *injuria;* but nevertheless, what must be upheld [because of the private] may be demolished because of the public welfare, which is preferred to the private.[126]

I mention Bracton because he might have been the source, direct or indirect, of Livingston's point. There seems, indeed, to be another reminiscence, direct or indirect, of Bracton in Judge Spencer's remark that the plaintiffs would have been remediless if they "had declared on the loss of custom to their mill . . . it is a *damnum absque injuria"*—precisely an example used by Bracton.[127]

What did appear to be new in Livingston's opinion was that he based his view of public advantage on the benefits of competition.

A very different view of the case was taken by Judge Thompson and Chief Judge Kent. Both held that on the facts the plaintiffs had suffered loss, and the latter would have found for them simply on the basis of priority of use. Thompson, though, would have wished to find for the plaintiffs unless the defendants' occupation had existed so long that a grant could be presumed:

> Lord Ellenborough in a late case decided in the court of King's Bench, in England, says, the general rule of law is, that, independent of any particular enjoyment used to be had by another, every man has a right to have

the advantage of a flow of water, in his own land, without diminution or alteration; but an adverse right may exist, founded on the occupation of another, and if this occupation has existed for so long a time as may raise the presumption of a grant, other parties must take the stream subject to such adverse right, and that twenty years' exclusive enjoyment of the water, in any particular manner, affords a presumption of right in the party so enjoying it, derived from grant or act of parliament. If the rules there laid down are, as I apprehend them to be, undeniable principles of the common law, and we apply them to the present case, they will establish, beyond contradiction, the plaintiffs' right to the use of the water, in the same manner it was enjoyed before the erection of the defendants' mill and dam. No presumption of the right derived from a grant can attach to the defendants, they not having been in possession more than eight or ten years.[128]

The point Judge Thompson was making is that where there is priority of use, adverse use would prevail over priority only when the use was acquiesced in long enough to establish the presumption of a grant. The opinions of both Kent and Thompson were thus also free from any novelty.

In a later New York case, *Platt v. Johnson,* Chief Judge Thompson used the notion of prescription rather differently, but made the same point. He held in effect that when a plaintiff has a mill and dam on a stream, and the defendants subsequently build a mill and dam on higher ground, thus diverting some of the water and injuring the plaintiff, the plaintiff has no right of action simply on account of priority of use. Lapse of time sufficient to establish that there was a grant allowing the prior use would be needed.

I cannot persuade myself, however, that the claim set up by the plaintiff can be sustained upon any principles of law recognized in our Courts. The principle sought to be established is, that a previous occupancy of land upon a stream of water, and an appropriation of the water to the purposes of a mill, gives such a right to the stream in its whole extent above, as to control the use of the water, so as to prevent any subsequent occupant from using or detaining the water, to the least injury or prejudice of the first occupant. Unless the principle thus broadly stated can be supported, the plaintiff must fail in the present action: for there is no color for charging the defendants with having diverted the natural course of the stream, or unnecessarily wasting the water, or wantonly detaining it longer than was reasonable and necessary for their own machinery and water works; nor is there any pretense that the plaintiff had been so long in the previous use and enjoyment of this stream of water, as to afford the presumption of a grant of the same beyond the bounds of his own land. The plaintiff's right, therefore, if any legal right exists, must grow out of the mere fact of his having first erected his mill. To give such an extension to the doctrine of occupancy, would be dangerous and pernicious in its consequences. The elements being for general and public use, and the benefit of them appropriated to individuals, by occupancy only, this occupancy must be regulated and guarded, with a view to the individual rights of all who may have an interest in their enjoyment; and the maxim *Sic utere tuo, ut alienum non laedas,* must be taken and construed with an eye to the natural rights of all. Although some conflict may be produced in the use and enjoyment of such rights, it cannot be considered, in judgment of law, an infringement of the right. If it becomes less useful to one, in consequence of the enjoyment by another, it is by accident, and because it is dependent on the exercise of the equal rights of others.[129]

Thompson insisted that the principle of simple priority of use had never been established as giving that landowner the right to such continued use when other landowners had an interest in the development of their land.[130] Indeed, though Blackstone's text was in favor of holding that priority of use by itself establishes the right, there were in fact English cases that insisted on the need for such long use as to establish the presumption of a grant. *Luttrel's Case* of 1600 may be singled out for special mention.[131] There, it was taken for granted that prescription was needed to acquire right to a watercourse. What was in issue was whether a plaintiff who had acquired such a right to the use of water for two ancient fulling mills and who later pulled them down and erected in their place two mills for grinding corn retained the right by prescription. The decision was that prescription of a right was not lost by alteration in the subject of the right, provided the use of the right was to be similar. To show that some English judges continued to require prescription for the acquisition of water rights it is enough to refer to the 1823 case of *Wright v. Howard.*[132]

Indeed, the idea that prescription was needed for the acquisition of water rights by priority had been around so long that we find it even in Bracton:

> And so if a servitude is imposed upon another's land by law, not by man, as above, by which one is prohibited from doing on his own land what may damage a neighbour, as where one raises the level of a pond on his land, or makes a new one by which he harms his neighbour, as where his neighbour's land is flooded, this will be to the wrongful nuisance of his neighbour's free tenement, unless he was granted permission by his neighbour

to do it. Just as one may have a servitude in his neighbour's land if it is constituted, so may he have it by long use without any constitution, through the knowledge and acquiescence of the lords, for long acquiescence is taken for consent, as in commons of pasture and the like.[133]

In this passage, Bracton was talking not only of servitude in general but expressly of a servitude right to increase the flow of water into a neighbor's land.

Commenting on the two cases of *Palmer v. Mulligan* and *Platt v. Johnson,* Horwitz writes:

These two cases marked a turning point in American legal development. Anticipating a widespread movement away from property theories of natural use and priority, they introduced into American common law the entirely novel view that an explicit consideration of the relative efficiencies of conflicting property uses should be the paramount test of what constitutes legally justifiable injury. As a consequence, private economic loss and judicially determined legal injury, which for centuries had been more or less congruent, began to diverge.[134]

Again I find little of the substance of this comment in the cases. It is quite incorrect to state that they introduced the view that relative efficiencies of conflicting property use should be the paramount test for determining legally justifiable injury. Not only was that not considered to be the paramount test, it was not even considered as a test.[135]

"The most dramatic departure from common law riparian principles took place in Massachusetts," says Horwitz,[136] and he concentrates on *Cary v. Daniels.* It is well to quote in full Chief Justice Shaw's statement of the law in that case:

It is agreed on all hands, that the owner of a parcel of land, through which a stream of water flows, has a right to the use and enjoyment of the benefits to be derived therefrom, as it passes through his own land; but as this right is common to all through whose lands it flows, it follows that no one can wholly destroy or divert it, so as to prevent the water from coming to the proprietor below; nor can a lower proprietor wholly obstruct it, so as to throw it back upon the mills or lands of the proprietor above. We, of course, now speak of rights at common law, independent of any modification thereof by statute. But one of the beneficial uses of a watercourse, and in this country one of the most important, is its application to the working of mills and machinery; a use profitable to the owner, and beneficial to the public. It is therefore held, that each proprietor is entitled to such use of the stream, so far as it is reasonable, conformable to the usages and wants of the community, and having regard to the progress of improvement in hydraulic works, and not inconsistent with a like reasonable use by the other proprietors of land, on the same stream, above and below. This last limitation of the right must be taken with one qualification, growing out of the nature of the case. The usefulness of water for mill purposes depends as well on its fall as its volume. But the fall depends upon the grade of the land over which it runs. The descent may be rapid, in which case there may be fall enough for mill sites at short distances; or the descent may be so gradual as only to admit of mills at considerable distances. In the latter case, the erection of a mill on one proprietor's land may raise and set the water back to such a distance as to prevent the proprietor above from having sufficient fall to erect a mill on his land. It seems to follow, as a necessary consequence from these principles, that in such case, the proprietor who first erects his dam for such a purpose has a right to maintain it, as against the proprietors above and below; and to this extent, prior occupancy gives a prior title to such use. It is a profitable, beneficial, and reasonable use, and therefore one which he has a right to make. If it necessarily occupy so much of the fall as to prevent the proprietor above from placing a dam and mill on his land, it is *damnum absque injuria.* For the same reason, the proprietor below cannot erect a dam in such a manner as to raise the water and obstruct the wheels of the first occupant. He had an equal right with the proprietor below to a reasonable use of the stream; his appropriation to that extent, being justifiable and prior in time, necessarily prevents the proprietor below from raising the water, without interfering with a rightful use already made; and it is therefore not an injury to him. Such appears to be the nature and extent of the prior and exclusive right, which one proprietor acquires by a prior reasonable appropriation of the use of the water in its fall; and it results, not from any originally superior legal right, but from a legitimate exercise of his own common right, the effect of which is, *de facto,* to supersede and prevent a like use by other proprietors originally having the same common right. It is, in this respect, like the right in common, which any individual has, to use a highway; whilst one is reasonably exercising his own right, by a temporary occupation of a particular part of the street with his carriage or team, another cannot occupy the same place at the same time.

But such appropriation of the stream to mill purposes, upon the principles stated, gives the proprietor a prior and exclusive right to such use only so far as it is actual. If, therefore, he has erected his dam and mill, with its waste ways, sluices and other fixtures necessary to command the use of the water to a certain extent, and there is a surplus remaining, the proprietor below may have the benefit of that surplus. If he erects a dam and mills, for the purpose of using and employing such surplus, he is, as to such part of the stream, the first occupant, and makes the first appropriation. As to that, therefore, his right is prior and exclusive. And although the proprietor above might, in the first instance, have raised his dam higher, keeping within the limits of a reasonable use, yet after such appropriation by the proprietor below, he cannot raise his dam and take such surplus; because, as to that, the lower proprietor has acquired a prior right.

So the proprietor above may, in like manner, make any reasonable use of the stream and fall of water which he can do consistently with the previous appropriation of the proprietor below. If, with a view of gaining an advantage to his mill, in low stages of water, which may occur perhaps during the greater part of the year, he places his mill so low that, in high states of water, the dam below will throw back water on his wheels, he may do so if he choose, because he thereby does no injury to any other proprietor. But if he sustains a damage from such back water, it is a damage resulting from no wrong done by the lower proprietor who had previously established his dam, and it is an inconvenience to which he subjects his mill for the sake of greater advantages; and he has no cause to complain.

Another consequence from this view of the rights of successive proprietors to the use of the fall of water, on their respective lands, is this; that where one has erected a dam and mill on his own land, to a given height, and thereby appropriated as much water as he has occasion for, and there is still a surplus, he has the same right as any other proprietor to appropriate that surplus . If, therefore, before any other person has erected a dam above him or below, so near as to be injured by the change, he elects to appropriate the surplus, or a part of it, he may either raise his dam higher, and thus create a greater head above, or place his wheels lower, so as to discharge the water at the race at a lower level, and thus appropriate to himself such surplus water and power of the stream. In regard to such surplus, he will still be the first occupant.

One other consideration of a general nature, applicable to this subject, it may be proper to advert to. It is obvious that these rights to the use and power of flowing water, whether it be the original right belonging to each successive proprietor to the flow of the water in a natural channel over his own land, or the same right modified by actual appropriation, may be granted away, or acquired, or may be limited, enlarged or qualified, by grant from the proprietor in whom either of them is vested, or by that exclusive, adverse and continued enjoyment which is regarded in law as evidence of a grant. If, therefore, one has enjoyed a particular use of the stream and water, or water power, for a period of twenty years, even though such use would not have been warranted by his original right to the natural flow of the stream—as by diverting it, or raising it unreasonably high, or otherwise—he will be presumed to do it by virtue of a grant from all those whose rights are impaired by such use; and thus his right to continue so to use it will be established. But if he shall thus exceed the equal, common and original right, thus belonging to him as a proprietor, and not justify such use by grant or prescription, it will be deemed a disturbance of the rights of those whose beneficial use and power of the stream are thereby diminished.[137]

Horwitz comments:

> Chief Justice Shaw pondered this question in Cary v. Daniels (1844). "One of the beneficial uses of a watercourse," he began, "and in this country one of the most important, is its application to the working of mills and machinery; a use profitable to the owner, and beneficial to the public." Proceeding from this new utilitarian orthodoxy, Shaw stated a legal doctrine strikingly different from Story's earlier formulation. Not only did the law require "a like reasonable use by the other proprietors of land, on the same stream, above and below," but it also took account of the "usages and wants of the community" and "the progress of improvement in hydraulic works." It required that "no one can wholly destroy or divert" a stream so as to prevent the water from flowing to the proprietor below, nor "wholly obstruct it" to the disadvantage of the proprietor above. Thus, despite its invocation of "reasonable use," Shaw's formulation tended to erode a standard of proportionality: a mill owner who did not "wholly" obstruct a stream might claim that "the needs and wants of the community" justified his using more than a proportionate share of the water.
>
> That Shaw intended this result is clear from Cary v. Daniels itself, in which the Chief Justice expressly rejected proportionality under the circumstances "growing out of the nature of the case." Under manufacturing conditions then existing, he observed, beneficial uses of water were often, of necessity, mutually exclusive. Where the power needs of particular manufacturing establishments were such that maximum exploitation of limited water resources required a monopoly, "it seems to follow, as a necessary consequence from these principles, that . . . [the] proprietor who first erects his dam for such a purpose has a right to maintain it, as against the proprietors above and below; and to this extent, prior occupancy gives prior title to such use."[138]

In contrast, it seems to me that there was no real departure from common-law principles in *Cary*. "Reasonable use" cannot be so regarded.[139] It was implicit in statements of the law from Bracton onward. It was accepted that most water use will change the flow somehow. In the general situation landowners would make use of water flowing through their land and, again in the general situation, no landowner would be entitled to prohibit his neighbor's using water in a particular way precisely because he wanted to use the same water in the same way. To this there were two provisos. By some views, priority of use (which was not at the time injurious to a neighbor) established a right to use and to prohibit the neighbor's engaging in a new usage that would affect the supply in a harmful way. By other views, not priority but prescription or a presumed grant was needed to establish such a right. That it was proper for a landowner to use water on his land to power his mill had also been accepted since early times. "Proportionality" of use, moreover, had never been a doctrine of the common law.[140]

It is time to return to *Evans v. Merriweather*. The approach of the *Evans* court had been foreshadowed by various judgments, including some that have already been discussed in this section,[141] but it was nonetheless a remarkable attempt to define exactly the competing needs of riparian proprietors. Justice Lockwood said:

> Each riparian proprietor is bound to make such a use of running water as to do as little injury to those below him as is consistent with a valuable benefit to himself. The use must be a reasonable one. Now the question fairly arises, is that a reasonable use of running water by the upper proprietor, by which the fluid itself is entirely consumed? To answer this question satisfactorily, it is proper to consider the wants of man in regard to the element of water. These wants are either natural or artificial. Natural are such as are absolutely necessary to be supplied, in order to his existence. Artificial, such only as, by supplying them, his comfort and prosperity are increased. To quench thirst, and for household purposes, water is absolutely indispensable. In civilized life, water for cattle is also necessary. These wants must be supplied, or both man and beast will perish.
>
> The supply of man's artificial wants is not essential to his existence; it is not indispensable; he could live if water was not employed in irrigating lands, or in propelling his machinery. In countries differently situated from ours, with a hot and arid climate, water doubtless is absolutely indispensable to the cultivation of the soil, and in them, water for irrigation would be a natural want. Here it might increase the products of the soil, but it is by no means essential, and can not, therefore, be considered a natural want of man. So of manufactures, they promote the prosperity and comfort of mankind, but can not be considered absolutely necessary to his existence; nor need the machinery which he employs be set in motion by steam.
>
> From these premises would result this conclusion: that an individual owning a spring on his land, from which water flows in a current through his neighbor's land, would have the right to use the whole of it, if necessary to satisfy his natural wants. He may consume all the water for his do-

mestic purposes, including water for his stock. If he desires to use it for irrigation or manufactures, and there be a lower proprietor to whom its use if essential to supply his natural wants, or for his stock, he must use the water so as to leave enough for such lower proprietor. Where the stream is small, and does not supply water more than sufficient to answer the natural wants to the different proprietors living on it, none of the proprietors can use the water for either irrigation or manufactures. So far, then, as natural wants are concerned, there is no difficulty in furnishing a rule by which riparian proprietors may use flowing water to supply such natural wants. Each proprietor in his turn may, if necessary, consume all the water for these purposes. But where the water is not wanted to supply natural wants and there is not sufficient for each proprietor living on the stream, to carry on his manufacturing purposes, how shall the water be divided? We have seen that, without a contract or grant, neither has a right to use all the water; all have a right to participate in its benefit. Where all have a right to participate in a common benefit, and none can have an exclusive enjoyment, no rule, from the very nature of the case, can be laid down, as to how much each may use without infringing upon the rights of others. In such cases, the question must be left to the judgment of the jury, whether the party complained of has used, under all the circumstances, more than his just proportion.[142]

The judgment speaks for itself. For natural wants or essential needs the proprietor could use up all the water; for artificial wants or uses that are beneficial even to the public but not essential to the proprietor, no proprietor could have exclusive enjoyment, and the issue of whether the defendant has exceeded his just proportion was to be left to the jury.[143] This balancing of interests to determine what use of water by neighboring proprietors was reasonable, and was similar to article 645 of the French Code civil. Both approaches left the task of balancing to the courts.

Finally, with respect to the cases, we should look to a much earlier case that Horwitz emphasizes. He believes that legal doctrine was fundamentally changed by the minority opinion of Justice Gould in *Ingraham v. Hutchinson,* which subsequently met with considerable approval. Gould argued that for prescription to occur it was not enough for a lower owner to have a mill on the river and to make use of the water for the necessary period. He claims:

> Now, in the present case, the parties, or those under whom they respectively claim, had, originally, a natural and equal right to the use of the stream in question. If the defendant had diverted the stream from the plaintiff's land; or if the plaintiff had, by obstructions, cast it back, and

overflowed the land of the defendant; and the injury had been acquiesced in, for fifteen years, on either side; a grant might now be presumed, in favour of one, or the other, of the parties. And the same thing might be said of any wrong, in general, of the same continuance, on one side, submitted to, on the other. But no such case as this is before us. The use, which the plaintiff has made of the stream, has been neither a legal injury, nor an inconvenience of any kind, to the defendant. It was nothing, of which the defendant had any right to complain. He has, therefore, acquiesced in no usurpation of his rights; and has been guilty of no neglect, in not asserting them sooner. For it would seem extraordinary, to charge a man with neglect, for omitting to seek redress, where there is no wrong; or for not complaining, where there is no ground of complaint. And the only principle, upon which the defendant can be supposed to have forfeited his natural right to use the stream in question, as he now does, must be, that he did not build his mill, within the fifteen years, whether it would, then, have been of any use to him, or not—and whether he was in a condition to build it, or not.

And what, on the other hand, is the injury of which the plaintiff complains? It is not, that the stream has been diverted from his mill. If this had been done, he would, undoubtedly, have a right of action, whether his mill had stood fifteen years, or but one year. But the water is still transmitted to him, in its natural channel; and the only wrong complained of is, that part of it is interrupted in its course, and delayed in arriving at his wheel.[144]

Gould cited considerable authority for his argument. There was nothing novel in his opinion. It was simply the common-law version of the doctrine of positive prescription. Prescription is the usurpation of a right, to which validity is given after lapse of time. There had been no usurpation of a right of the defendant by the plaintiff, because the defendant had no right to complain of the plaintiff's use of the water, so long as he himself was not using it. The plaintiff had committed no tort of nuisance on the defendant. Hence prescription against the defendant could not begin. Yet, as was often the case with lawyers dealing with prescription, Gould wove various strands of the doctrine together: for the plaintiff to have acquired a right by prescription to the use of the water, it was enough that he had had the mill there for the requisite time. He had acquired the right that the water not be diverted; he had not acquired the right that the water not be delayed.

The difference between positive prescription in the French Code civil and that in the common law was derived from the nature of the right to receive water. The French lower proprietor had no right to receive the continued supply of water from a spring. If he erected obvious works on his land that required the supply of water for their effective use, pre-scription began to run against the higher proprietor. In the common law both the lower and the higher proprietor had the right to the supply of water. If the lower proprietor made a greater use of it than before but the higher proprietor still had enough for his needs, the former was not infringing the rights of the latter, so prescription could not begin. Pre-scription could begin only when the lower-lying proprietor used water that the other then needed.

A great change was made in the common law by the Mill Acts passed in various states, beginning in Massachusetts in 1713,[145] but becoming generally important only from the beginning of the nineteenth century. Horwitz properly stresses that their purpose was to aid economic ex-pansion and the public good in light of the greatly increased significance of water power. The Mill Acts of the various states could be broadly di-vided into two types.[146] One type, of which the prototype is the Mas-sachusetts' act, allowed a landowner to build a mill upon his land though the consequence would be to cause flooding on another's land. But the millowner then had to pay damages, which were annually assessed. The second type, with prototypes in Kentucky and Virginia, provided that a landowner who wished to erect a mill or other engine useful to the public could make application to the court to be allowed to use the op-posite bank and to have the right to let the water flow onto the lands of others. A writ could be issued by the court, executed, and returned, and this procedure would vest ownership in the state. The former owner was entitled to receive damages. Further into these various Mill Acts, I do not intend to go. It is enough to claim that here we did have a leg-islative response to perceived economic and social needs.

The judges did not transform American property law with regard to riparian rights—at least not to the extent described by Horwitz. In America in the period studied, industrialization caused the water rights of riparian owners to be much discussed, and the number of lawsuits in-creased dramatically.[147] But that, of itself, is no indication that the common law greatly changed. To become convinced that one cannot chart an orderly progression of legal rules on this subject in nineteenth-century America, it would be enough to read the appropriate chapters of John M. Gould's nineteenth-century work, *A Treatise on the Law of Waters Including Riparian Rights*. Indeed, the state of the law was such that the distinguished John Bouvier—of *Dictionary* fame—could give in 1851 the basic rules of the French Code civil as a statement of Amer-ican law. He wrote that the owner of a spring that arose on his land was entitled to it without having regard to the convenience or advantage of his neighbors. This right, Bouvier wrote, was very different from the much more restricted right of use by the owner of an estate through which a watercourse flowed. He added that a neighbor could acquire an easement to the use of his neighbor's spring.[148] The fact is that whether the economy is agricultural or industrial, precisely the same issues will affect riparian owners, including some at a considerable distance from where the work was done, and the wider public. The individual owner and the public will, no matter what type of economy is dominant, have the same concerns: too much water or too little, resulting from another landowner's activity. It is not the case with water rights that the most effective law will vary according to whether the use is for agricultural or industrial purposes.

We have also seen that in an area where it is difficult to set out precise rules, conflicting approaches may coexist for a considerable period. Nor is it the case that particular approaches come into being as a result of specific types of economic situation. Nor is there a neat progression under economic pressure. Prescription is a good example. In Rome, prescription of servitude was abolished in the late republic, but by the third century A.D. it was creeping back in a different guise: long use—longer than was needed in other cases—implied that there had been a lost grant. Under Justinian, the general rules for *longi temporis praescriptio* seem to have applied to servitude but there is no real evidence for its application in connection with water law. France took over the Roman rules on *aqua pluvia,* but not prescription. Prescription of the right to receive water came into French law in the Code civil. In the common law, prescription was needed at some times for the acquisition of water rights, notably, perhaps, in England of *Luttrel's Case* and in the United States after 1818. At other times and for other judges or writers, priority of use was sufficient for the acquisition of the right. In that light it is very difficult to claim that particular economic circumstances dictated the nature of the legal rules. Whether priority or prescription was needed, whether the prescription could be negative or had to be positive, and what was needed for positive prescription to begin to run were all issues that were primarily affected by the basic approach to the nature of the general legal right. Thus, in Rome and France there could be no question of using the notion of priority, and in Rome there could—still in this context—be no issue of negative or positive prescription because the only private law action was in regard to warding off rainwater. In the common law, given that the appropriate action was the tort of nuisance, the notion of positive prescription involved something more than did the equivalent notion in France of the Code civil. The original approach of the legal system to the issue of a neighboring owner's rights continued to have an impact many centuries later.

Yet, despite the different legal approaches, all three legal systems managed to bring in somehow and to some extent the ideas of reasonableness and of public utility.

CONCLUSIONS

This chapter, I believe, is illuminating in various ways for an understanding of law and its development. The law itself in this instance is not riddled with difficult technicalities, but the subject matter itself poses serious problems. The issue is the extent to which one person may use flowing water to the detriment of another. The legal issues may vary between an agrarian or pastoral society and an industrial society, but even more because of geographic and climatic conditions.[149]

Another conclusion seems to emerge incidentally. For a sound explanation of the causes of change in any branch of law at any time in America or elsewhere, it is necessary to consider both the antecedents of the law and any other legal system that may have been influential, and also to examine (for patterns of similarity or difference in change) the same branch of the law in other legal systems that were subject to different economic, social, and political conditions. I would draw the following conclusions:

1. Legislation is sparse on a matter of consuming interest, of private and public concern.
2. Legislation, when it does occur, may be halfhearted, as in Napoleonic France, or concerned with one aspect of the problem, as with the Roman *actio aquae pluviae arcendae* or the eastern U.S. Mill Acts. There was no attempt by American legislatures to set up in the Mill Acts a comprehensive system, even in the public interest, to determine the general use that could be made of flowing water by neighboring riparian owners. The reforms were restricted to the urgent but limited need for mill construction.
3. The starting point of the law may be decisive for future development: again the *actio aquae pluviae arcendae* for Rome, tort law for England.
4. The extent of legal borrowing is enormous.

5. Authority, especially in juristic opinions and judicial decisions, is very significant in the development of the law.
6. When needed, fake authority is used.
7. The significance, when it comes to borrowing, of one system over another is evident.
8. The power of authority, when it comes to borrowing, overrules geographic conditions.
9. In law there is not necessarily a logical progression from point A through point B to point C.
10. Despite the foregoing it is often the case that societal concerns have an input.
11. Scholars trying to explain legal development in one country may neglect, at their peril, developments elsewhere.[150]

CHAPTER 7

LEGAL TRANSPLANTS I
The Cause of the Reception
of Roman Law

With a significance that is hard to grasp, borrowing has been the most important factor in the evolution of Western law in most states at most times. We have seen something of its impact on new juristic constructs, such as conflict of laws by Bartolus and Huber, and the constructs can in their turn be transplanted, as in the case of Huber, to Scotland, England, and the United States. We have seen something of its impact, even on legislation, in the example of délit and quasi-délit in the French Code civil; on judicial and juristic reasoning in instances from Scotland and South Africa; and its prominence in customary law that is supposed to emerge from what the local inhabitants do. We have noticed its impact on general approaches in particular areas, such as diverting water from or onto neighboring land: France and the United States have different approaches, deriving from Rome and England respectively. Even the artificiality of some borrowing betrays the importance of legal transplants. Again, the great *Digest* of the Christian Byzantine emperor Justinian is, in its contents, a transplant from the pagan Roman jurists, a world away.

From the eleventh century to the eighteenth and even beyond, the main feature of legal change in western continental Europe was the Reception of Roman law. At the beginning of that period law was above all custom, and throughout the period the main development in private law lay in the interaction between custom and Roman law. Certainly there were also statutes, but for private law they were relatively few, did not provide the main thrust of change, and were not at the center of legal interest. In their own spheres also, canon law and feudal law came to be supreme, but for convenience they may be left aside in this chapter, not least because to a considerable extent their history is also a parallel one of interactions with Roman law. The main question to be answered in Western legal history is an old one, one posed, for example, by Paul Vinogradoff at the very beginning of his famous work, *Roman Law in Medieval Europe.*

> Within the whole range of history there is no more momentous and puzzling problem than that connected with the fate of Roman Law after the downfall of the Roman State. How is it that a system shaped to meet certain historical conditions not only survived those conditions, but has retained its vitality even to the present day, when political and social surroundings are entirely altered? Why is it still deemed necessary for the beginner in jurisprudence to read manuals compiled for Roman students who lived more than 1500 years ago? How did it come about that the Germans, instead of working out their legal system in accordance with national precedents, and with the requirements of their own country, broke away from their historical jurisprudence to submit to the yoke of bygone doctrines of a foreign empire?[1]

The main thrust of this chapter is to explain the cause of this so-called Reception in the eleventh century. But some theorizing and earlier history are needed first. The theorizing is required to illuminate legal institutions as something different from, but related to, the corresponding social institutions; to illustrate the nature of legal ideas; and to account for legal borrowing from a society that has or had very different economic, social, religious, and political conditions and opinions. The earlier history serves to show that the Reception was not a one-off thing but corresponds to cultural rules of legal borrowing. The main issue, of course, is to explain how one system, Roman law, could have such an impact on so many others with such different contours. After all, the societies that gave rise to the law in the Corpus Juris Civilis, whether that of pagan Rome of the second century A.D. or that of Christian Constantinople of the sixth, were unlike the states of western Europe in the eleventh and subsequent centuries; and they in turn could be very different from one another. And even earlier, the Germanic tribes that borrowed pre-Justinianic Roman law have always been considered to be very different from the Romans of their time in their mores, their economic development, their political structure, and their religion.

SOME THEORY

Everyone would accept that, in the developed world, law is a separate entity in society, a distinct social institution. Yet somehow it is difficult to conceptualize legal ideas, in the way that one can conceptualize philosophical or religious ideas, as something different in kind from other ideas. The nature of the problem becomes apparent when we consider a legal institution, such as slavery, for example. Slavery (when it exists) is a legal institution with a bundle of legal rules. Slavery is also a social-economic-political institution: for brevity I will use "societal" institution to express this notion. Whether a society accepts or rejects slavery will, of course, depend on social circumstances. Slavery as a societal institution will not be brought into existence because a law of slavery exists or to complement a law of slavery. Rather, a law of slavery is wanted or needed because slavery is wanted or needed for societal reasons.[2] In other words, a legal institution is a social institution that has been given legal effectiveness and is being regarded from the legal point of view. A legal institution, to be at all meaningful, depends on a societal institution.

But let us break down the legal institution of slavery. There are certain matters typically regulated by law, such as enslavement and manumission. Who is to become a slave—only persons of certain racial groups, only persons belonging to and captured from a foreign society that has no treaty of friendship, criminals convicted of particular offenses, children born to a slave mother—is an issue that will be resolved primarily by societal values. Likewise, societal concerns will determine whether any owner can free any slave, whether the owner or the slave has to be above a certain age for manumission, whether the consent of state authorities is required, whether an owner can free only *inter vivos* or by testament, whether there are restrictions on the number of slaves who can be freed, and the standing in the community of slaves who have been freed. At what level do legal ideas, if they are distinct from societal ideas, come in?

The problem may be approached by picturing a society that has as yet little in the way of law. Imagine that in the society the issue is raised for the first time whether an individual of a particular type is a slave. A decision will be reached on societal grounds (at least in the absence of a sophisticated legal analogy). Plus, perhaps, justice. But justice, too, is a societal notion, though it is conceptually distinct from law. But if the issue is raised several times, or if in the first instance the ruling was treated as decisive for subsequent like cases, then there may in turn emerge, in a similarity of approach, a rule that can be termed a legal rule. What is a legal rule? At this level it is a crystallization of particular societal values organized so as to enable problems or disputes to be resolved with less trouble.

The means for resolving the disputes are also originally rooted in societal and not legal values. Judges will be those persons who are considered in societal terms to be fit to judge; what is regarded as probative will be determined by societal notions of proof. Likewise, legal rules will come into being in ways that have societal approval: if, for example, kings or councils have the requisite authority, they may make general declarations that will be regarded as creating legal rules.

Thus, legal institutions are societal institutions; the detailed rules derive from societal values; even the elements of the trial-process and the ways of creating law will stem from societal facts.

Yet, even if we accept that the legal derives from the societal, it is prima facie obvious that law also exists as something distinct from other institutions in society. It is to some extent autonomous, and exists and operates within its own sphere, as we saw in the earlier chapters. Law for our purposes may reasonably be regarded as the means adopted to institutionalize dispute situations and to validate decisions given in the process whose specific object is to inhibit further unregulated conflict.[3] The picture of law and society just given, if it is ever historically accurate, is so only at a very early stage. But when does law come to take on this life of its own, and cease to be simply a reflection of other aspects of society? First, it occurs when factual situations come to be determined according to a standard, a standard that has emerged from the societal norm, but is treated as having its own existence. A standard implies some degree of uniformity, but what is involved is rather more. Uniformity, for instance, in deciding similar cases in the same way may result from a consideration of the societal factors. But there is determination according to a standard when judges wish to give the same results in suits that have similar facts *primarily because* of the other rulings, and when a ruler announces that whenever and as often as a named factual situation arises he will do or cause to have done some particular thing. Determination according to a standard involves a kind of shorthand. A solution to a problem is to be arrived at by the application of the shorthand: the individual societal factors that previously would have been taken into account are not resorted to; the standard, which is in effect a legal rule, has usurped the role of the societal factors. The main reasons for this occurring are plain. To begin with, it makes the decision making much simpler: the obvious efficiency is enhanced when one takes into account that the standard can be regarded as the crystallization of the societal factors. Second, the existence of a standard gives greater certainty for regulating the future. Third, the application of a standard does, as it is meant to, lead to some equivalence of treatment, which gives at least the appearance of one kind of justice. Fourth, the party against whom the judgment is given will accept it more readily, feel less aggrieved, if he thinks a standard is being applied and the judge is not arbitrary.

But whenever and wherever this change occurs, there ceases to be a necessary, entire congruence between the standard and society. With regard to decision making, the standard—that is, the legal rule—now stands in the stead of all the societal factors once thought relevant. Societal factors may change without a corresponding change in the standard. Or the standard may have been imposed because of a very temporary situation that may have concerned the whole society or only a segment. Or the standard may have been formulated inexactly or in a primitive way for the societal conditions of the time. In any event, the very erection of a standard amounts to proof that societal values may not prevail in a particular case. Judging is to be in accordance with the standard. It is precisely the standard that is to prevail.

A standard according to which determination should be made is not to be equated with what happens in practice in court. In practice a great deal may happen in court that has nothing to do with the standard and is even extralegal—for instance, bribery of a witness or of the judge. Or again the standard may exist prior to any court deliberation: for instance, a statute may set out rules that will be obeyed, that will have an impact, before there is any question of a process. Further, to give a concrete example, the Roman jurists created the standards by their writings and discussions, but they seem, so far as our evidence goes, to have been quite indifferent to what happened in court.

Further (and it is almost simply the other side of the coin), law takes on a life of its own whenever and wherever the decision is regarded as authoritative, not because it is thought necessarily to encapsulate societal values but because the judge is treated as the right person to give the decision—in other words, when the authority of the decision derives from the way the judge is appointed and from the fact that he has followed the procedure of judging rather than from the intrinsic quality of the decision. The judgment can be appealed only to a higher judge, and the authority of his decision rests on his senior status, not on his necessarily being better acquainted with societal values.[4]

On the model so far proposed, legal rules and deliberations are purely the result of societal ideas, even though the stage may be reached that the legal rules do not by any means exactly fit the dominant societal ide-ology. The reason is apparent: law is not an end in itself but is always a means to other ends.

But the model so far proposed is obviously oversimple in another way. The ends may be societal ends, but the means to the ends require human ingenuity, and they inevitably involve standards having a distinct status. In addition, in the Western tradition at least, law becomes the province of specialized groups who may loosely be termed lawyers.[5] Lawyers themselves may be divided into groups, and in every society there will be one or more elite legal groups who to a very great extent control law making or law finding. Legal ideas and legal tradition result from the amalgam of law as involving standards having a distinct status, as human ingenuity, and as an elite making or finding the standards, all depend-ent on societal ends that may to some extent be not expressed, or be for-gotten or ignored.

The elite of lawmakers or law finders may be emphasized. They be-come so involved with law as law that they often talk of it as if it ex-isted for its own sake, and they cease to regard it—or at least to treat it—as existing for specific societal purposes. Thus, the Roman jurist Ju-lian, of the second century A.D., claims (and he is talking about law): "The reason cannot be given for all matters established by our ances-tors"; and this text is followed in Justinian's *Digest* by one of Neratius, who is slightly earlier: "And therefore it is not proper to seek the reasons of those matters that are established, for otherwise many of those things that are certain are overturned" (*D*.1.3.20, 21). In the eighteenth century, in his *Institutions du droit belgique* (1736), George de Ghewiet, who refers with approval to those Roman jurists, also says: "On this principle one must stop at the provisions of the homologated customs without wor-rying about the *why*. It is enough that they are as we find them" (1.1.5.2). In the twentieth century it is still the typical practice for the authors of English legal textbooks not to give the reason for the rules that they set out.

The notion that the law and the legal tradition powerfully affect the way the law develops is one that I have argued for on several occasions elsewhere,[6] and it appears prominently in every chapter of this book. Here the reminder of one example from Chapter 2 may suffice. Barter as a societal institution exists in many societies, but not all such societies recognize a contract of barter. Thus the city of Rome was traditionally founded in 753 B.C. (and may be older), and a contract, the *stipulatio*, was well established by 451 B.C., the date of the codification known as the Twelve Tables. Coined money was introduced in the third century B.C., and the consensual contract of sale (*emptio venditio*), followed hard upon. Yet, as we saw, barter (*permutatio*) as a legal institution is centuries later, and it was never fully accepted into the Roman system of contracts. As a contract it was very unsatisfactory; the Sabinians tried to include it within the satisfactory contract of sale but were blocked by the successful counterarguments of the Proculians. Neither side used societal arguments. Law was being treated as if it were an end in itself. In these circumstances only the most blinkered modern ideologue would deny that just as mercantile needs to some extent shape legal development, so the existing law to some extent shapes mercantile practices. It would be a grave mistake to suppose that because the mercantile elite can take more advantage than others of the law that the law is necessarily shaped to their advantage.

Legal rules and the legal tradition are therefore separated from society, though connected with it. The legal tradition as something distinct is most obvious in two spheres: first, in societal institutions, which appear to require support as legal institutions but do not receive it; second, in categorization, in the drawing of boundary lines, whether in the boundaries between two clearly defined, separate legal institutions such as barter and sale, or in determining whether one or more legal institutions is to provide for what may be regarded as more than one societal or legal institution, as in the hire of a thing, hire of labor, or hire of work to be done.

This separation of law from, but partial dependence on, societal institutions must be stressed. The law created by a society for its use is often by no means a perfect fit. And the historical reasons for the precise contours of the legal institution may well be forgotten. Yet people for the most part accept the law they have. They do not demand perfection. All this is a necessary precondition for one of the strangest of legal phenomena: the prodigious extent of legal borrowing. We need not concern ourselves here with the other prerequisites for successful legal transplants. It is enough to know that transplants occur in great number, that the recipient society may have very different values from the donor, and that the reasons justifying the acceptance of the foreign law may be different from those that created it in the first place. A general example of these propositions is provided by the influence of the French Code civil throughout the world;[7] a particular example, by the enshrinement of the Visigothic law of matrimonial property in the constitution of California,[8] and its acceptance in several German states (before unification) and Latin American countries. Societies with systems of customary law also, as mentioned, frequently resort to extensive borrowing: the *Sachsenspiegel,* an early-thirteenth-century account of the law of a part of East Saxony, was used throughout northern Germany and far beyond; medieval German towns adopted another as their "mother" town on points of law (Magdeburg is the supreme example, but others, too, had many "daughters"; thus, Lübeck had about 100 and Soest, 65); medieval French jurisdictions frequently accepted the law of another, often Paris, as subsidiary law whenever the local custom failed to provide an answer.[9]

If legal ideas evolve from societal ideas, yet come to have a (semi-) independent but subordinate existence; if, moreover, societal ideas and practices can exist without corresponding law; if the corresponding law may be inadequate; if one societal institution may be divided arbitrarily between more than one legal institution, each with its own imperfections; if several societal institutions may be brought within the same legal institution because of the legal tradition; but if, still, the subordination of law continues; and if, further, one can accept that with law in general, and also with customary law, borrowing is at least one of the most fruitful sources of legal development, then even on a priori grounds one can set out some general propositions about the grafting of Roman law onto customary systems.

To start with the extreme position. It would seem at first glance that there can be no transplanting of the legal institution where the possible donor's societal institution is the reverse of the recipient's societal institution. For example, a society having a system of bride price but not of dowry will not (or is not very likely to) borrow the corresponding law from a society having a system of dowry but not of bride price. But this immediately invites and even demands serious qualification. If the societal institution of dowry is not adopted, then the central core of the law of dowry also will not be borrowed; but surrounding rules may be, and then be attached to bride price—rules such as those determining the amount to be paid, the times for payment, and the rights of retention if the marriage fails. But this borrowing of these surrounding rules implies some degree of precision and clarity in the donor system and a felt need, which may be real or imaginary, in the recipient system. Hence, in general this type of borrowing implies greater precision and clarity in the donor. Borrowing of this type, of surrounding rules but not of the central core of the legal institution because the societal institutions are very different, will generally be from the more advanced by the less advanced. But the recipient need take only what it requires at any one time. Hence the reception can take a very long time.

If the outline just given is accurate, then we have the beginnings of an explanation of some phenomena of the Reception of Roman law into customary systems. First, many different systems can all be borrowers from the same sources: each takes, or need take, only what it wants, irrespective of the borrowings of others. Second, the pace of the Reception varies from place to place: each system takes only when it needs or wants. Third, systems of customary law are peculiarly susceptible to this type of borrowing from elsewhere precisely because they are notoriously lacking in precision and clarity: when a need for a rule arises it may not be found or easily found in what the people do. Fourth, a sophisticated system of Roman law may exist and be studied extensively in a society whose main law is customary. The main advantage of this for the society at large, as distinct from the professors of Roman law, is precisely that Roman law may be called upon to fill gaps in the customary system. Of course, where the societal institution in the two societies is very similar, the borrowing even of the central core of the legal institution from the more advanced legal system is easier, especially if the borrower's legal institution has not developed at all or only very partially.

In fact, the tenor of the foregoing paragraph is almost entirely encapsulated by a seventeenth-century judge and jurist, Lord Stair, in his *Institutions of the Law of Scotland*: "*Our Customes*, as they have arisen mainly from Equity, so they are also from the Civil Canon and Feudal Laws, from which the Terms, Tenors and Forms of them are much borrowed; and therefore these especially (the Civil Law) have great weight, namely in cases where a custome is not yet formed; but none of these have with us the Authority of Law."[10] Here we have the frank declaration that in Scotland customary law is often borrowed—especially when a Scottish custom is not yet formed—from a more developed system that is also accessible in writing; that even where there is local custom, it will come to be expressed in the terminology of the donor system and given its form and also its content; and that the borrowing is optional, though some outside systems will be particularly persuasive. If one can extrapolate from Scotland, as I think one properly can, then other countries differing in their societal structure would likewise borrow what they needed. The borrowing could be little by little, when an individual problem arose. To illustrate the process, an example from another Scottish attorney's speech to the court is quoted and discussed in Chapter 6.

SOME HISTORY

Let us look at two extensive instances of legal borrowing before the Reception of Roman law, which began in the eleventh century. The first is the influence of pre-Justinianic Roman law on Germanic customs, which becomes very apparent from the fifth century. The second is the spread of Visigothic law throughout Spain under and after Moorish domination. I am not outlining this history for its own sake but to show that the more famous Reception corresponds to the same cultural rules of legal borrowing, and hence that the explanation of its occurrence presents no special problems. The argument here rests on an acceptance of the principle known as Ockham's Razor, whether that principle be expressed as "Plurality is not to be assumed without necessity" or "What can be done with fewer is done in vain with more." Thus, if the borrowing of pre-Justinianic law by the Germanic tribes, the acceptance of Visigothic law by the Christian communities in Spain, and the Reception of Roman law are similar in their essentials, then a satisfactory general causative explanation of one ought to be a satisfactory general causative explanation of the others. There will, of course, also be individual causes of borrowing in each instance.

To consider the influence of Roman law on Germanic customs I begin with the *Edictum Theoderici,* treating it as the oldest surviving example and as the work of the Visigothic king Theoderic II (453–66).[11] Although there is no agreement as to the author, Theoderic II (or Magnus of Narbo, the *praefectus praetorio Galliarum* of his time)[12] seems to be the current favorite, and I believe he is the most likely candidate. The course of influence of Roman law is most simply explained if we begin with him, even though this starting point is the least helpful for my general thesis.

The other main contender for the authorship of the edict has always been Theoderic the Great, king of the Ostrogoths (493–526), who was supported by the first editor, Pierre Pithou in 1579, who had at his disposal two manuscripts that have now disappeared. Against this identification is the fact that, though his reign is well documented, he is never cited by contemporaries as responsible for a legal compilation—not by Cassiodorus, Jordanes, Epiphanius, Ennodius, Procopius, or others. Moreover, the imperial constitutions are cited in the *Edictum Theoderici* for no date later than 458. In favor of Theoderic II of the Visigoths, on the other hand, speak this dating of the constitutions in the *Edictum* and the fact that Sidonius Apollinaris (born around 430) says that

Seronatus—usually thought to be *praefectus praetorio Galliarum* or governor of Aquitanica Prima around 469 or holder of some other office, it does not matter which—tramples on the laws of Theodosius and issues laws of Theoderic.[13] One might also want to give some weight to Sidonius's claim (*Carmina* 7.495–96) that, thanks to Avitus, the laws of Rome had long appealed to Theoderic II; and perhaps even some to the obvious fact that of all the Germanic peoples, the Visigoths showed most interest in law and also borrowed most from Roman law.[14] For our present purposes it would not matter whether one said that Theoderic II issued the *Edictum* or Magnus of Narbo as the Roman magistrate or, as Vismara hypothesizes, that Magnus was the jurist entrusted by Theoderic to draft the *Edictum*.[15] It should be noted, though, that the text of Sidonius treated as indicating Magnus's authorship (*Carmina* 5.561–62) seems to be misunderstood and must actually refer to Theoderic. Sidonius's poem is a panegyric on Majorian, and in stressing the good qualities of the emperor's assistants, he has just referred to the prefect: "qui dictat modo iura Getis, sub iudice vestro pellitus ravum praeconem suspicit hostis" (The enemy dressed in skins, who now gives law to the Goths, under your judgeship, admires the hoarse auctioneer). But he who now gives law to the Goths (*qui dictat modo iura Getis*) must grammatically and logically be the enemy dressed in skins (*pellitus hostis*), who cannot be Magnus and must be the king of the Visigoths.

The *Edictum Theoderici* consists of 154 provisions plus a prologue and epilogue. The immediate purpose—irrespective of any wider political motive—was to set out, as the prologue and epilogue expressly state, the legal rules that were to apply both to Romans and Goths.[16] Thus not all of the law was covered. But what is remarkable is that, with this purpose, the provisions all seem to have a Roman origin, whether in juristic writing or in imperial rescripts.[17] Many of the provisions relate to criminal law and punishment, others to such diverse topics as testation, gifts, transfer of property, slavery, and marriage.

This purpose and the scope of the rules give a straight, conclusive answer to at least one possible puzzle: why the earliest collection of legal rules applying to a Germanic tribe was written in Latin, thus setting a trend that was to continue. This approach renders unnecessary a further explanation which may nonetheless have some validity: that the Germanic languages did not have the vocabulary needed to cope with law.[18] If we give some credence to this idea, it further entails holding that the *Edictum Theoderici* is giving a precision to the Germanic customs that was previously lacking. In any event, the use of Roman vocabulary means that, in Stair's words, "the terms, tenors, and forms of them [i.e., Roman legal institutions] are more borrowed."[19] Although we have no real evidence for the previous state of the Visigothic law, it would be a remarkable coincidence if so much Roman law was also common to the Visigoths. We have here, in all probability, a massive transplant.

On the view here proposed, the term *Edictum* would be used either technically or at least figuratively. Roman public officials did not have the power to legislate, but they could declare by *Edicta* how they would carry out their duties. Above all, the republican praetors, the officials in charge of the most important courts of private law, issued annual *Edicta* setting out the circumstances in which they would grant an action.[20] Thus the *Edictum Theoderici* is not *lex*, statute law. Only the emperor could issue statutes for Roman citizens. The term *Edictum* is very appropriate for legal rules that apply to Romans as well as Goths, set forth by someone other than the emperor, though we do not know that Theoderic had any legal right to issue an edict in the technical sense. If the lines from Sidonius about Theoderic that have just been quoted do refer to the *Edictum Theoderici*, we have the beginning of an understanding of the obscure phrase *sub iudice vestro*. Theoderic is giving law—*iura*, not *leges*—to the Goths with the emperor as his judge, or with the emperor's judicial representative in charge of court procedure. Whatever translation is appropriate, the implication is the same: the law of Theoderic is subject to the emperor.

Whatever the nature of the *Edictum Theoderici* and its origins, the Visigoths soon had another code of laws. The *Codex Euricianus* has reached us only in part and is the work of Euric (466–84), successor to Theoderic II as king of the Visigoths. According to Isidorus of Seville (*Historia Gothorum* 35, written in 624), the Goths first obtained written laws under Euric and previously lived according to their customs. It is usually thought, however, that at least individual laws were promulgated under Theoderic I and Theoderic II. The *Codex* is dated to 475 or 476, immediately after the fall of the Roman Empire in the West.[21]

Insofar as the *Codex Euricianus* survived, it has been in the *Antiqua* (the "old texts" in the later Visigothic Code) and in a fragmentary palimpsest containing chapters 276–336.[22] The work is in Latin, and it has long been recognized that the law has been heavily Romanized. This is also the conclusion of Alvaro d'Ors, the most recent editor, who has also produced a palingenesia, though he does find details and traces of Germanic law.[23] Thus, the oldest surviving corpus of law produced for Germans was very much the result of massive borrowing. In its turn, it was to be very influential, and even serve as model for other Germanic codes (even apart from those of the Visigoths). Clear traces of it are found in law for the Franks in the *Lex Salica* of Chlodwig (486–511); for the Burgundians in the *Lex Gundobada,* which seems to be not before 483; for the Lombards in the *Edictum Rothari* of 643; and, above all, for the Swabians in the *Lex Baiuwariorum* of the eighth century.[24]

In 506, another Visigothic king, Alaric II, produced a very different legal work, the *Breviarium Alaricianum* or *Lex Romana Visigothorum.* This work, which has survived, does not contain the laws of Visigothic kings, but Roman imperial constitutions and writings from Roman jurists. It is usually thought to have been issued with a political motivation: to try to retain the loyalty of Alaric's Gallo-Roman subjects who were Catholics—the Visigoths were Arians—and inclined to join with the Franks. The *Breviarium* was to provide some materials for the Visigothic Code. But more significantly, it served as a vehicle for the dissemination of law, and hence of Roman law, for many centuries in France. Its influence can be shown in the style of documents, in the redaction of formularies, and in conciliar canons from the sixth to the ninth centuries. In the eighth century especially there were numerous epitomes, and from the sixth to the tenth centuries legal science in France was largely restricted to using extracts from these epitomes and the Theodosian Code.[25]

The traditional view long held was that the Visigoths operated a system of personal, not territorial, law and hence that the *Codex Euricianus* was meant only for the Visigoths, the *Breviarium Alaricianum* only for the Romans living under Visigothic control. This view was challenged in 1941 by Alfonso García Gallo, who maintained that the Visigoths operated a system of territorial law and thus both the *Codex Euricianus* and the *Breviarium Alaricianum* (and other legislation) applied to Visigoths and Gallo- or Hispano-Romans alike: hence the *Codex Euricianus* was abrogated by the *Breviarium.*[26] A lively debate has followed,[27] and no consensus has been reached, but there is now considerable agreement that the *Codex Euricianus* was territorial, as, according to common belief, was probably the *Breviarium,* though more doubt is expressed on this second point.[28]

The arguments thought persuasive for the territoriality of the *Codex Euricianus* are its profound Romanization and its edictal character.[29] Evidence of the edictal character of the work seems to me to be lacking, because we do not have the formulas of its promulgation, and other explanations of the Romanization can be provided. The general correctness of the traditional view I would maintain for the following reasons.[30] First, it is no real explanation of the profound Romanization that the code was meant to apply to Romans as well as to Visigoths and thus is a hybrid. The latter had just achieved political domination over the Romans. Why should they, to keep the Romans content, adopt for themselves as well a system based on Roman law? The Visigoths' adoption of Romanized law can only have occurred because the Visigoths themselves (or their leaders) wanted it as law: hence, an explanation extending its operation to Romans is unnecessary. Second, the *Breviarium* contains only Roman law texts and no laws of Visigothic kings. It is inconceivable that with this scope it was intended as law for the Visigoths as well, replacing the *Codex Euricianus,* especially in view of known Visigothic legislation. That the Visigoths had their own legal tradition is evidenced both by the prior *Codex Euricianus* and the subsequent Visigothic Code.

A second approach is to claim that the *Breviarium* did not derogate from the *Codex Euricianus* but was a work complementary to the *Codex,* "a subsidiary source principally destined for the Roman population."[31] The first part of that claim is easily admitted. Alaric begins the *Commonitorium* to Thimotheus: "Utilitates populi nostri propitia divinitate tractantes hoc quoque, quod in legibus videbatur iniquum meliore deliberatione corrigimus, ut omnis legum Romanarum et antiqui iuris obscuritas adhibitis sacerdotibus ac nobilibus viris in lucem intelligentiae melioris deducta resplandeat ac nihil habeatur ambiguum unde se diuturna aut diversa iurgantium impugnet obiectio" (We, in this also considering the advantage of our people with the help of God, correct after better deliberation what seemed unjust in statute law, so that all the obscurity of Roman statutes and of the ancient law, brought forth with the help of priests and honorable men into the light of better understanding, shines forth and contains nothing ambiguous, and hence the continuous and opposing squabbles of those who quarrel reduce themselves to naught). Thus, any derogation is expressly from the preceding Roman *leges* and *ius.* But this is precisely what one would expect if the *Breviarium* was intended solely for the Roman population to whom the *Codex Euricianus* did not apply. The game is up for the claim of territoriality as soon as it has to be suggested that the *Breviarium Alaricianum* was destined principally for the Roman populace. How could it be, if one law applied to all? And if it were complementary to the *Codex,* which applied to both people, but the *Breviarium* was mainly for the Romans, why was the Visigoths' own law not given equal supplementation? If the ground of the argument were to be changed to the proposition that the *Codex Euricianus* and the *Breviarium* were territorial and that the latter was complementary for Romans and Visigoths alike, then we would be faced with an acute form of the converse of the issue, which led to the notion of territoriality of Visigothic law: the Romanization. If the serious Romanization of the *Codex Euricianus* leads to the belief that it must have been intended for Roman and Visigoth alike, can the total Romanization of the *Breviarum* lead to the belief that it also must have been intended for Roman and Visigoth alike? And how can one then explain the subsequent serious Visigothization of the Visigothic Code?

Third, if at this time Visigothic law was personal and the *Codex Euricianus* was promulgated for the Visigoths, the *Breviarium* for the Romans, then we would have almost an exact parallel from another Gothic people, the Burgundians. As we shall see, Gundobad, king of the Burgundians from 474 to 516, was responsible for the *Lex Burgundionum* (or *Lex Gundobada*) for his Burgundian subjects (and for conflict cases between Burgundian and Gallo-Roman) and the *Lex Romana Burgundionum* for his Gallo-Roman subjects.

Other Visigothic legislation followed. Teudis, king from 531 to 548, promulgated in 546 a law on procedural costs and ordered that it be included in the corresponding part of the *Breviarium*. Thus, this law was territorial, but the order to include it in the *Breviarium* would seem to indicate both that laws were not automatically for both peoples, and also that the *Breviarium* was not.

Leovigild (568–86) revised the *Codex Euricianus,* adding, cutting out, and modifying laws. This work has not survived in its own right. Subsequent kings, especially Chindasvind (642–53) and his son Recesvind (653–72), also legislated. But the most important work of Visigothic law was Recesvind's compilation of laws that had been promulgated until 654, the Liber Iudiciorum or Liber Iudicum or Visigothic Code. This massive compilation in twelve books, like Justinian's *Code* (though it is not certain that the compilers used that work),[32] replaced earlier law and was intended for all the people in the territory subjected to Visigothic domination. Roman law is the predominant element. Subsequent kings continued to legislate. Ervigius (680–87) revised the Liber Iudiciorum, introducing many statutes of his own and of Wamba, correcting and interpolating earlier laws. Egica (687–702) intended a new revision: we do not know if this was carried out, but statutes of his were included. In addition to the official versions, anonymous jurists produced private, vulgarized versions with a new preliminary title. The result was the version known as the *vulgata,* which was the most widespread in the High Middle Ages. This legislative activity of the Visigoths came to an end in 711 with the conquest by the Moors.

Savigny places the texts of the Liber Iudiciorum that reproduce Roman law in three categories.[33] First, there are those that reproduce Roman sources textually—for instance, on degrees of relationship, legitimate defense, and interest.[34] Second, very many texts reproduce Roman principles that have been adopted, imagined, modified, or completely changed. Savigny gives examples from the law of persons and related rules in succession. The Visigothic Code (*L. Visigoth.* 3.12) permits, with the authorization of the count, marriage between Goth and Roman. The prohibition is in *Codex Theodosianus* 3.14.1. A law that nuptial gifts by the husband may be equaled by the amount of the dowry is said to be that permitted by Roman law (*L. Visigoth.* 3.1.6). Another law forbids remarriage during the year of mourning (3.2.1), a rule that is found in more than one of the Roman sources. A widow becomes tutor of her children (4.3.3; from *C. Th.* 3.17.4). Minority ends at the age of twenty-five (*L. Visigoth.* 4.3.1), capacity to make a will begins at fourteen (2.5.10), and spouses inherit from one another in the absence of relatives (4.2.11). Manumission of slaves may take place in church (*L. Visigoth.* 5.7.2; from *C. Th.* 4.7.1). Third, some rules seem to be borrowed indirectly from Roman law by means of the *Lex Baiuwariorum.*

During the period covered by the foregoing summary the Visigoths were on the move. In 412, under Athaulf, they left Italy, which they had exhausted, and settled in Gaul. After many quarrels they entered Roman service and fought and defeated the Siling Vandals and the Alans in Spain. From there they were withdrawn to settle as federates in Aquitania in 418. In 435 a peasant revolt in Gaul gave the Visigoths (and the Burgundians) the opportunity to expand. From time to time the Visigoths intervened south of the Pyrenees, and, apparently in 457, a relatively large number of Visigothic peasant families settled in the Tierra de Campos. Euric himself seems to have wanted to extend Visigothic rule over the whole of Gaul and Spain. He extended the Visigothic kingdom in Gaul so that it was bounded by the Loire, the Rhine, and the Pyrenees. Southern Provence also came under his control. Within the Visigothic and Burgundian kingdoms the confiscation of land was more drastic than in other territory controlled by other barbarians; in the *Codex Euricianus* the Visigoths took two-thirds, the Roman owner retaining only one-third. This rule was retained in subsequent legislation. In time the Visigoths had to face war with the Franks, and Alaric II was defeated and killed at the battle of Vouillé (near Poitiers). Then followed a massive immigration of the Visigoths into Spain, always suffering further displacement to the south until Leovigild (568–86) situated his capital in Toledo.

Before we look at other Germanic codifications we should perhaps pause to consider some of the implications of the Visigothic experience. Visigothic law was the best-developed of all Germanic laws, but what is most striking is the massive Romanization at an early stage, as early indeed as the *Codex Euricianus,* and so massive that modern legal historians are unwilling to believe that it was intended by the Visigothic king for the Visigoths alone. For the sake of the argument let us assume that it was also intended to apply to the Gallo- or Hispano-Romans under Visigothic rule. This assumption would in no way diminish the impact of Roman law on the Visigoths, an impact they accepted freely, at their king's free choice. And the Romanization continued to increase even until the Liber Iudiciorum itself. We began by accepting that the starting point for the codification was in the *Edictum Theoderici,* which we treated as representing an edict of a Roman magistrate setting out the law that applied to Romans and Visigoths alike. A beginning of this type made it easier to understand why Latin was the language—which could be thought to set the tradition—and why the law was Roman, but does not explain why then or subsequently the Visigoths borrowed so much law from Rome. The borrowing continued over a long period of time. And it should again be stressed that Visigothic social mores, political structure, economic conditions, and religion were, and have always been accepted as being, vastly different from the Roman society for which Roman law was created.

But just as other societal conditions were very different among the Romans and the Visigoths, so were the systems of law at the beginning of this reception: not just in substance but in structure—custom as distinct from written law—and in the amount of detail and sophistication. Writing of the Germanic tribes in general at the time of the codification of their laws (and not excluding the Visigoths), the famous French legal historian A. Esmein follows the opinion of Sir Henry Maine: "Germanic law, at the period of the *Leges barbarorum,* was less advanced in its development than Roman law at the time of the Twelve Tables"—that is, in the mid-fifth century B.C.[35] Yet borrowing was not only possible but also massive.

The Burgundians were a second Gothic group prominent in code making. The *Lex Burgundionum*—also called, for instance, the *Lex Gun-*

dobada—an official collection of royal Burgundian laws, is mainly the work of King Gundobad, who ruled from 474 to 516. There are thirteen surviving manuscripts, none earlier than the ninth century; and, of these, five have a text of 105 titles, the others having only 88 or a number of appendixes. The work, in fact, is a composite, of which the first 88 titles constitute an earlier stage. Two manuscripts contain a short preface in which Gundobad claims to have given great thought to the laws of himself and his predecessors. Then follows in all manuscripts a heading to the effect that King Sigismond issued a new edition of the code in 517, the second year of his reign.[36] Of the first 88 titles, numbers 2–41 stand together as the work, though revised, of Gundobad; 42–88 are rather different and stem from Sigismond. Title 1 has certainly been revised. Whether there are laws older than the time of Gundobad in the code is not certain.[37]

The date of the *Lex Burgundionum* is not known. It was intended to apply to the Burgundians and in lawsuits between Burgundians and Romans. The Roman subjects of King Gundobad were to continue to be ruled by Roman law, and the preface expressly states that the Romans should know they will receive their own law book so that ignorance will excuse no one.[38]

The *Lex Burgundionum* contains many rules of Roman law, whether drawn directly or indirectly from Roman sources. Thus, a woman married for a second time retains only a usufruct of the gift given in contemplation of the first marriage, and ownership of it goes to the children (*L. Burg.* 24.1; *C. Th.* 3.8.2). The title on divorce is contradictory, but the provisions of 34.3, 4 permit a husband to divorce his wife if she is guilty of adultery, witchcraft, or violation of a tomb; if he leaves her otherwise, his property is forfeit to his wife and children. This is ultimately derived from the *Codex Theodosianus* 3.16.1, but the provisions there referred to divorce by a wife. Gifts and wills become valid provided five or seven witnesses append their marks or signatures (*L. Burg.* 43.1), a formality established by *Codex Theodosianus* 4.4.1 for the validity of wills and codicils. The requirement of an *inscriptio* in criminal charges also comes from Roman law.[39] The title on prescription, number 79, seems much influenced by Roman law; the legal treatment of documents comes from Roman vulgar law, and two texts show the use of the Roman vulgar law *Interpretationes*.[40] For Otto Stobbe this influence is explained by the fact that the *Lex Burgundionum* was intended to apply to Romans as well as to Burgundians (of course, only where there was a process between a Burgundian and a Roman).[41] But this explanation will not serve. There are two Burgundian codes, one for Burgundians, one for Romans. Each should contain what is appropriate for each people. There will be cases of conflict of law. If one set of rules is chosen to settle such issues, we could reasonably expect it to be the Burgundian, because the Romans were the subject people. Roman rules in the Burgundian code that would also apply in cases where all interested parties were Burgundians cannot be explained on this basis. The reason for their presence simply must be that they are wanted by the Burgundians themselves. It seems as if legal historians like Stobbe are unwilling to believe the ease with which Roman legal rules could be accepted by the Germanic tribes.

But just as interesting, and possibly even more significant, are the numerous borrowings in the *Lex Burgundionum* from Visigothic law, and in fact from the *Codex Euricianus.* The borrowings are shown from the parallelisms or similarities in the *Antiqua* texts in the Liber Iudiciorum, or in the *Lex Baiuwariorum,* which itself borrowed from the *Codex Euricianus,* or in the *Lex Salica* or the Lombard *Edictum Rothari,* which also were influenced by Visigothic law.[42]

The *Lex Burgundionum* remained in force after Burgundy became part of the empire of the Franks, and it is mentioned as personal law in documents of the tenth and eleventh centuries.

Gundobad's *Lex Romana Burgundionum* for his Roman subjects contains no new law but only that from Roman *ius* and *leges* and from the *Lex Gundobada.* It was not a complete account of Roman law, so that the Roman subjects also had to make use of the collections of imperial rescripts and juristic writings. Hence, it lost most of its significance when the *Breviarium Alaricianum,* which was intended to be complete, became known in Burgundy. It has often been rightly stressed that to a great extent the Roman law that was the source of borrowing was not the pure, classical Roman law but the simplified law for the conditions of the time, known as Roman vulgar law.[43] It is easily conceivable that borrowing would become difficult if the cultural level of the source system was so high above that of the possible borrower that its law was virtually incomprehensible. But what matters to us here is simply that Roman vulgar law was in fact much more sophisticated and developed than Germanic customs, and still could be borrowed.[44]

It is not to our purpose to examine the other numerous Germanic codes from the fifth to the eighth centuries. The pattern is plain. To a greater or lesser extent each subsequent codification shows borrowing from Roman law and often from Visigothic law. The borrowings by the Germanic tribes were not always of the same rules or to the same extent.

Rather it is appropriate to look briefly at the spread of Visigothic law within Spain, and first from the perspective of an old problem and a more recent, authoritative, rhetorical question. The old problem was the apparent profound Germanization of Spanish customary law in the High Middle Ages. The theory, developed principally by Ficker and Hinojosa, and widely supported, started from the observation that there was an intimate relationship between some high-medieval institutions in Spain and the corresponding Germanic ones in Norway and Iceland. These, it was argued, derived from a common ethnic Germanic source; hence there must have been a continued presence of Visigothic (i.e., Germanic) customary law in Spain from the eighth to the twelfth centuries along with and beneath the "legal law." In other words, because the Visigothic "legal law" was so Romanized and was in opposition to the customary law, its force in practice was limited and in many cases did not apply. The theory is not now considered acceptable[45] and in itself need not detain us here, but it did give rise to the important rhetorical question of the distinguished legal historian F. Tomás y Valiente: "Is it possible, historically and humanly speaking, that foreign and tiny minorities—though certainly dominant—who were extremely localized, and who lost their language, their culture, and their religion, could show themselves so terrifically expansive in the field of law, right to the point of imposing a profound Germanization on it?"[46] The Visigoths numbered somewhere between 80,000 and 200,000, less than 5 percent of the population of Spain, and they were in the main peasants settled around Toledo. Tomás y Valiente's question was obviously intended, as he goes on to suggest, to elicit a massive response in the negative. The question raises issues of fundamental importance for the growth and borrowing of law, but for us the focus of the question should be changed from the Visigoths' imposition of their customary law to imposition—if that term can be applied to a voluntary acceptance—of their Liber Iudiciorum. For, as is well known and as we shall see, the Liber Iudiciorum came to prevail as the main law of Christian Spain. The obvious glib answer should be discarded. The more one might be tempted to say that the Liber Iudiciorum could easily be accepted by the Hispano-Roman population because it was so Romanized, the more difficult becomes the issue of why the Visigoths, with a legal system based on Germanic custom, could borrow all that Roman law in the first place. And, of course, it should not be forgotten that the Liber Iudiciorum contains much that is not Roman.

"With the exception of Justinian's legislation, this seventh-century Visigothic lawbook has enjoyed a wider authority during a longer time than any other code of secular law."[47] Although the Visigothic era in Spain ended in 711 as a result of the Moorish invasion, the Liber Iudiciorum did not vanish from sight. Law was, of course, much localized, and customary law remained powerful. With time, in those territories and for those people to whom the Liber Iudiciorum applied, it either had its force and scope of application reduced or it had them increased.[48]

In Septimania and Catalonia, the Liber Iudiciorum continued in force as the personal law of the *hispani*. Pipin declared in 769 that the inhabitants of Aquitania should live according to their personal law, and this was confirmed for all the *hispani* of Septimania and Catalonia by subsequent Carolingian rulers in a number of capitularies: this personal law was Visigothic law. The capitularies also weakened the applicability of the Liber Iudiciorum, because they settled questions of political order, military service, and criminal law, but the materials of the Liber Iudiciorum were much used for private law. It was the most widely used law in Catalonia in the eighth to the tenth centuries, but it decayed with the growth of other local law. The local charters given to recovered territory had precedence over the Liber Iudiciorum. Count Ramón Berenguer (1035–76) promulgated usages (*usatges*) to supplement the Liber Iudiciorum, above all with regard to feudalization. In contracts there were frequent renunciations of the Liber Iudiciorum, and in 1251 the Catalan Cortes forbade its invocation. The Mozarabs—that is, Christians living under Moorish rule—received the Liber Iudiciorum as their personal law, and they retained it whether they fled into Christian kingdoms as a result of the persecution in the second half of the ninth century or whether the place in which they lived was reconquered. Elsewhere, throughout the Iberian Peninsula, there are also signs that the Liber Iudiciorum was used: in Asturias, Galicia, northern Portugal, Navarre, and Aragon. But the deepest penetration was in Leon, where, from the tenth century, it was customary to decide lawsuits by its rules. Local *fueros* prevented it from having general force during the eleventh and twelfth centuries, but afterward, until the reign of Alfonso IX, it was used as the law in force to cut down on appeal the judgments in the king's court and became ever more the general law of the kingdom. A similar happening occurred in Toledo.

Of course, the acceptance of the Liber Iudiciorum was not complete.

What was borrowed was not everywhere the same and was not everywhere to the same extent. What matters to us, though, is simply the fact that its contents were accepted in a greater or lesser degree as the law throughout the peninsula, centuries after its promulgation, by peoples differing in many respects from the Visigoths. And its history does not stop with Alfonso IX. Ferdinand III of Castile (1230–52), the son of Alfonso IX, had the Liber Iudiciorum officially translated into Castilian with the title of Fuero Juzgo. The Fuero Juzgo was then given, as if it were the local, individual *fuero,* to the towns as they were reconquered from the Moors: for instance, to Cordobá (1241), Cartagena (1243), and Seville (1248). His son, Alfonso X (1252–84) gave the Fuero Juzgo as the local *fuero* on an even grander scale: to Alicante, Elche, Lorca, Murcia, and Talavera, for example. Subsequent kings continued the process, even spreading the Fuero Juzgo as part of the law of Castile to the New World.

SOME PROBLEM

After considering the growth of legal institutions, rules, and ideas and the nature of customary law, and after looking at two major examples of legal borrowings, we are in a position to turn to the real issue of this chapter, the cause of the Reception of Roman law in western Europe, which began in the eleventh century, traditionally in Bologna with the teaching of the Corpus Juris Civilis, by Irnerius.[49] The cause of the Reception, you will recall, was described by Paul Vinogradoff as among the most momentous and puzzling problems within the whole range of history. And the heading of this section should be understood, as a Glaswegian Scot would say, "*Some* problem nae problem." This most momentous and puzzling problem within the whole range of history turns out to be a nonproblem.

As we have seen, legal development is to some considerable extent distinct from other developments in the society and in large measure is dictated by the tradition, relating to the law, that prevails among the legal elite. Law is by no means a perfect fit for the society, not even for the society in which and for which it is created. But in addition, the borrowing of another's law is a very potent means of legal growth. Even societies governed by custom frequently borrow much law from elsewhere, and customary legal systems may even be particularly susceptible to borrowing. I put it no stronger only because developed legal systems also borrow an enormous amount,[50] and I know of no way to measure the extent of borrowing. But on a priori grounds it makes sense to think that given the lack of law, especially clear law in customary legal systems, the relative lack of expertise in judges, and the common psychological need for authority in establishing legal rules,[51] the desire for borrowing would be relatively greater in customary systems.

Two major instances of massive legal borrowing—of much pre-Justinianic law by Germanic tribes from the fifth century onward and of Visigothic law by Spanish peoples—give concreteness to the issues raised earlier in the chapter. Some legal institutions and rules will be borrowed entire, some with modifications that may be major; some will be replaced; some will be ignored entirely. A massive borrowing may continue over a long span of time. But the Reception of Roman law in the Germanic codes and of Visigothic law in Spain show much more than this.

First, and above all, the codes show that (when the conditions are right) a great deal of law from a system constructed on very different lines or containing very different rules may be borrowed.

Second, they—and above all the Germanic codes—show that a great deal of law can be borrowed from a society in which very different political, social, economic, and religious conditions prevail.

Third, they show the tendency, which is natural enough, to borrow from the more developed and detailed system. The cause of borrowing is often the search for a better rule, but it may be no more than the search for an established rule. Let us postulate in the latter case the borrowing of an apparently neutral rule. Let us suppose, as may have been true though we do not know, that the Burgundians previously had no fixed age for the attainment of majority or for the capacity to make a will. Let us further suppose that they have no firm opinions on the matter but the time has come for it to be used to fix such ages. Nothing much, let us also suppose, turns upon the exact choice. So they choose the Roman ages of twenty-five and fourteen, respectively. Is that all there is to the matter? Not quite, I think. To begin with, the habit is being established of borrowing from one particular system whenever the rule there is not obviously inappropriate. Again, law develops ever more by analogy and by further borrowing. Other gaps in the law relating to majority or minority or capacity to make a will will require to be filled, and harmoniously they ought now to be filled for the Burgundians from Roman law.

Fourth, our two instances of borrowing show (what is amply documented in other instances) that law that is in writing, hence readily accessible, is *an* or *the* obvious source for borrowing: the success of the *Sachsenspiegel* in medieval Germany,[52] of the French Code civil in Europe and Latin America,[53] of Blackstone's *Commentaries* in North America, are other powerful examples.[54]

Points three and four lead on to a hypothesis. If Justinian's Corpus Juris Civilis, especially his *Code*, had been known in Spain at the time of the reception of the Visigothic Code, as we know that it was not,[55] then it would have been a formidable rival to the Visigothic Code. It would have had all the right credentials: it was in writing, hence accessible (if known), and was more sophisticated and detailed than the law of the possible borrowers. In addition, it had a further, attractive, but not necessary, quality as a prospective quarry: like the Visigothic Code its contents, as a result of previous transplanting, had much in common with the law of the possible borrowers. The Hispano-Romans had pre-Justinianic Roman law as their law even if largely drawn from Roman vulgar law; the Corpus Juris Civilis contained much of the preceding Roman law. Similarly, the Visigothic Code, containing much Roman and Germanic law, had a great deal in common with the law of the *hispani*.

Imagine then the situation of one detailed, massive, advanced system of law in writing coming within the orbit of a number of legal systems, each involving a relatively small number of persons (hence with limitations on the amount of original legal talent available), each primarily a customary system with regard to the legal institutions dealt with by the system in writing; imagine also no intense hostility—for instance, on religious grounds—toward the culture whose legal system was in writing. In such circumstances it would be inconceivable, even if the system in writing arose from a very different society, that the customary systems would not, one by one, each within its own time frame and for its own purposes and to varying extents, begin to borrow legal rules, approaches, and ideas. What was borrowed for one customary system would not necessarily be the same as what was borrowed for another, but the process of borrowing would continue, each borrowing suggesting the appropriateness of another borrowing.

A further factor should be thrown into the equation. It seems reasonable to think, even if it cannot always be proved, that when one legal system is habitually chosen as the source from which to borrow, then that system is regarded as having high quality.[56] I know of no evidence, other than circumstantial, to indicate that the Germans of the fifth and immediately following centuries had such an opinion of Roman law, or that inhabitants of Spain at the time of the reconquest felt that way about the Visigothic Code. But there is direct evidence of enormous respect for Roman law on the eve of the Reception. In the Frankish Empire there were numerous "capitularies," in the sense of royal legislation. One distinct type, *capitula legibus addenda* (capitularies to be added to laws), were issued in order to supplement or amend existing law, and they might be added to a particular lawbook such as the *Lex Saxonum, Lex Salica, Lex Baiuwariorum,* and so on. But in the Frankish Empire Roman law was also personal law. And, as has been pointed out,[57] it is remarkable that no capitularies supplementing Roman law have been found. King Carolus II in a capitulary of A.D. 864 modifying existing law expressly excludes its operation on Roman law: "But in these places where lawsuits are judged according to Roman law, let those persons committing such acts be judged in accordance with that law: because neither did our predecessors issue any capitulary nor do we lay down anything to supplement that law or against that law."[58] The reason is plain: no one could imagine Roman law to be capable of improvement. And at this time the Corpus Juris Civilis was not known.

Nothing more need be said. The cause of the Reception of Roman law is sufficiently explained. Other causes might be adduced, and ought to be adduced in the right place, to explain why it began where it did, and when it did, and why it took the particular forms that it did. But to deal with these here would only complicate and confuse the issue. The task here is finished once it is demonstrated that the most momentous and puzzling problem of history is no problem, that it corresponds to the cultural norms of massive, voluntary legal borrowing, and that it is a non-Reception that would have constituted the most puzzling problem of history. The first (and most) important step in understanding the Reception is to know that we should explain its cause by not explaining its causes.

CHAPTER 8

LEGAL TRANSPLANTS 2
Other Receptions

FEUDAL LAW

Many of the arguments adduced in this book, and not just about bor-rowing, are strikingly confirmed when we bring into discussion the me-dieval *Libri Feudorum* (Books of the feus), which in its own field of feu-dal law was almost as significant for development as was Justinian's Corpus Juris Civilis for private law in general. Eight relevant points may be made.

First, although it contains some imperial legislation, the *Libri Feu-dorum* was a private work by Obertus de Orto, a judge of the imperial court of Milan. It appears to have been composed primarily in Milan in the first half of the twelfth century. A second version contained some expressly quoted legislation, the constitutions of 1154 and 1158 of Em-peror Frederick I. A third version was completed by the celebrated Bolognese jurist Hugolinus in 1233. The very success of the *Libri Feudo-rum* is testimony to the absence of much governmental law making, by legislation, in this area. Subsequent major legislation also would have sup-planted them. Governments often do not legislate much on private law.

Second, the very fact that the *Libri Feudorum* does contain or report some imperial legislation[1] shows that the general absence of legislation is not to be explained on the basis that there could be no legislation; it is simply that governments were insufficiently interested. Rulers had bet-ter things to do. It is not easy to determine the extent of statute law in the *Libri Feudorum*, for statutory provisions may be included without being expressly mentioned. Again, the most frequent source of statutes referred to is the old collections of Lombard law from the seventh and eighth centuries, legislation meant for very different social conditions. Old law survives in different circumstances.

Third, a failure to accept that governments are uninterested in law making has led learned men—who ought to know better—to make fundamental mistakes. Thus the splendid Scot Thomas Craig says in his *Jus Feudale,* which was first published in 1655 though written much earlier (Craig died in 1608), at 1.6.7:

> But it may seem a surprise, since the authors of these books were private men and attorneys (however great intellectually, and leaders in their own assembly), how it could come about that their opinions were not only treated as if they were statutes, but even caused imperial and pontifical laws to be subordinate to them, and took to themselves supremacy of law in their own field; since it is certain that only the pope and emperor (in the term emperor I include all rulers who recognize no superior) have the right and power of laying down the law.

And he reminds us that even the great Roman jurists Ulpian, Scaevola, and Paul had their authority not from their eminence but from Emperor Justinian's approval and decree. And he goes on at 1.6.8:

> But the solution of this problem is easy. For the authority of the *Digest* received its authority not from the authors themselves but from the day of the constitution promulgated by Justinian, which is prefixed to the pandects, namely the 24th December, 533 A.D. . . . Likewise it should be considered in the case of the Libri Feudorum that, plausibly, they received their authority not from Gerardus nor from Obertus [the reputed authors] but from imperial constitutions. One might reasonably believe that when these were founded on and produced in the Lombard courts, Gerardus and Obertus set down in brief notes the extent of their use and observance.

Thus, he continues, the *Libri Feudorum* was a product of imperial statute, a select digest of laws of such emperors as Lothair, Conrad, and Frederick. Craig was deceived, of course, but it should be made clear that he was a victim of self-deception, and a very willing victim at that. For his purpose it should have been enough that the *Libri Feudorum* had authority: the origin of that authority did not have to be specified by him, especially since his main subject was Scots law (and Scotland never came under the rule of imperial legislation). He was also too good a historian not to be aware—as, indeed, he makes plain—that there was no evidence that the *Libri Feudorum* was a digest of imperial law. But he believed, and this alone can explain his approach, that such authoritative works must, of necessity, be based on direct governmental law making—imperial legislation. Incidentally, he was too good a lawyer to have failed to notice that the parallel he drew with the *Digest* was no parallel. The writings of the jurists contained in the *Digest* became authoritative because, and at the time when, the *Digest* was enacted as statute. That is very different from saying that the *Libri Feudorum* had authority because it contained a summary of legislation. A private work cannot be said to be authoritative because it paraphrases, summarizes, or reports legislation.

Fourth, the success of the *Libri Feudorum* is another instance of massive reception, of legal transplants. They were treated as having considerable authority for the law not just in Lombardy but elsewhere in France, Germany, the Netherlands, and Scotland. A remark of G. L. Boehmer (1715–97) in his *Principia Iuris Feudalis* (Principles of feudal law) published at Göttingen—Boehmer was an illustrious professor there, a subject of the king of Great Britain and of the elector of Saxony—is instructive: "The *sources* of *common* German feudal law are the *feudal* law *of the Lombards* received throughout Germany; universal *German feudal customs;* the *common law of the empire* contained in imperial sanctions, in Roman and in canon law."[2] Thus the *Libri Feudorum* is given pride of place among the sources of feudal law common to all Germany. As W. H. D. Sellar convincingly argues:

> The feudal law was in a very real sense the common law of post-Carolingian Europe, and the Libri Feudorum, which incorporated the Constitutions of several of *Charlemagne's* imperial successors, were often regarded as an appendix to the civil law of the Emperor Justinian himself.[3]

Indeed, for early-seventeenth-century Scotland, Thomas Craig could write:

> Nay, if we wish to judge the whole matter in an exact fashion, this [feudal law] can be called the proper law of this kingdom (if we wish to extend broadly the term of "proper law") because from its spring and sources all the law flowed that we use today in court, and all the usages and practice, and if any doubt arises, the beginnings are always to be searched out, so that from them what is fair may be recognized.[4]

But the history of Craig's *Jus Feudale* further alerts us to the enormous extent of the reception of feudal law. As I have already mentioned, it was first published in 1655 half a century after it was written in Edinburgh, Scotland. But it was republished, more than half a century later, in Leipzig, Saxony. Not only that, but the Leipzig title page describes it as *Opus in Germania Dudum Desideratum* (A work long longed for in Germany). And the editor of this edition, Lüder Mencke, in his preface continues in this vein, and insists that it was longed for because of its usefulness in court. But assuredly what the Saxons wanted for court practice was not law peculiar to Scotland. Yet it was useful enough for Scots law to be reprinted in Edinburgh in 1732.

But if the *Libri Feudorum* was widely received, it in its turn was greatly infiltrated by the law in the Corpus Juris. The accepted rule was that when the *Libri Feudorum* did not provide an answer, recourse was to be had to the Corpus Juris and to common law.[5] However, the converse did not apply. Arguments drawn from the *Digest* and the *Code* abound in commentaries on the *Libri Feudorum*, as do references to famous scholars of Roman law. Roman categories and classifications was treated as important resources. Thus, to give an example from a very basic level, Henricus Zoesius (1571–1627) in his *Praelectiones Feudales* (Feudal lectures) given at Louvain in 1623 (first published in 1641) put the questions whether the feu should be classified among the nominate or the innominate contracts, and then whether it should be classified among the *contractus bonae fidei* (contracts of good faith).[6] The notions of nominate contracts, innominate contracts, and contracts of good faith come from discussions on Roman law.

Fifth, feudal law lasted as an important legal system long after the real demise of feudalism as a meaningful social system. Thus, for many scholars, the end of feudalism as a social system came in the twelfth century, the time when the *Libri Feudorum* was just being written;[7] for others, it came in the later thirteenth century.[8] What is sometimes seen as a continuation of feudal society should rather be regarded as a survival of feudal law, above all of land tenure but now with the obligation of the recipient being to pay with money, not fealty. Yet the work of J. L. Boehmer just cited ran into at least eight editions and was last published in 1819. Thomas Craig's *Jus Feudale* was, as already emphasized, written in the early seventeenth century, published in 1655, and republished in Leipzig in 1716 and again in Edinburgh in 1732. The Prussian Henricus Coccejus's (1644–1719) *Juris Feudalis Hypomnemata* (Notes on feudal law) had four editions and was last published in Louvain in 1624. Sam Stryk's (1640–1710) *Examen Juris Feudalis* (Examination of feudal law) appeared in numerous editions, probably the last at Vienna, undated but of 1750 or later. And so it goes on. In France, feudal law was abolished at the Revolution.[9]

Sixth, the primary lawmakers here were professors. This is so not only with regard to the authorship of the *Libri Feudorum* but also with regard to its subsequent history. Even before the third version, an *apparatus* was produced by Pillius, which in turn was used by Accursius, who produced a standard *glossa,* here as for the Corpus Juris. The gloss remained in Hugolinus, who produced the third version of the *Libri Feudorum,* to add it, with the gloss, to the traditional arrangement of the Corpus Juris: in the fifth volume, the *Volumen Parvum,* where it is placed after the *Authenticae.* Thereafter the fate of the *Libri Feudorum* was tied up with the Corpus Juris and they were regarded as part of the learned law. Many jurists, including Baldus, Bartolus, Duarenus, Hotman, Cujas, Zasius, and Paulus de Castro, who are celebrated for their work on Roman law, also contributed important writings on the *Libri Feudorum.* Cujas, indeed, produced a new arrangement with the *Libri Feudorum* divided into five books instead of the traditional three.

The professors were the main cause of the territorial expansion of the realm of the *Libri Feudorum* just as they were for the development of the law. Thus it is not surprising to find that the great Hermann Conring claims in his *De origine juris Germanici* of 1643 that these feudal customs were transported into Germany in the fifteenth century when law was first taught and universities were founded.[10] But, of course, the feudal system and feudal customs had existed long before. Conring says: "For the Goths, Vandals, Alemanni, Franks, Burgundians, Angles, Saxons, all the German nations who occupied by war the richest parts of the Roman Empire, each had their own laws or customs on feus no less than had the Lombards." And Conring's view found favor.[11]

Seventh, it is in harmony with this that the justification for the authority of the *Libri Feudorum* was the subject of much doubt, though the authority itself was not. For some, the authority was the same as that of the other Libri Juris Civilis. Where local statute or local custom was lacking, the *Libri Feudorum* prevailed.[12] Others expressed the view that the *Libri Feudorum* had the force of statute as if it had been approved by the emperors and incorporated into the Corpus Juris.[13] Or: "By being received; that is, in so far as by a certain spontaneous decision, they were brought into the schools with the knowledge of the emperor who does not oppose the fact, and explicated and validated by the common observance of judgments."[14] Others insisted on the private category of the work, approved by no public authority of prince or people, and they maintained that private writings make no law. Despite the form, then, on that view the *Libri Feudorum* does not exceed the authority of custom.[15] This confusion as to the source of authority of the *Libri Feudorum* testifies to the lack of interest on the part of the governments as to who makes the law or how it is made. The authority exists by default.

Eighth, these subordinate lawmakers see law in part, I maintain, as their culture. Part of the traditional culture of these learned lawyers was the *Institutes* of Justinian, which had an enormous impact, for instance, on the structure of many later books dealing with local law.[16] So powerful was the impact of this tradition that we find this structure of the *Institutes* even where it was entirely inappropriate, even in feudal law, as in Sam Stryk's *Examen Juris Feudalis* (1685).[17] An example from Scotland is Alexander Bruce's *Principia Iuris Feudalis* (1713).

Feudal law presents us with a very convenient counterweight to Roman law. From it we can see again that the history of Roman law conforms to a pattern of human experience with law. Both were created in and for a particular society. In no way should the particular societal conditions of their origins be ignored. But they long outlived the social and political conditions of their origins. Their impact is noticeable even today. Then both spread from their country of origin to distant shores: Roman law roots are evident in modern South Africa; and feudal law has a prominent place in contemporary U.S. property law, even if this is unremarked.

FRENCH CODE CIVIL

The first steps in the reception of the French Code civil were the direct result of Napoleon's conquests.[18] Belgium was incorporated into France in 1797, and the Code civil automatically came into force in 1804, and remained in force despite Napoleon's fall. The Netherlands, despite its neutrality, was forced more and more into the French sphere of influence, and in 1806 the Dutch were forced to accept Napoleon's brother Louis as king. In 1809 Napoleon compelled them to accept a version of the Code civil that was slightly altered to take account of some Dutch legal practices. In 1810 Napoleon annexed the Netherlands, and the original Code civil was introduced. After Napoleon's fall, Belgium and the Netherlands were united. The Code civil was to remain in force until a fresh code could be issued, but Belgium separated in 1830, and a new Dutch commission was appointed, whose proposed code, the Burgerlijk Wetboek, came into force in 1838. The Burgerlijk Wetboek is itself strongly based on the Code civil, and indeed the majority of provisions are straight translations. There are, however, changes in structure. This code is in four books. The first deals with persons, and a significant change is that matrimonial property appears here sandwiched between marriage and divorce, whereas in the Code civil the subject is treated in book 3. Book 2 concerns things, including—unlike the Code civil—

succession. Book 3 concerns obligations, and book 4 deals with proof and prescription. Procedure and commercial law are excluded, as they are from the Code civil. In contrast to Justinian's *Institutes,* book 4 is much shorter than the others. Since 1947 a very different Dutch code has been in active preparation, and parts of it are already in force. The code includes commercial law, in which regard it is in line with a current trend.

In Italy, too, with the exception of Sicily and Sardinia, Napoleon's conquest introduced the Code civil with a few necessary changes. French law, in fact, was influential even before the promulgation of the Code civil. For instance, a *projet* was produced for the Roman Republic in 1798, and this was very much influenced by the French *projet* of 1796.[19] The Codice civile di Napoleone il Grande was repealed almost everywhere in 1814; Italy was then again a land of many independent territories, which began to produce their own civil codes, all of them based on the Code civil. Lombardy and the Veneto, being under Austrian rule, were subject to the Allgemeines Bürgerliches Gesetzbuch (ABGB). Italy became a unified kingdom in 1861, and since the individual civil codes were based on the Code civil, it was no difficult matter to frame an Italian civil code, heavily indebted to the Code civil, which was enacted in 1865. Plans for a reformed code existed in the 1920s and 1930s, but a new approach was devised in 1939: a code was to be prepared that would comprehend not only traditional private law but all the possible personal and professional relationships of the citizen. The new Codice civile of six books came into force in 1942, and it also deals with commercial law, with book 4 concerning labor law.

Napoleon's conquests meant that in Germany also the Code civil came into operation in the Rhineland in 1804, and later in Westphalia, Baden, Frankfurt, Danzig, Hamburg, and Bremen. After Napoleon's defeat the Code civil remained in force in the Rhineland, and in a translation called the Badisches Landrecht it was the law of Baden. Likewise in Switzerland in the cantons of Geneva and the Bernese Jura the Code civil applied from 1804 as the result of conquest. The Code civil served as the model for the civil code of cantons in western Switzerland: Vaud (1819), Fribourg (1834–50), Ticino (1837), Neuchâtel (1854–55), and Valais (1855). These codes survived until 1912.

In Europe even countries unconquered by Napoleon felt the power of the Code civil. The Rumanian civil code above all was simply a translation. In Spain, a commercial code based on Napoleon's Code de commerce was issued in 1829, and a modernized version appeared in 1885.

The Spanish Código civil appeared only in 1889 and in substance owes much to the Code civil, especially with regard to obligations, though much of family law and succession is native to Spain. The structure has original features. After a preliminary title the Código civil divides into four books. Book 1 is "persons"; book 2 is "things, ownership, and its modifications"; book 3 is "the different ways of acquiring property," namely occupation of unowned property, gift, and succession; and book 4 is "obligations and contract." Spanish law has had a complicated legal history, in that law in Spain, as elsewhere in western Europe, underwent a Reception of Roman law while retaining vigorous indigenous elements. Different kingdoms of Spain had their own laws, which remained important and were not all displaced by the code. In fact, of the Código civil only the general introductory provisions on statutes and private international law and the sections on matrimonial law applied throughout Spain. Where the fueral system, a system based on local chapters and customs, prevailed, the Código civil had only subsidiary effects in other matters. The fueral laws are now being codified.

Portugal, too, adopted in 1833 a commercial code based on that of France, and this was replaced in 1888. The Portuguese Civil Code of 1867, though heavily influenced by the Code civil, is less dependent on it than other codes of the nineteenth century. A new Portuguese Civil Code of 1967 still excludes commercial law and labor law.

France was also until recently the holder of a great colonial empire, and into the colonial territories, most noticeably in sub-Saharan Africa, the Code civil and the Code de commerce were introduced, though sometimes with modifications. These codes did not apply to "French citizens of local status" who were subject to African customary law or to Islamic law if they were Muslims. The various systems of law were dealt with in separate courts. Since the former colonies have become independent, they have been remodeling their law, using French techniques and French terminology. In Algeria the two main French codes were introduced in 1834, while Tunisia in 1906 and Morocco in 1913 received a Code des obligations et des contrats, which was largely a modified version of the appropriate sections of the French codes.[20] French influence still dominates in these areas. For political reasons French law also dominated these fields of law in Egypt and Lebanon.

In North America Louisiana, which was ceded by France to the United States in 1803, adopted a civil code in 1808. The main direct sources for the substantive provisions and even more for the structure of this code were the French Projet de code civil of 1800 and the Code civil itself.[21] The Louisiana code did not include commercial law. New codes were issued in 1825 and again in 1870.

REVOLUTION IN LAW

To all of what has been said in this and the previous chapters a possible objection might be raised. What, it might be asked, about revolution in law? It seems that there can be sudden drastic change in law: the introduction of the French Code civil for instance, or its acceptance in some South American states, or the approach to law in Russia after the Bolshevik Revolution, or Atatürk's legal reforms. How does sudden massive legal change affect the picture of legal development that I have presented? The answer, I believe, is that an examination of revolution in law confirms the general thesis of the enormous impact of the legal tradition on legal change.

Revolutions in law occur, I believe, in four sets of circumstances that, it should be emphasized, shade into one another: first, where the law has, largely through the impact of the legal tradition, become cumbrous and remote from societal realities, and there is a profound call for improvement; second, where the realistic possibility is presented of borrowing a foreign system in large measure; third, where there has been an actual political revolution, and societal conditions have changed; and fourth, where the ruling elite wishes to change society drastically, to revolutionize society, and chooses to use law as one tool.

For the first case, the best examples are, I believe, to be sought in some modern codes such as the Codex Maximilianeus Bavaricus civilis of Bavaria (1756), the Prussian Allgemeines Landrecht für die Preussischen Staaten (1794), and the Austrian Allgemeines Bürgerliches Gesetzbuch (1812). But they are all, as legal historians know, deeply rooted in the preceding legal tradition.[22] The concern of the lawmakers was much more to make the law more comprehensible and accessible than to change drastically the legal rules.[23] The formulation of these codes represents a decisive stage in the development of the law of their territory: from now on the authority of the territorial law is to rest primarily on statute rather than on custom and the Corpus Juris Civilis. Most of what could usefully be borrowed from the Corpus Juris has been. There is a turning toward new sources of legal growth but no rejection of the existing heritage of legal rules.

Two private initiatives from the same period for a code for all Germany are revealing of attitudes, as even the titles of their work show. In

1777 Johann Georg Schlosser published his *Vorschlag und Versuch einer Verbesserung des deutschen bürgerlichen Rechts ohne Abschaffung des römischen Gesetzbuchs* (Recommendation and attempt at an improvement of German civil law without the abrogation of the Roman code). And in 1800 came Johann Friedrich Reitemeier's *Ueber die Redaction eines Deutschen Gesetzbuchs aus den brauchbaren aber unveränderten Materialien des gemeinen Rechts in Deutschland* (On the redaction of a German code from the usable but unchanged materials of the common law in Germany). The Bavarian Code, too, had kept the previous law as law in force. That could not be the way forward. But, nonetheless, such books and that code indicate there was to be no break with the legal tradition. The draftsmen of the codes were not seeking a new set of very different legal rules, but the same or very similar rules, with modifications, made clearer, simpler, and less controverted. Acceptance of a code does require official, political intervention, but history shows that codification can occur under any type of government.[24]

For the second case, that of borrowing, the best examples are to be found in the wholesale adoption of the French civil code as a model for a civil code in Latin American countries and in parts of Europe.[25] Here, too, it was the legal tradition that dictated the changes. The borrowing nations might have had a very different economy or political structure from France at the time of Napoleon. What they had in common was a system of law similar to that of France before codification, a civil-law system that accepted the authority of the Corpus Juris,[26] and a desire to set out the law in a more accessible form. They did not necessarily want to create a society like that of France. For those imbued with this legal tradition the French Code civil was often the most obvious, if not the only, model. Significantly, no country without a civil-law tradition followed this path.

For the third case, involving revolution, the obvious examples should be chosen from the French Revolution and the Bolshevik Revolution. Here again we should remember that a legal institution is a social institution looked at from the legal point of view. If the social institution disappears, then so should the legal institution (though it may leave traces); if a new social institution emerges, then it is likely to be surrounded by applicable legal rules. The French Revolution destroyed the social institution of feudalism in France: with that destruction disappeared all the legal incidences of feudalism. But no one has, I believe, ever doubted that France remained what it had been before, a civil-law country and, indeed, for many became the civil-law country par excellence. However much society changed, the basic civilian approaches and rules remained.

The Bolshevik Revolution was much more drastic in its attempt to change both the basis of society and law. According to Marxist doctrine, law is only a superstructure: it is an instrument of those who exercise their dictatorship because they have under their control the instruments of production. Law in a capitalist state, for instance, is unjust, suppressing the interests of the exploited classes.[27] This attitude to law is therefore in strict contrast to the bourgeois notions of law that preceded it. If in such circumstances no trace remained of the preceding legal tradition, that would not be contrary to the thesis of this book. Naturally political will and political power have an impact on legal rules and the legal tradition; and here we would have an extreme case of political will using political power to change society, using law as one instrument of this change. Because the previous law and legal tradition were wicked, they, too, would have to change. One legal tradition would be replacing another. And in many regards Soviet law is very different from earlier Russian law. Yet when that is said, it must also be maintained that the preceding legal tradition has not relinquished its influence. Before the revolution Russian law could be classed within the civil-law family though it was not a full member.[28] Today, among Western jurists at any rate, the issue is still discussed whether Russian law should be classed as a civil-law system. For some there is no doubt that Soviet law should, even though stress is laid on the impact of Marxist-Leninist principles. According to E. L. Johnson,

> Soviet law, like Imperial Russian law (at any rate after 1864), clearly falls within the civil-law group of legal systems. This presents particular problems for Anglo-American students of the Soviet system, whereas for the continental students, there is much, especially in the way of principle and terminology, that a French or Dutch student may be able to take for granted; he is, in effect, enabled to concentrate on the differences between Soviet law and his own system, just by reason of the fact that certain basic assumptions and, in particular, certain matters of terminology are similar. The French research worker, for example, who finds some Soviet rule, institution, or juridical technique that differs from his own, will usually want to find out whether that particular rule, institution or technique was paralleled in the Imperial Russian legal system, for only then can he decide whether it is to be regarded as a specific feature of the Soviet legal system or whether it is part of the Russian legal heritage acquired and taken over, perhaps with modifications, by the Soviet. In other words, he asks himself,

does this rule or institution have a specifically Soviet or a specifically Russian character? The Anglo-American lawyer researching into Soviet law, however, who finds some rule or institution of an unfamiliar nature, has first to pose a preliminary question; is this rule or feature a common characteristic of civil law systems in general, as distinct from common law systems? Only when he is satisfied that it is not can he go on to consider whether he is dealing with some specifically Russian or specifically Soviet rule or institution.[29]

Others preferred to class socialist law as a separate family.[30] Among them some stress that, outside of Russia, much of the old law was retained in the socialist states: "Techniques known from experience to be valuable and which were in no way incompatible with a renewal of the law were preserved. Substantively, legal provisions in which class characteristics were evident were abrogated; but the whole of the law was not condemned since it contained a portion of the national cultural heritage that was worthy of admiration and confidence."[31] Others emphasize even for Russia the continued influence of German law in the Civil Code of the RSFSR of 1922.[32] Prerevolutionary drafts of codes were heavily based on German law. The RSFSR civil codes of 1922 and 1964 both have a "General Part" which corresponds closely in nature, intention, and contents to the "Allgemeiner Teil" of the German Bürgerliches Gesetzbuch, and both treat the specific types of contract in a manner very similar to that found in the BGB. This survival of the preceding legal tradition is deeply significant.

The fourth situation, involving the elite, should be discussed for the sake of completeness, but here, I wonder what is to be learned for or against the impact of the legal tradition on legal development. In the extreme case, one legal tradition is to be replaced by a second, in order to change societal institutions. If the result is a total and immediate success for the transplant, we would know that (in particular circumstances) societal (and with them legal) institutions can be rapidly altered by the imposition of political will using law as one instrument of change. If the result is a total failure, we would know (in particular circumstances) societal (and with them legal) institutions cannot be rapidly altered by the imposition of the political will. This kind of case is very common, especially perhaps in countries that have just won their independence. In the absence of sustained political opposition, the result is a more or less slow acceptance of the new legal rules. The speed of transition depends on many facts, including education in the new tradition. Penetration is thus often slowest in villages, where there is least impact on daily living from the official law and more acceptance of the traditional law, where illiteracy, including that of legal officials, makes understanding of the new law difficult, and where established local procedures are often cheapest.[33]

What the four situations have in common, especially first, third, and fourth, is that they represent the legal tradition in crisis, when law is seen and treated most clearly as a means, not an end.[34] The force of the legal tradition is, in fact, threatened. The remarkable fact then is not that that occurs, but that when it does, the legal tradition retains so much of its authority and power. Theoretically at least the legal tradition may be entirely superseded. When it is, it is replaced by another legal tradition.

OTHER INSTANCES

Massive transplants are incredibly common—for example, the largely complete borrowing of Swiss private law by Turkey, discussed in Chapter 1. A recent and ongoing example concerns the independent Republics of the former Soviet Union. They are preparing modern codes with the explicit aim of westernizing their law. But despite that, the impact of Russian law is enormous. Thus, in April 1997, 97 percent of the second part of the draft of the Civil Code of the Republic of Armenia, on obligations, derived directly from the Civil Code of Russia.[35] The draft was even composed in Russian, not in Armenian. When the United States of America was created in 1776, it accepted very largely the common-law system of the English enemy. Much of English law was already in place, but it was to be further greatly elaborated. Worth emphasizing is that the immediate source was often an unofficial private work, William Blackstone's *Commentaries on the Law of England* (1765–69). The source to be borrowed from need not have previous governmental authority.[36] And small legal works may often be the most influential in faraway lands.[37] One must not forget that often a reception can be very gradual.

ONE MORE CASE

From a very early point in this book the major themes emerged: the importance of the legal tradition for legal development, the nature of customary law, the central role of legal borrowing (especially of Roman law in past centuries), and the pivotal need for authority. In this connection I discuss in Chapter 6 one seventeenth-century Scottish case. In this the legal debate centered on the provisions of Roman law, although they were not economically appropriate and were not a necessary part of Scots law. Judging is rooted in the legal tradition often to the neglect of local societal conditions. No legal case, I maintain, can be understood as law in action if one neglects the legal tradition that sets the parameters of debate. The tradition is not noticed by the actors who live it, and they are unaware of its impact. They know not what they do.

Elsewhere, in Chapter 3, I give examples from other systems in which to outsiders judges had acted in an extreme way and obtained inappropriate results, but in which the judges thought of themselves as good judges acting out the rules of the judging game according to their own particular tradition.

Naturally enough, courts such as those in Scotland and South Africa do not always show themselves to be unaware of changed circumstances when they reason from Roman or Roman-Dutch law. But even then the legal culture may also emerge clearly. Another example from Scotland, *Halkerston v. Wedderburn* of 1781, merits attention:

> Mr. Halkerston, thinking his garden at Inveresk injured by a row of elms, the branches of which hung over it from the garden of Mr. Wedderburn, applied to the Sheriff for redress. After various steps of procedure, the cause was moved to the Court of Session by advocation; when the following abstract question came to be considered, viz. Whether a person is bound to allow his property to be overshaded by the trees belonging to a conterminous heritor?
>
> *Pleaded* for Mr. Wedderburn; The climate of Scotland is such as has induced the legislature to encourage the planting of forest-trees in hedge rows, for the sake of shelter; and, for some time, it was even imposed as a duty upon every proprietor: act 1661, cap. 41. This, however, would have been an elusory enactment, if the common law permitted a conterminous heritor to lop such trees, whenever their branches extended beyond the line of march. By the common law, an heritor may plant so near the march, *in praediis rusticis,* that the trees will protrude their branches into the air, over the adjacent ground; nor is there any thing in that law, which authorises the conterminous heritor to lop off such branches, unless he can qualify a material damage arising from their protrusion.
>
> In England, as well as in Scotland, the highways are understood to be vested in the King, for behoof of the public; yet in both kingdoms, statutes have been found necessary to authorize Justices of the Peace, Way-wardens, &c. to cause prune trees hanging over the road; which could not have been the case, had the common law allowed any such power to a conterminous heritor.

In like manner, though the Roman law allowed the proprietor of a *praedium rusticum* to prune such trees to the height of fifteen feet, yet this was not a right inherent in him upon the principles of common law, but was derived from the laws of the twelve tables, and confirmed by an edict of the Praetor; L.I. §7, 8, 9. D. De arb. caed. And this very limitation of the right shews, that the Romans did not think the protrusion of branches in itself any encroachment upon the right of property; except so far as it obstructed or impeded the immediate exercise of it. They considered the air as a *res communis*, incapable of appropriation; and thought, that no encroachment upon it afforded a proper ground of challenge.

Answered for Mr. Halkerston; It is understood to be a general rule of law, that no person is entitled to encroach upon the property of another, unless he can show a right of servitude to that effect. One may dig a trench upon his own property, though the effect of it may be, to cut the roots, and destroy the whole of his neighbour's trees. He may raise his wall to any given height; and, in doing so, he may cut down every branch that stands in his way. While a branch from his neighbour's tree does him no harm, he will allow it to remain, upon the same principle of good neighborhood, that he allows him to hunt over his fields, or to angle in his stream. But the moment this branch does him a real or an imaginary injury; whenever, in short, he wishes to remove it, the law entitles him to do so, in the same manner, and upon the same principles, that it entitles him to protect his property from any other kind of encroachment.

The regulations for the encouragement of planting and inclosing, introduced by the act 1661, can never apply, with any propriety, to two contiguous gardens in the village of Inveresk; and it is not very obvious how the powers given by statute to the public officers entrusted with the care of high-ways, at all derogate from the private right of parties to demand what they are empowered to do.

Neither does the argument on the other side derive any support from the Roman law. The edict referred to, related only to *praedia rustica;* but, where a similar encroachment was made upon a *praedium urbanum,* as seems more properly to be the case here, another edict of the Praetor authorised the whole tree to be cut down; L. I. § 2. D. De arb. caed. At any rate, it is nothing to us, in what manner the Romans chose to limit the natural right now contended for. Under an Italian sun, it might probably be thought, that there could not be too much shade; but the same idea can never be entertained in a northern climate; and, accordingly, the learned Groenewegen, in his treatise, *De legibus abrogatis et inusitatis, in Hollandia vicinisque regionibus,* says expressly, "*Si arbor fundo, vel aedibus alienis impendeat, nostris et Gallorum moribus, non totam arborem a stirpe exscindere sed id quod super excurrit in totum adimere licet; tit. De arb. caed.*"

The Court had no doubt upon the principle; and, therefore, adhered to the Lord Ordinary's interlocutor, "Remitting the cause to the Sheriff, with this instruction, that he find Mr. Wedderburn is bound to prune his trees in such a manner, as they may not hang over the mutual wall, and thereby be of prejudice to Mr. Halkerston's fruit and garden."[38]

As is usual for the time, the advocates' arguments are given much more prominence than the judges' reasoning. For the defender maintaining his right to have his trees overhang and overshadow the pursuer's garden, it was argued that there was no obstacle thereto at Roman common law; though it was conceded that by statute, namely, the Twelve Tables, the aggrieved neighbor could prune such trees up to fifteen feet from the ground, and that this was confirmed by edict. This distinction between common law and statute is based on the notion that statute is an encroachment and ought to be interpreted strictly. The notion itself came into Scots law from England and was unknown to the Romans. The argument is a blending of the two foreign elements in Scots law: the scope of a Roman rule should better be determined by Roman principles, not by much later English ideas. In fact the Twelve Tables, the codification of the fifth century B.C., was regarded as the foundation of all Roman law.[39] Thus, the defender wants to give as restricted a scope as possible to the Roman rules, but never does he argue that they ought to be treated as irrelevant. Yet Roman law was not the law in Scotland, though it could be treated as of great authority.

The argument for the pursuer is of more interest for us. First, it is claimed that under the edict the overhung neighbor had full right to cut down the offending tree. Then comes the argument from changed circumstances. Even if, it is suggested, the Romans did restrict the right to prune or cut down overhanging trees, that is of no relevance for Scotland: "Under an Italian sun, it might probably be thought, that there could not be too much shade; but the same idea can never be entertained in a northern climate." Yet the presumption that Roman law applies has to be rebutted by legal authority and since there was none for Scotland the pursuer looks to Holland and France: [40] "If a tree overhangs another's land or buildings, then, by our and French custom it is not permitted to cut out the whole tree from the root, but to remove completely what overhangs." This quotation he takes very significantly from Groenewegen, *De legibus abrogatis et inusitatis, in Hollandia vicinisque regionibus* (1649), a work that, as the title shows, is dedicated to setting out the Roman rules that were not accepted or were abrogated in Holland and neighboring territories.[41]

CHAPTER 9

THE CASE OF ENGLISH COMMON LAW

In the preface I stressed that the Western system of law has two strands: English common law and continental civil law. Much of the book has focused primarily on civil law. But now I must try to explain the split. It is frequently suggested to me that if the Reception was so natural, then I ought to explain why it did not also occur in England. What follows then is a preliminary attempt at that explanation.[1]

First, within the areas most affected by the Reception there were particular reasons for accepting easily the authority of Roman law. For the Italian city-states there was no problem in their seeing themselves as the direct descendants and heirs of the Roman legal tradition. Moreover, even during the period of personal rather than territorial law Roman law remained powerful: the Catholic Church in particular was governed by it. It had also had a powerful influence on Lombard law, both on the codifications and on its subsequent development, and the Lombard lawyers at the University of Pavia used Roman law as a universal subsidiary system to fill gaps.[2] In France, the Reception was powerful in the south, the *pays de droit écrit,* from a line on the coast just west of the Île d'Oléron, proceeding roughly eastward along a line just north of Saintonge, Languedôc, Lyonnais, Maconnais, and Bresse. Apart from Poîtou, Berry, and Haute-Bourgogne, which were territories of customary law, this territory was, in earlier times when personal law flourished, precisely the land of the Burgundians and the Visigoths who issued for their Gallo-Roman subjects the *Lex Romana Burgundionum* and, more particularly, the highly prized and influential *Breviarium Alaricianum.*[3] In these circumstances it is not surprising that Roman law was treated as the law of the land, but as law by custom; and in force only insofar as it was not replaced by a subsequent, dissonant custom. As for the Holy

Roman Empire of the German Nation, that was regarded as a continuation of the Roman Empire from as early as the twelfth century; indeed the notion that the German Empire was a continuation of the Roman Empire appears as early as the Carolingian period.[4] In fact, some legislation of the emperors Frederick I and II was interpolated into the Corpus Juris, and some doctrines of Roman law were seen as favoring the emperor. In 1165 Frederick I spoke of "the example of our divine Emperors who are our predecessors."[5] In a constitution in the *Libri Feudorum*, 2.27, he describes himself as *romanus imperator;* and in another constitution recorded in the same work, 2.52, dated 7 November 1136, Lothar calls himself the third *imperator romanorum.*

Present-day Netherlands and Switzerland also experienced the Reception. But precisely at the most significant time, that of the *translatio imperii,* they formed part of the Holy Roman Empire.

Second, it is easily overlooked that for a very long time England was by no means an exceptional case. The Reception was, even where the soil was fertile, as we shall see in the case of Germany and France, not fast. Thus, despite the "theoretical Reception" in Germany (the notion that the Holy Roman Empire was a continuation of the Roman Empire), the "practical Reception" (the actual acceptance of Roman legal rules as living law) came much later. No sharp distinction can really be drawn between the "theoretical" and the "practical Reception" but, for the latter, 1495 is usually regarded as a significant date when the Reichskammergericht was created as the supreme court of the Holy Roman Empire and when it was enacted that half of the judges of it should be *doctores iuris,* that is, judges trained in Roman law. Despite the enormous boost given to the Reception of Roman law in Germany by the theory of the continuation of empire, the real Reception in the sense of actual acceptance in practice is to be dated to the fifteenth and sixteenth centuries.[6] It was then that the Corpus Juris Civilis so far as glossed—*Quidquid non agnoscit glossa, non agnoscit curia* (What the gloss does not recognize, the court does not recognize)—was accepted as a whole as law, though indeed only as subsidiary law that was overcome by local statute or custom.

The so-called Lotharian Legend, that the emperor Lothar of Supplinburg had expressly received Roman law as statute in 1135, which was apparently the invention of Phillip Melancthon, was refuted by Hermann Conring in his *De origine juris Germanici* of 1643. Thereafter, both Italy and Germany had need of new theoretical answers to the question why the Corpus Juris Civilis was given authority. Into these we need not go.[7] The Reception had already basically occurred.

In France, in the *pays de droit coutumier,* the progress of the Reception was even slower. The various local *coutumes* were eventually to be reduced to writing (and converted into statute law) as a result of Charles VII's Ordonnance de Montil-les-Tours which was dated April 1453. The slow redaction of the *coutumes* was virtually complete by the middle of the sixteenth century.[8] These written *coutumes* were influenced to various degrees by Roman law but in none did it appear as the predominant element. Much for the future was to depend on the outcome of a famous doctrinal battle. Some authorities, notably Pierre Lizet (1482–1554), first president of the Parlement of Paris, wanted Roman law to be the common law of France as *lex scripta,*[9] but this was opposed vigorously by others such as Cristophe de Thou (1508–82), also first president of the Parlement of Paris, Guy Coquille (1523–1603), Estienne Pasquier (1529–1615), and later by Nicholas Catherinot (1628–88), who wanted Roman law treated only as *ratio scripta.* The distinction was crucial. If Roman law was only *ratio scripta* then, in the absence of a rule in the *coutume,* it would have authority for a judge only if it were in harmony with the principles of the *coutume,* only if it appeared just (and then for the judge its authority was precisely because it was just); and the judge could prefer the authority of another *coutume* such as the Coutume de Paris. But if Roman law were *lex scripta* and was thus the law in force in the absence of a contrary custom, then the judge would have to apply it. In the event, in accordance with the spirit of the Ordonnance of Phillipe-le-Bel of 1312, Roman law was treated only as *ratio scripta* in most of the *pays de droit coutumier.*[10] The main exceptions, where the *coutumes* expressly adopted Roman law in the absence of a relevant provision, were the *coutumes* of Berry, Haute-Marche, Auvergne and Bourbonnais which were adjacent to the *pays de droit écrit,* the *coutumes* of Burgundy, Franche-Comté, and les Trois-Evêchés which were close to the territory of the Holy Roman Empire, and some of the *coutumes* in Flanders.[11] This apparent influence of geography is very revealing.

The debate on the nature of the authority of Roman law may be seen as part of, or related to, a larger issue, namely the unification of the *coutumes.* This was above all the great desire of Charles Dumoulin or Molinaeus (1500–1566), who was to have a preponderant influence in future development, though not perhaps in a way that he envisaged. The Coutume de Paris of 1510 was very short and incomplete. In 1539 Dumoulin published his treatise on fiefs, which was the beginning of a commentary on this *coutume*. Here he expressed his criticisms and proposed new approaches, most of which were adopted by the Parlement of Paris. Consequently there was discord between the *coutume* and the case law, and this led to the promulgation in 1580 of a much larger and improved Coutume de Paris under the guidance of Christophe de Thou. The Parlement of Paris operated in effect as a court of appeal for many other towns; its *ressort* covered the jurisdiction of fifty municipal and local *coutumes*. Estienne Pasquier, who had participated in the preparation of the new Coutume de Paris, held that in these fifty jurisdictions the Coutume de Paris should be known and followed "because," as he put it, "Paris was in this kingdom what Rome was in the Empire." This called forth the wrath of Guy Coquille, who believed that other *coutumes* should be used equally with the Coutumes de Paris to supplement the local law.[12]

In fact the Coutume de Paris was to prove very acceptable in other jurisdictions. A significant step in that direction occurred in 1747 when François Bourjon published *Le Droit commun de la France et la Coutume de Paris* (The common law of France and the custom of Paris). The opening paragraph of this work seems obscure until one realizes that he is treating the common law of France and the Coutume de Paris as the same thing. This treatment in itself is indicative of the success of the *coutume* but in its turn Bourjon's large and clear text spread the message that the Coutume de Paris was the law of France.

But one must not exaggerate the extent to which there had not been a Reception of Roman law in France, on the eve of the Revolution. First, of course, there was a full Reception in the *pays de droit écrit*. Second, this Reception had a continued effect on the *pays de droit coutumier* because, through it, Roman rules and solutions were known since books on the law of France set out the law in the *pays de droit écrit* as well as the provisions of the various *coutumes*. Third, even when a jurisdiction looked to the Coutume de Paris or some other *coutume* to fill gaps, when a solution was not found in that way recourse was still had to Roman law. And even the reformed Coutume de Paris had many gaps, with only 372 articles. Fourth, French jurists, even those most addicted to their *coutumes*, had deep knowledge of and great respect for Roman law. Roman law is prominent in their works. The influential Robert Pothier (1699–1772) may serve as an example. Fifth, many books, including that of Bourjon, show the influence of Justinian's *Institutes* on their structure. This is especially true of institutional writings[13] such as Gabriel Argou's *Institution du droit français,* which was first published in 1692 and reached its eleventh edition in 1787. The structure of the French Code civil is similar to that of the works of Bourjon and Argou. Thus, the Reception, even in favored locales such as Germany and France, was slow.

A third point that is frequently downplayed is that much Roman law was actually borrowed by English common law. Around 1600 Thomas Craig, in his *Jus Feudale,* at 1.7.22–23 puts it this way:

> The Civil Law is rarely used in England, and although among the English are found very learned men in every branch of learning, still there are few who devote themselves to the Civil Law, they are content with a bowing acquaintance with it, since native institutions and customs are more in use with them: hence the learned say that the English use municipal law when the Scots are governed by the Civil Law. But so little are they free from the Civil Law in their judgments, that reasons and decisions of it, as if living sparks, are found in all matters and controversies which they, however, prefer to ascribe to their own men than to owe to the ancient jurists. In the event a great dependence on the Civil Law shines forth in all controversies to such an extent that an expert in Civil Law understands that the greatest controversies of English law can be decided according to the sources of the Civil Law and the replies of the jurisconsults or Emperors, as often appears from the reports of Plowden and Dyer.

As elsewhere, Craig exaggerates: his motivation is to indicate that the differences between Scots law and English law are not so great as are often supposed. And yet, without some considerable admixture of Roman law into England, his claim would have appeared simply ridiculous. Accuracy, in the state of the evidence, is difficult to attain, but what can surely be stated is that the influence of Roman law in England varied from time to time and from type of court jurisdiction to jurisdiction.[14]

In this instance, as often, it is perhaps sensible not to begin at the beginning. Writing of formularies, of collections of writs, Milsom claims:

> In one respect the most illuminating of these formularies was that which acquired the title *Brevia Placitata.* Dating from soon after the middle of the thirteenth century, it is a conflated formulary giving both writs and counts. But the writs, which in real life were always in Latin, are here translated into French, the language in which counts, at any rate in the king's courts, were actually spoken, the ordinary language of the upper classes.

This collection was for the use, or more probably the instruction, of professional men, literate men, but men not at home in the Latin tongue and not interested in the riches to which it gave access. The common law had started its career as an alternative learning, cut off from even the legal learning of the universities which until the eighteenth century taught only Roman and canon law.

Almost at the same time as the counters' modest *Brevia Placitata* Bracton gave final shape to a much larger and more ambitious book; and it is one of the important facts in the history of western thought that the former was to prove fruitful, the latter sterile.[15]

By the last sentence of his first paragraph, Milsom means, I think, not that the origins of the developed common law lay in an alternative learning, cut off from the universities, but that it was at this time around the middle of the thirteenth century that the common law cut itself off from the universities and became an alternative learning. If this interpretation is correct then Milsom's position, I suppose, would be that in England, as elsewhere in Europe in, say, the eleventh century, the local law was more or less free from Roman influence but that influence began to be felt in England as elsewhere, though not necessarily so early or so powerfully, until it was disrupted in the age of, or succeeding, Bracton.

Thus, the lawbook written apparently shortly before 1118, which is known as *Leges Henrici Primi,*[16] cites for instance Salic and Ripuarian laws and Frankish capitularies; hence, it is significant as John Barton, the leading expert on Roman law in medieval England, observes that there are so few traces of Roman law.[17] No attempt was being made by the author to Romanize. Another private work of the time, the *Leis Willelme,* contains some Roman law, but of this Barton endorses Maitland's judgment: "It shows us how men were helplessly looking about for some general principles of Jurisprudence which would deliver them from their practical and intellectual difficulties."[18]

The treatise, which was written in the 1180s and goes under Glanvill's name, is a very practical work based on what was happening in the royal courts. "The author is writing of matters which are in regular use and within his own experience. If there are cases which the King's court is not prepared to deal with, he says so. He is under no temptation to fill the gaps with matter borrowed from Salian or Ripuarian Franks or, for the matter of that, from Roman law. By the same token, when he does borrow from the civil law, this is a very much more significant circumstance than the use of a few maxims by the author of the *Leis Willelme.*"[19] Some use is made of Roman terminology though not always with the Roman meaning,[20] and book 10, which treats of the English equivalents of Roman contracts, shows some acquaintance with Roman law. But, despite the use of the Roman contractual terms, the substantive law looks very different: "The most striking feature of this book of the treatise is the conflict, if this be not too strong a term, between the form and the substance."[21]

Henry of Bracton was a royal judge who died in 1268. The treatise *De Legibus et Consuetudinibus Anglie,* which goes under his name, shows very considerable knowledge both of Roman law directly and of the learned continental jurists, notably Azo.[22] The arrangement of the work also owes much to the structure of Justinian's *Institutes.* What is not so easily determined is the extent to which Roman law had influenced the substance of English law. As Barton puts it, at times Bracton Romanizes but at other times he is clearly Anglicizing. How far Bracton accurately depicts the common law and the extent to which English rules in resembling Roman rules betray their origin are questions too difficult to be resolved here. What concerns us more is the likelihood that, because of the Romanized appearance of the *De Legibus,* if Bracton's treatise had been influential and if he had been followed on the Bench by others trained as he was, England would have undergone a Reception. But as Milsom noted, it was the *Brevia Placitata* that was to prevail.

Yet, to contrast England with continental states of the period, one should not ignore the success of the un-Romanized works, such as the *Brevia Placitata.* After all, not so long before—certainly before 1235, probably between 1221 and 1224—had been written the enormously successful *Sachsenspiegel.*[23] Originally in Latin it was rapidly turned into low German, probably East Saxon, by its author, Eike von Repgow. It was in turn translated into other German dialects, Dutch, and back into Latin. Of its two parts, over 200 manuscripts survive of the "Landrecht" and nearly 150 of the "Lehnrecht." Its influence was great well beyond the confines of the area whose customary law it described. And, in France too, even much later than Bracton's time, books such as the *Très Ancienne Coutume de Bretagne* of 1315 were to prove influential. The clue to the different development that is taking place and will continue lies not in the use made of Roman law in these works. In England, France, and Germany alike, there were books very much influenced by Roman law and books that were very much less so. Both existed side by side. But whereas books such as the *Sachsenspiegel* and French works on customary law set out the substantive law, the English works such as the *Brevia Placitata, Novae Narrationes, Placita Coronae,* and the *Court*

Baron are formularies setting out writs and pleadings.[24] The successful English works are geared very narrowly to aiding the practicing lawyer to bring the suit in the proper formal manner. This was to be the direction for English law in the succeeding centuries. And here Roman law had no role to play.

Bracton may be regarded as the high-water mark of the influence of Roman law in medieval England. The attitude to Roman law in medieval England, as in Scotland and continental Europe, corresponded to that described in Chapter 7 of the Reception of Roman law: customary systems of law are very much disposed to borrow from a mature, detailed system in writing, even when the latter is constructed on very different lines and was created for very different social, economic, and political conditions. But the borrowings may be very slow and piecemeal. The reasons are not hard to find.

What is in issue here, in fact, is not that England did not borrow from Roman law when others were doing so—it also did—but why England alone did not come to accept the Corpus Juris Civilis as authoritative. We have already seen part of the answer. Lands prominent in the Reception had particular reasons for accepting the Corpus Juris as authoritative. And for a long time England was not so different from other territories. But more must be said to explain why, in the result, England was the odd man out.

A word must be said, though, about Roman law in later England. In the sixteenth and seventeenth centuries there was an upsurge of the influence of Roman law, particularly in substance, which lends some credence to the paragraph of Craig set out at the beginning of this section. But after Bracton there was never a danger of a Reception in the sense of the Corpus Juris Civilis becoming authoritative.[25]

A fourth point to be emphasized is that, before the Corpus Juris Civilis is treated as the law of the land or as directly and highly persuasive, Roman law is influential and infiltrates other systems by filling the gaps. The greater the gaps, the greater the potential for Roman law influence. As Craig (1.2.14) puts it: "In Scotland there is the greatest scarcity of written laws and therefore, naturally, in most matters we follow the Civil Law. Not because we are learned or well grounded in it, because to this point no one—so far as I am aware—were professors of law who taught law publicly (which is of course to be regretted), but almost against our will, since we are deprived of our own written law we are led there by the sole beneficence of nature or the worth of that law."

Here I am, of course, speaking of private law, the sphere in which lay the achievement of the Romans. But English private law developed precociously. Statutes were very important for private law from an early date. Thus, Henry II (1154–89) can be characterized as "a great legislator," and Edward I (1272–1307) was responsible for some of the most important laws in English history.[26] Maitland, indeed, goes so far as to say that "the vigorous legislation of the time has an important consequence in checking the growth of unenacted law."[27] This consequence, he believes is revealed both in the check to the further advance of Roman law, which had been growing in importance under Henry III (1216–72), and in hampering further development by case law. And early there was developed a system of king's courts, applying the same law through the country. National courts, as distinct from local courts, apply to far more people: there are more cases, and relevant law is more readily established. And, as we shall see, precedent was regarded early on as important in England for fixing the law.

The mention of the king's courts brings us to a fifth point, the writ system, which has Anglo-Saxon roots.[28] The need to have a writ to bring the cause before the court meant that high priority was centered on that and on proof, rather than on systematic development of legal rules. S. F. C. Milsom goes so far as to claim that from, say, the thirteenth to the early sixteenth century the lawyers did not see the law as a system of substantive rules at all, and he contrasts them with Bracton and his kind, who "were accustomed to think in terms of substantive law." But Bracton's was the last English lawbook for centuries to be written with such terms in mind.[29] With such a framework the infiltration of Roman law would be no easy matter. It could either take the citadel by storm— which did not happen—or leave the field.

And the emphasis in England on what happened in court led early to the high practical standing of precedent. Craig (1.7.20) says:

> If nothing is settled by the principles of the common law or by custom (general or manorial) then in similar cases the authority of previous decisions, especially of the King's Bench, prevails. And now disputes are settled primarily in this way if it is shown that it was previously decided otherwise. Nor is there any defense to this form of judging unless the case can be distinguished for it very often happens that the whole situation of fact for the decision is changed by minute circumstances of fact. Hence come the many volumes of cases (for so the situations of fact are called) in Plowden, in Dyer and others.

And he demonstrates the rather lower value of precedent in Scotland (1.8.13, 14, 15). Yet Scotland and England, were the main countries where institutional writers cited precedent as authority for propositions of law.[30] This is as true of Lord Stair, *Institutions of the Law of Scotland* (first edition 1681) as of John Cowell, *Institutiones Iuris Anglicani* (first edition 1605). But even much earlier, Bracton's *De Legibus et Consuetudinibus Anglie* of the thirteenth century (now thought to have been written in the 1220s and 1230s and brought up to date by Bracton in the 1240s and 1250s)[31] contains about 500 references to decided cases. Case law was an important source of legal growth in the reign of Henry III (1216–72) and the first Year Books, the earliest English law reports, date from 1292.

The use of precedent also militates against the infiltration of Roman law. First, there are fewer gaps to be filled. Second, gaps can be filled by analogy with previous cases. Third, where judges are given the high social status of lawmakers—even if they talk as if their role was that of law finders—they will bolster their own position and prestige by relying on the authority of other judges rather than looking elsewhere for authority.

One final factor, which is by no means the least important and which perhaps deserves pride of place for England being different from the other states of western Europe in its attitude to Roman law, is feudalism and the different standing of feudal law in England.

To begin with, feudalism by its very nature ought to operate as a powerful barrier to the encroachment of Roman law. The law flowing from feudalism affects the most powerful interests. Landholding is central to the feudal system, and land was the basis of wealth in the Middle Ages. The feudal relationship was primarily knightly and military. Wealth and high social status go together in ensuring that legal rules deriving from feudalism will have a major impact on law in general. But the concepts and categories that flow naturally from feudalism into feudal law cut across those of Roman law to such an extent that they make Roman law seem irrelevant within their sphere of influence. Thus, first, by its very nature feudal law makes no distinction between public and private law, partaking of both, whereas the foremost distinction in Roman law is between public and private, with the stress in the surviving materials almost entirely on the latter. As Maitland puts it, "we may describe 'feudalism' as a state of society in which all or a great part of public rights and duties are inextricably linked with the tenure of land, in which the whole governmental system—financial, military, judicial—is part of the law of private property."[32] Second, for the law of persons in feudal law the most important division is into lord and vassal, a division that has no place in Roman law. Third and more important, fealty, a central element in the feudal system, is an obligation or one side of an obligation or partly an obligation. But it does not fit neatly into Roman notions: looked at from a Romanist point of view, it is in some sense a contract but it has very different effects from contract. Moreover, the other contracts which are so familiar from Roman law have no role to play in feudal law. Fourth, Roman law, especially as set out in the Corpus Juris Civilis, made scarcely any distinction between land and movable property. But for feudal law, only land (and some offices) was usually relevant. Moreover, the feudal grant of land in England was of an estate in the land, a time in the land, and not of ownership. The whole doctrine of estates as it was to develop was unknown to Roman law. In addition, the acquisition of an estate involved a formal ceremony, of fealty, and such ceremonies were unknown to the Corpus Juris. Fifth, the nature of the feudal grant had an automatic impact on the law of succession. Because originally an estate in land ended on death, there would be no feudal succession to land. Gradually, it came to be expected that the lord would renew. Still, this would mean in the case of land that there would be no testate succession: the lord would not want the vassal to have a right of choosing the next vassal. Also it would mean that primogeniture would be favored: the lord would not want the vassal's obligations to him to be divided among a number of people. And there would be a preference for males: the main obligation of the vassal was military service which could not be performed by a female.

These characteristics are very different from those of Roman law, where testacy was freely permitted, where no distinctions were drawn for inheritance between land and movables, where there was no primogeniture, and where for the most part male and female were equally entitled to inherit, both under a will and on intestacy. Thus, in all branches of substantive law, feudal law presented a very different face from Roman law. In addition, in all feudal relations the superior retained the power of jurisdiction over his vassal.[33] The more important feudal law was in a society, the greater the obstacle it presented to the Corpus Juris becoming authoritative.

But feudal law was bound to have a greater impact in England than elsewhere. On the one hand, it was only in England that landholding involved the doctrine of estates that resulted in so much convoluted legal reasoning and learning. Such was the overwhelming importance of this subject that it is scarcely surprising that Milsom can say that "Littleton could write his *Tenures,* which can properly be regarded as a text-book of land law, nearly four centuries before text-books were written on other branches of the law."[34] But such massive emphasis on a topic where Roman law was irrelevant would reduce the general authority of Roman law. And borrowing is often from a system that has achieved general respect. Moreover, pride in one native English achievement would increase the native self-confidence to go it alone in other fields of law. On the other hand, England, with Normandy and Brittany following hard upon, was the only territory where all of the land was held in feudal tenure. Where land is allodial, or not in feudal tenure, nonfeudal principles will determine ownership, transfer, rights of succession, and so on. Another system will have to apply, and Roman law is an obvious resource. On this argument it is not surprising that at the time of the French Revolution, Normandy and Brittany had received relatively little of Roman law. And it is consistent with this argument that Friesland, whose law was notoriously more Romanized than the other United Provinces, had relatively more of its land held allodially than had the others.

In a very different way feudal law would be more of a barrier to the penetration of Roman law in England than elsewhere. The *Libri Feudorum*, already discussed, is the greatest monument of the feudal law and seems to have been composed mainly in Milan in the first half of the twelfth century. A second version contained constitutions of the Emperor Frederick I, dating from 1154 and 1158. Hugolinus, the Bolognese jurist, completed a third version, and the book acquired a semiofficial status[35] when he inserted it in the *volumen parvum* of the Corpus Juris, which contained the *Institutes* and the *Authenticum* (a version of the *Novellae*). In fact, it was treated as an appendix to the nine *collationes* of the *Authenticum* and hence was even called the tenth, *decem collatio*. It was glossed like the parts of the Corpus Juris Civilis—that name is later—and the gloss was accepted into the *Glossa Ordinaria* of Accursius. Its fate and fortune were thus linked with those of the Corpus Juris. It was even taught along with it, and the same celebrated European scholars like Cuiacius, Baldus, Julius Clarus, and Hotman, wrote on both.

But this linking of the *Libri Feudorum* with the Corpus Juris Civilis would restrict the impact of feudalism to feudal law. To begin with, the elements of the Corpus Juris, in particular the *Digest* and *Code*, had such a high status and were so detailed that the *Libri Feudorum* could scarcely encroach. Then again, the *Libri Feudorum* was much less detailed, and treating it with the Corpus Juris would result in the gaps, inconsistencies, and ambiguities in the *Libri Feudorum* being resolved or filled by the Corpus Juris. Craig puts it this way in discussing the nine characteristic qualities of feus (1.9.36): "Third, any point in relation to a feu which is not expressly settled in the *Libri Feudorum* ought to be decided by the Jus Civile or the law of the Romans. Feudal decisions, on the other hand, have no relevance except in relation to feudal questions." Again, and even more significant, with this continental attitude toward the *Libri Feudorum* and feudal law, when feudalism as a social system declined, as it began to do early with the decline of knight service, there would be no obstacle from feudal law to using the rules and categories of the Corpus Juris to develop the local law.

But the *Libri Feudorum* was used in this way only in continental Europe and in Scotland, not in England. There is no trace of their having influence on English law, and no sign of any knowledge of them in English works such as Littleton on *Tenures*. But where the *Libri Feudorum*, restricted and reined in by the Corpus Juris, was not used, there were not these obstacles to feudal law dominating the legal scene and hindering legal growth on other principles, and to remaining dominant long after feudalism itself had declined.

As we have seen, there is a strong tendency for legal rules, structures, and concepts to continue in life long after the social structure has died. So it was with feudal law in England after the death of feudalism. And feudal law was the dominant part of English law, and its ideas were very different from those of Roman law.

Feudal law was thus a major factor in preventing the Corpus Juris from becoming authoritative in England while being much less of an obstacle elsewhere. I am tempted by a paradox: it was above all the early failure to receive the Corpus Juris Civilis as authoritative in England that led to the failure in England to accept the Corpus Juris Civilis as authoritative. Failure to receive the Corpus Juris Civilis as authoritative involves the failure to receive the *Libri Feudorum* as authoritative—at a certain stage in western European history, feudalism, and with it the legal rules relating to the feudal system, is very potent for development; rules of feudal law cut across the notions of Roman law; for the rest of western Europe the most important ideas of feudal law are contained in the *Libri Feudorum*; where the Corpus Juris Civilis is treated as authoritative, the *Libri Feudorum* is appended to it and treated as subsidiary; and this relationship keeps feudal law to its proper sphere and causes its decline when feudalism declines. Where feudal law is not studied through the *Libri Feudorum* as interpreted through Roman law in the gloss, feudal law is not restricted by the Corpus Juris which accordingly seems less important.

I conclude with two observations of extreme importance. First, William M. Gordon has recently and vigorously reminded us that in any discussion of a non-Reception in England the emphasis is always on the common law, "ignoring or marginalizing those parts of English law which were administered elsewhere, in particular in Chancery, in the ecclesiastical courts, in the courts of admiralty and in the conciliar courts."[36]

Second, Michael Clanchy authoritatively states:

> The distinctive style of English common law derived from many sources and traditions: Anglo-Saxon, Norman, ecclesiastical, Roman and Scholastic. The system took the form it did because it developed in the period of the twelfth century Renaissance and it retained that form for centuries thereafter because bureaucracy perpetuated it. Hence later lawyers praised as peculiarly English something that was really peculiarly twelfth century and cosmopolitan. . . . Its distinctive form was therefore a product of England's close contacts with the continent at the time and not in opposition to them.[37]

HUMANISM, THE LAW OF REASON, CODIFICATION

As I insisted at the outset, this book is not a work of legal history but an attempt to distinguish the general factors that caused Western private law to evolve the way it did. But these factors can only be isolated and their importance shown by means of individual, even detailed examples. Still, to explain the course of evolution I had to present two particular episodes that I regard as pivotal for this evolution: the Roman Twelve Tables of the mid-fifth century B.C. and the Byzantine Corpus Juris Civilis of the sixth century A.D.

At the close of the book, though, I feel it appropriate to discuss in rather general terms three movements important in the development of legal thought: legal humanism in the sixteenth century, the law of reason in the seventeenth and eighteenth centuries, and codification from the mid-eighteenth through the nineteenth century. I look at the movements through the lens of their relationship to legal evolution.

The great humanist jurists such as Cujas (1522–90), Donellus (1527–91), Hotman (1524–90), Zazius (1461–1536), and Balduinus (1520–75), and also of the Dutch "Elegant School," most notably Gerard Noodt (1647–1725), have an important place in the history of legal ideas, and of legal education. Yet their impact on practical law and legal development was limited, or indirect. Franz Wieacker puts it this way:

> We have seen that while humanist lawyers were able to find a new legitimation for Roman law, to purify and refine the way texts were read, and to offer through the Platonic theory of ideas, a new basis for legal education, they did nothing to change the idea of law or the methods used by lawyers in the late Middle Ages, especially not in the countries of the Reception. Nor was this just happenstance. Law is in debt to humanism for the return to the ancient sources, for textual criticism, and for educational

248

reform, but legal humanism was just one aspect of a general revitalization which was taking place in early modern times—the return to the model of the classical world, which started in Italy and which so raised the quality of life there that its name was lifted from the discourse of religion (renaissance, *rinascimento* = rebirth, just as spiritual man is born again in Christ). In the rest of Europe it merely replaced medieval authorities with classical ones: it did not yet encourage people to think for themselves.[1]

Why did the humanists fail to have much direct influence on the way law was practiced? To begin with, their main researches were focused on recovering classical Roman law, whereas what was accepted as authoritative was the law set out in the Byzantine emperor Justinian's Corpus Juris Civilis. That authority was not going to give way to an "antiquarian" zeal for the law of three centuries before Justinian. Again, medieval as it was, the gloss had established its authority as almost equal to that of the Corpus Juris itself. Or, at least, both were read together. In Germany the maxim came to be, *Quidquid non agnoscit glossa, non agnoscit curia* (What the gloss does not recognize, the court does not recognize).

I am not, of course, denying that individuals might have a direct impact on legal rules but that would not be in their capacity as humanists. In any event, it is not possible to see much direct impact on the development of practical law.

Still, they did have an indirect impact on law at one remove and, I believe, two other indirect cases of impact at a second remove.

The indirect impact at one remove was that the very thrust of their scholarship downgraded the authority of the Corpus Juris Civilis and of the gloss. The most vivid example comes from the short *Antitribonianus* of François Hotman, which was apparently written in 1567 but first published, in French, in 1603, and in Latin not until 1647. The very title sets the scene. Tribonian was Justinian's chief minister for the construction of the *Digest. Antitribonianus* is thus a manifesto against the *Digest.*

Hotman begins with a declaration of the supreme importance of law and a statement that a part of the French youth is seriously engaged in the study of Justinian's law. "But if I draw a big distinction between the civil law of the Romans and the books of the Emperor Justinian, I do not think I am saying something remote from the truth." Hotman's procedure is, first, to proceed as if that method of legal study was the best regulated in the world and the books of Justinian were made in all perfection and, second, to investigate the quality of these books and their effects. He claims that at all times wise men have accepted that the laws of a country must be fitted to the state and form of the commonwealth, not the commonwealth to the laws. Among his illustrations is Rome, where as soon as kings were destroyed and the republic established, all effort for 150 years was on making new laws fit for the democracy. He then argues that the state of France is so different from Rome that nothing for France can be learned from Roman public law. Moreover, Roman public law of the republic and high empire cannot really be known from the Corpus Juris.

His chapters 4 through 9 are devoted to showing how far Roman private law also differed from that of France. Hotman compares Roman and French legal education in chapter 10 but also draws more general conclusions. Thus, "And if one must speak of the civil law of the Romans, I will say further that it was never made or composed to serve as equity or natural reason, suitable to every nation without distinction, but only by a particular prerogative expressly invented to support Roman citizens, and in a higher degree and dignity than the other inhabitants of Italy." Again, "These two points have been sufficiently recognized; first that it is only very mistakenly that one calls the study of the books of Justinian the study of Roman law, since only a twentieth part has remained for us; second, that of the little which has survived to us, not even a tenth part can be used and put into practice in our France."

From chapter 11 onward Hotman deals with his second principal point, namely, the quality of the Corpus Juris. He notes the numerous disputes as to the law among the followers of the two Roman schools, Sabinian and Proculian, and implies that rescripts of notorious emperors such as Helagabalus, Commodus, Caracalla, and Diocletian would not be noteworthy for their equity. He stresses the iniquity of Justinian's chief minister, Tribonian, who according to Suidas despised God and all religions, especially the Christian; who was so avaricious that he sold law and justice, and for money changed the tenor of the laws; and who, according to Procopius, did not let a single day pass without changing the law for the profit of an individual. Justinian, Hotman avers, was regarded as no better. Chapter 12 is devoted to a discussion of some peculiarities in the work of Tribonian. Having completed his work, for example, Tribonian suppressed and abolished all the old laws, the praetorian Edict, and the decrees of the Senate. While vaunting that he had left the expositions of the jurists, Tribonian actually suppressed the works of those great jurists who were truly Roman such as the Catos and the Mucii, Manilius, Caecilius, and Servius Sulpicius, but retained the works of Greeks, Syrians, and Africans like Africanus, Tryphoninus, Modestinus, Javolenus, and Ulpian. Tribonian's work, says Hotman, is composed of broken extracts, useless and out of context, and he has not kept to the original order, not even of statutes. Many contradictions remain, as well as many interpolations of Tribonian himself and many repetitions. Formalities of Roman law that had been abolished nonetheless appear throughout the work. Thus runs Hotman's criticism of Tribonian. The rest of Hotman's book then concerns the subsequent history of the Corpus Juris, with chapter 18, the final one, expressing the hope of reform.

Even apart from Hotman's plea for a reformed attitude to law, the message of legal humanism for local law is plain. Roman law was not intended to be eternal or to serve as natural reason but was created for a particular people at a particular time: nor was it ever perfect for its purpose. Moreover, Justinian's law books do not really give Roman law, and they were the work of men famous for their iniquity. Respect for classical antiquity should therefore not lead to admiration of the Corpus Juris. For the humanist jurists' attitude to the gloss we may consider the humanist, nonjurist François Rabelais (c. 1490–1553?): "So from thence he [Pantagruel] came to Bourges, where he studied a good long time, and profited very much in the faculty of the Lawes, and would sometimes say, that the books of the Civil Law were like unto a wonderfully precious, royal and triumphant robe of cloth of gold, edged with dirt; for in the world are no goodlier books to be seen, more ornate, nor more eloquent than the texts of the Pandects, but the bordering of them, that is to say, the glosse of Accursius is so scurvie, vile, base, and unsavourie, that it is nothing but filthinesse and villany."[2]

The indirect impacts at the second remove are the result of this downgrading of the authority of the Corpus Juris. One of these is the writing by scholars of institutes of local law which number probably into the hundreds. These range from France to Holland to Scotland and elsewhere. Famous examples are Hugo Grotius *Inleidinge tot de Hollandsche rechtsgeleerdheid* written between 1619 and 1621, and Sir George Mackenzie's *Institutions of the Law of Scotland,* first published in 1684. What most of these books on local law have in common is the structure of Justinian's *Institutes.* They contain the subject matter of the *Institutes,* though often omitting procedure and criminal law; anything that was not in Justinian is excluded from the local Institutes. Their parentage is apparent.

These institutes do not change the course of evolution. The local law was already there. If anything they strengthen the impact of Roman law: local law systematized according to the structure of Justinian's *Institutes* tends to emphasize the common elements and to deemphasize what is purely local.[3]

The other indirect impact at a second remove was the systematization of the *ius commune*. The *ius commune* may briefly be described as the law deriving from the Corpus Juris Civilis and the Corpus Juris Canonici that was close to being the same in many European territories. Again, this systematization was not a breach in the legal tradition.[4]

The philosophical notion of "natural law"—that is, law existing without being necessarily accepted in a particular state—has existed almost as long as we have evidence of law. Theories of natural law may be based on divine revelation, on nature and in particular human nature, and on reason. Such theories are multifarious and often overlap. But from the seventeenth century onward a strong new current of natural law as the law of reason is evident. The most eminent early exponent is again Hugo Grotius, this time in his *De Iure Belli ac Pacis* (On the law of war and peace), first published in 1625. This is regarded as one of the founding texts of international law, and it is no coincidence that this law of reason was first prominent there, not in a discussion of territorial law. The authority of Roman law for private law could not easily be displaced.

Grotius sets out his general view of natural law in the prolegomena. Man is a very superior animal, one of whose characteristics is an impelling desire for society, not society of any sort but peaceful and organized society according to the measure of his intelligence. It is not a universal truth that every animal is impelled by nature to seek only its own good (§6). Man, moreover, alone among animals, is endowed with the faculty of knowing and of acting in accordance with general principles (§7). The maintenance of the social order that is consonant with human nature is the source of law: hence come the legal obligations to abstain from anything that is another's, to restore to another anything of his that one has plus any gain one has received from it, to fulfill promises, to make good a loss suffered through one's own fault, and hence also to inflict punishment in accordance with deserts (§8). A more extended meaning of the term *law* flows from these obligations; as man has the power of discrimination, to act contrary to this discrimination is to act contrary to the law of nature (§9). To the exercise of such discrimination belongs the rational allotment to each individual or social group of that which is properly theirs, such as preference at times to the more wise over the less wise, to a kinsman and not to a stranger, to a poor man not to a wealthy man (§10).

All the foregoing, claims Grotius, would have some validity even if it is conceded—which it cannot be, without great wickedness—that there is no God, or that men's affairs are of no concern to Him. The opposite of this view, namely, the understanding that God exists, has been implanted in man, partly by reason, partly by tradition, and is confirmed by many proofs. Thus, all people must all render obedience to God their creator (§11). The free will of God is thus another source of law (§12). Again, to obey pacts is part of the law of nature, and this source of law gives rise to bodies of municipal law, since those who have associated with a group have subjected themselves to a man or men (§15). The principles of natural law, being always the same, can easily be systematized, whereas elements of positive law are outside systematic treatment since they often undergo change and are different in different places.[5]

This theoretical discussion of the nature of law is carried further by Grotius in the body of the work, particularly at 1.1.2–1.1.15. At 1.1.10, for example, Grotius claims that the law of nature is unchangeable even in the sense that it cannot be altered by God. Again, some things are in accordance with this law not in a proper sense but "by reduction"; that is, the law of nature is not contrary to them. Presumably Grotius means here, as in section 15 of the prolegomena, that when established municipal law is not directly derived from natural law but is not contrary to it, then it is in a secondary sense natural law "by reduction."

This theoretical foundation justifies the individual legal rules. Grotius does not set out either the Roman rules or local rules but, by the use of reason, attempts to deduce what the rules should be according to the law of nature. One example of the method is his account of contracts in book 2, chapter 12. Of simple acts, some are mere acts of kindness, others involve a mutual obligation (II). Of these acts that are reciprocal, some separate the parties, others produce a community of interests. The Romans rightly divide the former into three classes: I give that you may give; I do that you may do; I do that you may give. The Romans omitted from this classification the specific named contracts, not so much because they had a name but because their more frequent use gave them a certain force and character. But the law of nature ignores these distinctions (III). The law of nature requires that there be equality in contracts, and the party who receives less acquires a right of action from the inequality (VIII). Thus, a person making a contract ought to point out to the other any faults in the thing concerned in the transaction, but he need not disclose circumstances that have no direct connection with the thing (IX). Equality is also required with respect to freedom of choice; no fear should be unjustly inspired for the sake of making a contract (X). Likewise, except in the case of beneficence, there should be careful observance that the exchange of considerations is equally balanced (XI). Finally, there should be equality in the subject matter of the contract, so that if subsequently an inequality, even one not due to the fault of a party, is spotted, it should be made good. The Romans properly established this rule not to apply to every inequality, since otherwise there would be a great many lawsuits, but it applies above one-half of the just price (XII). The most natural measure of the value of a thing is the need of it. But this is not the only measure. Desire—for instance, for luxuries—sets a measure, and the most necessary things are of less value because they are abundant. The view of the jurist Paul is acceptable that the prices of things are not fixed by the desire or the use of individuals but by common estimation (XIV).

In the preceding chapter on promises, Grotius had already made other relevant points. For instance, the first requisite in a promise is the use of reason; hence the promises of lunatics, idiots, and children are void. But the promises of minors and women are not void since they have judgment, though it is rather weak. The time when a boy begins to exercise reason cannot be absolutely fixed but must be assumed from his daily behavior. Various states fix the commencement of capacity at different times, but this has nothing in common with natural law except that it is natural that the individual local rule be observed in the places where it is in force.

These particular points are part of a systematic and comprehensive treatment in which Grotius seeks to build up a structure of law founded neither on Roman law nor on revealed religion. Certainly arguments are at times drawn from Roman law or religion, and either may even be cited occasionally as if it were of some authority. But the final product is far removed from the Corpus Juris. Thus, quite gone is the Roman concentration on the individual contracts such as sale or stipulation, each with its emphasis on its own requirements. Instead, the *omnium gatherum* attributed to Paul—with the omission here of "I give that you may do"—comes to the fore although it has little prominence in the Corpus Juris and was never part of the Roman contractual system. Formalities of contracting have disappeared, and the stress is on agreement. Even more striking is the emphasis on the equality of the agreement, including the equality of the prestation. Not only was the role of enorm lesion limited to sale in the Corpus Juris, where it appears only in the *Code*,[6] but many of the individual contracts such as stipulation are unilateral in form and theory, although in practice they might be balanced by a second stipulation.

In view of the nature of *De Iure Belli ac Pacis,* the basic divisions, even as they relate to private law, are very different from those of Justinian's *Institutes.* Thus, instead of a division of contracts into the four genera each with its species, contractual obligation is treated in three chapters, 11–13, of book 2—on promises, contracts, and oaths.[7] Again, the overall arrangement is by no means the same as that of the *Institutes.* For instance, the first seven chapters of the book are titled: "The Cause of War: First, Defense of Self and Property," "Of Things Which Belong to Men in Common," "Of Original Acquisition of Things, with Special Reference to the Sea and Rivers," "On Assumed Abandonment of Ownership and Occupation Consequent Thereon: and Wherein This Differs from Ownership by Usucaption and by Prescription," "On the Original Acquisition of Rights over Persons: Herein Are Treated the Rights of Parents, Marriage, Associations, and the Rights over Subjects and Slaves," "On Secondary Acquisition of Property by the Act of Man: also Alienation of Sovereignty and of the Attributes of Sovereignty," and "On Derivative Acquisition of Property Which Takes Place in Accordance with Law: and Herein, Intestate Succession."

But the law of reason did not break the tradition or evolution of Western private law. Several features should be emphasized.

First, many of the transformations had already occurred. This is possibly most noticeable in the field of contract law where already had emerged the general notion of contract, displacing the Roman idea of individual types of contract. Of course, despite the general theory of contract, individual types of contract retained particular features, as can be seen very clearly in the much later civil codes.

Second, when scholars attempted to naturalize the law of reason in territorial law they tamed it. They gave it more and more a structure akin to that of Justinian's *Institutes,* and of course they cited the Corpus Juris as authority. Roman law was still in large measure *ratio scripta,* "written reason." And it should be emphasized that the Reception was of private law, and private law is the subject of this book.

Third, and most important for us, What was this law of reason? How was it to be found? Is it to be discovered only after deep reflection, only by a handful of scholars? That approach was widely rejected. The basic approach, not always fully expressed, was straightforward in the extreme. The law of reason was that which appeared to reason, without deep thinking. It was what was obviously the law. But what law was that? The law to be found everywhere, at least in civilized nations, or at least in most civilized nations. But what law was that? The answer at this distance is blindingly obvious for private law: it is the law that derives from the Corpus Juris. Once again, Roman law as it evolved was to be the law, this time as Reason.

The third movement that I want to discuss, but in very brief terms, is codification. In this context I mean by the term *code* a legislative enactment that in brief form covers a whole area of law: for instance, private law in a civil code, all of criminal law in a criminal code. Codes are, of course, the central feature of almost all present-day civil-law systems, but are almost totally absent from common-law systems.

Successful modern codification leads to four conclusions about legal evolution. First, successful codification was not simply the response to a felt need for it in the sense that the greater the complexity of the law and the difficulty in finding the law, the greater the demand for simplification, hence codification. Certainly, one strong impulse toward codification has frequently been the complexity and amount of the existing law. According to Suetonius, Julius Caesar formed the project "to reduce the civil law to fixed limits, and from the enormous and prolix mass of laws to place only the best and necessary in a few volumes" (*Divus Iulius* 44.2). As a motive for his *Digest,* Justinian alleges that "we find the whole course of our statutes, such as they come down to us from the foundation of the city of Rome and from the days of Romulus, to be in a state of such confusion that they reach to an infinite length and surpass the bounds of all human capacity" (*C. Deo auctore* 1). The publication regulations (*Publikationsprotokol*) of 20 March 1791 of the *Allgemeines Landrecht für die Preussischen Staaten* declare "that the whole law will be produced in a coherent order, in the language of the nation and presented in a generally understandable way so that any inhabitant of the state, whose natural capacities have been trained through education even only to a moderate standard, may be himself able to read the laws in accordance with which he should conduct his dealings and be judged, to understand them and in future cases be attentive to their provisions."[8]

However great was the difficulty of finding and understanding the law in continental countries, it can scarcely have been greater than in England, where the law was not systematized, even after the appearance of Blackstone's *Commentaries on the Law of England* in 1765–69, where different courts enforced common law and equity, where local custom remained important, and where much law was hidden in inaccessible law reports. Yet English law was not codified, nor was there ever much chance of it.

Second, the introduction of "original" codes, that is those prepared fresh without deriving in structure and content from an existing code, is not sufficiently explained by social upheaval or complexity, as Frederick H. Lawson argued: "All the original codes have been in countries which have just undergone a revolution and wish to recast their law quickly from top to bottom, or in countries which had in the past suffered from a diversity of legal systems or had just found themselves in that position because they have incorporated new territories or had come into existence by a union of territories governed by different laws. One or the other of these factors must be at work if the lawyers of a country are willing to undergo the immense trouble and inconvenience of transforming their law and learning it afresh."[9] Lawson is right in stressing the difficulty of successfully preparing and introducing an original code.[10] But he does not take sufficient account of the eighteenth-century codifications in Bavaria, which he describes as "too old-fashioned to fit into the movement" of codification.[11] Work on codification in Bavaria was in fact begun in 1750, and the code of criminal law, Codex iuris Bavarici criminalis, was issued in 1751; of procedure, Codex iuris Bavarici judicialis, 1753; and of private law, Codex Maximilianeus Bavaricus civilis, in 1756. Historically this codification is undoubtedly part of the general movement and was inspired by initiatives already taken in Prussia. Moreover, the Bavarian Civil Code is thoroughly modern in its arrangement. Above all, whether the Bavarian codification was or was not old-fashioned is irrelevant, for the codes are original, despite the fact that neither of the factors postulated by Lawson for the appearance of an original code was present to any important extent. Again, Lawson emphasizes "original" codes. The stress seems inappropriate. The upheaval in the law and in learning would be at least as great where the code was largely borrowed. Furthermore, his emphasis on social upheaval does not explain why there was no really successful codification in the United States after the American Revolution or the Civil War. The power of the individual states of the Union cannot have precluded codification, for Germany, which introduced the Bürgerliches Gesetzbuch, was and still is a federation; and other countries, notably Switzerland, that have civil codes are also federal. Still another federation that has codes is Mexico, but here the individual states have each their own civil codes.

Third, the introduction or nonintroduction of a code in a particular territory cannot be attributed to the power or persuasiveness of one individual. Thus, no doubt Napoleon's energy and power counted for much in the promulgation of the Code civil, but in the French Revolution there had already been attempts at codifying the law. Despite all his persuasiveness, learning, and political power, Friedrich von Savigny could, at the most, greatly delay the preparation of a code for Germany, most noticeably by his *Vom Beruf unserer Zeit für Gesetzgebung und Rechtswissenschaft*, first published in 1814. And in non-civil-law countries, Jeremy Bentham could not move the English to codification, nor could David Dudley Field move the Americans in the populous East.

Finally, even for civil-law countries, systematic codification of private law is a relatively modern phenomenon. The earliest codification is that of Bavaria in 1756. In any account of codification as a phenomenon related more to civil-law than to common-law systems, this matter of dating also requires explanation. The success of codification in the civil-law systems and its relative failure in common-law systems is explained primarily by general factors in the legal systems themselves.[12] The distinctive element of civil-law systems is the acceptance, past or present, of the Corpus Juris or part of it as authoritative. This acceptance has profound consequences for the legal system, apart even from the acceptance of individual legal rules. But these consequences do not appear immediately or all at the same time. They include an academic and systematic, as distinct from a practical and pragmatic, emphasis on law. Roman law dominates legal education, and particular prominence falls on Justinian's *Institutes,* because it is both the fundamental book for beginners and is the authoritative attempt to give a systematic structure to law. When the insufficiency of Roman law for contemporary needs becomes apparent and respectable to notice, books on local law—law that already existed—then emerge. These books are of various kinds and of different scope. But Justinian's *Institutes* show that it is possible to set out the basic rules of even a complex system in a comprehensive and organized way. This leads to a desire likewise to set out in one work the basic rules of a local system.

Almost inevitably, these books of local rules model themselves in length and arrangement on Justinian's *Institutes,* though with variations. The role of Justinian's *Institutes* in legal education increases the influence of such local institutes vis-à-vis other books on contemporary law.

In addition, a system in which the Corpus Juris is authoritative is more open than is a common-law system to the influence of powerful general intellectual currents, such as the Enlightenment. A great boost was given to natural law's capacity to influence private law by the genius of Hugo Grotius. The Enlightenment led to the belief that law can be established on the basis of reason, and this intellectual impetus toward reform, married with the civil-law tradition, led on to official codes of law. With the coming of institutes of local law and of natural law, the civil-law tradition became more receptive to the idea of codification. Justinian's *Institutes* show that it is possible for a brief outline of the law to have legislative effect. But successful codification in the civil-law tradition, at least in the forms that the codification takes, has to wait for the emergence of institutes of local law.

Proof that codification can be regarded as the natural product of the civil-law tradition is twofold. First, no explanation, other than one based on the legal tradition itself, can account for codification flourishing in civil-law systems to a degree unknown in common-law systems. "Many of the most civilized modern societies have felt the need to codify their laws. One can say that it is a periodical necessity for societies"—so begins the message of the executive to the Congress in Chile, proposing approval of the Chilean Civil Code in 1855. But these "most civilized modern societies" are in the main only those of the civil-law tradition. The second proof is the similarity between institutes, whether of Justinian or local law on the one hand and of civil codes on the other. Many oddities of construction of modern codes can be explained only by reference to these institutes. More particularly, modern scholars profess to see two different "families" among civil-law systems or two branches of the civil-law "family," one deriving from the Germanic sphere of influence, the other from the Latin or, more particularly, the French. This distinction is best explained in terms of the preceding civil-law tradition, the juristic reaction to it, and the penetration of it by natural law.

In a very real sense codification is a reaction against the existing state of the law. But it is a reaction that continues the legal tradition in a new guise. Some of the impact of the old on the new is brought out in Chapter 5, on French délit.

Some readers will be surprised that I have not devoted a separate chapter or chapters to canon law, or even in fact a separate section in this chapter. If I were writing a history of Western law my approach would be inexcusable. But this is not a work of history but an attempt to explain legal evolution, and, at that, only of private law. I would explain my omission by emphasizing that with regard to private law, canon law was very much within the tradition of Roman law. From the earliest days of the renewed teaching of Roman law at Bologna in the eleventh century, clerics were prominent as law students.[13] And canonists always gave a place of particular honor to the Corpus Juris Civilis.[14] Some of the most particular features of canon private law can be traced to Roman law. For example, the prohibited degrees for marriage on the ground of consanguinity are Roman and do not derive from Jewish rules as one might have expected; the church's special concern for jurisdiction to aid poor people and widows has precedents in Roman law;[15] likewise *laesio enormis;*[16] likewise private prescription.[17] Of course, canon private law went beyond Roman law—for instance, in emphasis on agreement for sale—but that is the nature of evolution.

CHAPTER II

CONCLUSIONS

By the very fact of becoming law, ideas and claims of right come to exist in their own right as legal ideas and legal rules, and they form their own societal unit. To some extent they coincide, and perhaps ideally they ought entirely to coincide,[1] with other societal institutions and with the needs and desires either of the people forming the society or of the ruling elite. But those working with the law estimate the rules by their "lawness," by their being or not being law. Law has its own standard for existence. Law is a means to an end and cannot be an end in itself, but lawyers—however widely one may define the term—have an inherent tendency to look upon legal rules as if they were ends in themselves; for them a course of action is properly to be followed because it is in accordance with law, even if the reason for the law can no longer be discovered or if the society has changed and the legal rule is no longer appropriate.

Of all law, custom should most closely match society. Indeed, in its own sphere (i.e., the sphere of law), it should be a mirror image. Custom is not imposed from above, arbitrarily perhaps, but, as the standard theory has it, it is law because the people follow it as law, and it corresponds to their normative behavior and changes when the behavior changes. But all this is far from the truth. The truth is patent in the sources; it is noted by legal historians and anthropologists; yet the obvious conclusions are not drawn.

Those writing down their customs stress the antiquity of those customs, but the social mores may have changed. They stress the difficulty of finding the law, so how can it have emerged from normative behavior accepted by the people as law? They say at times that after strenuous effort they have found the custom in antique decisions and documents, so the problems raised by the issues just mentioned are compounded.

Legal questions are continually asked to which there is no answer in the custom and for which there is no legal machinery to settle the scope of principles or rules. Standard methods develop to help fill gaps in the law, whether this is to choose other folks' custom as one's own subsidiary custom, or to treat another town as one's "mother" in legal matters and send there for a reply to a legal problem, or habitually to resort to the rules of another system. But whatever approach is adopted, the overwhelming tendency is to turn to a more developed legal system. Great disparity in legal structure or sophistication is no bar to borrowing. But the more complex law is likely to have been the product of a more developed economy: the Custom of Paris is looked to by small, rural southern French towns; the law of thriving Magdeburg, by remote Polish settlements; Roman law, by wandering German tribes. Not only is the borrowed law "foreign" law; it is also the law of economically and politically different cultures. Customary law is above all to be found in court decisions, and is discovered by the judges whether there was a custom or whether a "custom" was invented by the judge or, more likely, borrowed by the judge from elsewhere. Customary law when it is accepted as law is judge-made law and hence is subject to the influence of the legal tradition. As judge-made law, it is, moreover, "official" law; customary law is law only insofar as it is acceptable to the rulers.

The extent to which legal rules in customary (and, indeed, other) systems do not fit the society particularly well and are even disfunctional is often concealed by a failure to distinguish clearly between the societal institution and the legal institution. A legal institution is a social institution that has been given legal effectiveness and is being regarded from the legal point of view. Without the social institution of slavery there will be (in almost all cases at least) no legal institution of slavery. In a society exclusively of small peasant farmers there may be law for small peasant farms but not for high-rises. We have been told nothing about how well law functions in a society when we learn that it does not exist apart from its relevant social institution. That without peasant farms or high-rises there will be no law about peasant farms or high-rises does not entail the conclusion—apparently often assumed—that, because in a society there is law about peasant farms and there are peasant farms and there are no high-rises and no law about high-rises, the law is in congruence with the society.

When we turn to more developed law, we find the same phenomena. Society has its input, which may be vigorously expressed or be tacit but demonstrated by obvious needs, overwhelming or minor. The legal tradition shapes the law that comes out: divisions, classifications, types of remedy, scope of rules and exceptions, all matters of great practical consequence. As a result of societal pressure, say, the law has to be changed: the resulting law will usually be borrowed, from a system known to the legal elite, often with modifications, to be sure, but not always those deemed appropriate after full consideration of local conditions. The input of the society often bears little relation to the output of the legal elite. This remains true no matter what the principal sources of law are, though the relative impact of societal forces and the legal tradition on these varies from one source to another.[2]

Thus, the direct link between a society and its law is tenuous, whether the law is customary or formed by professional full-time lawyers. Legal development depends on the lawyers' culture. When an issue arises, whether in theory or in practice, and requires a legal answer, the lawyers habitually seek authority. Hence it is that to an enormous extent law develops by borrowing from another place and even from another time. This borrowing may follow a systematic search for the best law, but typically some system is chosen to be the prime quarry; Roman law after the rediscovery of the Corpus Juris Civilis, the French Code civil after its promulgation. The principal reason for the choice of quarry is that its law is accessible because it is written down. This law will also be more elaborated (because it has to provide an answer) and will have the *general* admiration of the lawyers. The full appropriateness of the particular foreign rule for the borrowing system will not then be investigated: it is usually enough that the foreign rule is not obviously and seriously inappropriate. That does not mean that such a foreign rule will inevitably be borrowed or be borrowed without alteration, but only that within the legal tradition there exists a strong predisposition in favor of borrowing and, at that, from the individual preselected system.[3] When no authority can be found, false authority may be adduced.

A revolution may occur in law or in society. With revolution in law, the legal tradition continues but with appropriate modifications: the basis of the law has been changed. With revolution in society the aim must also be to revolutionize law. The legal tradition is then replaced by another legal tradition in whole or in part.

Law, then, despite its practical impact, is very noticeably the culture of the lawyers and especially of the lawmakers—that is, of those lawyers who, whether as legislators, jurists, or judges, have control of the accepted mechanisms of legal change. Legal development is determined by their culture; and social, economic, and political factors impinge on legal development only through their consciousness. This consciousness results from the lawmakers' being members of the society and sharing its value and experiences, though of course they are members with a particular standing. Sometimes this consciousness is heightened by extreme pressures from other members of the society, but always the lawmakers' response is conditioned by the legal tradition: by their learning, expertise, and knowledge of law, domestic and foreign.

This book has been both descriptive and explicative; but I should like to conclude with a message. The theme of this book (as of others I have written) is that law is largely autonomous and not shaped by societal needs; though legal institutions will not exist without corresponding social institutions, law evolves from the legal tradition. To understand law in society, one must be fully aware of the impact of the legal tradition. Whether, for reform of the law in the future, the impact of the legal tradition can be reduced is very doubtful. But the message is that for satisfactory law in society one must have a satisfactory legal tradition. The main thrust of law reform must be to ensure that the means of making law are the best possible for the society. In this context, specific, abiding—indeed, natural—features of the culture deserve express mention. Law is treated as existing in its own right: it is being in conformity with "lawness" that makes law law. Hence, first, the means of creating law, the sources of law, come to be regarded as a given, almost as something sacrosanct, and change in these even when they are obviously deeply flawed is extremely difficult to achieve.[4] Second, law has to be justified in its own terms; hence, authority has to be sought and found.[5] That authority (in some form, which may be perverted) must already exist; hence, law is typically backward-looking. These two features make law inherently conservative.[6]

My conclusions are simple. Legal change comes about through the culture of the legal elite, the lawmakers, and it is above all determined by that culture.

But law is not the culture of the legal elite alone and it is not the only culture of the legal elite. As to the first of these conclusions, law is also the cultural heritage of other lawyers and of society at large. But to effect change, other lawyers and other members of society have to operate on and through the legal elite, whereas the elite can initiate change on its own.[7]

As to the second of these, the law-making elite also partakes of the general culture of society. Thus, where the society as a whole or its ruling elite is cosmopolitan or innovative, the law-making elite will tend to be cosmopolitan or innovative. The general culture has many strands and many roots, resulting from geography, history, economics, politics, religion, and so on and it is as part of the general culture that these factors influence law making. But what has to be stressed is, as we have seen, the very powerful role that the legal culture itself has on law making. The law-making elite comes to regard law as existing in large measure in its own right, as an end in itself, as having its being distinct from other institutions of society.

Legal change also comes about by organized pressure from outside of the legal elite. But when it does, the emerging law is still given its contours by the law-making elite.[8]

Two restrictions should be set forth right at the end of this book so that their importance should not be ignored. The first is that the argument here is *not* that the law-making elite is never aware of, and fully responsive to, wider societal conditions. It may well be and often is, and the legal rules on a particular topic may well be entirely satisfactory for those making use of them. At times, for instance, the business community may have such close contacts with some part of the legal elite in the shape of academics whom it hires as consultants that their concerns are very much the same, and a view of law is preferred that is in harmony with commercial interests. Even then, of course, in a developed system that view of law put forward by academics will prevail only if it is also adopted by judges and legislators, who, in their turn, are also of course blinkered by their own part of the tradition. My point is only that members of the legal elite shape the legal rules, that they are fixed within their cultural tradition, and that to a very considerable extent the rules often do not meet the needs and desires of those who use them, which is not a matter of immediate concern to the legal elite. No better illustration of this can be found than in English land law, which for centuries until 1925 (at the earliest) was very unsatisfactory for landowners and was beneficial to no one (except practicing lawyers). Those who had no property had no concern with the rules; those who had were also those who as judges and legislators were in a position to change the rules. But (in Oliver Cromwell's phrase) the "tortuous and ungodly jumble" of English land law was to prevail for centuries.[9] A glance at the confused and unsatisfactory state of the law (for those using it) in the contemporary United States on copyright infringement with regard to the fair use of factual works should point a warning to those who believe American law is in harmony with the needs of law users.[10]

The second restriction ought not need mentioning; I am concerned with the development of the legal rules themselves, not with how the legal rules operate in society. For reasons at least partly connected with the wider society, the same legal rule may operate to different effect in different societies; and in the same society to different effect in different groups. The present book is written on the premise that actual legal rules, as authoritatively set forth, have themselves an impact.[11]

Notes

FREQUENTLY CITED WORKS

Buckland, *Textbook*	W. W. Buckland, *A Textbook of Roman Law from Augustus to Justinian*, 3d ed., ed. P. Stein (Cambridge, 1963).
Civilian Tradition	*The Civilian Tradition and Scots Law*, ed. David L. Carey Miller and Reinhard Zimmerman (Berlin, 1997).
Fenet, *Travaux préparatoires*, 13	P. A. Fenet, *Recueil complet des travaux préparatoires du Code Civil*, vol. 13 (Paris, 1827).
Jolowicz and Nicholas, *Historical Introduction*	H. F. Jolowicz and B. Nicholas, *Historical Introduction to the Study of Roman Law*, 3d ed. (Cambridge, 1972).
Kaser, *Privatrecht*, 1	Max Kaser, *Das römische Privatrecht*, vol. 1, 2d ed. (Munich, 1971).
Kunkel, *Herkunft*	Wolfgang Kunkel, *Herkunft und soziale Stellung der römischen Juristen*, 2d ed. (Graz, 1967).
Milsom, *Historical Foundations*	S. F. C. Milsom, *Historical Foundations of the Common Law* (Boston, 1981).
Pollock and Maitland, *History*, 1, 2.	Frederick Pollock and Frederick William Maitland, *The History of English Law*, vols. 1 and 2, 2d ed. (Cambridge, 1968).
Robinson, *Introduction*	O. F. Robinson, T. D. Fergus, and W. M. Gordon, *European Legal History*, 2d ed. (London, 1994).

Rotondi, *Leges Publicae* G. Rotondi, *Leges Publicae Populi Romani* (Milan, 1912).

Thomas, *Textbook* J. A. C. Thomas, *Textbook of Roman Law* (Amsterdam, 1976).

Tómas y Valiente, *Manual* Francisco Tómas y Valiente, *Manual de historia del derecho español*, 4th ed. (Madrid, 1983).

T.v.R. *Tijdschrift voor Rechtsgeschiedenis*

Watson, *Comity* Alan Watson, *Joseph Story and the Comity of Errors* (Athens, Ga., 1992).

Watson, *Failures of the Legal Imagination* Alan Watson, *Failures of the Legal Imagination* (Philadelphia, 1988).

Watson, "Legal Change" Alan Watson, "Legal Change: Sources of Law and Legal Culture," *University of Pennsylvania Law Review* 131 (1983): 1121–57.

Watson, *Making of the Civil Law* Alan Watson, *The Making of the Civil Law* (Cambridge, Mass., 1981).

Watson, *Obligations* Alan Watson, *The Law of Obligations in the Later Roman Republic* (Oxford, 1965).

Watson, *Society and Legal Change* Alan Watson, *Society and Legal Change* (Edinburgh, 1977).

Watson, *Sources of Law* Alan Watson, *Sources of Law, Legal Change, and Ambiguity*, 2d ed. (Philadelphia, 1998).

Watson, *Transplants* Alan Watson, *Legal Transplants: An Approach to Comparative Law*, 2d ed. (Athens, Ga., 1993).

Weill and Terré, *Droit civil* A. Weill and F. Terré, *Droit civil: Introduction générale*, 4th ed. (Paris, 1979).

Wieacker, *Private Law* Franz Wieacker, *A History of Private Law in Europe*, trans. Tony Weir (Oxford, 1995).

ZSS *Zeitschrift der Savigny-Stiftung (romanistische Abteilung)*

Zweigert and Kötz, *Introduction* Konrad Zweigert and Hein Kötz, *An Introduction to Comparative Law*, 2d ed., trans. Tony Weir (Oxford, 1992).

PREFACE

1. For the argument, see Watson, *Making of the Civil Law.*

2. The nature of the legal process will not be much discussed in this book because from Roman times onward the basic approach in the West has been unitary, but see Chapter 10.

3. *An Inquiry into the Law of Negro Slavery in the United States of America* (Philadelphia, 1858), p. xxxvi.

4. Thus, parts of Chapter 1 derive from my *Making of the Civil Law* (chap. 1), *Roman Law and Comparative Law* (Athens, Ga., 1991, chap. 12), *Failures of the Legal Imagination* (chap. 2), and my paper, "The Evolution of Law: Continued," *Law and History Review* 5 (1987): 537–70; of Chapter 2 from *Making of the Civil Law* (chap. 4); of Chapter 3 from *Roman Law and Comparative Law* (chap. 23) and "Evolution"; of Chapter 4 from "Evolution"; of Chapter 5 from *Failures of the Legal Imagination* (chap. 1); of Chapter 6 from "The Transformation of American Property Law: A Comparative Law Approach," *Georgia Law Review* 24 (1990): 163–221, and "Aspects of the Reception of Law," *American Journal of Comparative Law* 44 (1996): 335–51; of Chapter 8 from *Making of the Civil Law* (chap. 8), *Roman Law and Comparative Law* (chap. 24), and "Evolution"; of Chapter 9 from "Evolution"; and Chapter 10 from *Making of the Civil Law* (chaps. 7 and 8).

CHAPTER I. LEGISLATION

1. On the question of dating, see D. Liebs, *Hermogenians Iuris Epitome* (Göttingen, 1964).

2. *C. Deo auctore* §§ 7, 9–10.

3. A typical exaggeration occurs in Jolowicz and Nicholas, *Historical Introduction,* p. 481: "Full power was given to cut down and alter the texts, and this extended even to the works of ancient *leges* or constitutions which were quoted by the jurists." But *C. Deo auctore* §7 gives power to change quotations from laws and constitutions only where the compilers find they are *non recte scriptum* (incorrectly set down). It is only to be expected that the decision of the commissioners on the correct reading was to be treated as final. For the full argument against interpolations of substance, see Alan Watson, "Prolegomena to Establishing Pre-Justinianic Texts," *T.v.R.* (1994): 113–25; J. H. A. Lokin, "The End of an Epoch: Epilegomena to a Century of Interpolation Criticism," in *Collatio Iuris Romani,* vol. 1, ed. R. Feenstra et al. (Amsterdam, 1995), pp. 261–73.

4. For this proposition, see now, above all, Watson, *Failures of the Legal Imagination,* pp. 35–61.

5. I use this term *government* as consistently as possible to indicate the individual or group that has, individually or collectively, both the highest ex-

ecutive powers in the state and the right to issue legal commands in the form of statute or a close approximation.

6. See, e.g., Buckland, *Textbook,* p. 4; Kaser, *Privatrecht,* 1:181; Thomas, *Textbook,* pp. 4–5, 40–54.

7. *Advances* is, of course, an ambiguous term. I do not think a precise explanation need be proffered, but I am thinking of changes in the law that had a long-term impact.

8. See, e.g., Rotondi, *Leges Publicae,* p. 241. But A. M. Honoré, for instance, prefers a date between, say, 209 and 195 B.C: "Linguistic and Social Context of the *lex Aquilia,*" *Irish Jurist* 7 (1972): 138–50, esp. 149.

9. On all of these, see *G.*3.118–125.

10. See, e.g., Rotondi, *Leges Publicae,* pp. 271–72.

11. See, e.g., Kaser, *Privatrecht,* 1:357.

12. For details, see, e.g., Alan Watson, *The Law of Succession in the Later Roman Republic* (Oxford, 1971), pp. 163ff.

13. For the argument, see Alan Watson, *The Spirit of Roman Law* (Athens, Ga., 1995), pp. 60–63.

14. We need not consider which assemblies were responsible for private law legislation.

15. As can be calculated from Rotondi, *Leges Publicae.*

16. See, e.g., the Portuguese *Ordenaçoes Filipinas* (1643), 3.64.

17. See, e.g., Robinson, *Introduction,* pp. 37–38.

18. See Watson, *Failures of the Legal Imagination,* pp. 145–54.

19. Ibid., pp. 47–59.

20. See, e.g., Milsom, *Historical Foundations*; F. Reynolds, *The Judge as Lawmaker* (London, 1967), p. 7.

21. See now Alan Watson, *Law Out of Context* (Athens, Ga., 2000), pp. 19ff.

22. Wieacker, *Private Law,* pp. 261–62. The original idea of Frederick William of 1714 was even more a redaction of Roman law; see W. Wagner, "Die Wissenschaft des gemeinen römischen Rechts und das Allgemeine Landrecht für die Preussischen Staaten," in *Wissenschaft und Kodifikation des Privatrechts im 19 Jahrhundert,* ed. H. Coing and W. Wilhelm (Frankfurt am Main, 1974), pp. 191ff.

23. Gerald Strauss, *Resistance, and the State* (Princeton, N.J., 1986), p. 85. See his subsequent pages for information on these reformations.

24. See, e.g., Eckhard Maria Theewen, *Napoleons Anteil am Code civil* (Berlin, 1991).

25. See L. Juliot de la Morandière, *Droit civil,* vol. 4 (Paris: Dalloz, 1959), p. 1.

26. See Fenet, *Travaux préparatoires,* 13:492ff.

27. Ibid., 13:550.

28. Ibid., 13:551–52.

29. Ibid., 13:758.

30. See, e.g., C.-B.-M. Toullier and J.-B. Duvergier, *Le Droit civil français,* 6th ed. (Paris, n.d.), 6.2, pp. 5ff.; 7.2, pp. 25–26.

31. Fenet, *Travaux préparatoires,* 13:758.

32. Estienne Pasquier, *Recherches de la France,* bk. 4, chap. 21. To be found in his *Oeuvres* (Amsterdam, 1723), cols. 411, 412.

33. Bozkurt is quoted (in German) in E. E. Hirsch, *Rezeption als sozialer Prozess* (Berlin, 1981), pp. 33–34.

34. See, e.g., H. V. Velideoğlu, "Erfahrungen mit dem Schweizerischen Zivilgesetzbuch in der Turkei," *Zeitschrift für Schweizerisches Recht* 81 (1962): 53.

35. E. E. Hirsch, "Die Einflusse und Wirkungen ausländischen Rechts auf das heutige Türkische Recht," *Zeitschrift für das gesamte Handelsrecht* 116 (1954): 206.

36. Hirsch, *Rezeption,* pp. 11–12.

37. See, e.g., Hirsch, *Rezeption;* M. Zwahlen, "L'application en Turquie du Code civil reçu de la Suisse," *Zeitschrift für Schweizerisches Recht* 95 (1976): 249ff.

38. See Hirsch, *Rezeption,* pp. 56–57.

39. *Annales de la Faculté de Droit d'Istanbul* 5 (1956).

40. *Fünfzig Jahre Türkisches Zivilgesetzbuch, Zeitschrift für Schweizerisches Recht* 95 (1976): 217ff.

41. Kurt Lipstein, "The Reception of Western Law in Turkey," *Annales de la Faculté de Droit d'Istanbul* 6 (1957): 18.

42. June Starr, *Dispute and Settlement in Rural Turkey* (Leiden, 1978), p. 276.

43. Eugen Huber, *Erlauterungen zum Vorentwurf des Eidg. Justiz- und Polizeidepartementes,* 2d ed. (Bern, 1914), p. 2.

44. Virgile Rossel, *Amtliches Stenographisches Bulletin der Schweizerischen Bundesversammlung, Nationalrat* (1905), p. 438.

45. For an illuminating example of largely inappropriate rules being borrowed "just because they were there," see S. B. Burbank, "Procedural Rulemaking under the Judicial Councils Reform and Judicial Conduct and Disability Act of 1980," *University of Pennsylvania Law Review* 131 (1982): 283ff.

46. B. N. Esen, "Die Entwicklung des Türkischen Eherechts seit der Rezeption des Schweizerischen Zivilgesetzbuches" (Ph.D. diss., Göttingen, 1966), pp. 141–42.

CHAPTER 2. JURISTS

1. The main exception is the contemporary United States.

2. In this chapter, to lay the groundwork, I propose to sketch these events and describe in outline their consequences for the spirit of Roman law. For

the full argument, see Alan Watson, *The State, Law and Religion: Pagan Rome* (Athens, Ga., 1992).

3. Instructive is, e.g., J.-L. Halpérin, "Tribunat de la plèbe et haute plèbe (493–218 av. J.C.)," *Revue Historique du Droit Français et Étranger* 62 (1984): 161ff.

4. See, e.g., Rotondi, *Leges Publicae,* p. 236

5. See, e.g., ibid., pp. 216ff.

6. See, e.g., ibid., pp. 212–13.

7. See Watson, *State, Law and Religion,* pp. 76–77.

8. For this struggle, see Livy, 3.9.1ff.; 3.10.5ff.; 3.11.3, 9, 12–13; 3.15.1; 3.18.6; 3.19.11; 3.31.5ff.; 3.32.1; 3.32.5ff.; 3.34.6; 4.3.17; Dionysius of Halicarnassus, 10.1.1ff.; 10.2.1; 10.4; 10.51.5; 10.55.4ff.; 10.57.6; 10.58.4.

9. See Watson, *State, Law and Religion,* pp. 21–29.

10. See Kunkel, *Herkunft,* pp. 38–61; cf. A. Schiavone, *Giuristi e nobili nella Roma repubblicana* (Rome, 1987).

11. Complications need not concern us here.

12. Oddly, it is sometimes claimed that this narrow interpretation of "killing" is the result of a Roman limited view of the notion of causation; see, e.g., Dieter Nörr, "*Causam mortis praebere,*" in *The Legal Mind,* ed. Neil Mac-Cormick and Peter Birks (Oxford, 1986), pp. 203–17. But then two matters became incomprehensible: (1) the narrow interpretation is not applied in other contexts such as the *lex Cornelia de sicariis* for murder; and (2) the restricted interpretation is later, from the empire, not the republic.

13. See, e.g., Watson, *Obligations,* pp. 241–47.

14. *Aequitas* (fairness) may be cited as a reason for a rule *having been* accepted. But then the rule is usually exceptional.

15. See Alan Watson, *The Spirit of Roman Law* (Athens, Ga., 1995), pp. 98–110, 117–23.

16. See, e.g., Alan Watson, *Law Out of Context* (Athens, Ga., 2000), pp. 92–139, and the sources there cited.

17. See, e.g., Franz Horak, *Rationes Decidendi,* vol. 1 (Innsbruck, 1969), pp. 267–75; David Daube, *Roman Law: Linguistic, Social, and Philosophical Aspects* (Edinburgh, 1969), pp. 176–94.

18. See now Alan Watson and Khaled Abu el Fadl, "Fox Hunting, Pheasant Shooting, and Comparative Law," *American Journal of Comparative Literature* 48 (2000): 1ff.

19. See, e.g., R. Dekkers, *Het humanisme en de rechtswetenschap in de Nederlanden* (Antwerp, 1938), pp. 8ff.

20. See, e.g., ibid., pp. 14ff.

21. It is a great service of Joseph Plescia to show how little of conflict of laws in the modern sense appears in the Roman Empire: "Conflict of Laws in the Roman Empire," *Labeo* 38 (1952): 30ff.

22. On Justinian's *Code* 1.4, *De summa trinitati,* gloss *Quod si Bononiensis.*

23. For another example of this approach of Bartolus on conflict of laws, see Watson, *Comity,* pp. 5–6.

24. *Pantagruel,* chap. 5; see infra, Chapter 10. For Rabelais and law, see now Barbara C. Bowen, *Enter Rabelais, Laughing* (Nashville, 1998), pp. 160ff.

25. *Praelectiones juris romani et hodierni* 2.1.3. On the whole subject, see Watson, *Comity.*

26. Bernhard Windscheid, *Lehrbuch des Pandektenrechts,* 8th ed. (Frankfurt am Main, 1900), pp. 744ff.

27. Published as Alan Watson, *The Contract of Mandate in Roman Law* (Oxford, 1961).

28. Windscheid, *Lehrbuch des Pandektenrechts,* 8th ed., pp. I, II, IV.

29. See Glanvil (d. 1190), *Tractatus de Legibus et Consuetudinibus Regni Anglie* 10.18–19; A. W. B. Simpson, *A History of the Common Law of Contract* (Oxford, 1975), p. 4.

30. For the argument, see Watson, *Transplants,* p. 15.

31. *Mancipatio* was a formal ceremony needed to transfer certain important kinds of property; its obligational content was an inherent warranty against the eviction of the transferee from the property. *Nexum,* though obscure, was probably a variant form of *mancipatio;* it involved a creditor's having real rights over the person of the *nexus:* see Kaser, *Privatrecht,* 1:165ff.; Alan Watson, *Rome of the XII Tables* (Princeton, 1975), pp. 11–14, 134–49; Gy. Diósdi, *Contract in Roman Law* (Budapest, 1981), pp. 30ff. It is Diósdi who would add *in iure cessio* as involving an obligation. This was a fictional lawsuit to effect the transfer of ownership in which the defendant, the owner, put up no defense to a claim of ownership from the plaintiff, the transferee. None of these three institutions had a major impact on the later development of the law of contract.

32. See, e.g., Thomas, *Textbook,* p. 226.

33. *Rhetorica ad Herennium* 2.13.19.

34. See Max Kaser, *Das altrömische Ius* (Göttingen, 1949), pp. 256–67; H. van den Brink, *Ius Fasque: Opmerkungen over de Dualiteit van het archaïsch-romeins Recht* (Amsterdam, 1968), pp. 172–80; Okko Behrends, *Der Zwölftafelprozess* (Göttingen, 1974), pp. 35–36; and the authors they cite.

35. Kaser, *Privatrecht,* 1:168–70.

36. Ibid., 1:170–71.

37. See for the argument Alan Watson, *Roman Private Law around 200 B.C.* (Edinburgh, 1971), pp. 126–27.

38. The *condictio furtiva,* which is exceptional, need not concern us here.

39. Kaser, *Privatrecht,* 1:492–93.

40. In French law any noncommercial (in the technical sense) transaction above a very small amount can be proved only by a notarial act or a private signed writing except, under article 1348 of the Code civil, when it is not possible for the creditor to procure writing. "Possible" here refers to moral pos-

sibility as well as physical, and in certain close relationships—such as, at times, those involving one's mother, mistress, or physician—the obtaining of a writing is regarded as morally impossible.

41. Some scholars—e.g., Kaser, *Ius,* p. 286—suggest that a real action, the *legis actio sacramento in rem,* was available for *mutuum* before the introduction of the *condictio.* There is no evidence for this, and the availability of such an action would make it more difficult to explain the introduction of the *condictio.* But the suggestion would not adversely affect the idea expressed here that *mutuum* was given specific protection because the arrangement was among friends and *stipulatio* was morally inappropriate. At whatever date, a commercial loan would involve interest, a *stipulatio* would be taken, and there would be no need for specific legal protection of *mutuum.*

42. D. Daube, "Money and Justiciability," *ZSS* 92 (1979): 1–16, 11; see earlier D. Daube, "The Self-Understood in Legal History," *Juridical Review* 18 (1973): 129–30.

43. *Collatio* 10.7.11. The action has often been thought to be something other than an action for deposit or to be an action for what was later called *depositum miserabile,* but see Watson, *Private Law,* p. 151, and Kaser, *Privatrecht* 1:160, n. 49.

44. E.g., Watson, *Private Law,* p. 157; Kaser, *Privatrecht,* 1:160.

45. E.g., Kaser, *Privatrecht,* 1:160.

46. Otto Lenel, *Das Edictum Perpetuum,* 3d ed. (Leipzig, 1927), pp. 288–89. Praetors were elected public officials who, among other things, had control over particular courts. They had no power to legislate, but in practice they modified the law enormously by issuing edicts setting out actions they would give and special defenses they would allow.

47. The literature is enormous, but see, e.g., W. Litewski, "Studien zum sogenannten 'depositum necessarium,'" *Studia et Documenta Historiae et Iuris* 43 (1977): 188ff., esp. 194ff., and the works he cites.

48. Diósdi, *Contract,* pp. 44–45.

49. See Watson, *Obligations,* pp. 40–43.

50. See Kaser, *Privatrecht* 1:546; Jolowicz and Nicholas, *Historical Introduction,* pp. 288–94; and the works they cite.

51. Th. Mommsen, "Die römischen Anfänge von Kauf and Miethe," *ZSS* 6 (1885): 260ff.

52. Scholars who take any one of these approaches—especially the first two—also wish to give a central role in the invention to the peregrine praetor. This seems to me to be unnecessary, but the point need not detain us here; see Alan Watson, *Law Making in the Later Roman Republic* (Oxford, 1974), pp. 63–83.

53. This appears even in Mommsen, "Anfänge," p. 260; see also E. I. Bekker, *Die Aktionen des römischen Privatrechts,* 1 (Berlin, 1871), pp. 156ff.; V. Arangio-Ruiz, *La Compravendita in diritto romano,* 1, 2d ed. (Naples, 1956):

57ff. Diósdi objects, asking why it would be necessary to cut up "the uniform contract of spot transactions into two separate contracts, to confirm the two promises with a *stipulatio*, then abandon the *stipulationes* shortly so that at the beginning of the preclassical age the contract appears as already in its classical shape." *Contract*, p. 45. By "spot transaction," he appears to have *mancipatio* in mind. There are two flaws in this argument. First, the object of the sale-type transaction would not always be a *res mancipi*, in which case *mancipatio* would be inappropriate. Second, even in the earliest times, even when the object was a *res mancipi*, the parties would not always want a spot transaction, but delivery at a future time, and *mancipatio* would not then be used.

54. Alan Watson, "The Origins of Consensual Sale: A Hypothesis," *T.v.R.* 32 (1964): 245–54.

55. In fact, the *stipulatio* could not be taken from a son or slave with full protection until the introduction of the *actio quod iussu*. That action appears to be based on an edict of the praetor (Lenel, *Edictum*, p. 278), and actions based on an edictal clause giving the plaintiff a new right of action cannot be safely dated earlier than c. 100 B.C.: see Watson, *Law Making*, p. 38.

56. B. Nicholas does not agree, and suggests for the persistence of the stipulations that they imposed strict liability, whereas liability on sale would be based only on good faith: Jolowicz and Nicholas, *Historical Introduction*, p. 289, n. 8 (at p. 290). This does not address the problem, which is not the continued use of *stipulatio* but the absence of implied warranties in sale. Those who wanted strict liability could still have demanded a *stipulatio* even if *emptio venditio* had implied warranties (which could be excluded). Again, this approach does not lessen the commercial inconvenience of the lack of implied warranties. Moreover, it must be surprising in a contract of sale based on good faith that there is no warranty of title or of quiet possession.

57. Strict textual proof is lacking, but a development from the strict law *stipulatio* to good faith *emptio venditio* can have been no other.

58. For this, see Watson, *Making of the Civil Law*, pp. 14–22.

59. The impact of the defects in early consensual sale would be less noticeable, of course, where what was sold was a *res mancipi* and it actually was delivered by *mancipatio*, which did have an inherent warranty against eviction. Even here, however, there was no warranty against latent defects.

60. For views see, e.g., Jolowicz and Nicholas, *Historical Introduction*, pp. 294–97. Significantly, one writer on ancient hire, H. Kaufman, offers no view on the origins of the consensual contract; see *Die altrömische Miete* (Cologne, 1964).

61. Actually, *locatio conductio* is so obviously a residual category—every bilateral transaction involving a money presentation that is not sale is hire—that one need not start with the assumption of the priority of sale. From the very fact of the residual nature of hire one can deduce the priority of sale. Unless, that is, one were to argue (as I think no one would) that originally sale

transactions were within the sphere of *locatio conductio* and that *emptio venditio* was carved out of this all-embracing contract.

62. *Rhetorica ad Herennium* 2.13.19. See Alan Watson, *Contract of Mandate in Roman Law* (Oxford, 1961), p. 22.

63. K. Visky, *Geistige Arbeit und die Artes Liberales in den Quellen des römischen Rechts* (Budapest, 1977), pp. 146-58.

64. Watson, *Law Making*, pp. 31-62, esp. p. 38.

65. See, e.g., Lenel, *Edictum*, pp. 254-56, who thinks there was such an action; and Kaser, *Privatrecht*, 1:537, who apparently tends to think there was not.

66. Watson, *Obligations*, pp. 182-84.

67. Though the *actio quod iussu* is not evidenced for the republic: see ibid., pp. 187-88.

68. A further reason for the introduction of the new contractual action was that it could allow more of a role for reliance on good faith, even though the praetorian action did not have a condemnation clause framed *ex fide bona*. In favor of this explanation is the fact that *fiducia*—the older form of real security (and not contractual in terms of the definition given at the beginning of this chapter)—was erected by using *mancipatio* with a special clause relating to trust and faith; see ibid., pp. 172-79. Indeed, it is possible that the existence of *fiducia* was influential by way of analogy for the creation of *pignus*. *Fiducia* had two limitations: its dependence on *mancipatio* meant that only *res mancipi* could be so pledged (unless the cumbrous *in iure cessio* were used) and that only citizens (or those with *commercium*) could be creditors or debtors. The praetor might thus have introduced the very different contract of *pignus*, also because of the difficulties involved in framing stipulations that would adequately cover the debtor's rights.

69. Thomas, *Textbook*, pp. 267-69.

70. Watson, *Obligations*, pp. 21-24.

71. See, above all, Alan Watson, "Consensual *societas* between Romans and the Introduction of *formulae*," *Revue Internationale des Droits de l'Antiquité* 9 (1962): 431-36.

72. *D.*17.2.29.pr., 1; see Alan Watson, "The Notion of Equivalence of Contractual Obligation and Classical Roman Partnership," *Law Quarterly Review* 97 (1981): 275-86.

73. *Laesio enormis* is postclassical, whether it is to be attributed to Diocletian or Justinian: C.4.44.2; 4.44.8.

74. *G.*3.159; *D.*17.1.12.16. That damages were doubled for breach in *depositum miserabile* is not a problem. *Depositum miserabile* could still be subjected to special regulation.

75. *D.*45.1.122; 45.1.126.2; 45.1.140.pr. There is something illogical in accepting a written document as evidence of *stipulatio*. It can show the intention of the parties, but scarcely that they went through the formalities.

76. D. M. MacDowell, *The Law in Classical Athens* (Ithaca, N.Y., 1978), p. 233.

77. M. Crawford, *Roman Republican Coinage* (Cambridge, 1976), pp. 35–37.

78. The state of development of barter before the time of Justinian is very obscure, much disputed, and need not be gone into here. For literature, see, e.g., Thomas, *Textbook,* pp. 311–12, and Kaser, *Privatrecht* 1:381.

79. David Daube, "Three Quotations from Homer in *D.*18.1.1.1," *Cambridge Law Journal* 10 (1949): 213–15.

80. A relatively satisfactory outcome, I believe, from the Sabinian viewpoint would be that barter is sale, and both parties have the obligations of sellers.

81. Daube, "Money," pp. 8, 9.

82. See Watson, *Obligations,* p. 257.

83. The literature is immense, since authors often have to take a position, but see, e.g., Reuven Yaron, "Semitic Elements in Early Rome," in *Daube Noster,* ed. Alan Watson (Edinburgh, 1974), pp. 343–57; Watson, *Law Making,* pp. 186–95.

84. See already Alan Watson, *Sources of Law.*

85. For the argument, see Watson, *Spirit,* pp. 60–61.

CHAPTER 3. JUDGES

1. Milsom, *Historical Foundations,* p. 20.

2. See, e.g., A. W. B. Simpson, *Introduction to the History of the Land Law* (Oxford, 1961), p. 8.

3. Milsom, *Historical Foundations,* p. 21.

4. See, e.g., E. H. Burn, *Cheshire and Burn's Modern Real Property,* 14th ed. (London, 1988), pp. 23–24; R. E. Megarry and H. W. R. Wade, *The Law of Real Property,* 3d ed. (London, 1966), p. 29; 5th ed. (1984), p. 32.

5. Milsom, *Historical Foundations,* p. 165 (subsequent page citations are in text).

6. M. Krygier, "Critical Legal Studies and Social Theory: A Response to Alan Hunt," *Oxford Journal of Legal Studies* 7 (1987): 26.

7. *Amtliches Stenographisches Bulletin der Schweizerischen Bundesversammlung, Nationalrat* (1905): 436.

8. But I have argued elsewhere that the humanists, by showing that to a great extent the Corpus Juris Civilis was not of classical origin, weakened its authority and thus academics could more respectably pay attention to other aspects of local law. This was an important factor in the codification of civil-law systems. See Watson, *Making of the Civil Law,* pp. 71–72. There are implications for "schools" of jurists in Douglas Osler, "A Star Is Born," *Rechtshistorisches Journal* 2 (1983): 194–95.

9. See G. Manna, *Della Giurisprudenza e del Foro Napoletano della sua Origine fino alla Pubblicazione delle nuove Leggi* (Naples, 1859), pp. 186–87.

10. Examples of such books are F. Rapolla, *De jure regni neapolitani Commentaria in ordine redacta* (Naples, 1746); C. Fimiami, *Elementa juris privati neapolitani in duos libros redacta* (Naples, 1782); M. Guarani, *Syntagma romani juris ac patrii secundum seriem Institutionum Imperialium* (Naples, 1773); G. Maffei, *Institutiones juris civilis Neapolitanorum* (Naples, 1784); G. Basta, *Institutiones juris romani neapolitani* (Naples, 1782); O. Fighera, *Institutiones juris regni neapolitani* (Naples, 1782).

11. See Giuseppe Sorge, *Jurisprudentia forensis universi juris materias,* 11 vols. (Naples, 1740–44); Giuseppe Sorge, *Enucleationes casuum forensium, sive additamenta ad opus jurisprudentiae forensis,* 11 vols. (Naples 1756–58).

12. For the group see, e.g., the bibliography of Critical Legal Studies by Alan Hunt in *Modern Law Review* 47 (1984): 369–74; Mark Kelman, *A Guide to Critical Legal Studies* (Cambridge, Mass., 1987); James Boyle, ed., *Critical Legal Studies* (New York, 1992).

13. I say most types of appellate civil cases rather than all because it may be that one party believes so passionately in the morality of his position that, despite the clear meaning of the law, he insists on going to court to make a point or in the faint hope of winning the verdict. Such was the situation on the rendition of fugitive slaves after the U.S. Fugitive Slave Act of 1850; see, e.g., R. Cover, *Justice Accused* (New Haven, Conn., 1975), pp. 119–30. Such cases, where the judge is caught between the demands of his role and the voice of conscience (ibid., pp. 6ff.), where he may be asked to go beyond the law in the direction of freedom, are not discussed here, although they raise similar issues.

14. *Brown v. Allen,* 73 S.Ct. 397, 427 (1953).

15. Practice Statement (Judicial Precedent) [1966] 1 W.L.R. 1234.

16. *London Street Tramways Co. v. London County Council* [1898] A.C. 375; and see, e.g., R. B. Stevens, *Law and Politics* (Chapel Hill, N.C., 1978), pp. 88–90.

17. For their practice, see above all Alan Paterson, *The Law Lords* (Toronto, 1982), esp. 162–69.

18. *President of India v. La Pintada Compañía Navigación,* at p. 13.

19. This, of course, was one of the insights of the American legal realists. To say that a well-fought appellate civil case can always be decided either way is not to deny the existence of legal rules. The rules decide many issues before they come to trial, but appellate cases are either about the boundary lines of legal rules or, as here, about changing the rules when the court has the power to do so.

20. *President of India v. La Pintada Compañía Navigación,* p. 13.

21. Ibid.

22. See also the note by P. M. N. in *Lloyd's Maritime & Commercial L.Q.*

(1984), pp. 305ff. On discovering the intention of the legislature, see, e.g., H. Friendly, "Mr. Justice Frankfurter and the Reading of Statutes," *Benchmarks* 9 (1967): 196ff., esp. 200, 207, 219ff.

23. See the materials and discussion in Watson, *Sources of Law,* pp. 78ff.

24. See, e.g., the remarks of various politicians during the passage of the Land Registration (Scotland) Act of 1979, quoted in *Journal of the Law Society of Scotland* 24 (1979): 235ff.; Lord Hailsham of Marylebone, "Obstacles to Law Reform," *Current Legal Problems* 34 (1981): 279ff., esp. 286ff.

25. See Watson, *Sources of Law,* pp. 80–83; *Society and Legal Change,* pp. 61ff.

26. That is, in fact, to interpret a statute only in terms of the words used.

27. *President of India v. La Pintada Compañía Navigación,* p. 23. On the question of statutory and common law remedies existing together one might refer to *Illinois v. City of Milwaukee,* 599 F.2d 151 (1979).

28. I am reminded of article 1 of the Swiss Civil Code: "The law regulates all matters to which the letter or the spirit of any of its provisions relates. In the absence of an applicable legal provision, the judge pronounces in accordance with customary law and, in the absence of a custom, according to the rules that he would establish if he had to act as legislator. He is guided by the solutions consecrated by juristic opinion and case law.

29. *President of India v. La Pintada Compañía Navigación,* p. 14.

30. Ibid., p. 30.

31. See, e.g., W. Dale, *Legislative Drafting: A New Approach* (London, 1977), pp. 331–35; the publications of the Statute Law Society entitled *Statute Law: The Key to Clarity* (London, 1972), and *Renton and the Need for Reform* (London, 1979); Michael Zander, *The Law-Making Process,* 4th ed. (London, 1994), pp. 14–25.

32. R. H. S. Crossman, *The Diaries of a Cabinet Minister* (London, 1975), p. 628.

33. See, e.g., W. J. Hosten, A. B. Edwards, C. Nathan, and F. Bosman, *Introduction to South African Law and Legal Theory* (Durban, 1977), p. 222; H. R. Hahlo and E. Kahn, *The South African Legal System and Its Background* (Cape Town, 1968), p. 581.

34. *Mann v. Mann,* p. 94.

35. On *infamia* in Roman law, see above all A. H. J. Greenidge, *Infamia: Its Place in Roman Public and Private Law* (Oxford, 1894).

36. The translations are by R.W. Lee, *Hugo Grotius: The Jurisprudence of Holland* (Oxford, 1953), pp. 121, 123.

37. *Mann v. Mann,* p. 99.

38. Ibid., p. 98.

39. See, e.g., Grotius, *Inleidinge,* 3.34.2; Voet, *Commentarius ad Pandectas,* 9.2.11; Matthaeus, *De Criminibus,* 47.3.3.4; Groenewegen, *Tractatus de Legibus Abrogatis et Inusitatis in Hollandia Vicinisque Regionibus,* D.9.3.7.

40. See, e.g., J. C. Macintosh and C. Norman-Scoble, *Negligence in Delict,* 5th ed. (Cape Town, 1970), p. 41. N. J. Van de Merwe and P. J. J. Olivier, *Die Onregmagtige Daad in Die Suid-Afrikaanse Reg,* 4th ed. (Cape Town, 1980), 302, 355, accept Rohloff for the proposition that a delictal action lies between husband and wife not married in community but keep Mann for the proposition that an action does not lie when the marriage is in communion.

41. For a modern extreme and illuminating South African example, see *Du Plessis NO v. Strauss* 1988 (2) SA 105.

42. There are, of course, exceptions, including the earliest of the modern civil codes, that of Bavaria, the Codex Maximilianeus Bavaricus Civilis (1756), which had only subsidiary force.

43. See, e.g., Watson, *Making of the Civil Law,* p. 101; "Legal Change," p. 1132; J. P. Dawson, Review, *University of Chicago Law Review* 49 (1982): 602.

44. But an early group of interpreters of the French Code civil, the *école de l'exégèse,* did look at legislative history; and in the early days of the Code civil old authorities were frequently cited in court.

45. *Dalloz,* 1876.1, p. 193.

46. See, e.g., A. Weill and T. Terré, *Droit civil: Introduction générale,* 4th ed. (Paris, 1979), p. 184.

47. *Traité du contrat de Louage,* art. 113.

48. See also along the same lines *D.*50.17.23.

49. See Fenet, *Travaux préparatoires,* 13:54. The sole discussion related to the last sentence. Portalis successfully suggested the deletion of "contractées et" before "executées." See also C. Baudry-Lacantinerie and L. Barde, *Traité théorique et pratique de droit civil: Les obligations,* 3d ed. (Paris, 1906), 1:381ff.

50. See Baudry-Lacantinerie and Barde, *Traité,* 1:383 and n. 1.

51. See, e.g., Richard Schröder, *Geschichte des Ehelichen Güterrechts in Deutschland,* pt. 2, sec. 3 (1874; Leipzig, 1967), pp. 187ff.

52. It appears as number 123 of the first book of the collection of *Schöffen* opinions of the town of Pössneck: *Die Schöffenspruchsammlung der Stadt Pössneck,* ed. Grosch (Leipzig, 1957), 1:1118ff. See also vol. 3, ed. Buchda (1962), p. 7.

53. Whereas the *Schöffen* of Leipzig did attempt to judge according to the law of the petitioners.

54. For what is now modern Belgium, see J. Gilissen, *Introduction historique au droit* (Brussels, 1970), pp. 247ff. He observes that there were very many jurisdictions, even in small communities, and that the *échevins,* who were both administrators and judges, had no legal training. When difficulties arose in a lawsuit, it became habitual to send the issue to the *échevins* of a larger town or village that "followed approximately the same custom." In the twelfth and thirteenth centuries the law of many towns was granted to other towns: Bruges, for example, was mother town to more than twenty others.

55. See, e.g., J. M. Lacarra, *Fueros Derivados de Jaca,* vol. 1, *Estella–San Se-*

bastián (Pamplona, 1969), p. 21; J. M. Lacarra and A. J. M. Duque, *Fueros Derivados de Jaca,* vol. 2, *Pamplona* (Pamplona, 1975), p. 56.

56. The reply is reprinted by Lacarra and Duque, *Fueros Derivados,* pp. 235ff.; but the accurate version of four chapters was sent.

57. Ibid., p. 57.

58. Jaca was by no means the only town whose *fuero* spread widely. Estella itself is another notable example. See in general Tomás y Valiente, *Manual,* pp. 150ff.

59. There is no direct evidence that it was the judges of, say, Pamplona, and not the parties to the lawsuit, who appealed to the judges of Jaca, but it is difficult to imagine that the decision of Jaca would have any impact otherwise on the enforceability of the decision in Pamplona. Moreover, the reply from Jaca of 27 August 1342 makes little sense if it was not the judges of Pamplona who raised the appeal. No such decisions of the *"jurados y hombres buenos"* of Jaca seem to have been published.

CHAPTER 4. CUSTOM

1. For the development of a theory of custom in Roman law, insofar as there is one, see D. Nörr, "Zur Entstehung der gewohnheitsrechtlichen Theorie," in *Festschrift für W. Felgentraeger* (Göttingen, 1969), pp. 353ff. A very different view of the formation for customary rules, particularly in international law, is given by J. Finnis, *Natural Law and Natural Rights* (Oxford, 1980), pp. 238ff. Custom as a source of international law is not discussed in this chapter.

2. It is presumably on this account that Rudolf von Jhering described custom as the "pet" of the German Historical School; see *Geist des römischen Rechts* 2.1, 5th ed. (Leipzig, 1894), p. 29.

3. But this chapter is not directly an essay on the history of legal theory, and I have done little more than read the appropriate pages in the gloss and typical authors such as Oinotomus, Wesembecius, J. Voet, Vinnius, and Heinecius.

4. K.C.W. Klötzer, *Versuch eines Beytrags zur Revision der Theorie von Gewohnheitsrecht* (Jena, 1813), esp. pp. 189ff.; S. Brie, *Die Lehre von Gewohnheitsrecht,* vol. 1 (Breslau, 1899).

5. I have translated this quotation from K. Larenz, *Methodenlehre der Rechtswissenschaft,* 2d ed. (Berlin, 1969), p. 338; see also his *Allgemeiner Teil des deutschen Bürgerlichen Rechts: Ein Lehrbuch,* 5th ed. (Munich, 1980), p. 10. In later editions Larenz is much less explicit, although he seems to have basically the same opinion; see *Methodenlehre,* 4th ed. (1979), pp. 345ff. He expressly adopts the view of Nörr that the theory of customary law, as such, is unsatisfactory.

6. F. von Savigny, *System des heutigen Römischen Rechts* (Berlin, 1840), 1:174–75.

7. *D.*1.3.39. And this view is generally accepted within the tradition.

8. No comparison can be drawn with desuetude of statute, for which there is no need for a belief that the contrary acting is in accord with the law.

9. See, e.g., the remarks of C. K. Allen, *Law in the Making,* 7th ed. (Oxford, 1964), p. 136.

10. Savigny, *System,* I, p. 171.

11. Watson, *Sources of Law,* pp. 175–76.

12. See, e.g., Allen, *Law in the Making,* pp. 87ff. Yet, oddly, it survives indirectly, without the theoretical trappings, in a number of writers; for instance, add to the authors quoted in Watson, *Society and Legal Change,* pp. 1–2, L. M. Friedman, *A History of American Law,* 2d ed. (New York, 1985), pp. 694–95. In a curious way Guido Calabresi seems a modern distorting mirror of Savigny, and for him the judges (like jurists) "represent" the people at one remove, the current "legal landscape" generally reflects popular desires, and legislation inhibits law from giving the people what they want and need; see *A Common Law for the Age of Statutes* (Cambridge, 1982).

13. J. Austin, *Province of Jurisprudence Determined* (London, 1954), pp. 30ff., 163ff.; J. Austin, *Lectures on Jurisprudence,* vol. 2 (London, 1863), 222ff.

14. But J. C. Gray argues that statutes are not law but only sources of law, because their meaning is declared by the courts, and "it is with the meaning declared by the courts, and with no other meaning that they are imposed upon the community as law." *The Nature and Sources of Law,* 2d ed. (New York, 1927), p. 170.

15. Allen, *Law in the Making,* p. 70.

16. J. A. Brutails, *La Coutume d'Andorre* (Paris, 1904), p. 55.

17. Ibid., pp. 47–74.

18. Ibid., p. 342; P. Ourliac, ed., *La Jurisprudence civile d' Andorre: Arrêts du tribunal supérieur de Perpignan, 1947–1970* (Andorra, 1972), p. 12, n. 7.

19. Further reports appear in subsequent volumes.

20. C. Obiols i Taberner, *Jurisprudéncia civil andorrana: Jutjat d'apellacions, 1945–1966* (Andorra, 1969).

21. See Watson, *Sources of Law,* pp. 45–46.

22. Ibid., pp. 46–47.

23. But not all contemporaries saw borrowing of a neighbor's custom as borrowing it as the custom of the borrower; see the preface of Guy Coquille (d. 1603) at his Coutume de Nivernais.

24. Of course, none of this is to be taken as meaning that it is not also often the case that the customary law does derive from preceding local behavior. But even where this is so, there are great difficulties in regarding *opinio necessitatis* as providing the factor that turns behavior into law, as is discussed later in this chapter.

25. Austin, *Province,* p. 31.

26. *In quattuor libros Institutionum Imperialium Commentarius* 1.2.7.

27. It may be worth mentioning in this connection that the Bavarian civil

code of 1756, Codex Maximilianeus Bavaricus Civilis, 1.2. sec. 15, expressly requires for customary law both the will of the people and the consent of the ruler.

28. Alan Watson, *The Nature of Law* (Edinburgh, 1977), p. 3.

29. Pollok and Maitland, *History,* 1:399–400.

30. For this practice, see Watson, *Sources of Law,* pp. 31–36.

31. Ibid., pp. 28–31.

32. Ibid., pp. 47–50.

33. Tomás y Valiente, *Manual,* p. 133.

34. Certainly the compilers of unofficial collections of customary law frequently praise the quality and the descent from their forefathers. But we cannot generalize from these writers. They wrote these works because they were attached to the customs, but this does not imply the same feeling in other members of the community. Indeed, the authors often lament that the customs are not being kept.

35. An *Oberhof* was the *Schöffen* of another place selected as a mother town, who gave replies on points of law submitted to them.

36. Watson, *Sources of Law,* pp. 37–38.

37. Ibid., pp. 42–43. With time, the use of the *enquête par tourbes* became more complicated.

38. Ana Maria Barrero Garciá, *Fuero de Teruel* (Madrid, 1979), p. 7.

39. Tomás y Valiente, *Manual,* p. 150.

40. See, e.g., R. Besnier, *La Coutume de Normandie. Histoire externe* (Paris, 1935), p. 32. If, as often the privileges of one town were granted to another by the ruler, then the result is statute, not customary law. Nonetheless, as with the redaction of *coutumes* in France in general, the written redaction was regarded in fact as containing customary law.

41. Ibid., p. 22.

42. Soulatges, *La Coutume de Toulouse* (Toulouse, n.d.), p. ix. The work is not dated, but the latest reference is to 10 November 1769.

43. See P. Loscertales de Valdeavellano, *Costumbres de Lérida* (Barcelona, 1946), pp. 10ff.

44. "Dum memorassem quod venientes homines nostri, in praesentiam nostram, adduxerint caussas, inter se altercantes quae nec per usum fuimus certi ad terminandum, nec in Edicti corpore anteriori incerto." See also for slightly different issues the preambles from his fourteenth (A.D. 726) and fifteenth (A.D. 727) years.

45. See., e.g., Soulatges, *La Coutume de Toulouse,* pp. xi ff.

46. "Ego Guillelmus Botetus dedi aliquantulam operam ut consuetudines civitatis varias et diversas in unum colligerem et scriptis comprehenderem ut aufferretur quibusdam occasio malignandi qui quando erat pro eius consuetudo et esse consuetudinem affirmabant. Si contra eos in consimili casu allegabatur non esse consuetudinem asserebant. Unde processus causarum probacio consuetudinis retardabat et litigantes inde dispendia gravia senciebant."

47. "Quoniam igitur humana labilis est memoria nec rerum turbe potest sufficere ob hoc cautele sagaci actum est arbitrio leges autentice institutionis et iura civica, que consulta discretione ad sedendam seditionem inter cives [et incolas] de regali auctoritate manarunt, litterarum apicibus anotari, ut majori, quia regali tuicione munitas, malignantium versucia nullatenus possint infringi, vel alicuius subreptioris molestia deinceps eneruari"; to be found in R. De Ureña, *Fuero de Cuenca* (Madrid, 1935), p. III. Of course, because the compilation is official, it has become statute, and the *fuero* does contain legislative materials but that does not affect the issue.

48. J. F. Holleman, *Shona Customary Law* (London, 1952), p. x.

49. It is common for authorities on customary law to regard their law as ancient; see Watson, *Sources of Law*, pp. 44–50.

50. L. Shapera, *Handbook of Tswana Law and Custom*, 2d ed. (London, 1965), pp. 39–40.

51. F. A. Ajayi, "The Judicial Development of Customary Law in Nigeria," in *Integration of Customary and Modern Legal Systems in Africa*, ed. Law Faculty, University of Ife (Ife-Ife, Nigeria, 1971), p. 126.

52. Hans Cory, *Sukuma Law and Custom* (London, 1953), p. vii.

53. But see, e.g., A. N. A. Allott, *Essays in African Law* (London, 1960), pp. 3ff., and *New Essays in African Law* (London, 1970), pp. 9ff.

54. See also, for instance, the volumes of *Restatement of African Law* by various authors, under the general editorship of A. N. A. Allott, for the School of Oriental and African Studies, University of London, and published by Sweet & Maxwell, London.

55. See above all, Cory, *Sukuma Law*, pp. xiii–xiv.

CHAPTER 5. LEGISLATION AND JURISTS: FRENCH DÉLIT

1. See, e.g., William M. Evans, *Social Structure and Law* (Newbury Park, Calif. 1990), pp. 34ff.; cf. already Watson, *Transplants*, pp. 107, 114–17. For two recent views, see Pierre Legrand, "The Impossibilities of Legal Transplants," *Maastricht Journal of European and Comparative Law* 4 (1997): 111–24; Charles Donahue, "Comparative Legal History in North America," *T.v.R* 65 (1997): 14–15.

2. See C. Calisse, *General Survey of Events, etc.*, in *Continental Legal History*, by various European authors (Boston, 1912), p. 286.

3. Paul Viollet, *Histoire du droit civil français*, 3d ed. (Paris, 1905), p. 220. Viollet would not refuse some place to Roman law (pp. IIff.).

4. Now in Rudolf B. Schlesinger et al., *Comparative Law*, 6th ed. (New York, 1998), p. 257.

5. Code civil: 1382. Tout fait quelconque de l'homme, qui cause à autrui un dommage, oblige celui par la faute duquel il est arrivé, à le réparer.

1383. Chacun est responsable du dommage qu'il a causé, non seulement par son fait, mais encore par sa négligence ou par son imprudence.

1384. On est responsable, non seulement du dommage que l'on cause par son propre fait, mais encore de celui qui est causé par le fait des personnes dont on doit répondre, ou des choses que l'on a sous sa garde.

Le père, et la mère après le décès du mari, sont responsables du dommage causé par leurs enfans mineurs habitant avec eux;

Les maîtres et les commettans, du dommage causé par leurs domestiques et préposés dans les functions auxquelles il les ont employés;

Les instituteurs et les artisans, du dommage causé par leurs élèves et apprentis pendant le temps qu'ils sont sous leur surveillance.

La responsabilité ci-dessus a lieu, à moins que les père et mère, instituteurs et artisans, ne prouvent qu'ils n'ont pu empêcher le fait qui donne lieu à cette responsabilité.

1385. Le propriétaire d'un animal, ou celui qui s'en sert, pendant qu'il est à son usage, est responsable du dommage que l'animal a causé soit que l'animal fût sous sa garde, soit qu'il fût égaré ou échappé.

1386. Le propriétaire d'un bâtiment est responsable du dommage causé par sa ruine, lorsqu'elle est arrivée par une suite du défaut d'entretien ou par le vice de la construction.

6. See, e.g., Weill and Terré, *Droit civil,* p. 184.

7. The terms *délit* and *quasi-délit* do appear in article 1370, along with *quasi-contrat* as types of obligations that arise without agreement, but they are neither defined nor explained.

8. The rules are complicated and of no consequence here, but see, e.g., Watson, *Obligations,* pp. 274ff.

9. I believe that the occupier was liable only if he placed or knew of the placing of the object: "Liability in the *actio de positis ac suspensis,*" in *Mélanges Philippe Meylan,* 1 (Lausanne, 1963), pp. 379ff. My view and its accuracy are irrelevant in the present context, where what matters is the traditional view that the occupier was liable even without fault.

10. See *Pauli Sententiae,* 1.15.1; also see Otto Lenel, *Das Edictum Perpetuum,* 3d ed. (Leipzig, 1927), p. 198.

11. Jean Domat, *Les Lois civiles dans leur ordre naturel* (Luxembourg, 1689), 2.7.3; Fenet, *Travaux préparatoires,* 13:477.

12. We need not go into details; see, e.g., Kaser, *Privatrecht,* 1:408–9.

13. There were a few other special remedies, such as the *actio aquae pluviae arcendae,* the action for warding off rainwater.

14. See, above all, Lenel, *Edictum,* p. 551.

15. But French case law has held that article 1386 also applied to damage from defective trees: see Cour d'Appel, Paris, Première Chambre, 20.8.1877; S.1878 II.48.

16. Domat, *Les Lois civiles,* 13.9.

17. See the first paragraph of Domat's preface to *Les Lois civiles.*

18. On peut distinguer trois sortes de fautes dont il peut arriver quelque dommage: celles qui vont à un crime ou à un délit; celles des personnes qui manquent aux engagemens des conventions, comme un vendeur qui ne délivre pas la chose vendue, un locataire qui ne fait pas les réparations dont il est tenu; et celles qui n'ont point de rapport aux conventions, et qui ne vont pas à un crime ni à un délit, comme si par légèreté on jette quelque chose par une fenétre qui gâte un habit: si des animaux mal gardés font quelque dommage; si on cause un incendie par une imprudence, si un bâtiment qui menace ruine, n'étant pas réparé, tombe sur un autre, et y fait du dommage.

De ces trois sortes de fautes, il n'y a que celles de la dernière espèce qui soient la matière de ce titre; car les crimes et les délits ne doivent pas être mêlés avec les matières civiles, et tout ce qui regarde les conventions, a été expliqué dans le premier livre.

19. See Pothier, *Traité des obligations,* 1.1.2.2.

20. See, e.g., C. de Ferrière, *La Jurisprudence du Digeste* (1677), on *D.*9.2; cf. A. Dumas, *Histoire des obligations dans l'ancien droit français* (Aix-en-Provence, 1972), p. 33; Helmut Coing, *Europäisches Privatrecht* (Munich, 1985), 1:504ff.

21. There were other reasons for neglecting the *lex Aquilia,* because it could well be doubted whether that statute had been "received" into later law. See the discussion of the opinions of Christianus Thomasius (1655–1728) and J. H. Heineccius (1681–1741) in Watson, *Transplants,* pp. 79ff.

22. Article 16. Si, d'une maison habitée par plusieurs personnes, il est jeté sur un passant de l'eau, ou quelque chose qui cause un dommage, ceux qui habitent l'appartement d'où on l'a jeté sont tous solidairement responsables, à moins que celui qui a jeté ne soit connu, auquel cas il doit seul la réparation du dommage.

Article 17. Les hôtes qui n'habitent qu'en passant la maison d'où la chose a été jetée, ne sont point tenus de la réparation du dommage, à moins qu'il ne soit prouvé que ce sont eux qui ont jeté, mais celui qui les loge en est tenu.

23. *Procès-Verbaux,* 3:311ff. Cf. C.-B.-M. Toullier, *Le Droit civil Français,* 11, 5th ed. (Paris, 1830), pp. 192–93; C. Baudry-Lacantinerie and L. Barde, *Traité théorique et pratique de droit civil, les obligations,* vol. 4, 3d ed. (Paris, 1908), pp. 653–54.

24. See Fenet, *Travaux préparatoires,* 13:464ff.

25. Toullier, *Le Droit civil,* pp. 433ff.; cf., e.g., the remarks of A. Tunc, "A Codified Law of Tort—The French Experience," *Louisiana Law Review* 39 (1979): 1051–75.

26. F. Mourlon, *Répétitions écrites sur le code civil contenant l'exposé des principes généraux,* vol. 2 (Paris, 1877), pp. 892ff., esp. p. 895. The same silence is observed by V. Marcadé, *Explication théorique et pratique du code Napoléon,*

vol. 5 (Paris, 1859), pp. 267ff.; J.-B.-C. Picot, *Code Napoléon expliqué article par article* (Paris, n.d.), pp. 58ff.; A. Duranton, *Cours de droit civil,* vol. 7, 4th ed. (Brussels, 1841), pp. 508ff. The same is true for the famous work of C. S. Zachariae, *Cours de droit civil français,* revu et augmenté par C. Aubry et C. Rau, vol. 3 (Strasbourg, 1839), pp. 202–3, and also A. M. Demante with E. Colmet de Santerre, *Cours analytique de Code civil,* vol. 5, 2d ed. (Paris, 1883), pp. 660ff. The explication of Bosquet is illuminating. On article 1384 he writes: "Les choses qu'on a sous sa garde sont mobilières ou immobilières, elles sont sans vie ou avec vie. Ce ne peut être que du fait de ces dernières, dont le présent article a entendu parler. Mais, dans cette acceptation, l'article 1385 n'est-il pas suffisant?" (Things which one has under one's guard are movable or immovable, they are inanimate or animate. The present article can have intended to speak only of those last named. But, with this understanding, is article 1385 not sufficient?) *Explication du code civil,* vol. 3 (Avignon, 1805).

27. S. 1897.1.17 (to be found in English in A. T. von Mehren and J. R. Gordley, *The Civil Law System,* 2d ed. [Boston, 1977], pp. 608–11).

28. See G. Viney, *Les Obligations, la responsabilité: Conditions* (Paris, 1982), p. 749. In the case of Jand'heur c. Galéries Belfortaises, P. Matter claimed that liability for things under one's guard derived from old French customary law; see Dalloz, *Recueil périodique et critique,* vol. 1 (Paris, 1930), p. 65.

29. "Les maîtres d'école, les artisans et autres qui reçoivent dans leurs maisons des écoliers, apprentis, ou d'autres personnes pour quelque art, quelque manufacture ou quelque commerce, sont tenus du fait de ces personnes."

30. The idea had already appeared in practice that an employer was liable for loss caused by the fault or clumsiness of mule drivers, carters, or coachmen; see Ferrière, *Jurisprudence,* on D.9.2.

31. Reported in J. G. Locré, *Législation civile, commerciale, et criminelle de la France* (1827–32), 13:42.

32. Quoted from ibid., 13:58.

33. Ibid.

34. Domat, *Les Lois civiles,* 1.2.7.2.

35. However, although he bases his idea on Roman law authority, he seems to hold that for the *actio de pauperie,* in some situations at least, liability depends on the owner's knowing about his animal's bad habits and still not taking care; see ibid., 1.2.7.2.6, 7, 8.

36. For a few examples chosen almost at random, see Guy Coquille, *Conférence des coustumes de France* (Paris, 1642), p. 211; *Coustumes générales de Berry,* title 10, art. 1–4 (pasturage); *Coustumes générales du bailliage de Troyes,* art. 118 (wandering animals); art. 121, arts. 167–72 (pasturage), *Coustumes de Melun,* arts. 302–9 (pasturage); M. Petitjean and M. L. Marchand, *Le Coutumier Bourguignon glosé* (Paris, 1982), pp. 232 §273, 239 §300 (delict), pp. 32 §3, 236 §287, 291 §402. Interestingly, despite the practical importance of dam-

age by animals, nothing is said on the subject by writers such as A. Loysel, *Institutes coutumières* (first published in 1607) or G. Argou, *Institution au droit françois* (first published in 1692). Very different, though, is de Ferrière, *Jurisprudence,* on *D.9.1.*

37. This last sentence may perhaps be misleading. If Domat's treatment of responsibility for other persons was the sole *fons et origo,* then Roman noxal surrender may never have been directly relevant for subsequent French law because it has no place in the *actio de effusis vel deiectis.*

38. Treilhard said nothing apropos, and the words of Tarrible are vague but suggestive of liability only for fault (contrary to the wording of the article); see Locré, *Législation* 13:58.

39. Fenet, *Travaux préparatoires,* 13:455.

40. Locré, *Législation* 13:31, 40–41, 59–60.

41. Pothier, *Traité des obligations,* 1.1.2.2.

42. Already J. J. Bugnet in his notes on Pothier at this point observed that the redactors of the Code civil who followed Pothier seemed to intend to talk of "délits" in article 1382 and of "quasi-délits" in article 1383.

43. See, e.g., Watson, "Legal Change," pp. 1151ff.

44. Milsom, *Historical Foundations,* p. 6.

45. And there must be a collapse or fall: see, e.g., M. Planiol and G. Ripert, *Traité pratique de droit civil français,* vol. 6, *Les Obligations* (by P. Esmein), 2d ed. (Paris, 1952), pp. 849–50.

46. For the variety of interpretations of this part of article 1384, see, e.g., Tunc, "A Codified Law of Tort," pp. 1064ff.; F. H. Lawson and B. S. Markesinis, *Tortious Liability for Unintentional Harm in the Common Law and Civil Law,* vol. 1 (Cambridge, 1982), pp. 146–47. There is nothing in that work that is relevant to the argument of this chapter. For an interpretation of liability for persons for whom one is responsible under article 1384, see, e.g., Tunc, "A Codified Law of Tort," pp. 1062ff. See also A. Tunc, "It Is Wise Not to Take the Civil Codes Too Seriously: Traffic Accident Compensation in France," in *Essays in Memory of Professor F. H. Lawson,* ed. P. Wallington and R. M. Merkin (London: Butterworths, 1980), pp. 71–85. Traffic accident law was revised by the "loi de 5 juillet," 1985: cf. A.Tunc, "La loi française du 5 Juillet, 1985," *Revue Internationale de Droit Comparé* 37 (1985): 1019–23.

47. Articles 1300–1304. Additional provisions are in articles 1305–7; these too have Roman law roots.

48. See, e.g., J. G. Wolf, *Error im römischen Vertragsrecht* (Cologne, Graz, 1961), esp. pp. 112–65, and V. Zilletti, *La dottrina dell'errore nella storia del diritto romano* (Milan, 1961), esp. pp. 59–93.

49. *Procès-Verbaux* 3:243.

50. Locré, *Législation* 12:319.

51. Ibid., 12:554.

52. Ibid., 12:424–25.

53. See, e.g., Maleville, *Analyse raisonné*, 13:20; R. Feenstra, "The Dutch *Kantharos* Case and the History of 'Error in Substantia,'" *Tulane Law Review* 48 (1974): 846–58.

54. Pothier, *Traité des obligations*, no. 18.

55. Argou, *Institution au droit français*, 3.23.

56. For the argument that Argou's *Institution* may have provided a model for the structure of the Code civil, see Watson, *Making of the Civil Law*, pp. 111–12. P. Viollet in this connection calls attention to F. Bourjon, *Droit commun de la France et la coutume de Paris: Histoire du droit civil français* (1747), p. 251. See also C. Chêne, *L'Enseignement du droit français en pays de droit écrit* (Geneva, 1982), pp. 298–301.

57. The classic modern account is in E. Gaudemet, *Théorie générale des obligations* (1937; Paris, 1965), pp. 11131, esp. pp. 119–20.

58. For an informative short statement of *causa* in Roman law, see Buckland, *Textbook*, pp. 428–29.

59. See, e.g., Coing, *Privatrecht*, pp. 402–5.

60. Domat, *Les Lois civiles*, 1.1.1.5, 6; 1.1.5.13.

61. Pothier, *Traité des obligations*, §§42–47.

62. Locré, *Législation* 12:138ff.; 14:77–85.

63. See, e.g., Toullier, *Le Droit civil Français*, 6:170.

64. For various accounts, see, e.g., Gaudemet, *Théorie générale*, pp. 111–31; J. Carbonnier, *Droit civil*, vol. 4, *Les Obligations*, 10th ed. (Paris, 1979), pp. 106–9: B. Nicholas, *French Law of Contract* (London, 1982), pp. 112–15.

65. Indeed, until later: see, e.g., Toullier, *Le Droit civil français*, 6:170.

66. I am, of course, well aware that the compilers of the Code civil declared that absolutely new civil legislation for a great people would be above human powers, that they expressed great respect for Roman law, and that they sought a compromise between Roman law and customary law; see the "discours préliminaire" to the first *projet*, by Portalis, Tronchet, Bigot-Préameneu, and Maleville in *Conférence du code civil* (Paris, 1805), pp. xvii, xxxii, xxxiii.

67. P. Ourliac and J. de Malafosse, *Histoire du droit privé*, vol. 1, *Les Obligations* (Paris, 1961), p. 365.

CHAPTER 6. JURISTS, JUDGES, CUSTOM, LEGISLATION: WATER RIGHTS

1. See Alan Watson, *Rome of the Twelve Tables: Persons and Property* (Princeton, 1975), pp. 160–61.

2. Aulus Agerius and Numerius Negidius are the standard names for the Roman plaintiff and defendant, respectively.

3. "Se paret opus factum esse in agro Capenate, unde aqua pluvia agro Ai

Ai nocet, quam ob rem NmNm eam aquam Ao Ao arcere oportet, si ea res arbitrio iudicis non restituetur etc." The reconstruction of the *formula* is the work of Otto Lenel, *Das Edictum Perpetuum,* 3d ed. (Leipzig, 1927) p. 375.

4. Buckland, *Textbook,* p. 598.

5. See Kunkel, *Herkunft,* pp.18, 28.

6. Ateius even allowed the action in these circumstances to compel the neighbor to clear a ditch: *D.* 39.3.2.4.

7. The text may be corrupt at this point. Theodor Mommsen suggests that it spoke expressly of the action for fraud: *The Digest of Justinian,* vol. 3, ed. Theodor Mommsen, Paul Krueger, and Alan Watson (Philadelphia, 1985), p. 396, n.2.

8. See, e.g., *D.* 39.3.8 (Ulpian, Edict 53), 39.3.11 (Paul, Edict 49), 39.3.17 (Paul, Plautius 15).

9. On the general phenomenon of legal development, see Alan Watson, *Slave Law in the Americas* (Athens, Ga., 1990), pp. 1–21.

10. For present purposes I do not intend to go into the meaning of "rainwater," *aqua pluvia.* It is enough to know that generally it meant any water that was increased by rain. For a more extended discussion, see Alan Watson, *The Law of Property in the Later Roman Republic* (Oxford, 1968), pp. 155–75; Alan Rodger, "Roman Rain-Water," *T.v.R.* 38 (1970): 417–31. Nor do I address the question of impure water flowing onto another's land, or of any distinction between public and other rivers.

11. E.g., the *actio pro socio* (action on partnership); *actio finium regundorum* (action for regulating boundaries); *actio communi dividundo* (action for dividing common property); and the *actio familiae erciscundae* (action for dividing an inheritance). Buckland, *Textbook,* p. 252.

12. E.g., the *actio tutelae* (action on guardianship); *actiones empti et venditi* (actions on sale); and the *actio mandati* (action on mandate).

13. See, e.g., *D.* 39.3.13 (Gaius, Urban Praetor's Edict), 39.3.14 (Paul, Edict 49), 39.3.23 (Paul, Sabinus 16).

14. See Rotondi, *Leges Publicae,* p. 414.

15. *D.* 39.3.1.23 (Ulpian, Edict 53). *Precarium* was the grant of use of land by one private person to another, where no date was set for termination but the grant could be revoked at any time; *h.t.* 43.26.

16. Buckland, *Textbook,* p. 266; Thomas, *Textbook,* pp. 200–201. *Vetustas* literally means "ancient times" and "was of particular importance in relations between neighbors when the owner of land from time immemorial had certain profits from a neighbor's property (e.g., use of water)." A. Berger, *Encyclopedic Dictionary of Roman Law* (Philadelphia, 1953), p. 763.

Buckland, discussing "long enjoyment," explains that "[t]he earlier law is obscure. Perhaps the most probable view is that . . . a practice grew of treating very long enjoyment . . . as raising a presumption that the right had been duly created." Buckland, *Textbook,* p. 266.

17. Watson, *Making of the Civil Law,* pp. 144–67. The Roman jurists also dealt to a moderate extent—and no more—with criminal law and procedure.

18. *D.* 43.13.1; see Mommsen, *Digest,* 4:580, n. 18.

19. See, e.g., the apparatus in the edition of Mommsen, *Digest.*

20. *D.* 43.13.1.8 (Ulpian, Edict 68): "The interdict renders liable anyone who has caused a river to flow otherwise than it flowed last summer."

21. Interdicts such as *de aqua cottidiana et aestiva, D.* 43.20, and *de fonte, D.* 43.22, are not relevant in this context. They were concerned with the acquired servitude right of drawing off water from a neighbor's land, and simply prohibited force being used to impede the drawing off.

22. There is nothing on the subject in the work of Pothier's great predecessor, Jean Domat, *Les Loix civiles dans leur ordre naturel* (Luxembourg, 1689).

23. R. Pothier, *Traité du contrat de société* (Paris, 1775), §§236, 237, 239.

24. See Watson, *Failures of the Legal Imagination,* p. 11 (describing Domat's grand plan to set out a scheme of law in an easily comprehensible arrangement, his view that public "crime" should not be mixed with civil matters, and his primary concern with civil law).

25. Jean Domat, *Le Droit Public, suite des loix civiles dans leur ordre naturel* (Luxembourg 1702), liv. 1, tit. VIII, sec. II, §11.

26. Pothier, *Traité du contrat,* §239.

27. P. Merlin, "Cours d'eau," in *Répertoire universel et raisonné de jurisprudence,* vol. 4, 5th ed. (Paris, 1827), p. 43.

28. See, e.g., G. Argou, *Institution au droit françois,* vol. 1, 11th ed. (Paris, 1787), p. 219. This was the main French textbook from its first edition in 1692 until codification.

29. Cambacérès, *Troisième Projet de Code civil,* §§447, 448: Fenet, *Travaux préparatoires* 11:248.

The corresponding articles of the first *projet* (1793) are 37, 38 of title 2; of the second *projet* (1974), 80.

30. This corresponds to article 640 of the Code civil as it was promulgated.

31. Fenet, *Travaux préparatoires,* 11:256.

32. Pothier, *Traité du contrat,* §§236, 237; Argou, *Institution,* 1:218.

33. Fenet, *Travaux préparatoires,* 1:43, 117, 248; Argou, *Institution,* 1:218.

34. Pothier, *Traité du contrat,* §236; Merlin, "Cours d'eau."

35. These correspond to articles 641 to 645 of the promulgated Code civil.

36. See Merlin, "Cours d'eau." These cases were not concerned, however, with prescription after the recipient had built to facilitate the flow.

37. Fenet, *Travaux préparatoires,* 11:256–59. *Ouvrages extérieurs* can best be translated in this context as "visible works."

38. Fenet, *Travaux préparatoires,* 11:261.

39. This corresponds to the view expressed by Treilhard.

40. For a general explanation of servitudes and applicable rules under Roman law, see Buckland, *Textbook,* p. 267.

41. Articles 641–43 of the Code civil, which were articles 634–36 of the definitive draft, were replaced in 1898.

42. See Fenet, *Travaux préparatoires,* 1:xxxv–cxxxviii.

43. Sir George Mackenzie, *Works,* vol. 1 (Edinburgh, 1716), pp. 24–25 (of his Pleadings).

44. See Lord Stair, *The Institutions of the Law of Scotland,* 2d ed. (Edinburgh, 1693), 1.1.10, 16; cf. G. Mackenzie, *The Institutions of the Law of Scotland* (Edinburgh, 1684), 1.1.

45. In the first edition, of 1681, Stair appears to give more weight to a single decision than he does subsequently. Mackenzie observes that though the Lords of Session may depart from their own previous decision it is not their habit to do so: *Institutions,* 1.1.

46. Stair expressly lists feudal law as carrying weight, and here he is thinking of feudal law not previously accepted as part of Scots law. Stair also considers rules of Roman law once accepted into the law of Scotland as becoming part of Scots customary law.

47. The reference should be to book 43, not 53, of the *Digest.*

48. Sir James Balfour of Pittendreich, *Practicks,* vol. 2 (Edinburgh, 1963), p. 544.

49. James Craig, *Ius feudale,* 2.8.15 (2.8.7 in the Leipzig edition of 1716). This work was first published in 1655, but had been written half a century before.

50. David Hume, *Lectures,* vol. 4, ed. G. C. H. Paton (Edinburgh, 1955), pp. 245–46.

51. Stair, *Institutions,* 1.6.36–43.

52. See, e.g., J. Erskine, *Institute of the Law of Scotland* (Edinburgh, 1773), 2.1.2.

53. Stair, *Institutions,* 2.7.8. (The equivalent, almost identical passage in the first edition is 1.71.8.)

54. Erskine, *Institute,* 1.2.1.

55. *D.*39.3: cf. Watson, *Property,* pp. 155–75.

56. See the reconstruction of the *formula* in Lenel, *Edictum,* p. 375.

57. Hume, *Lectures,* vol. 3, ed. G. C. H. Paton (Edinburgh, 1952), p. 209.

58. Ibid., 3:225.

59. G. J. Bell, *Principles of the Law of Scotland,* 10th ed., ed. W. Guthrie (Edinburgh, 1899), p. 399. But see earlier A. McDouall (Lord Bankton), *An Institute of the Laws of Scotland,* vol. 1 (Edinburgh, 1751), p. 682.

60. Erskine, *Institute,* 2.1.2.

61. The further argument of the pursuers that there were particular restrictions by statute on an owner's use, and Mackenzie's reply need not detain us.

From *D.*39.3.3.pr. one might argue that in the Roman Republic at least, some jurists would give the *actio aquae pluviae arcendae* when water was polluted. But the law is not clear.

62. J. Rankine, *The Law of Land-Ownership in Scotland,* 4th ed. (Edinburgh, 1909), p. 564.

63. Bell, *Principles,* p. 434; cf. T. B. Smith, *Scotland: The Development of Its Law and Constitution* (London, 1962), p. 528.

64. Watson, *Making of the Civil Law,* pp. 83–98.

65. Case law that formed a custom shows the step-by-step way in which Roman law directly entered a mature system of law that was theoretically largely based on custom. But Roman law could also indirectly enter a system of law by being incorporated into a juristic book, from which it might gradually penetrate that system. Or it could be incorporated in statute.

66. The work is known by various titles such as *Loci argumentorum legales* and *Topicarum seu de locis legalibus liber.* It was first published in 1516.

67. In his comment on Justinian's *Code* 1.4 *de summa trinitati, gloss Quod si Bononiensis,* §19.

68. *Praelectiones juris romani et hodierni* 2.1.3 (1689 is the first publication date of the relevant volume 2).

69. See Watson, *Comity,* pp. 2–17.

70. D.43.12.1.pr. Part of the translation is omitted from Mommsen, *Digest,* 4; see *The Digest of Justinian,* vol. 2, 2d ed. Alan Watson (Philadelphia, 1998), on this text.

71. For other systems that will not be discussed here but where Roman law was relevant see, e.g., Hans Baade, "The Historical Background of Texas Water Law—a Tribute to Jack Pope," *St. Mary's Law Journal* 18 (1986): 2–98, 65–67.; "Springs, Creeks, and Groundwater in Nineteenth-Century German Roman-Law Jurisprudence with a Twentieth-Century Postscript," in *Comparative and Private International Law: Essays in Honor of John Henry Merryman,* ed. David S. Clark (Berlin, 1990), pp. 61–89.

72. Voet, *Commentarius in Pandectas* 1.8.8; Huber, *Heedendaegshe Rechtsgeleertheyt* 2.1.19.

73. *Libri feudorum* 2.56.

74. Erskine, *Institute,* 2.6.17.

75. Cf. Alan Watson, *Roman Law and Comparative Law* (Athens, Ga., 1991), p. 247. The importance of salmon fishing as a private right in a public river was recognized before there was much reception of Roman law in Scotland.

76. 1976 S.L.T. Reports (H.L.), p. 162.

77. For an instructive discussion of the distinctions "private" and "public," and "navigable and tidal" and "navigable and nontidal," see James Ferguson, *The Law of Water and Water Rights in Scotland* (Edinburgh, 1907), pp. 99–101, 126–28.

78. Hume, *Lectures,* vol. 4, ed. G. C. H. Paton (Edinburgh, 1955), p. 243.

79. *Transvaal Canoe Union v. Butgeriet,* 1986 4 SA (TPD) 207. For simplicity I am reducing the parties to one on each side.

80. It is not significant for us that by the Water Act 54 of 1956 the water in the river was public.

81. *Van Niekerk and Union Government (Minister of Lands) v. Carter,* 1917 A.D. 359.

82. *Transvaal Canoe Union v. Butgeriet,* p. 210.

83. But it should be emphasized that modern economic circumstances were stressed in Wills' Trustees, also in Lord Dilhorne's dissent.

84. See for a recent and judicious account Alan Rodger, "The Use of Civil Law in Scottish Courts," in *The Civilian Tradition and Scots Law,* ed. David Carey-Miller and Rheinhard Zimmermann (Berlin, 1997), pp. 225–37.

85. See Rudolf B. Schlesinger et al., *Comparative Law,* 6th ed. (New York, 1998), pp. 257–58.

86. See above all Rudolf B. Schlesinger (gen. ed.), *Formation of Contracts: A Study of the Common Core of Legal Systems,* vol. 1, pt. 2 (New York, 1968).

87. See now Gert Steenhoff, "The Place of Legal History in the Teaching of Law and in Comparative Formation," in *Rapports néerlandais pour le quinzième Congrès International de Droit comparé* (Antwerp, 1998), pp. 1–12.

88. Morton Horwitz, *Transformation of American Law, 1780-1860* (Cambridge, Mass., 1977), pp. 31–62.

89. For criticism of Horwitz's treatment of the history of contract law, see John Barton, "Contract and Quantum Meruit: The Antecedents of Cutter v. Powell," *Journal of Legal History* 8 (1987): 46; A. W. B. Simpson, "The Horwitz Thesis and the History of Contracts," *University of Chicago Law Review* 46 (1979): 533.

90. Horwitz, *Transformation,* p. 31.

91. Blackstone, *Commentaries* 2.1.

92. See, e.g., H. Grotius, *Inleidinge tot de Hollandsche Rechtsgeleerdheid* 2.3.2 (written between 1619 and 1621).

93. *Commentaries* 2:80–102. See also J. Baker, *Introduction to English Legal History,* 2d ed. (London, 1979), p. 194; Milsom, *Historical Foundations,* p. 99; T. Plucknett, *Concise History of the Common Law,* 5th ed. (1956), pp. 505–8; Pollock and Maitland, *History,* 1:129.

94. Blackstone, *Commentaries,* 3:217–18.

95. Ibid., 2:402–3.

96. Ibid., 3:217.

97. Bracton, *De Legibus et Consuetudinibus Anglie,* folio 221a (written in the thirteenth century). Bracton's work has been edited and translated into English by G. E. Woodbine and S. E. Thorne, *Bracton, On the Laws and Customs of England* (Cambridge, Mass., 1968). The cited passage may be found in the English version at Woodbine and Thorne, *Bracton,* 3:164.

98. Bracton, *De Legibus,* folio 231B; Woodbine and Thorne, *Bracton,* 3:189. See also Bracton, folios 232B, 234B; Woodbine and Thorne, *Bracton,* 3:191, 196.

99. "The assize of novel disseisin . . . provided a rapid means in the king's court whereby a person dispossessed of his free tenement might, by use of the royal writ and a jury of twelve, be restored quickly to his premises by establishing (1) that he had been seized of the premises, and (2) that he had been dispossessed of them." T. E. Lauer, "The Common Law Background of the Riparian Doctrine," *Missouri Law Review* 28 (1963): 67 (footnote omitted).

100. Bracton, *De Legibus,* folio 220B; Woodbine and Thorne, *Bracton,* 3:162.

101. Compare cases where the flow was diverted, diminished unreasonably or cut off, e.g., *Buddington v. Bradley,* 10 Conn. 213 (1834); *Westin v. Alden,* 8 Mass. 136 (1811); *Runnels v. Bullen,* 2 N.H. 532 (1823); *Sackrider v. Beers,* 10 Johns. 241 (N.Y. 1813); *Beissell v. Scholl,* 4 Dall. 211 (Pa. 1800), with those where the water backed up because of a lower dam (i.e., too much water), e.g., *Sherwood v. Burr,* 4 Day 244 (Conn. 1810); *Hatch v. Dwight,* 17 Mass. 289 (1821), and those where the flow was irregular (i.e., higher and lower at different times of the day), e.g., *Colburn v. Richards,* 13 Mass. 420 (1816); *Merritt v. Brinkerhoff,* 17 Johns. 306 (N.Y. 1820). See also *Hodges v. Raymond,* 9 Mass. 316 (1812): "Now there can be no difference whether the damage to the owner of a mill arise from the water below being stopped so as to flow back, and thereby prevent the mill from grinding. The mischief is the same, and the same remedy ought to be furnished" (319).

102. Between the times of Bracton and Blackstone, however, prescription was at times a requirement.

103. Horwitz, *Tranformation* p. 36.

104. Ibid., p. 32. The quoted maxim *sic utere tuo, ut alienum non laedas* means "use your own property in such a manner as not to injure that of another." *Black's Law Dictionary,* 6th ed. (St. Paul, 1979), p. 1238.

105. L.R. 3 E. & I. App. (H.L. 1868).

106. J. Angell, *Treatise on the Law of Watercourses* (1826–30). In the later editions, the discussion of natural use appears at §§21, 128.

107. J. Kent, *Commentaries on American Law* (1826–30). Natural use is first referred to in the 6th edition, vol. 4 (New York, 1848), p. 440.

108. 4 Ill. (3 Scam.) 492 (1842).

109. 20 Mass. (3 Pick.) 269 (1826).

110. 10 Conn. 213 (1834).

111. *Buddington v. Bradley,* p. 219 (emphasis in original); see also *Anthony v. Lapham,* 22 Mass. (5 Pick.) 175, 176–77 (1827) (holding that any landowner through whose land water passes has the natural right to use that water for watering cattle or irrigating land, but must do so in manner to do the least possible injury to a neighboring landowner who has the same right); Hoy v. Sterrett, 2 Watts 327, 329 (Pa. 1834) (holding that every riparian owner is entitled to the flow of water through his land, and that a prior occupant of the stream for purposes of a mill cannot preclude others from building mills along

same stream, even though the earlier occupant may be injured to some degree thereby).

112. *Merritt v. Parker,* 1 N.J.L. 526 (1795).

113. E.g., *Webb v. Portland Mfg.,* 29 F. Cas. 506, 510 (C.C.D. Me. 1838) (No. 17,322); Buddington, 10 Conn. at 219; *Elliot v. Fitchburg R.R.,* 64 Mass (10 Cush.) 191, 193 (1852); *Anthony v. Lapham,* 22 Mass. (5 Pick.) 175, 177 (1827); *Runnels v. Bullen,* 2 N.H. 532, 537 (1823); *Sackrider v. Beers,* 10 Johns. 241, 241 (N.Y. 1813); *Livezey v. Gorgas* (Pa. 1811), in H. Brackenbridge, *Law Miscellanies* (Philadelphia, 1814), p. 454.

114. E.g., *Buddington v. Bradley,* 10 Conn. at 218; *Twiss v. Baldwin,* 9 Conn. 291, 302 (1832); *Cook v. Hull,* 20 Mass. (3 Pick.) 269, 271 (1826); *Hatch v. Dwight,* 17 Mass. 289, 296 (1821); *Sackrider v. Beers,* 10 Johns. at 241.

115. In fact, the side note in the report misstates the case.

116. *Merritt v. Parker,* p. 530.

117. Ibid., pp. 532–33.

118. Horwitz, *Transformation,* p. 36.

119. See also *Elliot v. Fitchburg R.R.,* 64 Mass. (10 Cush.) 191, 194 (1852), where the court stated: "To take a quantity of water from a large running stream for agriculture or manufacturing purposes, would cause no sensible or practicable diminution of the benefit, to the prejudice of a lower proprietor; whereas, taking the same quantity from a small running brook passing through many farms, would be of great and manifest injury to those below, who need it for domestic supply, or watering cattle; and therefore it would be an unreasonable use of the water, and an action would lie in the latter case and not in the former."

120. See the interesting remark "Principles [of water law] so equitable and just, it would seem, could not be very difficult of application, and yet it is often found to be so" in "The Law of Water Privileges," *American Jurist* 2 (1829): 25, 27 (reviewing Angell, *Watercourses*).

121. 1 Root 535 (Conn. 1793).

122. *Palmer v. Mulligan,* 3 Cai. R. 307 (N.Y. Sup. Ct. 1805), at 313.

123. *Elliot v. Fitchburg R.R.,* 64 Mass. (10 Cush.) 191 (1852): "The Right to flowing water is now well settled to be a right incident to property in land; . . . as one of the beneficial gifts of Providence, each proprietor has a right to a just and reasonable use of it, as it passes through his land; and so long as it is not wholly obstructed or diverted, or no larger appropriation of the water running through it is made than a just and reasonable use, it cannot be said to be wrongful or injurious to a proprietor lower down" (p. 193); cf. *Anthony v. Lapham,* 22 Mass. (5 Pick.) 175, 176 (1827) (affirming judgment for a lower-lying proprietor plaintiff because, "Here the water was stopped by a dam . . . and the surplus was not returned into the natural channel; so that the plaintiff was deprived of the privilege which belonged to him"); *Snow v. Parsons,* 28 Vt. 459, 462 (1856) (stating "There is no doubt one must be allowed to use

a stream in such a manner as to make it useful to himself, even if it does produce slight inconvenience to those below"). But this doctrine was certainly not new, contrary to Horwitz's claims. Cf. *Weston v. Alden*, 8 Mass. 136, 137 (1811) (stating that reasonable use of water is not actionable even if the result exceeds slight damage). See generally *Livezey v. Gorgas* (Pa. 1811), in Brackenridge, *Miscellanies*, pp. 438, 454ff. (allowing plaintiff to recover damages resulting from defendant's unreasonable use, while equivocating between an opinion that there may be trespass even if there is not damage, and an opinion that the law does not regard damages *de minimis*).

124. *Palmer v. Mulligan*, at 312–13.

125. See, e.g., *Buddington v. Bradley*, 10 Conn. 213, 220 (1834) (holding that degree of obstruction required to constitute actionable injury in absence of malice must always be question of fact for jury); *Elliot v. Fitchburg R.R.*, 64 Mass. (10 Cush.) 191, 194–95 (1852) (rejecting plaintiff's argument that if diversion of water by defendant were proved, plaintiff would be entitled to nominal damages even if no actual damage shown); *Runnels v. Bullen*, 2 N.H. 532, 534 (1823) (allowing action where defendant infringed on rights of plaintiff to use dam water for his mills but would disallow action if plaintiff's property were only incidentally damaged).

126. Woodbine and Thorne, *Bracton*, 3:191 (footnote omitted).

127. *Palmer v. Mulligan*, p. 313; Woodbine and Thorne, *Bracton*, 3:164.

128. *Palmer v. Mulligan*, p. 316. The English case referred to is *Bealey v. Shaw*, 102 Eng. Rep. 1266, 6 East's Rep. 208 (1805).

129. *Platt v. Johnson*, 15 Johns. 213 (N.Y. Sup. Ct. 1818), pp. 217–18.

130. See, e.g., *Martin v. Bigelow*, 2 Aik. 184, 187 (Vt. 1827) (holding that "the mere prior occupancy of the water by the defendant does not give him a right to prevent the plaintiff from using the same water in a prudent way, as it flows down its channel").

131. 76 Eng. Rep. 1065, 4 Coke 86a (K.B. 1600). For a general discussion of this, and much else of importance in the development of riparian law, see Lauer, "Riparian Doctrine," pp. 83–84.

132. 57 Eng. Rep. 76, 1 Simons & Stuart 190 (1823). The case is referred to in this context by Chancellor Kent, *Commentaries*, 3:353.

133. Woodbine and Thorne, *Bracton* 3:189–90 (footnotes omitted).

134. Horwitz, *Transformation*, pp. 37–38 (footnote omitted).

135. See, e.g., *Elliot v. Fitchburg R.R.*, 64 Mass. (10 Cush.) 191, 194 (1852) (stating rule that "each proprietor has a right to a reasonable use of it, for his own benefit, for domestic use, and for manufacturing and agricultural purposes").

136. Horwitz, *Transformation*, p. 40.

137. *Cary v. Daniels*, 49 Mass. (8 Met.) 466 (1844), pp. 476ff.

138. Horwitz, *Transformation* p. 41 (footnotes omitted). I have chosen to pass over the rather earlier case of *Tyler v. Wilkinson*, 24 F. Cas. 472

(C.C.D.R.I. 1827) (No. 14,312). Horwitz regards Story's opinion as "filled with ambiguities." Horwitz, *Transformation,* p. 39. I deal with that case and with Chancellor Kent's treatment of this subject in his *Commentaries* and decisions in "Chancellor Kent's Use of Foreign Law," in *The Reception of Continental Ideas in the Common Law World, 1820-1920,* ed. Mathias Reimann (Berlin, 1993), pp. 45–62. But Horwitz, *Transformation,* p. 43, says that Kent "managed not only to defend the natural flow doctrine but to approve a rule of priority as well, [and] was also sympathetic to some form of reasonable use test." Indeed he was, and quite rightly. It should also be observed that the cases cited by Chancellor Kent along with Tyler v. Wilkinson reveal that there was nothing new in that case: Kent, *Commentaries,* 4:353.

139. See, e.g., *Twiss v. Baldwin,* 9 Conn. 291, 305 (1832) (stating that "[a] right to use merely, cannot confer a right unreasonably and unnecessarily to prejudice the rights of others"); *Runnels v. Bullen,* 2 N.H. 532, 537–38 (1823) (holding that "each may use his portion of the water, in any reasonable way he pleases, but neither can wantonly waste the water, to the prejudice of the other"). These statements are the equivalent of *sic utere tuo ut alienum non laedas* found in earlier cases.

140. Moreover, what really seemed to be on the judges' minds was equity, not efficiency and defense of monopoly as Horwitz claims. Thus, Judge Woodward delivering the opinion of the court in *Merritt v. Brinkerhoff,* 17 Johns. 306 (N.Y. Sup. Ct. 1820), stated:

> The common use of the water of a stream, by persons having mills above, is frequently, if not generally, attended with damage and loss to the mills below; but that is incident to that common use, and for the most part unavoidable. . . . The person owning an upper mill on the same stream has a lawful right to use the water, and may apply it in order to work his mills to the best advantage, subject, however, to this limitation; that if, in the exercise of this right, and in consequence of it, the mills lower down on the stream are rendered useless and unproductive, the law, in that case, will interpose, and limit this common right, so that the owners of the lower mills shall enjoy a fair participation; and if, thereby, the owners of the upper mill sustain a partial loss of business and profits, they cannot justly complain, for this rule requires of them no more than to conform to the principle upon which their right is founded. It cannot then be admitted that the defendants may use the water as they please, because they have a right to a common use, although their works may require all the water, in order to derive the greatest profit. The plaintiffs' rights must be regarded; they must participate in the benefits of the stream, to a reasonable extent, although the defendants' profits may be thereby be lessened. (Ibid., p. 321)

For an espousal of reasonable use for present-day law, see Lauer, *Riparian Doctrine,* 1.

141. Horwitz, *Transformation,* pp. 40–42.

142. *Evans v. Merriweather,* 4 Ill. (3 Scam.) 492 (1842), pp. 495–96.

143. This is by no means the only way in which the distinction was expressed. Bouvier, for example, said "It will be well to observe a distinction which exists in easements of which running water is the subject. The right to receive a flow of water and to transmit it in its accustomed course, may be called a *natural* easement: the right to interfere with the accustomed course, either by damming it and forceing it upon the land above, or transmitting it altered in quality or quantity, to the inferior inheritance, may be called an *artificial* easement." J. Bouvier, *Institutes of American Law,* vol. 2 (Philadelphia, 1851), p. 174.

144. *Ingraham v. Hutchinson,* 2 Conn. 584 (1818), pp. 594–95 (Gould, J., dissenting).

145. Originally enacted in 1713, the Massachusetts Mill Acts, as amended, are today codified at Mass. Gen. Laws Ann. chap. 253, 1–62 (West 1988).

146. J. M. Gould, *A Treatise on the Law of Waters Including Riparian Rights, and Public and Private Rights in Waters Tidal and Inland,* 2d ed. (Chicago, 1891), §592. For a good account of the Mill Acts generally, see §§579–623.

147. Horwitz, *Transformation,* pp. 31–62.

148. Bouvier, *Institutes* 2:173–76. Bouvier was born in France in 1787 and only came to the United States when he was fifteen.

149. Quite deliberately I have avoided discussing modern water law in the western states of the United States, and international issues in the Middle East. But there is fruitful material for study.

150. See in general Alan Watson, Review, *Yale Law Journal* 91 (1982): 1036–47, reviewing Mark Tushnet, *The American Law of Slavery, 1810–1860* (Princeton, 1981) (contending that "it is difficult to write with insight and accuracy about law and society unless one takes a long-term view, often extending over centuries, and unless one also bears in mind analogous situations and conditions in other societies").

CHAPTER 7. LEGAL TRANSPLANTS I: THE CAUSE OF THE RECEPTION OF ROMAN LAW

1. P. Vinogradoff, *Roman Law in Medieval Europe,* 3d ed. with preface by F. De Zulueta (Oxford, 1961), p. 11.

2. It is possible for a society to adopt a law of slavery—by borrowing, for instance—before it has slaves. But the societal wanting of slaves still comes before the desire for the law.

3. This is the definition of law that I proposed in *The Nature of Law* (Edinburgh, 1977). It is appropriate to restate it here, but the present argument would not be affected by its excision.

4. In the last few paragraphs I have been stressing the courts and the judges

for the emergence of a standard, since I am adopting the traditional hypothesis that law at first emerges from individual decisions rather than from general commands of the political sovereign. But if the standard were thought to be established by a general command and applied through the courts, then an exactly parallel argument could be constructed.

5. At this stage I wish to use the term *lawyers* very loosely to include, for instance, legislators, not all of whom have legal training.

6. E.g., my *Sources of Law,* and "Legal Change," pp. 111–31.

7. See, for an outline, Zweigert and Kötz, *Introduction,* pp. 100–120.

8. Watson, *Society and Legal Change,* pp. 107–11.

9. Watson, *Sources of Law,* pp. 25–50, 70–75.

10. Lord Stair, *Institutions of the Law of Scotland* (Edinburgh, 1681), 1.1.15. "Feudal Laws" here refers to the *Libri Feudorum* and the commentaries on them.

11. See, e.g., G. Vismara, *Edictum Theoderici,* in *Ius Romanum Medii Aevi,* pt. I, 2 b *aa* α (Milan, 1967); H. J. Becker, s.v. *Edictum Theoderici,* in *Handwörterbuch zur Deutsche Rechtsgeschichte,* vol. 1 (Berlin, 1971), pp. 802ff.; H. Schlosser, *Grundzüge der neueren Privatrechtsgeschichte,* 4th ed. (Heidelberg, 1982), p. 6.

12. A. D'Ors, *Estudios visigóticos* II: *El código de Eurico* (Rome and Madrid, 1960), p. 8; E. Levy, *ZSS* 79 (1962): 479ff.

13. "Leges Theudosianas calcans Theudoricianasque proponens." *Epist.* 2.1.3.

14. Other contenders for the honor of authorship of the *Edictum Theoderici* have been Odovaker (476–93) and the Burgundian Gundobad (472–516).

15. Vismara, *Edictum,* p. 29. The problem, of course, is one of jurisdiction: to this we will return.

16. Provision 32 speaks only of barbarians, but its purpose seems to be to give those who are soldiers of the state the same rights of testation that Romans had. I do not understand Vismara's comment (*Edictum,* p. 61) that a few provisions—especially 34, 43, and 44—are specifically for Romans or barbarians. These apply expressly to both peoples.

17. An edition such as that of Baviera lists for the provisions the corresponding Roman law texts: J. Baviera, *Fontes Iuris Romani Antejustiniani,* vol. 2 (Florence, 1940), pp. 684ff.; and see Vismara, *Edictum,* pp. 127ff.

18. See, e.g., E. Levy, "The First 'Reception' of Roman Law in Germanic States," *American Historical Review* 48 (1942): 22.

19. Stair, *The Institutions of the Law of Scotland,* 1.1.15.

20. In practice these edicts changed the law enormously.

21. C. Calisse, *General Survey of Events, etc.,* in *Continental Legal History,* by various authors (Boston, 1912), p. 51; H. Conrad, *Deutsche Rechtsgeschichte,* 2d ed., vol. 1 (Karlsruhe, 1962), p. 59; D'Ors, *Estudios II,* p. 4; Tomás y Va-

liente, *Manual,* p. 102. Schlosser puts the *Codex* just before the fall: *Grundzüge,* p. 6.

22. *Cod. Paris. lat.* 12161; for this see H. Brunner, *Deutsche Rechtsgeschichte,* 2d ed., vol. 1 (Leipzig, 1906), pp. 482–83. It is published in *Monumenta Germaniae Historica, Leges,* 1 (Hanover, 1902), pp. 3ff.

23. D'Ors, *Estudios II.*

24. Calisse, *General Survey;* K. F. Drew, *The Burgundian Code* (Philadelphia, 1949), p. 6.

25. See, e.g., Tomás y Valiente, *Manual,* p. 103; R. McKitterick, "Some Carolingian Law-Books and Their Function," in *Authority and Power: Studies on Medieval Law and Government,* ed. B. Tierney and P. Linehan (Cambridge, 1980), pp. 13ff.; and, above all, J. Gaudemet, *Le Breviaire d'Alaric et les Epitome,* in *Ius Romanum Medii Aevi,* pt. 1, 2b *aa ß* (Milan, 1965). Editions of these epitomes are to be found in G. Hänel, *Lex romana visigothorum* (reprint; Aalen, 1962).

26. A. García Gallo, "Nacionalidad y territorialidad del derecho en la epoca visigoda," *Anuario de Historia del Derecho Español* 13 (1941): 168ff.

27. See the bibliography in Tomás y Valiente, *Manual,* p. 110. García Gallo has modified his opinion.

28. E.g., ibid., p. 107.

29. García Gallo, "Nacionalidad," p. 194; D'Ors, *Estudios II,* pp. 6ff.

30. See also P. D. King, "King Chindaswind and the First Territorial Law-Code of the Visigothic Kingdom," in *Visigothic Spain,* ed. E. James (Oxford, 1980), pp. 131ff.

31. See P. Merêa, *Estudos de direito visigótico* (Coimbra, 1948), pp. 199ff.; quoted by Tomás y Valiente, *Manual,* p. 107.

32. F. C. Von Savigny, *Geschichte des Römischen Rechts im Mittelalter,* vol. 2, 2d ed. (Heidelberg, 1834), pp. 73ff.

33. Ibid., 2:77ff. Not all editions of the Visigothic Code have the same numbering of the texts. For the convenience of the nonspecialist reader I have in the citations that follow adopted the numbering of S. P. Scott, *Visigothic Code* (Boston, 1910).

34. On degrees of relationship: *L. Visigoth.* 4.1, taken from *Pauli Sententiae* 4.11. On legitimate defense: *L. Visigoth.* 8.1.2., taken from the *interpretatio* to *C. Th.* 4.22.3. On interest: *L. Visigoth.* 5.5.8–9, taken from the *interpretatio* to *C. Th.* 2.33.1–2.

35. A. Esmein, *Cours élémentaire d'histoire du droit français,* 14th ed., ed. Genestal (Paris, 1921), p. 35.

36. In the heading the name Gundobad is usual, but one manuscript has Sigismond.

37. It is sometimes said that there are references in the code to earlier Burgundian legislation, for instance in title 18.1: see, e.g., Drew, *Burgundian Code,*

pp. 8–9. But the wording in the text could as easily refer to a law (relating to horses) which has not come down to us but may be the law referred to in title 49.4 and be the work of Gundobad.

38. "Qui formam et expositionem legum conscriptam, qualiter iudicent, se noverint accepturos, ut per ignorantiam se nullus excuset." Sec. 8. But some provisions of the *Lex Gundobada* are made to apply to Romans also: e.g., 4.1; 4.3; 4.4; 6.3; 6.9.

39. *L. Burg.* 77.1. For this paragraph to this point, see, above all, Savigny, *Geschichte,* 2:5ff.

40. The *Interpretatio* to *C. Th.* 3.8.2, 3 in title 24.1; to *C. Th.* 3.16.1 in 34.3.

41. O. Stobbe, *Geschichte der deutschen Rechtsquellen* (reprint, Aalen, 1965), 1:110.

42. Thus, *L. Burg.* 4.6. = *L. Visigoth.* 8.4.1; *L. Burg.* 4.7 = *Roth.* 340, *Lex Sal.* 23; *L. Burg.* 4.8 = *L. Visigoth.* 8.4.9; *L. Burg.* 6.1, 3 and 20.2 = *L. Visigoth.* 9.1.14; *L. Burg.* 6.4.9 = *L. Visigoth.* 9.1.5; *L. Burg.* 23.4 = *L. Visigoth.* 8.5.1, *Roth.* 349; *L. Burg.* 25.1, 27.7, and 103.1 = *Lex Baiuw.* 9.12 (cf. *L. Visigoth.* 8.3.2. and *Lex Sal.* 27.6); *L. Burg.* 27.1–2 = *L. Visigoth.* 8.3.10, *Lex Sal.* 9, *Roth.* 344; *L. Burg.* 39.1–2 = *L. Visigoth.* 9.1.3 and 9.1.6; *L. Burg.* 68 = *L. Visigoth.* 3.4.4., *Lex Baiuw.* 8.1, *Roth.* 212; *L. Burg.* 72 = *L. Visigoth.* 8.4.23; *L. Burg.* 73.1–2 = *L. Visigoth.* 8.4.15; *L. Burg.* 73.3 = *L. Visigoth.* 8.4.3, *Lex Sal.* 38.8, *Roth.* 338, 341.

Code. Paris lat. 12161 has been identified with part of the *Codex Euricianus,* and of it we should pair cap. 320 with *L. Burg.* 14; cap. 277 with *L. Burg.* 17.1 and 79.5; cap. 305 with *L. Burg.* 1.3. For this and for the whole account of the *Lex Burgundionum,* see, above all, Brunner, *Rechtsgeschichte,* 1:497ff.

43. See, e.g., H. Maine, *Ancient Law,* Everyman Edition (London), chap. 8, pp. 174–75; E. Levy, "Reflections on the First 'Reception' of Roman Law in Germanic States," in *Gesammelte Schriften,* vol. 1 (Cologne, 1963), pp. 201–9.

44. See the very just remarks of E. Levy, "The Reception of Highly Developed Legal Systems by Peoples of Different Cultures," in *Gesammelte Schriften,* 1:210ff., esp. pp. 217ff. Furlani's edition of the *Lex Romana Burgundionum,* in Baviera, *Fontes Iuris Romani Antejustiniani,* 2:714ff., gives cross-references to the Roman sources.

45. See, e.g., Tomás y Valiente, *Manual,* pp. 108–10.

46. Ibid., p. 99: Tomás y Valiente relies heavily on Ramón d'Abadal i de Vinyals, "Del reino do Tolosa al reino de Toledo," *Discusso de ingreso en la R.A.H.* (Madrid, 1960).

47. E. N. van Kleffens, *Hispanic Law until the End of the Middle Ages* (Edinburgh, 1968), p. 80.

48. For what follows, see, above all, Tomás y Valiente, *Manual,* pp. 126ff.

49. For a full, if dated, account of the early history of the Bologna Law School, see Hastings Rashdall, *The Universities of Europe in the Middle Ages,* 2d ed., ed. F. M. Powicke and A. B. Emden (London, 1936), pp. 87–93. See

also S. Kuttner, "The Revival of Jurisprudence," in *Renaissance and Renewal in the Twelfth Century*, ed. R. L. Benson and G. Constable (Cambridge, Mass., 1982), pp. 299–305.

50. Watson, *Transplants.*

51. Ibid., pp. 57–60, 88–94.

52. Watson, *Sources of Law*, pp. 28–31.

53. Zweigert and Kötz, *Introduction*, pp. 100–122.

54. Watson, *Transplants*, pp. 93–94. The phenomenon need not be confined to the spread of law. David Daube suggests that Judaism (especially, I think he means, in its proselytizing form of Christianity) owes much of its attraction from the beginning of the current era to its possession of written books. "It is consistent with this explanation," he says, "that Jewish-Christian preaching has had scant success in the East—India, China—with comprehensive Scriptures of its own." And he adds in parentheses, "In my opinion, the predominance of Roman law from the Middle Ages on owes more to its availability in a written corpus than to quality." *Ancient Jewish Law* (Leiden, 1981), p. 11. And see, for the transmission of parables in the early Christian tradition, J. Jeremias, *The Parables of Jesus*, rev. ed. (London, 1963), pp. 33–37.

55. Tomás y Valiente, *Manual*, pp. 180–94. My friend Michael Hoeflich tells me that he believes Justinian's *Code* was known, but not widely.

56. Although the prestige might be in part the general or political prestige or power of the state that created the law, such as ancient Rome or Napoleon's France.

57. Calisse, *General Survey*, pp. 39–40, esp. p. 40, n. 1.

58. "In illis autem regionibus, in quibus secundum legem Romanam iudicentur iudicia, iuxta ipsam legem committentes talia iudicentur; quia super illam legem vel contra ipsam legam nec antecessores nostri quodcumque capitulum statuerunt nec nos aliquid constituimus." *Edictum pistense*, cap. 20, in *Monumenta Germaniae Historica, legum sectio*, 2.2:319.

CHAPTER 8. LEGAL TRANSPLANTS 2: OTHER RECEPTIONS

1. *Libri Feudorum* 1.9, 13*pr.*, 19.1; 2.1*pr.* (which states generally that cases involving feudal law are resolved some by Roman law, some by statutes of the Lombards, some by custom), 3.1, 9*pr.*; 9.4, 16, 22*pr.*; 24.12, 27; 33.3, 34*pr.*, 38 (custom sanctioned by statute), 39.2, 40, 44*pr.*, 52, 53, 55, 57; 58.1, 58.2, 58.3, 58.4, 58.5. Where a direct confrontation of texts is not possible there can be no sure way of measuring preceding legislation. Sometimes the preceding legislation will not be expressly mentioned. Sometimes authority will be given to a text by a reference to nonexistent legislation. To take an example from a different work: paragraph 2 of the prologue of the Assizes of Romania, the law code of Frankish Morea of the early fourteenth century (but probably resting in part on a shorter compilation of the thirteenth century), claims to

be based on the usages and customs of Jerusalem (i.e., Constantinople). It seems in fact not to derive from the Assizes de Jerusalem as it now exists, and the issue is whether the law code from Morea was based on a now lost earlier version. P. W. Topping gives a negative answer in "The Formation of the Assizes of Romania," *Byzantion* 17 (1944–45): 304. J. L. La Monte prefers the positive in "Three Questions Concerning the Assizes de Jerusalem," *Byzantina-Metabyzantina* 1 (1946): 210–11.

2. G. L. Boehme, *Principia Iuris Feudalis*, 5th ed. (Göttingen, 1796), 1.1.10.

3. W. H. D. Sellar, "The Resilience of the Scottish Common Law," in *The Civilian Tradition and Scots Law,* ed. David Carey-Miller and Rheinhard Zimmermann (Berlin, 1997), p. 154.

4. *Jus Feudale* 1.8.10 (in the Leipzig edition). "Imo si exacte rem omnem aestimare velimus, hoc jus proprium huius Regni dici potest. (Si latius iuris proprii nomen extendamus) cum ex ejus scaturigine et fontibus omne jus, quo hodie utimur in foro, omnisque usus et praxis defluxerit, et si quid dubii oriatur, origines semper repetendae sunt ut inde quod aequum est dignoscatur." The translation is my own.

5. See, e.g., for a few statements to that effect, Craig, *Jus Feudale,* 1.9.36; the Saxon S. Stryk, *Examen Iuris Feudalis,* 1.26; the Prussian Henricus Coccejus, *Juris Feudalis Hypomnemata,* 1.13.

6. Henricus Zoesius, *Praelectiones Feudales* (1641), 1.5, 6.

7. See, e.g., Robinson, *Introduction,* p. 61.

8. See, e.g., M. Bloch, *Feudal Society* (Chicago, 1961), pp. 48ff.

9. See, e.g., A. Esmein, *Précis élémentaire de l'histoire du droit français de 1789 à 1814* (Paris, 1911), pp. 57ff.

10. Hermann Conring, *De origine juris Germanici* (1643), chap. 32.

11. See, e.g., Stryk, *Examen,* 1.15.

12. See, e.g., Gudelinus, *De Iure Feudorum,* prol. 5.

13. Jason, *Super Usibus Feudalis,* 2 (*in fine*).

14. Stryk, *Examen,* 1.14, gives references to some who share his opinion.

15. Zoesius, *Praelectiones,* proem. 15; see also H. Coccejus, *Hypomnemata,* 1.12.

16. See, e.g., Watson, *Making of the Civil Law,* pp. 64–82.

17. See Watson, "Legal Change," p. 1128.

18. See Zweigert and Kötz, *Introduction,* pp. 100ff. See also J. Gaudemet, "Les transferts de droit," *L'année sociologique* 27 (1976), pp. 48ff.; R. Piret, "Le Code Napoléon en Belgique de 1804 à 1954," *Revue Internationale de Droit Comparé* 6 (1954): 753ff.

19. *Projet du code civil de la république romaine,* introd. F. Ranieri (Frankfurt am Main, 1976).

20. But N. J. Coulson argues that the 1906 code "rested squarely on Islamic sources, and was designed simply to achieve uniformity and certainty in the application of the law." *History of Islamic Law* (Edinburgh, 1964), p. 157.

21. There was once doubt whether the draftsmen had access to the Code

civil and it is now disputed whether the Code civil should be regarded as "Spanish" in substance or "French." See H. W. Baade, "Marriage Contracts in French and Spanish Louisiana: A Study in 'Notarial Jurisprudence,'" *Tulane Law Review* 53 (1978): 1–82.

22. See Zweigert and Kötz, *Introduction*, pp. 143, 163–72; Watson, *Making of the Civil Law*, pp. 104–11.

23. See the preface, secs. 15–23, of the *Project des Corpus juris Fredericiani*, or *Code Frédéric* (1749–51), quoted in part by Watson, *Sources of Law*, pp. 64–65.

24. Watson, *Making of the Civil Law*, pp. 99–130.

25. Zweigert and Kötz, *Introduction*, pp. 100–122.

26. Watson, *Making of the Civil Law*, esp. pp. 1–22.

27. We need not, I think, be more precise.

28. Zweigert and Kötz, *Introduction*, pp. 35–43; René David and Camilla Jauffret-Spinosi, *Les grands systemes de droit contemporains*, 10th ed. (Paris, 1992), p. 124.

29. E. L. Johnson, *Introduction to the Soviet Legal System* (London, 1969), p. 3: cf. W. E. Butler, *Soviet Law* (London, 1983), pp. 1ff., 25–26, 175–86.

30. R. David and C. Jauffret-Spinosi, *Les grands systèmes de droit contemporains*, 8th ed. (Paris, 1982), pp. 124ff.; Zweigert and Kötz, *Introduction*, pp. 296–307.

31. R. David and J. E. C. Brierly, *Major Land Systems in the World Today*, 2d ed. (London, 1975), p. 183.

32. For this see K. Zweigert and H. Kötz, *Introduction to Comparative Law*, trans. Tony Weir, vol. 1 (Amsterdam, 1977), p. 309.

33. One example, already cited, may stand for many: Atatürk's acceptance of Swiss law as the law of Turkey in 1926. For a long time there was great doubt as to whether the imposition, especially of civil marriage and especially in rural Turkey, had taken. See above all the papers in *Annales de la Faculté de Droit d'Istanbul*, 6 (1956): F. Ayiter, "The Interpretation of a National System of Law Received from Abroad," p. 43; H. Z. Ülken, "Le droit coutumier et le code civil," pp. 88–91; H. V. Velidedeoğlu, "De certains problèmes provenant de la réception du code civil suisse en Turquie," pp. 111ff. See also O. Kahn-Freund, "Uses and Misuses of Comparative Law," *Modern Law Review* 37 (1974): 16–17. By 1973, marriages registered legally amounted to 78 percent in communities under 2,000 souls, and well above 90 percent in larger communities; see W. F. Weiker, *The Modernization of Turkey from Atatürk to the Present Day* (New York, 1981), p. 56. For the very powerful impact of Western law now on rural Turkey, but also the survival of traditional law, see J. Starr, *Dispute and Settlement in Rural Turkey* (Leiden, 1978), esp. pp. 275ff.

The case of the imposition of a state's law on a conquered territory need not be separately discussed: it is a composite of the other situations, especially of two, three, and four.

34. In this context it is entirely unsurprising that so often the initiative comes from someone outside of the legal tradition; see Watson, "Legal Change," p. 1156.

35. See Alan Watson, *Ancient Law and Modern Understanding: At the Edges* (Athens, Ga., 1999), pp. 84–90.

36. See already Watson, *Transplants,* pp. 93–94.

37. See already Alan Watson, "The Importance of Nutshells," *American Journal of Comparative Law* 42 (1994): 1–23.

38. *Halkerston v. Wedderburn* (1781) M. 10495.

39. See, e.g., D.1.2.2.6; Cicero, *De oratore,* 1.44.195.

40. On the paucity of Scottish authority, see J. Rankine, *The Law of Land-Ownership in Scotland,* 4th ed. (Edinburgh, 1909), pp. 631ff.

41. For a South African case in which changed circumstances—this time of law—were taken into account, see *Simons and Others v. Board of Executors* 1915 C.P.D. 479.

CHAPTER 9. THE CASE OF ENGLISH COMMON LAW

1. "Preliminary" because I do not feel I have sufficient expertise.

2. See, e.g., Hastings Rashdall, *The Universities of Europe in the Middle Ages,* 2d ed., ed. F. M. Powicke and A. B. Emden (Oxford, 1936), p. 105. F. Calasso, *Medio Evo del Diritto,* vol. 1 (Milan, 1954), pp. 161ff., 215ff., 235ff., 267ff., 305ff.

3. See, above all, E. Chénon, *Histoire générale du droit français public et privé des origines à 1815,* vol. 1 (Paris, 1926), p. 488.

4. See, e.g., H. Conrad, *Deutsche Rechtsgeschichte,* vol. 2, 2d ed. (Karlsruhe, 1962), pp. 233–34.

5. MGH Const I, n. 227. 322 c.3; Conrad, *Rechtsgeschichte,* 1, p. 234.

6. Conrad, *Rechtsgeschichte,* 2:339ff.

7. But see, above all, K. Luig, "Der Geltungsgrund des römischen Rechts in 18. Jahrhundert in Italien, Frankreich und Deutschland," in *La Formazione storica del Diritto moderno in Europa* 2 (1977), pp. 819ff.

8. For more detail and references, see, e.g., Watson, *Sources of Law,* pp. 47–50.

9. In fact, he inserted much Roman law into the customs he drew up, such as that of Berry; see R. Filhol, *Le Premier Président Christofle de Thou* (Paris, 1937), esp. p. 67.

10. For the doctrine debate, see, above all, V. Guizzi, "Il diritto comune in Francia nel xvii secolo," *T.v.R.* 37 (1969): 1ff.; Luig, "Geltungsgrund," pp. 832ff.

11. See, above all, E. Chénon, *Histoire générale,* vol. 2 (1929), pp. 331–32.

12. See ibid., pp. 317ff.; Watson, *Sources of Law,* pp. 57, nn. 70–71.

13. For this notion, see K. Luig, "The Institutes of National Law in the Seventeenth and Eighteenth Centuries," *Juridical Review* (1972): 193–226; John

Cairns, "Institutional Writings in Scotland Reconsidered," *Journal of Legal History* 4 (1983): 76–117. For France and the Code civil, see now, above all, C. Chêne, *L'Enseignement du droit français en pays de droit écrit (1679-1793)* (Geneva, 1982), esp. pp. 323ff.

14. See the end of this chapter.

15. Milsom, *Historical Foundations,* pp. 40–41.

16. Pollock and Maitland, *History* 1:99–100.

17. John Barton, *Roman Law in England* (Milan, 1971), p. 7.

18. Pollock and Maitland, *History,* 1:102; quoted by Barton, *Roman Law,* p. 8.

19. Barton, *Roman Law,* p. 9.

20. See G. D. G. Hall, ed., *The Treatise on the Laws and Customs of the Realm of England Commonly Called Glanvill* (London, 1965), p. xxxvi.

21. Barton, *Roman Law,* p. 11.

22. See, above all, Barton, *Roman Law,* pp. 13ff.

23. See Watson, *Sources of Law,* pp. 28–32.

24. G. T. Turner and T. F. T. Plucknett, eds., *Brevia Placitata,* Selden Society, vol. 66 (London, 1951); E. Shanks and S. F. C. Milsom, eds., *Novae Narrationes,* Selden Society, vol. 80 (London, 1963); J. M. Kaye, ed., *Placitata Coronae,* Selden Society, suppl. ser. 4 (London, 1966); F. W. Maitland, ed., *Court Baron,* Selden Society, vol. 4 (London, 1890).

25. See, e.g., W. Holdsworth, *History of English Law,* vol. 4, 3d ed. (London, 1945), pp. 283ff.; B. P. Levack, *The Civil Lawyers in England* (Oxford, 1973), pp. 122ff.; J. H. Baker, *Introduction to English Legal History,* 2d ed. (London, 1979), pp. 36–37. Significantly, Milsom does not mention any danger of a reception in that period: *Historical Foundations.*

26. F. W. Maitland, *Constitutional History of England* (Cambridge, 1920), pp. 10, 18ff.

27. Ibid., p. 21.

28. See, e.g., R. C. van Caenegem, *The Birth of the English Common Law* (Cambridge, 1973), p. 30.

29. Milsom, *Historical Foundations,* pp. 43–44. English law with its multiplicity of courts and competing jurisdictions appears very different from and much less comprehensible than Roman law: see Alan Watson, *Roman Law and Comparative Law* (Athens Ga., 1991), pp. 250–65. For the development of German procedure, see Wieacker, *Private Law,* pp. 138–41.

30. But elsewhere, too, an institutional writer might refer to precedent. A notable example from southern France is Claude Serres, *Les Institutions du droit françois suivant l'ordre de celles de Justinien* (Montpellier, 1753).

31. See, e.g., Baker, *Introduction,* p. 101.

32. Maitland, *History,* pp. 23–24.

33. See, e.g., Craig, *Jus Feudale,* 1.9.3.6.

34. Milsom, *Historical Foundations,* pp. 3–4.

35. See, e.g., C. Calisse, *General Survey of Events, etc.*, in *Continental Legal History*, by various European authors (Boston, 1912), p. 74.

36. William M. Gordon, "A Comparison of the Influence of Roman Law in England and Scotland," in *The Civilian Tradition and Scots Law*, ed. David Carey-Miller and Rheinhard Zimmermann (Berlin, 1997), p. 143. He also reminds us that in England legal education for those who intended to practice the common law was distinctive: at the Inns of Courts, not as in continental Europe at universities by professors who were not primarily practitioners (p. 143).

37. M. T. Clanchy, *England and Its Rulers 1066-1272* (London, 1983), pp. 158–70.

CHAPTER 10. HUMANISM, THE LAW OF REASON, CODIFICATION

1. Wieacker, *Private Law*, p. 200.

2. *The Works of Mr. Francis Rabelais*, trans. Urquhart (1653), book 2 [Pantagruel], chap. 5.

3. For a brief, general introduction to local Institutes, see Watson, *Making of the Civil Law*, pp. 62–82.

4. For the humanist input on this systematization, see Wieacker, *Private Law*, pp. 124–25; for the authorities of the *ius commune*, see, e.g., Helmut Coing, *Europäisches Privatrecht*, vol. 1 (Munich, 1985), pp. xiii–xv, 7–9.

5. The terminology used here is adopted from the translation of F. W. Kelsey, in *De jure belli ac pacis* (Oxford, 1925), II.

6. Cf. already Alan Watson, *Roman Law and Comparative Law* (Athens, Ga., 1991), pp. 201–6.

7. Then come three chapters, on promises, contracts, and oaths of those who hold sovereign power; on treatise and sponsions; and on interpretation.

8. Cf. the prefatory remarks of Franz I of Austria to the Allgemeines Bürgerliches Gesetzbuch of 1811 that the law should be in an understandable language and in an orderly collection.

9. Frederick H. Lawson, *A Common Lawyer Looks at the Civil Law* (Ann Arbor, Mich., 1953), p. 49.

10. Cf. Watson, *Sources of Law*, pp. 111–31.

11. *Common Lawyer*, p. 48n13. See also A.T. von Mehren and J. R. Gordley, *Civil Law System*, 2d ed. (Boston, Toronto, 1977), pp. 59–60.

12. The position is very different where codification may be imposed by an absolute autocrat like Atatürk in Turkey, or by a foreign conqueror, or is intended for a territory where there is no deeply established legal tradition.

13. Cf., e.g., Wieacker, *Private Law*, p. 54.

14. Cf., e.g., Wieacker, *Private law*, pp. 47ff.; R. H. Helmholz, *The Spirit of Classical Canon Law* (Athens, Ga., 1996), pp. 17–20.

15. See, e.g., Helmholz, *Canon Law*, pp. 121–26.

16. For this in canon law, see Helmholz, *Canon Law*, pp. 114, 304, 388; for the law in Justinian's *Code*, and how it could be understood, see Watson, *Roman Law and Comparative Law*, pp. 201–6.

17. See, e.g., Helmholz, *Canon Law*, pp. 174–99.

CHAPTER 11. CONCLUSIONS

1. I would not agree, but this is not the place for a discussion.

2. See Watson, *Sources of Law*.

3. For this paragraph, see also Watson, *Transplants*.

4. See Watson, *Sources of Law*.

5. See Watson, *Transplants*, pp. 57–60, 88–94.

6. This does not mean there are not radical lawyers. But except when they are legislators, they are "bad" lawyers—not in an ethical sense, but in the sense that they have to use arguments outside the reach of the accepted mode of legal reasoning. They therefore appear to the generality of lawyers to be at the intellectual mercy of the traditionalists. Pointing this out is in no sense to be construed as support for conservative positions. In fact, precisely because of the force of the legal tradition, legal change is frequently the result of efforts of nonlawyers or of lawyers outside the tradition.

7. See already Watson, "Legal Change," pp. 1121–70, esp. pp. 1151–53.

8. See already Alan Watson, "Comparative Law and Legal Change," *Cambridge Law Journal* 37 (1978): 313–36.

9. For the argument, see Watson, *Society and Legal Change*, pp. 47ff.

10. See G. Francione, "Facing the Nation: The Standards for Copyright, Infringement and Fair Use of Factual Works," *University of Pennsylvania Review* 134 (1986): 519ff.

11. See already Watson, "Legal Change," pp. 1138–39.

Glossary

actio aquae pluviae arcendae: the Roman action against a neighbor whose work might change the flow of rainwater in a way that might cause damage on the plaintiff's land.

actio certae pecuniae: the Roman action available to recover a sum of money that had been lent.

actio quod iussu: the Roman action against a head of household in respect of a contract made by his slave or son on his authorization.

advocate: the Scottish equivalent of the English barrister. In both countries the legal profession is split, and the advocate or barrister specializes in litigation.

capitularies: royal legislation under the Carolingians.

cas fortuit: in French law "chance," which operates as a defense when injury has been caused.

cause étrangère: in French law an "external cause" that cannot be imputed to a defendant and excuses him from liability for damage to person or property.

commodatum: the Roman contract of loan for use.

condictio: the Roman action in which a nonowner claimed that the owner of something was under a legal obligation to deliver it to him.

contrectatio: the physical element, wrongful handling, which was needed to constitute theft in Roman law.

Corpus Juris Civilis: the name given since the seventeenth century to Justinian's codification of Roman law and his subsequent enactments.

Cour de Cassation: the highest French civil court.

damnum infectum: in Roman law, damage not yet done but threatening as a result of a neighbor's defective property.

delict: the Roman and later civilian equivalent of a tort.

délit: French tort.

depositum: the Roman contract of deposit.

depositum miserabile: Roman deposit made following a shipwreck, fire, earthquake, or collapse of a house.

edict: the setting down by a high elected Roman public official of the rules he would follow in carrying out his office. The individual clauses are usually written as "edicts." The most important edicts for us were those of the praetors, who had control of the lawcourts.

emptio venditio: the Roman contract of sale.

enquête par tourbes: a method in medieval France to establish the existence of a custom that was not known to the judge.

ercto non cito: the oldest form of partnership at Rome. When a head of family died, all those subject to his power who became free of power on his death were partners in the inheritance until it was divided.

exceptio: a clause of defense inserted into the Roman *formula* by which a defendant did not deny the plaintiff's pleadings but claimed some other fact had to be taken into account.

fiducia: a Roman form of security of *res mancipi* in which ownership was transferred to the creditor.

force majeure: in French law "force" that cannot be foreseen or averted and operates as a defense for damage to person or property.

formula: the pleadings in an action in classical Roman law.

furtum: theft in Roman law, which was treated primarily as a private wrong, not a crime.

in iure cessio: a Roman method of transferring property, using a fictitious lawsuit. The defendant owner put up no defense, and the thing was adjudged to the plaintiff.

interdict: an order issued by an authorized official to prohibit someone from a particular course of conduct.

ius commune: "common law," a mix of Roman and canon law.

laesio enormis: in late Roman law a ground for setting aside a sale of land if the agreed price was less than one-half the land's value.

legis actio: the archaic form of Roman procedure.

legis actio per condictionem: the archaic form of the Roman *condictio.*

legis actio per iudicis postulationem: an archaic form of Roman procedure in which a judge was appointed immediately after the assertion and denial of the claim.

legis actio sacramento in rem: archaic Roman procedure claiming property in which an oath was sworn on the validity of the claim, and the action proceeded on whether the oath was justly sworn.

locatio conductio: the Roman contract of hire.

mancipatio: a formal method of transferring ownership of *res mancipi.*

mandatum: a Roman contract in which one person agreed to do something gratuitously for another.

mutuum: the Roman contract of loan for consumption. The borrower's obligation was to return an equivalent.

nexum: an institution related to *mancipatio* in which a free person became bound to another on account of loan or debt.

Oberhof: the *Schöffen* of a town who gave rulings on points of law submitted from other towns. Despite the name, the *Oberhof*—except that of Lübeck—did not function as a court giving binding decisions.

pays de droit coutumier: territories in medieval northern France where the law was primarily custom.

pays de droit écrit: territories in medieval southern France where Justinian's codification was regarded as the primary law, supplemented by local custom and later legislation.

permutatio: the Roman contract of barter.

pignus: the main Roman form of real security and the relevant contract.

pourvoi: in effect a French form of appeal.

praetor: the second highest elected Roman official, whose duties included control over courts.

Proculians: one of the two main schools of law in ancient Rome. Despite numerous attempts, no convincing theory has been advanced for the basis of their differences with the Sabinians.

prodigal: a person legally determined as a spendthrift and allowed only restricted dealings with his property.

quasi-délit: French negligent tort.

res mancipi: types of property regarded as of particular importance in early Rome and transferrable only by a formal method.

Sabinians: one of the two main schools of law in ancient Rome. See "Proculians," above.

Schöffen: nonprofessional judge-jurists of medieval Germany.

servitude: an easement.

societas: the Roman contract of partnership.

stillicide: the right to allow water to drip onto a neighbor's land.

stipulatio: a Roman contract formed by oral question and answer, which could be used for any type of transaction.

sui heredes: those persons at Rome who became independent of any person's paternal power on the death of the ancestor in question.

Weistümer: collections setting out the law of a German village.

Index

Library of Congress Cataloging-in-Publication Data

Watson, Alan.
  The evolution of western private law / Alan Watson.—Expanded ed.
    p.   cm.
  Rev. ed. of: The evolution of law. 1985.
  Includes bibliographical references and index.
  ISBN 0-8018-6484-4 (hbk. : alk. paper)
  1. Law—History.   2. Roman law—History.   I. Watson, Alan. Evolution of law.
  II. Title.
K150 .W37 2001
340'.09—dc21

                                                              00-055274